RESEARCH METHODS

Roger L. Dominowski
University of Illinois, Chicago Circle

PRENTICE-HALL, INC., *Englewood Cliffs, New Jersey* 07632

Library of Congress Cataloging in Publication Data

DOMINOWSKI, ROGER L (date)
    Research methods.

    Bibliography: p.
    Includes index.
    1. Research—Methodology. I. Title.
Q175.D69   502'.8   79-17780
ISBN 0-13-774315-7

Editorial/production supervision and interior design by Alison D. Gnerre
Cover design by Frederick Charles Ltd.
Manufacturing buyer: Ed Leone

Prentice-Hall Series in Experimental Psychology
  James J. Jenkins, editor

© 1980 by Prentice-Hall, Inc., Englewood Cliffs, N.J. 07632

Printed in the United States of America

10   9   8   7   6   5   4   3   2   1

PRENTICE-HALL INTERNATIONAL, INC., *London*
PRENTICE-HALL OF AUSTRALIA PTY. LIMITED, *Sydney*
PRENTICE-HALL OF CANADA, LTD., *Toronto*
PRENTICE-HALL OF INDIA PRIVATE LIMITED, *New Delhi*
PRENTICE-HALL OF JAPAN, INC., *Tokyo*
PRENTICE-HALL OF SOUTHEAST ASIA PTE. LTD., *Singapore*
WHITEHALL BOOKS LIMITED, *Wellington, New Zealand*

CONTENTS

PREFACE

This book is intended to help students to acquire basic knowledge about research methods and to develop analytic skills that will enable them to evaluate and do research. My basic assumption is that research is a complex, problem-solving activity. "The perfect study" is an ideal to be sought after rather than an attainable achievement. Presented with a completed research study, people must decide what conclusions might reasonably be drawn from the results, which requires a careful analysis of what was done. People doing research face a similar task; the research *plan* must be examined to determine what problems (if any) might be involved, with steps then taken to correct deficiencies. The book is guided by this orientation. I discuss the advantages and disadvantages of different methods of doing research, the interpretive difficulties that can arise, and the methods that can be used to avoid or minimize such difficulties.

The book focuses on research in psychology, although the material also applies to research in other fields (e.g., education, sociology, biology). There are many examples in the book that represent a variety of research areas and include some examples from "everyday life."

It is impossible to cover research methods without some discussion of statistical concepts and techniques. This is, however, a text on research methods, *not* a statistics text. In writing the book, I have *not* assumed that the student has had a prior statistics course. In the text, I emphasize those statistical concepts that are fundamental to understanding research and stress the logic of statistical analysis. Although the text requires no statistics background, the book is also suitable for more advanced methods courses (where students have had statistics). There is relatively little overlap between the discussions of statistical issues in this text and the content of the typical undergraduate statistics book. Instructors who wish to provide more extensive coverage of particular statistical techniques will find popular methods (e.g., chi square, *t* ratio, analysis of variance) summarized in an appendix. Also, since many instructors require their students to conduct and report research projects, another appendix deals with writing research reports.

The book is organized, in a general sense, to proceed from broader issues to more specific techniques and to proceed from simpler, basic concepts to more complex methods. Chapter 1 presents a discussion of the role that research plays in science and provides an orientation for the material to follow. Chapter 2 deals with essential components of research, namely, measurement, control, and ethics, while Chapter 3 covers the factors most relevant to research in psychology and related disciplines. Chapters 4, 5, and 6 are concerned with the treatment of data and the use of research findings for making decisions and inferences, from both statistical and psychological perspectives. Chapters 7 and 8 cover methods that are both specific and complex; the uses of correlational methods are discussed in Chapter 7, while Chapter 8 concerns factorial designs and multiple-stage research.

A distinguishing feature of this book is the inclusion of problems as an integral part of the text. At various points in each chapter, the student will encounter a problem that requires the application of the material to a specific example. The problems provide a check on understanding of the material and allow the student to develop the analytic skills needed to evaluate and conduct research. There are 65 problems in the text, 10 of which constitute a "posttest" presented in Chapter 9.

I have tried to make the material understandable to students, avoiding technical jargon where simpler language will do the job and explaining necessary technical concepts in some detail. I have attempted to make the book resemble as much as possible an instructor talking with his students. I believe that this approach works better than the more formal, "third-person" style.

Many people have contributed, directly and indirectly, to this book. As faculty members during my own graduate study and through their writings, Donald T. Campbell, Carl P. Duncan, Albert E. Erlebacher, and Benton J. Underwood have contributed greatly to my education in research methodology. For a number of years, I have had fruitful discussions with Herbert Stenson and Norman E. Wetherick. James J. Jenkins and Carol J. DeBoth made helpful comments about the manuscript, along with a number of anonymous reviewers. I am grateful to Donna Behnke Partyka for her help in typing the manuscript. Finally, I am indebted to the many students whose comments over the years have helped me to learn about teaching research methods.

Roger L. Dominowski

TO THE STUDENT

In this special section, I want to make some suggestions that are intended to help you learn as much as possible from the book.

In courses such as introductory psychology, it is quite common for instructors to emphasize that psychology is based on "facts" obtained by doing research. This book is concerned with the methods that researchers use. At the outset, let me emphasize that research is a difficult, error-prone activity. While there are rules and principles that can be used to guide research, there is no magic formula that guarantees that meaningful results will be obtained. Researchers try to do the best work they can, but they should not be expected to do "perfect" research. I want to help you develop a reasonable attitude toward research. It is foolish to simply believe everything researchers tell us, and it is equally foolish to believe that "all research is terribly flawed and doesn't tell us anything worthwhile." A research finding will justify some conclusions but not others; to decide what might reasonably be concluded (or what might be worth doing) requires a careful analysis of the methods used, in light of what we currently know. Even though each of us will make some mistakes, the effort is well worthwhile.

Clearly, there are differences between experts and novices. An expert has not only greater methodological expertise but also deeper knowledge of the topic under investigation. You might get the impression that, if you are not an expert, conducting or evaluating research is hopeless, but I do not believe that this impression is correct. There are issues that are relevant to a great many topics and that do not require "expert" knowledge to be understood. These are the issues that will be considered in this book. While there is a great distance between "novice" and "expert," it is possible to make meaningful progress toward becoming expert. My goal is to help you make such progress. As you go through this book, you will learn more and more about the problems that researchers face, the ways in which research flaws affect the kinds of conclusions that can reasonably be made, and what can be done to minimize or avoid such problems.

In reading this book, I strongly urge you to adopt the following approach. Since each chapter begins with a complete listing of the topics and ends with a summary, examine the topic list and read the summary *before* you begin reading a chapter. In this way, you will have an idea of what the chapter is about, which will help you to understand the material. As you progress through a chapter, you will encounter numerous tables and graphs. These illustrations are just as important as the text of a chapter. Be sure you understand the information in tables and graphs before you continue reading a chapter.

In each chapter, you will periodically encounter "problems," asking you to do something before reading further. To get maximum benefit from this book, try to do these problems before reading the answer and discussion. By trying to work the problems, you will be able to check your understanding of the material and you will have an opportunity to develop the analytic skills that are essential to understanding research.

Roger L. Dominowski

1

THE PURPOSE
OF
RESEARCH

People know many things. One might know one's own mind, how to ride a bicycle, that the moon isn't made of cheese, that Republicans are better than Democrats, or that vitamin B helps prevent nervousness. We use the term *know* in a number of different ways. When we try to be more precise, we usually distinguish between things we believe and things we know. When pressed during an argument, you might hear a person say, "Well, I don't really know, but I believe it is true that . . ." The distinction between beliefs and knowledge ordinarily lies in a person's reasons for accepting something as correct. *Beliefs* might refer to things I accept as true without any particular proof, while *knowledge* seems to refer to facts of some sort. It isn't critical for us to make a very precise distinction between beliefs and knowledge, but it is important to recognize that we know different kinds of things and that we accept things as correct for different reasons.

Research is a fact-finding activity. When people want "facts" before they will accept something as correct, they might well go out and try to collect relevant information. Frequently people differ about what the facts actually are—think of all the arguments that have started with statements like "The fact is you were leering at that girl all night!" On other occasions there are disagreements not about the facts but about what they mean. Two people might totally agree about the fact that the President endorsed a tax cut for large corporations, but one might argue that this action shows that the President has been "bought" by big business while the other argues that it shows that the President wants to help workers by encouraging corporations to hire more employees or lower prices. These examples illustrate that neither facts nor the meanings of facts are always obvious.

Everyone engages in fact finding or research of one sort or another from time to time. If you have ever concluded that the gas line in your car might be clogged because the car won't start but the engine turns over, you have used facts to reach an opinion or decision. Other informal examples of fact finding or research include testing to see whether the spaghetti sauce tastes better if you add an extra bay leaf, or watching to see whether people who drink more at a party have more (or less) fun. This book is concerned with more formal research, usually called scientific research.

Sciences are organized bodies of knowledge in which statements are based on facts, among other things. Scientific facts are not obtained in casual ways; rather, they are required to meet a number of standards or criteria. Scientific knowledge does not belong to a particular individual but is a kind of public knowledge. Note that *scientific knowledge is only one kind of knowledge.*

I think it is useful to distinguish between scientific goals and scientific practices. A broad scientific goal is organized understanding of "the world around us" (including outer space). This goal implies that some things will not be worth knowing from a scientific perspective because they do not fit into the organized system that scientists are trying to build. Scientists also follow certain kinds of procedures in building their systems of organized knowledge.

Let me give you an example of the possible value of distinguishing between scientific goals and scientific practices. Suppose I'd like to know whether my dog prefers Alpo or Purina Dog Chow. I doubt whether such knowledge, in this form, would ever be an integral part of scientific knowledge. The question of whether my dog prefers one or the other brand of dog food is *not* a good scientific question; it is not phrased properly, and the answer would not fit well into scientific knowledge. Nevertheless I could use some scientific procedures to get an answer to my question. In other words, I could use scientific procedures to answer an unscientific question.

Most of this book is concerned with the procedures scientists use to obtain and evaluate "facts." This collection of procedures or methods is called *research methodology.* We will of course give special attention to the methods used in psychological research—studies concerned with collecting facts about "behavior." Many of the issues and procedures we will discuss apply as well to research in other disciplines (e.g., education, sociology, biology). I will, however, "flavor" the discussion with examples from psychology. In this chapter I want to give you a broad perspective on what sciences are like—what scientists are trying to do, how they tend to think about things, and how they collect and use facts in trying to achieve their goals.

It is difficult to define science in such a way that it is clearly and unambiguously separated from other systems of knowledge, and I don't think it is very important to try to do so. There are, however, features that characterize scientific knowledge and scientific practices. Let me describe these features in order that you can achieve some understanding of what science is seeking and how it goes about its business.

CHARACTERISTICS OF SCIENCE

Scientific knowledge can be characterized as organized, abstract, public, and based in part on observable facts. Scientists tend to share some common assumptions, ask and answer questions in certain ways, and follow similar procedures in collecting facts and organizing those facts to create knowledge structures. Only in a very broad sense is there a single thing called SCIENCE or something called THE scientific method. First of all, there are many sciences—physics, psychology, chemistry, biology, and sociology, to name a few. The sciences differ in the topics they deal with, in the methods they use, and in the kinds of explanations or theories they construct. The emergence of hybrid sciences—biochemistry, social psychology, physiological psychology—suggests that the boundaries between sciences are fuzzy in places. There are broad similarities among the sciences. Roughly speaking, scientists believe that there is order in the universe and that it is possible for people to understand "how things work." Scientists try to create understanding by making observations in accordance with some general rules and by requiring that explanations meet specified criteria. Let's look at these characteristics of science more closely.

Assumptions

Scientists keep an open mind about many things, make a lot of tentative, qualified statements, and often argue that we should "wait and see." At the same time, they accept certain things as correct pretty much without proof—these are the beliefs or assumptions on which scientific work is based. Most scientific work is based on two general assumptions: that there is an external reality that we can know about and that this reality is ordered or organized.

External Reality. Scientists assume that there is an external reality that can be shared by many people and therefore known. This assumption probably doesn't shock you because it is made not only by scientists but by most people. There are, however, some philosophical problems with the concept of an external reality, and these problems are of greater concern to scientists because scientists are quite deliberately and formally involved with the nature of knowledge.

It is important to recognize that agreement among people is critical for what we call reality. Let me give you an example to illustrate in rough terms the problems involved in identifying reality. I'm sure you are familiar with the term *hallucination,* usually defined as an apparent perception of something that is not actually present. Notice that the words "not actually present" refer to an external reality. Suppose you are in a room with 999 other people. One person announces that he sees a "purple elephant with green stripes" in the room. You look around, carefully, and see no such thing. From your perspective, the other person must be hallucinating; from his, you must be hallucinating, seeing "blank" space where there is none. How can we decide who is hallucinating and who is perceiving reality? I'm sure you are thinking, "Ask the other 998 people," confident that they will agree with you and that the person who sees a purple elephant with green stripes will be properly recognized as hallucinating. But what if the other 998 people said they too saw a purple elephant with green stripes?

Philosophers who emphasize the weakness of the concept of external reality stress the point that what we call reality depends on interpersonal agreement. Scientists assume that the interpersonal agreements that occur are not arbitrary but reflect a source—external reality. This issue is not readily resolved, but I won't belabor it. At the same time, you should be aware that the concept of external reality does involve some problems. The assumption that we are perceiving and talking about "the same thing" has proved useful, and usefulness (in a slightly special sense) is important to scientists. To minimize difficulties, scientists try to base their system of knowledge at some point on observations about which there is near-perfect agreement.

There are two related points that you should be aware of. First, science does *not* deal with personal reality but with a form of shared or public reality. Something might seem very real to me or to you, but science cannot deal with it until some way is found to gain agreement about what is "real." The fact that science does not deal with something does not mean that that thing is unreal. Science operates on the assumption of one öf several possible conceptions of reality, which enables it to consider many things, but not everything.

Second, our conceptions of reality change over time, and so does scientific knowledge. Even if we assume that an external reality exists, our knowledge of it is limited. The way in which we view reality is not static. For example, at one time people assumed that the earth was the center of the universe, but that is no longer the case. At one time people assumed that the earth was flat, but that is no longer the case. Scientists once accepted the conservation of mass and energy, but Einstein successfully challenged that assumption. Scientists recognize that they are constructing a "picture" of reality, a representation that is limited by what we know. It follows that "usefulness" is important to scientists. If it no longer seems useful to view reality in a particular way, adopt a new conception of reality.

Scientists sometimes simultaneously hold incompatible views of reality. For example, for over a century there was a controversy over whether light was a wave form or moving particles. The modern physicist's answer to the question is "Yes, light is a wave form, and yes, light is moving particles." That is, sometimes it is more useful to view light as a wave form, while other times it is more useful to view it as moving particles.

Let me summarize these thoughts. Scientists generally accept the concept of an external reality, although they recognize the importance of interpersonal agreement for deciding what is "real." Scientific knowledge is affected by how we view reality; since these views can and do change, scientific knowledge changes. Scientists employ conceptions of reality that are useful, that help build an organized system of knowledge. Perhaps the essential point is this: Scientific knowledge is anchored in facts, and facts depend on how we view reality. Scientists are reluctant to say that they are *absolutely sure* that any part of scientific knowledge is correct. If asked to tell someone what is "really, absolutely, for-sure true about such-and-such," a scientist is likely, after some reflection, to say, "Well, I don't know what's absolutely true, but here's the best version of 'truth' we have arrived at so far."

Regularities. A related assumption is that there are regularities in "nature" or reality. In other words, there is order rather than chaos in nature. There is a pattern to events, rather than everything being unique unto itself. Scientists try to describe and explain regularities. The emphasis on regularities leads scientists to concentrate on what is common, repeatable, and predictable rather than attending to what appear to be unique or special qualities of events. Features of events are therefore described in abstract or general terms. Suppose my dog prefers Alpo to Purina Dog Chow; scientists would not treat this as a unique event specific to my dog, this particular occasion, or Alpo and Purina Dog Chow. They would assume that this event is part of some pattern, an example of some general regularity. (In rough terms, this is why the question of "Alpo vs. Purina Dog Chow" is not a good scientific question; it is stated in specific terms with no attempt to relate it to other concepts and facts.)

There are two important issues related to the assumption of regularities in nature. First, we can ask whether the observed regularities are stable over time. Are the observations, facts, and laws of science permanent? The basic answer is that we do *not* know, but scientists are likely to assume that the answer is "yes" in some fashion. To give an extreme example, suppose that what is "really true" is that objects heavier than air and unsupported some distance above the ground might move in any direction. We are used to seeing objects fall down toward the ground, but maybe this regularity has just "happened" up until now and that after, say, 2050 objects will fall up or sideways. Basically, we don't know whether the "law" of gravity will apply tomorrow—we assume that it will. If forced to conclude that some former regularity had changed, scientists would assume that there is some more complex regularity that fits the earlier pattern of events, the later pattern of events, and the change. The idea is that "we have described the regularity imperfectly," not that there is no regularity. However, we should recognize that the regularities we accept as established might change.

A related issue concerns the nature of regularities. This issue has been voiced as "determinism versus free will" and as "deterministic versus probabilistic laws." Ordinary folk like you and me are used to thinking that we make choices and exercise some control over our behavior. Most religions and societies assume some version of personal responsibility. But if everything in nature is part of a fixed regularity, where is the room for choice and freedom? Perhaps you can see why some people have asked whether it is possible to have a science of human behavior, why others have written about "the appearance of free will," why there have been conflicts between science and religion.

The determinism-versus-free-will issue arose in relation to human behavior. People who argued against determinism for human beings typically did not reject the idea of determinism for "animals" or inanimate objects. However, the argument has been made that all scientific laws are fundamentally probabilistic rather than rigidly deterministic. A deterministic law involves the concept of necessity—"A and B *must* be related." A probabilistic law is "looser"—"A and B are *likely* to be related." Another version of this distinction is the difference between "This *must* follow that" and "This *is likely to* follow that."

In brief, here is the situation: No regularity yet identified is perfect. There is always some uncertainty or slippage in the regularity; very little in some cases, more in others. The question is, Why is the uncertainty or slippage there? Is it because regularities are fundamentally probabilistic or because we just don't yet know something that, when it is known, will eliminate the uncertainty and lay bare a deterministic regularity? What is the answer? We simply do not know. At present a person could adopt either position with little apparent effect on scientific activity. It is abundantly clear that the regularities that psychological research has identified are uncertain; there is a lot of "on the average," "more or less," or "probably" associated with psychological phenomena. Whether such imperfect regularities will always be with us or will eventually give way to more complex but perfect regularities is not something that will be settled in the near future, if at all. In either case researchers can try, to the best of their ability, to study the regularities they can identify.

The Goal: Understanding

The regularities that scientists study are relations between variables. A *variable* is anything that takes on different values from time to time, person to person, situation to situation, and so forth. Such things as length, molecular structure, attitude toward the United Nations, and group cohesiveness are variables, as are many other things. Scientists are particularly interested in *relations among variables*—for example, how variation in age is related to variation in height or perceptual ability or social skills.

The observations made by researchers are referred to as data, results, or findings. Collecting data is an important part of scientific work, but it is a means to an end rather than an end in itself. The primary goal of science is *understanding* the relations among variables that have been observed.

Science is often said to have two other goals, *prediction* and *control*. That is, science presumably seeks to predict what will happen and to control what will happen. However, prediction and control are secondary or incomplete goals. By itself, predicting what will happen with some success is not enough. For example, Aunt Sadie might have some success in predicting whether or not it will rain on the basis of how her corns feel, but her predictive success would not be enough. Scientists would want to understand how and why her predictive system works. Scientists have criticized astrology on precisely this basis. They might well question whether predicting people's behavior on the basis of their "signs" really works, but they also argue that astrologers do not give any plausible reasons *why* such predictions should be successful.

If we understand relations among variables, we will be able to make successful predictions. Thus one consequence of understanding is success in prediction; the essential point is that prediction by itself is not enough. To scientists, successful predictions cry out for understanding.

Similarly, controlling events may be desirable, but control is not the primary goal of science. In a sense, control by itself might not be sufficient. People can "control" the illumination of the lights in their houses by flipping switches and "control" their cars by using pedals, gearshifts, switches, and steering wheels. However, we would not begin to attribute scientific knowledge to such people unless they understood how and why the switches allow them to control the lights or how and why the pedals, gearshifts, and so forth allow them to control the car.

Understanding events may or may not lead to control. Astronomers are not able to control the movements of the planets and stars, but this lack of control has not prevented them from developing a refined understanding of space, and the lack of control does not diminish the importance of this understanding. In some instances control might be theoretically possible but is not actually possible because of ethical or societal constraints. For example, if we understood the relation between a mother's characteristics and the well-being of her children, would we be able to or want to take infants away from "predicted-to-be-poor" mothers in an attempt to "control" their well-being? There are many things that scientists cannot control, and it is a mistake to assume that scientists want to control them.

"Mad scientist" movies and some antiscience movements portray scientists as driven to use their knowledge to control everything. These portrayals are grossly overstated. Scientists do have an intellectual interest in exercising control because successful control based on scientific understanding can provide strong support for the accuracy of that understanding. Just as it would be incorrect to state that scientists have *no* interest in control, it is incorrect to state that scientists are *necessarily* interested in control.

A useful distinction can be made between the development of scientific knowledge and the use of such knowledge (presumably to "control" things). This distinction is usually phrased in terms of the difference between "science" and "technology." The simple fact that the distinction is commonly made suggests that control is not a necessary part of science. Science does lead to technology (and vice versa). Can scientific knowledge be abused? The answer is yes. Knowledge really is power, and power can be used for good or ill. Deciding whether a particular use of knowlege is "good" is often difficult. There has been and continues to be a fair amount of concern among scientists over the possible misuse of scientific knowledge, for example by governments. A number of scientists who were involved in the initial work on atomic energy have advised, begged, and demanded that governments stop using such knowledge to make more fearsome weapons (to date, with little or no impact).

Some people, including some scientists, are sufficiently afraid of the possible abuses of certain kinds of knowledge that they propose that we should not try to develop such knowledge. This is a difficult and sensitive issue. Scientific knowledge can be used for both good and bad purposes. The same knowledge that might lead to a new weapon might also lead to better medical care; a "brainwashing" technique might be based on the same scientific principles as an improved method of teaching schoolchildren to read. Preventing the development of such knowledge will prevent both good and bad applications. It is difficult to predict what the future uses of any knowledge will be. Obviously this is a difficult issue, and I cannot offer even a tentative resolution. Scientists tend to believe that ignorance is *not* bliss, and they tend to be hopeful. Since scientific knowledge can be distinguished from the uses of that knowledge, it may be hoped that some means can be found for maximizing the good uses and minimizing the bad ones.

While scientific knowledge can lead to control, it should be clear that control of events is not a necessary part of science. The goal is understanding, which will lead to predictions and might, but does not have to, lead to control. The kind of understanding that science develops is limited—science does not provide "ultimate" solutions. At some point scientists stop trying to explain a given phenomenon; then the point has been reached at which science can offer no further understanding.

Science provides understanding at several levels of abstraction, some "close to the data," others more abstract and removed from the basic observations. What scientists try to do is develop as much understanding as they can; over time, understanding tends to increase or "deepen," but no "ultimate" level of understanding is reached. Philosophers debate the nature of ultimate answers, and I emphasize "debate." Remember, scientists work from certain assumptions and employ particular kinds of explanations; thus there are some questions that don't have scientific answers.

Criteria for Explanations

I have pointed out that science seeks to understand the relations among variables, to explain them in some way. It has been said that something has been adequately explained when people stop asking "Why?" Sometimes a distinction is made between explaining *how* something happens and explaining *why* it happens, but I do not think this distinction is critical; one person's "how" might be another person's "why." In general terms, something has been explained when it has been made more meaningful. There can, of course, be better and worse explanations, more and less complete explanations. Because the goal of science is an organized understanding of relations among variables, scientists use a number of criteria to evaluate explanations. We will consider these criteria in a moment; first I will make a few comments about *theories*.

Explanations vary in *scope,* that is, the range of observations to which they apply. There are, in a sense, "little" explanations and "big" explanations. Usually the term *theory* is reserved for broader, more abstract explanations that have a large scope. Thus a theory might be described as based on some general and fundamental assumptions, from which successive deductions are made, leading eventually to specific predictions for particular observations. Scientists seem to sometimes just "suggest" explanations, other times to propose theories; the theories are likely to be more encompassing, more formal, and more abstract (further from the data) than "mere" explanations. The dividing line between theory and mere explanation is very fuzzy, however, and I do not think it is important to spend time trying to decide whether some explanation "is" or "isn't" a theory. It is enough to recognize that explanations vary in scope and that the term *theory* usually implies some larger, more formal explanation.

Science does not employ an all-or-none approach to evaluating explanations. Rather than viewing explanations as true or false, right or wrong, scientists view explanations as differing from each other in degree. Some explanations are better or more accurate than others. The general criterion that scientists use to evaluate explanations is their *usefulness* for building an organized knowledge system. Some explanations (theories) are more useful than others, and an explanation that has some usefulness is likely to stay around until it is replaced by a better one. To decide how useful an explanation might be, scientists compare it to several criteria, which we will now consider.

Clear Terminology. Scientists desire explanations stated in clear, unambiguous terms. If a proposed explanation is couched in murky language and contains vague terms, it will not be very useful—it might sound good but it will be difficult to figure out what it means. For this reason many scientists prefer explanations stated in mathematical terms rather than in ordinary language, the reason being that mathematical formulations are less ambiguous and more precise. In psychology, many explanations are stated in ordinary language, which is relatively vague; the explanations or theories are sometimes difficult to decipher. For example, Sigmund Freud proposed that in the course of human development libido is concentrated in different areas of the body. Many psychologists have wondered what *libido* means, and some have decided that the term *libido* is so vague that Freud's theory is relatively useless. (Others, meanwhile, have tried to clarify its meaning.) Similar problems have arisen with respect to terms like *reinforcement, cognitive dissonance,* and *self-concept.* Much research effort has been directed toward trying to clarify the meanings of terms used in explanations.

Empirical Validity. Since science is concerned with the nature of external reality, an explanation or theory must make contact with data, or observations. Indeed, contact with observations is an important part of clear terminology. An explanation is supposed to explain the relations among variables that have been identified. To give a ridiculous example, suppose I were to announce a new psychological "theory": $G = R \times D + P$. You ask, "What does this mean?" I answer, "As anyone can see, G equals R times D plus P. G, R, D, and P are essentially abstract concepts, but, if you want word names, the equation reads 'Gorfooning equals rapidity times depth plus pedanticness.'" You say, "But what does that mean—how does your theory relate to observations of behavior?" I answer, "Well, I have not yet worked that out." It would be quite appropriate for you to conclude that I am some kind of crank whose "theory" has no scientific value.

Relating the terms of an explanation to observations is not always easy. The terms in actual explanations are not as divorced from observations as "gorfooning," but determining precisely how the terms connect with data can be troublesome. To be useful, an explanation must make contact with observations and needs to be consistent with the data that have been collected. Scientists often talk about the importance of a theory's being "testable." They are referring to the idea that an explanation should be consistent with existing observations and lead to predictions about future observations. That is, a theory ought to "take a position" regarding what should be observed in various circumstances; by making the observations, we could see whether the explanation is accurate or not.

An additional—and important—point about relating explanations to observations is that each of the major terms in an explanation must be related to a different aspect of the observation. For example, suppose we want to check the empirical accuracy of the theoretical statement "High anxiety is associated with poor learning." The observation of "high anxiety" must be separate from the observation of "poor learning" if either observation is to sensibly serve as a check on the accuracy of the explanation. Suppose I tell you that "poor learning" is associated with the observation that a person requires a greater-than-average time to learn some task. Now you ask how "high anxiety" is observed. Suppose I tell you that high anxiety is indicated by the need for a greater-than-average time to learn the task. In other words, "high anxiety" and "poor learning" are tied to the same observation. Clearly there would be no way to meaningfully check the accuracy of the explanation; a closer look reveals that the only observation is that some people require a greater-than-average amount of time to learn. It would explain nothing to refer to this observation as both "high anxiety" and "poor learning." It is necessary not only that explanatory terms be tied to specific observations but also that different explanatory terms refer to separate observations.

PROBLEM

It is quite common in psychology to define a *reinforcer* as "that which increases the frequency of a response with which it is associated." Consider the statement "Responses increase in frequency because they are reinforced." Given the preceding definition of a reinforcer, is this statement a testable explanation of increases in response frequency?

The basic answer is that this statement is not really testable unless some additional constraints are imposed. Notice that the term *reinforcer* is defined in terms of its effect; with this definition it is impossible for a reinforcer to fail to increase response frequency. How would you know that something is a reinforcer? According to this definition, the basic observation is an increase in response frequency. Suppose that you tried to increase the frequency with which your dog comes to you when you call him by giving him a "dog yummy" each time he does what you want. After repeated efforts you find that you have failed—your dog does not come when called any more frequently than before. Would this indicate that a reinforcer had failed? According to the definition just presented, the answer is no. All that your failure would mean is that "dog yummies" are not a reinforcer for this particular response.

From this viewpoint the statement that "responses increase in frequency because they are reinforced" is more of an assumption than an explanation. If you observe an increase in response frequency, then there must be a reinforcer, because reinforcers are those things that increase response frequency. You can't really prove this statement to be wrong. It is possible to test a hypothesis that a particular event is a reinforcer, as in the example of "dog yummies." However, the basic statement cannot really be shown to be false. If you had observed an increase in response frequency and had shown that none of a large number of events could be the reinforcer, it would still be possible to argue that you just haven't yet identified the reinforcer. Thus the statement represents a way of looking at things rather than an explanation. Only when a specific event is named as a reinforcer can the (modified) statement be tested.

Logical Consistency. To be "testable" and thus potentially useful, an explanation must not only use terms that make contact with observations but also lead in a logical fashion to specific predictions about observations. It must not contradict itself or lead to incompatible statements about observations. Suppose a theory is intended to explain why people will sometimes be cooperative and sometimes competitive. Variation from cooperation to competition among individuals or among situations constitutes the data to be explained. You work through the theory and determine that it leads to the prediction that people will be *more* cooperative in situation A than in situation B. Then someone says, "Wait a minute. You can also take the theory and derive the prediction that people will be *less* cooperative in situation A than in situation B. The theory can be used to make either prediction." This theory would not be considered very useful; although the explanation makes contact with the observations, there is something wrong or incomplete in the theory that allows incompatible predictions to be derived from it.

Scientists desire explanations that are consistent with observations. Notice, however, that an explanation that can be consistent with *any* observation is not considered useful. If a theory will be "right" no matter what is observed, it is hard to see how that theory helps us understand why observations vary from time to time, situation to situation, and so on. While science wants explanations that are "correct," a useful explanation is one that would be incorrect *if* certain events occurred.

Generality. Since science seeks to understand patterns of events, explanations are better to the extent that they account for more observations. Consider the limiting case: Each observation is explained in a different, unique fashion. If this happened, there would be no way for an organized system of knowledge to develop. Suppose we have one explanation for the way people learn lists of words and another explanation for the way they learn perceptual–motor skills. Researchers would like to develop a broader explanation that covers both kinds of learning; that is, in essence, they would like to fit word list learning and perceptual–motor learning into a larger pattern of understanding. As explanations become more general they also become more abstract and cover fewer details. For example, scientists might develop a general theory of learning within which certain special principles apply to word list learning and others apply to perceptual-motor learning. Such a theory would be better than two unconnected explanations, even though some special principles would be needed for different kinds of learning.

All explanations are assumed to have *boundary conditions*, limits within which the explanation applies. For example, an explanation might apply only to children or only in certain defined situations. A very clear theory, with clear terms and clear internal logic, is likely to be found to be "incorrect" under certain circumstances. Rather than discarding the theory, scientists would feel that they have identified one of the boundary conditions of the explanation. They would accept the theory as a limited explanation and seek a broader, higher-order explanation that links this and other limited explanations together.

It is possible to generate a very broad explanation by dealing with fewer details of observations. Such explanations might not be very useful; while they might seem to account for a broad range of observations, they might explain only a few aspects of each observation. Scientists have to make decisions about the amount of detail they want explanations to cover. Better explanations account for more details of observations and for a broader range of observations. Sometimes there is a trade-off between breadth and completeness, and scientists differ in the relative values they place on these two attributes. One theorist might decide that certain details of observations are not very important and try to develop a broad explanation covering fewer aspects. Another might argue that the details left out of the first theory are extremely critical, reject the first theory, and develop a different explanation. It is easy to say that, "other things being equal," a more general explanation is preferred over a less general one, but things are seldom equal. Deciding on the balance between detail and generality leads to differences among explanations and continual revisions of explanations.

Simplicity. If some observations can be explained in two different ways, one more complicated than the other, the simpler explanation will be preferred. If one explanation involves, say, 5 assumptions, 14 terms, and complex relations among the terms, while the other rests on 2 assumptions, 3 terms, and simple, direct relations among the terms, there appears to be no good reason to carry along the "extra baggage" of the first explanation. The desire for simple explanations is often called the "law of parsimony": Don't use a complex explanation if a simpler one will do the job. While the law of parsimony is eminently reasonable, it is important to realize that the simpler theory *must do the job.* That is, a theory is not good just because it is simple. The choice between a simple explanation and a more complex one rests on the same issue as the choice between more general explanations and less general ones: How much detail do we want explained? If the simpler explanation is not as complete as the complex one, the choice is not that obvious. A simple explanation that omits important details will not be very useful. Since scientists differ both in *the amount of* detail they think is appropriate and in *which* details they think are important, there are many differences of opinion about which explanation is better (i.e., more useful).

At this point I should mention some terms related to simplicity. Scientists often refer, very favorably, to *elegant* explanations, and sometimes call an explanation *beautiful.* There is an esthetic component to choosing explanations. A simple explanation that "does the job" will be appealing both for intellectual reasons and because it is esthetically pleasing. A neat, elegant explanation might be preferred even if it is not as complete as a more complex account. Let me give you a nonscientific analogy. Many people play tennis; players differ both in their success rates (wins and losses) and in the elegance of their play—one might scrape and scramble, hitting the ball any old way, while another seems to glide over the court, making smooth, fluid strokes. We might appreciate the determination, tenacity, and effectiveness of the "scrambler," but there is a kind of beauty in the actions of a player with very fluid motions. Here is the point: Many players, at all levels of ability, opt for elegance to the detriment of their success rates. They concentrate on form and tend to ignore the goal of winning the game (a choice any player is free to make). In a similar fashion the esthetic appeal of elegant explanations can lead to biases in choosing explanations; hence, it is important to remember that simple, elegant explanations must adequately account for the data.

A Note on Causality. You have now seen that scientists seek clear, internally consistent, simple, and general explanations of the relations among variables that are observed. In psychology it is often said that we seek *causal* explanations of events. Let's consider what causality might mean, using the familiar example "Smoking causes cancer." One logical possibility is that smoking is *necessary* for cancer to occur; if this were correct, there would be no nonsmokers with cancer (i.e., you have to smoke to get cancer). Another possibility is that smoking is *sufficient* for cancer to occur; what this means is that, while there might be people who don't smoke but do get cancer, anyone who smokes must get cancer (i.e., there could be no cases of smokers without cancer.) The observed facts are that there are people who smoke and get cancer, people who don't smoke but do get cancer (indicating that smoking is *not necessary* for cancer to occur), and people who smoke but don't get cancer (indicating that smoking is *not sufficient* for cancer to occur). Of course there are also people who don't smoke and don't get cancer. If smoking is *not* a *necessary* casue of cancer, and if smoking is *not* a *sufficient* cause of cancer, in what sense does smoking *cause* cancer? The best answer is that *smoking increases the chances of getting cancer;* this is the reasonable meaning of the statement "Smoking causes cancer."

PROBLEM

Consider the statement "A high level of intelligence is necessary but not sufficient for a high level of creativity." What kind of observation would contradict this statement?

The answer is that the statement would be contradicted by the observation that an individual with a low level of intelligence has a high level of creativity. If high intelligence is necessary for high creativity, then it is logically impossible to have high creativity without high intelligence. In principle, observing just a single instance of a "low (i.e., not-high) intelligence, high creativity" individual would invalidate this statement. In actual practice researchers seldom make statements about necessary or sufficient causes; most often statements are made in terms of greater and lesser probabilities. For example, the statement "The higher the intelligence level, the greater the probability of high creativity" does *not* predict anything to be impossible. Such loose, probabilistic statements are far more difficult to prove "right" or "wrong."

Few psychologists claim to have identified a necessary cause or a sufficient cause. Statements that "this causes that" are probabilistic statements with meanings like those of the statement "Smoking causes cancer." When a psychologist says something like "Lack of parental affection produces [causes, results in] neuroses," this actually means that as parental affection decreases there is a greater chance of neuroses occurring. (At this point it might be useful for you to review our earlier discussion of deterministic laws versus probabilistic laws.)

The distinction between causal and noncausal statements can be related to the likely effects of intervention. As we use the terms *cause* and *effect,* an effect occurs *after* a cause; it does not make sense to us for an effect to occur *before* a cause. If we want to intervene in nature, to manipulate something in the hope of later observing some change in another variable, we want to know *how* to intervene. If we have observed a systematic relation between two variables and can identify one variable as the "cause," we should know how to intervene.

Suppose we have observed a systematic relation between amount of education and attitude toward spending money for welfare—the greater the amount of education, the more positive the attitude toward spending money for welfare. If we look at the relation in terms of causality, there are three logical possibilities: (1) Differences in education "cause" differences in attitude toward welfare. (2) Differences in attitude toward welfare "cause" differences in education. (3) Neither variable is a cause; both are "effects" of some other, unidentified cause. In terms of possible intervention, the questions are, "If I manipulated amount of education, would differences in attitude toward welfare result?" and "If I manipulated attitudes toward welfare, would differences in level of education result?" We could get three understandable patterns of answers to these two questions: "yes and no," suggesting that education causes attitude toward welfare; "no and yes," suggesting that attitudes toward welfare cause differences in education; and "no and no," suggesting that neither variable is a cause of the other. ("Yes and yes" would be hard to understand.) In seeking a causal explanation of this relation, we would be guided by our current knowledge of the world and by the temporal order of the two variables. It would be hard to imagine that changing people's attitude toward welfare would later lead to changes in their amount of education. It might be reasonable to think that changing amount of education might lead to later changes in attitude toward welfare. Of course manipulating amount of education might lead to no change in attitude toward welfare (implying that no causal relation exists).

Suppose that level of education is the causal variable in this relation. If so, then in principle we could produce changes in attitude toward welfare by manipulating amount of education. On this basis we might recommend that, if society wants people to be more positive toward welfare spending, educational levels should be increased. If, however, no causal relation exists between amount of education and attitude toward welfare, then increasing educational levels will have no impact on attitude toward welfare (or vice versa).

It is easy to see how identifying causal variables can help us understand relations among variables. I must, however, emphasize the limited nature of such knowledge. First, causal statements are probabilistic (at least at present). It would be incorrect to state that increasing educational levels will *guarantee* more positive attitudes toward welfare spending (at best, it would only increase the chances of more positive attitudes). Second, even if we have considerable evidence that one variable in a relation is a "cause," we cannot be sure that we have properly identified the "cause."

To illustrate the second point, let me tell you a story about a superstitious child. Once upon a time there was a young child who noticed that the light in the kitchen was sometimes on, sometimes off. The child wondered what made the light go on and off. One day, while in the kitchen, the child moved an arm and the light went on! The child thought, "Oh, maybe moving an arm makes the light change." Trying again and again, the child observed that moving an arm could make the light go on (if it was off) or off (if it was on). Confidently, the child went away believing that moving an arm made the light go on or off. Unknown to him, his impish older sister had been flipping the light switch every time the child moved an arm. The child's arm movements had only *appeared* to be the cause of changes in the light.

This example is exaggerated, to be sure. The point is, however, that a scientist could at any time be playing the role of the superstitious child, thinking that a cause has been identified and failing to notice that some other variable, the "real cause," changes whenever the apparent cause changes and seems to produce its effect. Our knowledge is limited, and it is tentative.

Rules for Making Observations

Collecting data is an integral part of science. The goal is to understand the patterns of relations among variables, and we obviously need to know what relations exist. Observations are used to test the accuracy of scientific explanations and improve theories. Just as scientists evaluate explanations according to a particular set of criteria, they expect observations to be made in ways that conform to some rough rules. In other words, scientists will not try to explain just any observation; observations must be made in certain ways before they will be worthy of scientific attention. There are three general rules that indicate how data should be collected.

1. *Specify Procedures.* Earlier I pointed out that the terms of an explanation must "make contact" with observations. If I have a theory relating "anxiety" to "learning," scientists will want to know how these theoretical terms relate to observations. Scientists would eventually ask, "How did you measure anxiety?" or some similar question. Science distinguishes between "what the facts are" and "what the facts mean," and it does so much more seriously than we ordinarily do in everyday life. To a scientist, the statement "I have observed that people with high anxiety learn more poorly than those with moderate anxiety" is, despite the verb *observed*, a theoretical statement rather than an observational statement. Scientists want much more specific descriptions of what I did and will keep asking for more specific descriptions until they are satisfied.

Researchers are obligated to specify in a clear fashion all aspects of their procedures that might be relevant to determining what the observations mean. For example, I might indicate that "anxiety" refers to measurement of changes in heart rate during a two-minute period and that "learning" refers to the amount of practice time people required before they were able to ride a unicycle for one minute without falling off. I would also be required to specify much more—what the people I observed were like, how they wound up participating in my study, how many there were, what I told them, what equipment was used to measure heart rate, what went on during the two-minute heart rate measuring period, and so on. The goal is to describe the procedures in terms *other than those I use in my explanation* and in sufficient detail to allow another researcher, in principle, to do what I have done.

It is hard to say exactly *how* specific the description of procedures must be. Keep in mind that the rule of specifying procedures applies to observations that a researcher wants to offer for inclusion among the facts that science will seek to explain. If I want to form a personal opinion, then I can do whatever I want; of course scientists don't have to pay any attention to me. In rough terms, procedures must be specified in commonly understood, nontheoretical terms. The description of procedures must stop at some point and need include only things that might be relevant to understanding the observations. Scientists would want to know that what I had "observed" was that people showing larger changes in heart rate took longer to learn to ride a unicycle. This "observation," together with the other procedural specifications, can then be evaluated to see whether it justifies the statement "People with high anxiety learn more poorly."

I would be required to specify things like those mentioned earlier. I might be required to describe more specifically how time periods were measured (e.g., by hand-held stopwatch or automatic timing device) or how we determined that a person had "fallen off" the unicycle (e.g., one foot off a pedal, one foot on the floor, two feet off the pedals), but I would not be required to give more detail about "pedal," "stopwatch," "minute," or "foot." Nor is it likely that scientists would want to know what color clothes people were wearing, what day of the week it was, or what I had for lunch the day before making my observations. If there were some reason to suspect that heart rate or unicycle riding might be related to the color of a person's clothes, then this factor might need to be described. The level of concreteness that is required in specifying procedures is relative both to what is considered commonly understood, nontheoretical language and to what might be theoretically important.

② *Make Systematic Observations.* In everyday life, people often form opinions on the basis of rather casual observations. Some things capture our attention more than others, and we might base our "facts" on things that happened to catch our attention. For example, I might meet a red-haired person who captures my attention through an outburst of "temper"; sometime later I happen to notice another "hot-tempered" person with red hair, and I might begin to believe that "red-haired people have hot tempers." I have not made any deliberate attempt to observe any relation between hair color and "temper" but have simply noticed some things that caught my attention.

Scientific observations need to be made more systematically. A researcher must choose beforehand the variables whose values will be observed and must select the times and situations in which observations will be made. The immediate goal is to make a relatively large number of observations of different values of the variables that are of interest. The reason for describing procedures in detail is that such information allows scientists to decide whether the observations have been made in a systematic and unbiased manner. In broad terms, the idea is to have observations governed by a plan rather than by momentary fluctuations in attention.

Making observations systematically does not guarantee that accurate information will be obtained. My system might have some kind of bias in it. Here is a simple example. Suppose I want to know something about the relative popularity of rock music and classical music. I decide to collect information by systematically asking a number of people which type of music they prefer. What I actually do is get the opinions of all of the students in my course on Musical Compositions by Mozart. My observations would be systematic, but my plan has bias in it; I might get accurate information about the musical preferences of people who have chosen to take a course dealing with classical music, but it is doubtful that I would get accurate information about the musical preferences of people in general. As an alternative, I might ask a representative group of people but bias the information by asking a question like "You like rock music more than classical music, don't you?" Note that while systematic observations might yield inaccurate information, it is impossible to evaluate the information resulting from unsystematic, casual observations. There is really no substitute for making observations systematically.

③ *Make Public Observations.* Science deals with a shared version of reality. Therefore the observations that science considers must, in principle, be "makeable" by anyone who is interested. If observations are unique to a particular individual, they will not be a part of science. If I report some observations, other scientists basically ask, "How can we make the observations you have made?" If I say that they cannot, that only I can, they will dismiss my observations from their consideration. For example, suppose I report that I have made a large number of systematic observations and have found that "people with guilty consciences blink their eyes a lot." If scientists are interested in this relation, they will ask how I observed eye blinking and guilty consciences. Suppose I say that eye blinking was measured by asking each person a standard set of questions and counting the number of eye blinks during the first two minutes of the interview. The scientists might say, "Okay, we could do that, but what about guilty consciences?" If I answered, "Well, that's harder to describe. I seem to have this special talent—I can look at a person and tell whether or not he or she has a guilty conscience," the scientists would pursue the question: "How do you tell by looking at a person?" I would respond, "Well, I can just tell, that's all." In this case there is nothing science can do with my observation. Notice that while I might well "believe my own eyes," my observation will not become part of scientific information.

The requirement that observations be public might seem obvious, and my example is admittedly a bit farfetched. However, there are less extreme examples in which this requirement is precisely the point at issue. For example, if a psychiatrist should report that, on the basis of many years of experience, he has found that many people suffer from anxiety because of unresolved conflicts with their fathers, that report is not enough. Scientists must ask how anxiety and unresolved conflicts with fathers were observed, and until those questions are satisfactorily answered the status of the psychiatrist's observations will remain in doubt.

Consider a different example—assessing the creativity of an essay. It might be quite difficult to specify in great detail how one judges the creativity of an essay. Perhaps all a researcher can say is that in assessing creativity she follows a few general rules, and tell you what those rules are. Perhaps the "rules" are somewhat vague—"I look for innovative ideas, clever uses of the language, unusual meanings for words and phrases." We might well want to know more about what is meant by "innovative ideas," "clever uses of the language," and "unusual meanings." However, it might be possible to show that the researcher's observations of creativity are sufficiently public. We could give the rules to several people and ask each of them to independently assess the creativity of a set of essays. If those people agreed in their assessments of the creativity of the essays, then the observations would be public. Without knowing more precisely what the researcher means by her rules, different people are capable of making the same observations, which is the core of the requirement that observations be public.

To sum up, science distinguishes between observations and explanations; theoretical explanations are evaluated by checking their consistency with the "facts" of observation. For this process to make sense, the terms of observation must be different from the terms of explanation, making it possible to determine whether the explanation is consistent with the observations. Observations are described in concrete, commonly understood terms. Observations must also be public—capable, in principle, of being made by anyone. A systematic plan for making observations must be used, and the procedures must be described in sufficient detail to allow the accuracy of the observations to be evaluated.

The Relation Between Observations and Explanations

Making observations and devising explanations are both necessary parts of science. It might seem obvious that the observations come first and then are explained in one way or another. However, this is not quite correct. *There are no completely neutral observations.* What you observe depends on what you already believe about "what's going on," at least to some extent. After all, scientific observations are made by people, who are not cameras but organisms who know things that affect the ways they "see" things. A researcher might have a hunch or have casually noticed something that seems sensible and then make systematic observations to check out these ideas. As scientific work on any question continues, observations come to be guided more and more closely by the existing theories. The process of developing theories involves repeated recycling between theorizing (at various levels) and making observations. In rough terms, the sequence might be something like this: vague idea → observation → tentative explanation → observation → modified explanation → observation . . . → formal theory → observation → modified theory → observation, and so on. This sequence is only roughly accurate. In the history of science there are many instances of scientists inventing theories, even very formal ones, not to explain large amounts of existing data but because the theories seemed like good ones on intuitive grounds. Only after the theory had been proposed were systematic observations made to test it.

The key points in the relation between observing and explaining are these. First, there are no really neutral observations. People with radically different theoretical orientations might have difficulty agreeing on what observations need to be explained. Second, the purpose of making observations is to advance understanding, to help develop explanations. This means that researchers should be very aware of the possible theoretical relevance of any observations they might think of making. The history of science suggests that scientific progress is *not* made by making lots of observations guided by vague notions or simple curiosity in the hope that theoretical understanding will come later. Good ideas are most important, and observations are useful to the extent that they lead to better ideas.

SOURCES OF RESEARCH QUESTIONS

In the preceding section I stressed the point that the scientific purpose of observations is to advance theoretical understanding. Reasonable though this statement might be, it does not say much about how a researcher goes about choosing a question to investigate in a particular study. "Contributing to scientific progress" is too vague a goal to help a researcher actually do a research project—the question posed in any study must be more specific. We will now consider some of the ways in which researchers choose questions to study. In essence, we'll get a bit closer to the actual practice of research.

A particular research project might be done for several different reasons: to fill a gap in knowledge, to resolve contradictory findings, or to test a theoretical prediction. I will discuss these and other sources of research questions in a moment. Right now I want to emphasize two general points. First, the choice of a research question is strongly influenced by what is already known in a scientific community—it is important for the individual researcher to be aware of the current state of knowledge in the field (which is, in fact, easier said than done). Second, although I will discuss ways in which a question might be chosen for a *single* study, the simple fact is that no one study is likely to make a great difference in the long run—many observations are usually required to make a substantial change in scientific knowledge. Let's now consider how researchers "get into action."

Gaps in Knowledge

The idea here is that a person would like an answer to a specific question and doesn't find it in the reports of research already done. For example, you might want to know whether 2-year-old children find jigsaw puzzles interesting, and fail to find any research on this question in the existing literature. If you're really interested, you might collect data to try to get an answer. In psychology it is really rather easy to think of a specific question that has not been investigated previously. There are, however, two clear dangers involved in choosing a research question to fill a gap in knowledge.

First, the person must make sure that the gap lies in the collective knowledge of the research community and not just in his or her personal knowledge! If a particular question has been studied by other researchers but you are not aware that this has been done, you might well waste your time making observations that have been made a number of times already. Perhaps this point seems obvious, and you assume that any researcher would know what's already been done. There are, however, dozens of journals publishing research reports, and it is really difficult for any individual to stay informed about the research in any area. Professional researchers spend a great deal of time and effort trying to "keep up with the literature." At the end of this chapter, I provide some suggestions for searching through the research literature to find out what is known about questions that you find interesting.

A second and more important danger lies in the possibility that a gap in knowledge might not be very important. Evaluating the gap is crucial to choosing a good research question—the simple fact that a particular question has not yet been investigated does *not* mean that the question is worthwhile. To use the earlier example, why should we care whether 2-year-olds find jigsaw puzzles interesting? How will an answer to this question advance our understanding? For a gap in knowledge to be worth pursuing, reasonable answers to questions like these are needed.

In a thoroughly delightful article Henry Klugh (1969) satirized gap filling without critical evaluation. His article was entitled "A Problem-Finding Machine," referring to an "invention" of his that he suggested could be used by a person who wanted to become a "really famous psychologist." I'll describe an advanced version of this invention. Take two coffee cans and mount them on a stick such that they spin freely and separately. Run to the library and pick two psychological journals, one from each of two areas of psychology. Choose, for example, the *Journal of Experimental Social Psychology* and the *Journal of Comparative and Physiological Psychology*. Examine each journal and make a list of the variables researchers have used (you probably only need to read titles) for each journal. Type the "social" list on a sheet of paper and mount it on one can, and type the "physiological" list for the other can. Place some kind of window in front of the cans such that you can see only one line at a time on each can. Spin the two cans and see what two variables show up in the window. Check the literature to see if anyone has used this combination in a study. If not, do the study. Imagine a study titled "The Effects of Hippocampal Lesions on Bargaining in Conflict Situations." You can be fairly sure that nobody has done such a study, and you can also be rather sure that such a study would not be worth doing. Klugh's point is that without good evaluation a person could fill gaps in knowledge that are best left as gaping holes.

Contradictory Findings

As research findings accumulate, a set of contradictory findings sometimes emerges—several researchers seem to have studied the same question, but their findings do not agree. Here's an example. In the introduction to an article Laughlin (1969) pointed out that the findings of eight different studies did not agree regarding the question of whether performance on concept-learning problems improves as people become more practiced (solve more problems). Improvement had been found in four studies, while four others reported no improvement. Such contradictory findings surely present a puzzle that a researcher might try to solve by conducting another study.

There is a good way and a bad way to try resolving a set of contradictory findings. The bad way is to just do another study, in effect trying to change the "count" one way or the other. For example, doing a study that changes the "count" to five "yes, performance improves with practice" to four "no improvement occurs" would give little information—we still wouldn't know why practice effects sometimes occur and sometimes don't occur.

A far better approach is to carefully examine the studies producing the conflicting results to see if they are *really* contradictory. Even though several studies deal with the same question, they will differ from each other in a number of ways. The idea is to see whether you can find some difference(s) among the studies that can be used to organize the findings and to explain why researchers have obtained different results. This is what Laughlin (1969) tried to do. He noticed that the eight studies differed in terms of the procedure used to present stimuli to the subjects: In some studies the experimenter chose the stimuli, while in others the subject could choose the stimuli about which information would be given. Laughlin suggested the following, tentative hypothesis (which seemed to fit the set of "contradictory" findings): Subjects will improve with practice when the experimenter chooses the stimuli, but performance will not improve with practice when the subjects choose the stimuli. Notice that if this hypothesis were correct, the confusion would be eliminated—we would know that the question is more complex than it had originally been thought to be, and we would know to some extent when improvement with practice will or will not occur. If the hypothesis were not supported, we would still need an explanation for the contradictory findings, but we would at least know that one plausible explanation is not the answer. Thus when Laughlin did his study comparing the practice effects for the two kinds of stimulus selection procedures he was collecting data that held the promise of increasing our understanding. In fact, Laughlin (1969) found that improvement with practice did *not* depend on who chose the stimuli (experimenter or subject), and he went on to test other possible explanations in later research.

PROBLEM

One researcher found that fourth-grade students who studied in groups scored better on science tests than those who studied alone. Another researcher found that fourth-grade students who studied in groups scored worse on tests of English grammar than those who studied alone. These findings appear to be contradictory—one study reports that studying in groups is better, the other that it is worse. Formulate a hypothesis about the effects of studying in groups versus studying alone that is compatible with both results. Then indicate how your hypothesis could be investigated.

In these simplified descriptions there is one obvious difference between the two studies. One researcher looked at scores on science tests while the other studied performance on grammar tests. Therefore a plausible explanation for the difference in results would be the following: "Studying in groups is better than studying alone for science, but the opposite is true with respect to grammar." To test this idea one would compare "studying in groups" with "studying alone" with respect to both science and grammar, all in one study. In actual research, studies differ from each other in more than one way. Nonetheless if the studies yield apparently contradictory findings, it is useful to try to identify a way in which they are "not quite the same" and then check to see whether the difference that is identified provides a plausible explanation that can be supported by additional data.

Theoretical Predictions

Theories form the core of a science, and it is quite common for researchers to collect data to test theoretical predictions. Although it is tempting to think of theory-testing studies as "crucial," no single study really carries that much weight, for a variety of reasons. If the results support a theoretical prediction, the theory is *not* proved although researchers will have slightly more confidence in the theory. If the results do *not* support the prediction, it is seldom true that the theory is completely discarded because of the failure. One reason is that the connection between a theory and any specific prediction is usually complex and not all that obvious. Quite often it is possible to argue that "the theory doesn't really make that prediction." Let's consider an example.

A number of researchers have conducted studies in which they have tried to train young children to solve "conservation problems." (The details of conservation problems need not concern us here.) The stated reason for such studies is to test "a prediction from Piaget's theory of cognitive development." The researchers argued that, since Piaget's theory holds that children develop the ability to solve conservation problems gradually over time, his theory predicts that it should not be possible to train children to solve such problems. The issue *seems* simple: If training is successful, Piaget's theory is wrong; if training doesn't work, Piaget's theory is supported. However, as Kuhn (1974) and others have pointed out, the matter is not that simple. Here are some of the complexities.

If training doesn't work, this does not necessarily mean that Piaget is right; it might just mean that a poor training scheme was used (implying that a better scheme might work). Successful training results have also been ambiguous. It has been argued that Piaget's theory does *not* predict that training *cannot* be successful—training might well be predicted to work for children who have almost completed the development of conservation ability. It has also been argued that the kind of "success" claimed for training is *not* the "success" that Piaget's theory is concerned with (roughly, that Piaget's criteria for success are much more stringent than those used in training studies). As you can see, testing theoretical predictions is not as simple as it might seem at first.

Acceptance of a theory becomes more likely as the number of successful predictions increases. It is, however, critical for a theory to explain findings that other theories cannot account for. In other words, a theory succeeds by cumulating successful predictions and by eliminating competitive theories. Similarly, when data do *not* support a theory's prediction, the theory is seldom discarded. The theory may be modified in some way to make it fit the results better. As an alternative, an unsuccessful prediction may lead to the identification of a *boundary condition* for the theory—a statement of conditions under which the theory is applicable. For example, many years ago there were two clearly opposed theories of problem solving. Edward L. Thorndike proposed that problem solving was a gradual, trial-and-error process, while Wolfgang Kohler proposed that problem solving was an insightful, all-or-none process. It would seem that one of these proposals must be wrong and the other right, but that is not the case.

Over the years researchers showed that under some circumstances problem solving is a gradual, trial-and-error process while under other circumstances it is an insightful, all-or-none process. Each theory is correct under some conditions and incorrect under others.

Finally, keep in mind that if a theory helps us understand many findings it remains helpful even if one of its predictions is not supported by research findings. Basically, theories that are reasonably useful stay around until a better theory is generated. Doing research to test theoretical predictions is important, but no single study is decisive. Many research findings are needed for real theoretical change to take place.

PROBLEM

Which of the following is the better way of establishing a particular scientific explanation: (1) amassing as much evidence as possible that is consistent with the explanation or (2) eliminating alternate explanations of the evidence that has been collected?

The answer is (2)—eliminating alternate explanations. Keep in mind that no number of confirmations proves an explanation to be correct. Furthermore, even if an explanation (A) is consistent with, say, 100 observations, it has no advantage if the same 100 observations are also consistent with a different explanation (B). For an explanation to "rise above the crowd," as it were, it is necessary to demonstrate that that explanation can account for observations that are inconsistent with other, alternate explanations.

Programmatic Research

This category really includes all the sources of research questions that I have already discussed, but I want to emphasize that many research questions arise from a researcher's previous work. It is often said that "one good study suggests another." Keep in mind that no single study provides that much information or settles an issue. Many researchers operate research programs doing dozens of studies dealing with a fairly narrow topic and using the results of one study to suggest ideas for the next. Through a long series of studies dealing with basically the same problem, real advances in knowledge can be generated.

In my view there is one possible problem with programmatic research, which strikes me as a kind of "tunnel vision." It is actually rather easy to find some way to modify a study and thus come up with another—you might change the way behavior is measured, try different kinds of subjects, or make some other modification. The danger lies in the possibility of the researcher's losing sight of the general theoretical importance of the topic being studied, which might lead to collecting data to answer minor, unimportant questions (rather like gaps best left unfilled). It is difficult for researchers to decide that it might be best to stop a program of research that they have been following for some time, but surely this is sometimes the proper decision.

Outside Influences

I have now described several formal ways in which researchers select problems for study. In all cases the choice is based in some way on the existing knowledge in the field. There are, however, other influences on the choice of research questions, factors that arise not directly from the scientific literature but from outside sources. Research on particular topics has sometimes resulted from societal needs. For example, World War II produced an enormous amount of research on psychological testing because of the need to test and selectively place men who had been drafted into the armed services, as well as research on visual–motor skills, much of it in connection with pilot training. In the 1960s, because of a political decision to start a "war on poverty," there was a great increase in research on compensatory education and other remedial programs. When the use of marijuana reached a level sufficient to evoke public and political attention, studies of the effect of this drug on various kinds of behavior increased noticeably in frequency.

Over the years much research has become expensive to conduct, with the result that the availability of funds has come to have some control over which research questions will be investigated. Money for research is provided in the form of grants awarded on a competitive basis by private foundations and government agencies such as the National Science Foundation, the Department of Health, Education and Welfare, or a state department of mental health. While such agencies utilize panels of scientists to review grant proposals and help decide which projects will receive funds, the budgets and directions of these agencies are determined on fundamentally nonscientific grounds. For example, Congress passes appropriations bills specifying how much money the National Science Foundation will receive and how that money should be allocated among various broad areas of activity.

While there is obviously nothing intrinsically wrong with researching questions that are of concern to society, the social pressures and political decisions that influence research are not based on careful evaluation of the existing state of scientific knowledge. It is therefore possible that such influences can lead to relatively unproductive research being done and, conversely, to potentially fruitful research not being done. For example, when the Nixon administration announced a "war on cancer" in the early 1970s this resulted in a politically directed increase in funds for the support of research on cancer, which meant that some funds were taken away from programs supporting research on other issues. Many researchers were concerned that, as a consequence, good research on other questions might not be funded and thus would not be done, while relatively less productive research having some relevance to cancer might be funded and thus completed.

THE OUTCOMES OF RESEARCH

Now that you have some understanding of how researchers choose questions to investigate, let's consider what the products of research are like. There are two basic kinds of observations that might be made, two basic classes of *data* or *findings* that might be reported. A researcher might study some features of a *single* variable or the *relation* between two or more variables. Let's take a brief look at these two kinds of outcomes and then consider how research findings are evaluated.

Describing a Variable

The simplest research outcome is a description of some characteristics of a variable. Such research is a preliminary step in scientific work, although the data might have considerable practical value. For various reasons people often want information about a single variable. For example, a politician might have a poll taken to see what percentage of the population favors some legislative proposal, such as national health insurance. A manufacturer might want to know the percentage of products that leave the assembly line in defective condition. An educator might want to know the percentage of first-graders who know the meanings of various words, or the average speed at which they read.

Information about the distribution of values, the average value, or the spread of values of a single variable might be desired for practical decision making or to gain some knowledge about a variable that is of potential theoretical interest. With such outcomes there is one basic question to ask: Is the description accurate? I will shortly have more to say about the meaning of *accurate,* but first we'll look at outcomes dealing with relations among variables.

Relations Among Variables

From a scientific viewpoint information concerning relations among variables is extremely important. Research dealing with relations among variables can be done in many ways, and the way in which the information is obtained is critical for deciding what the observations mean (more on this shortly). At this point I want to alert you to two slightly different forms that statements about relations might take. These two research outcomes are *not* fundamentally different, but they "look" different.

Determining Whether a Relation Exists. The simplest question one can ask about a relation between variables is whether or not a relation exists. In psychological research this question is often phrased in terms of *differences*. Here are some examples: Do males and females differ in anxiety? Are learning scores different, depending on whether a large or small reward is given for correct responses? Do the grades of students in small classes differ from those of students in large classes?

Notice that, in each case, the question is phrased in terms of a difference, but actually concerns a relation between two variables. The first question can be rephrased, "Is there a systematic relation between variation in gender (male or female) and variation in anxiety?" Rephrasing the third question leads to "Is there a systematic relation between class size and students' grades?" The outcomes of psychological research are often stated in terms of differences or "effects." You might encounter statements such as "There is a difference . . .," "This variable does make a difference . . .," "There is an effect of . . .," or "This variable does not affect . . ." All such statements refer to a relation between variables even though they might not use the term *relation*. If you look closely, you will find that two (or more) variables are being described and that the difference or effect refers to their relation (or lack thereof).

Describing Relations. Deciding that a relation exists between variables leads to an obvious question: What kind of relation is it? Relations can differ in *form* as well as in *strength*. A relation might be *linear* or *curvilinear*, or even more complex. A linear relation means that a straight line describes the relation; a curvilinear relation might take several forms but will have a bend or curve in it. Figure 1.1 illustrates both forms.

Panels (a) and (b) illustrate linear relations; in these examples as entrance scores vary from low to high, the associated grades vary from low to high, following a straight line. The difference between panels (a) and (b) lies in the strength of the relation illustrated. Strength refers to the degree to which changes in one variable are associated with changes in the other. Comparing the panels, you can see that as entrance scores vary from low to high, there is a large linear increase in grades in panel (a) but only a modest linear increase in grades in panel (b).

Panel (c) illustrates a curvilinear relation—as arousal varies from low to high, performance values first increase and then decrease. There are other, more complex forms of relations that have been observed, but we need not consider them here. The essential point is that research findings about the type of relation that exists between variables provide a great deal of information.

Describing a relation is essentially an expanded, more precise version of research on whether a relation exists. Often, researchers who talk about

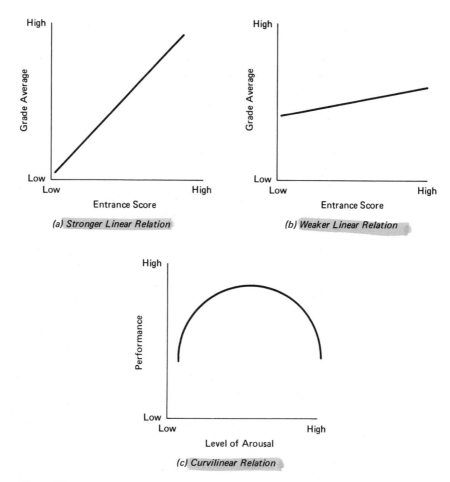

Figure 1.1. **Examples of different relations between variables.**

"differences" include just two values of one variable in their research. For example, research on the question "Do grades in large and small classes differ?" involves just two values of class size, large and small (two specific sizes would actually be used). Information about the "difference" would provide some information, but it would not tell us much about the type of relation between class size and grades. To describe the relation more precisely, more values of class size would have to be included.

Natural Versus Manipulated Variation

When evaluating information about a relation between variables, it is important to know how the different values of each variable occurred. A variable might take on different values either naturally or because of manipulation by the researcher. As we go about our everyday lives we observe a great deal of variation—some people are taller than others, some drive foreign cars while others don't, some things burn when others won't, and so on. The variation we observe is "natural"—we haven't done anything to produce variation but are just observing what happens under the circumstances. There are times when we do manipulate variables quite deliberately—on Tuesday I drink my coffee with sugar and cream, but on Wednesday I deliberately leave out the sugar to see whether I like the drink more or less that way. The variation in sugar content of my coffee has not "just happened"—I made it happen.

In any research study at least one variable will necessarily vary naturally. In psychological research one variable always concerns some aspect of the behavior or traits of organisms that is left (within some limits) to take on whatever values happen to occur. When another variable is involved it may vary naturally or through manipulation, and the difference is important for understanding the relation. Suppose I am teaching a course in a room having ten rows of seats and decide to study the relation between grades in the course and seating location (row). One way to do this would be to let the students sit wherever they want (but requiring them to keep the same seats throughout the course). In this way *both* seating location and course grades would vary *naturally*. Suppose that when the course is over I find that students who sat nearer the front of the room tended to get higher grades than those sitting toward the back. I have observed a relation, but the question is, What does it mean? Perhaps sitting near the front is helpful to students, or perhaps the better students just happened to sit nearer the front—it would be hard to figure out the meaning of the relation.

If, on the other hand, I manipulated seating locations, I would have an *opportunity* to clarify the situation. If I assigned the students to seats according to some plan, I might be able to make sure that better and worse students (in terms of past performance) were equally distributed over the rows in the classroom. If I were able to do this, and if I observed that students in the nearer rows got higher grades, I would have eliminated one possible meaning of this relation—it could not be true that "the better students just happened to sit in the front rows." The relation between seating location and grades would be easier to understand. Of course I could manipulate seating locations and do it poorly, in which case there would really be no advantage. For example, suppose I assign students to seats according to the order in which they show up for the first class—early arrivers are assigned to front rows and later arrivers to rows in the back. I would have manipulated seating location, but if better students tend to show up earlier than poorer students, I would not have eliminated the possibility that "better students were just sitting in the front rows." Manipulating variables does not guarantee clearer, more understandable observations, but it does give the researcher an opportunity to avoid some difficulties.

When a researcher manipulates one of the variables involved in a relation that is under study, we say that he or she is doing an *experiment*. (Remember, one of the variables in a relation always varies naturally.) As you can see, experiments have some potential advantages over studying the relation between two naturally varying variables. I will have much more to say about experimental and nonexperimental research in later chapters.

Evaluating Research Findings

A research outcome must be evaluated to determine the quality of the information. I have hinted at this in talking about the accuracy or clarity of a research finding; here I will discuss this issue more formally. Three broad criteria are applied to research findings. Two of these involve a careful examination of the observations and the procedures used to collect the data. Campbell and Stanley (1963) refer to these criteria as *external validity* and *internal validity*. External validity refers to the *generality* of a result—we can ask about the range of conditions over which a particular finding might be expected to occur. This criterion applies to all research findings. Internal validity concerns only findings dealing with relations among variables and refers to the *interpretability* of the observed relation. Before considering these criteria more closely, I will discuss a third criterion, *theoretical contribution,* which includes external and internal validity but may also be treated separately.

Theoretical Contribution. The purpose of collecting data is to advance understanding, to increase our knowledge of the world around us. A broad question that scientists ask about any research outcome is, "How (to what extent) does this finding increase our understanding?" The overall value of a finding depends on three basic components of a research project— the question that was asked, the methods used to make observations, and the actual nature of the data. Consequently there are three ways in which a finding might be judged as failing to make a sufficient theoretical contribution.

First, the question that was posed might not be very important; that is, it might not fit in well with the existing structure of knowledge. If so, the results, while providing some answer to the question, would not help complete the knowledge structure or advance our understanding. Second, a researcher might pose a good question but use flawed methods in collecting data, which reduces the value of the findings because interpretive problems exist (concern over external and internal validity is involved here). Third, a researcher might pose a good question and use reasonable methods but simply obtain poor data. The results might be "noisy," more confusing than illuminating. Of course better methods might lead to more understandable results, but it is not always obvious how the methods should be changed. Sometimes researchers need to collect more information to improve the finding rather than drastically alter their methods.

Most of this book concerns the evaluation of methods and data in a very direct and detailed fashion. At this point I want to emphasize that using good methods, while crucial, is not enough to ensure that a result will be viewed as valuable. Earlier I discussed how researchers try to choose good questions, and it should be clear that the choice of question can be critical for the later evaluation of the results.

External Validity. Any research finding is limited in a number of ways. In rough terms, reality is very large, and a researcher studies only a small part of reality in any project. It is therefore necessary to ask how limited or how general an observation might be. The importance of generality or external validity can be easily seen in the case of poll taking. Suppose we want to know how "the voting population of the United States" plans to vote in a particular national election. It is impossible to obtain information for the entire voting population; a researcher would collect data for only a part of the population. An important question is how well the information, coming from a part of the population, generalizes to the entire population. If I ask some of my friends and find that 80 percent of them say they plan to vote Democratic, it is obvious that this information does *not* clearly tell us anything about the whole population. I have no way of knowing how my friends' plans relate to the plans of "all voters."

Concern over *who* was observed is not the only basis for questioning external validity. Suppose a very reasonable attempt has been made to find out the voting preferences of a representative part of the population one week before the actual election. To what extent do the results of the poll generalize to the actual election results? There could be a significant change in voter opinions during the week between the poll and the election. Moreover, everyone who responds to a poll does not actually vote; this might reduce the external validity of the poll results. Or people might respond differently to the poll taker's question than they do to the voting machine itself—asking people whether they plan to vote for John Doe might yield a "yes" answer even though they will not vote for that candidate. Even in research that simply deals with describing a variable there can be many threats to external validity.

Similar considerations apply to research dealing with relations among variables that is done for "purely" theoretical reasons. Consider the example of a researcher who studies the question of whether large and small rewards lead to different learning scores. The question is phrased in rather general terms, but to actually do the research the investigator will collect data in a particular set of circumstances. The learners will be some particular kind of organism; there will be a particular learning task; a particular kind of reward will be used; "large" and "small" will have specific meanings; a particular method of measuring learning will be used—in short, the research project will have many particular features. When the results are in, it is reasonable to ask how general they are. Suppose the researcher finds that, on the average, large rewards lead to better learning scores than small rewards. We could ask whether this result would "hold up" if we studied people rather than mice or children rather than adults, if the reward were money rather than food, if the learning task involved auditory rather than visual discrimination or pictures rather than words, if performance were assessed in terms of accuracy rather than speed, and so on.

Evaluating the external validity of research findings is extremely difficult. If we adopt a strict position on the issue, the vast majority of research findings would be seen as very limited, that is, as having quite uncertain external validity. Researchers tend to adopt an attitude of cautious optimism toward this issue. They try not to overstate the generality of their findings, but they are inclined to believe that their results have *some* reasonable amount of external validity.

Campbell and Stanley (1963) emphasize the importance of the *plausibility* of any argument dealing with research. We can distinguish between *technical* flaws in research and *plausible* weaknesses in research outcomes. Plausibility takes into account the current state of knowledge. For example, if in a research project I have had people write answers to questions with a number 2 pencil, technically I could not claim that similar results would be obtained if a ball point pen were used. However, researchers would ask whether there is any plausible reason to expect that changing to ball point pens would change the results. If a researcher is criticized because all the subjects were third-graders in Milwaukee and you don't know whether the results would be the same for third-graders in San Francisco, the researcher is very likely to ask whether there is any plausible reason to expect the results to change.

I do not want to overstate or underestimate the importance of concern over external validity. But you should recognize that the generality of results is fundamentally important for scientific purposes, and that evaluating generality is difficult. A *plausible* argument that findings are critically limited is a serious matter. A number of critics have argued that psychological researchers do *not* pay enough attention to the external validity of their findings, and their criticisms are sometimes very plausible.

Internal Validity. When a relation between variables has been observed, an important question is how the relation might be explained. As the number of plausible explanations *increases,* the internal validity of the finding *decreases.* Let me give you a rather extreme example of a finding with very low internal validity. Suppose I tell you that I have found that the math scores of students who smoked marijuana before taking the test were, on the average, higher than the scores of students who didn't smoke before the test. I claim that my results show a relation between marijuana smoking and math scores. However, when you examine the details of my study you discover the mess shown in Table 1.1.

In this made-up study the basic fact that has been observed is that the math scores for Group A were higher than those for Group B. As soon as we ask the question "Why?," the messiness of the study becomes critically important. Perhaps the score difference does have something to do with smoking marijuana versus not smoking. Of course the observed score difference could also have something to do with group differences in time of testing, amount of prior education, or sex. In other words, we cannot propose a sensible answer to the question. We don't know whether the data reflect a relation between marijuana smoking and math scores, between time of testing and math scores, and so on. There are just too many plausible explanations for the finding to make much sense. Certainly it would be foolish to accept the claim that the results show that "smoking marijuana affects math scores."

When a number of variables are confused in this way, the study is said to be *confounded*. That is, the relation between marijuana smoking and math scores is confounded with the relation between time of testing and math scores, both of which are confounded with the relation between amount of education and math scores, and so on. Stated differently, as marijuana smoking varied from yes to no, time of testing varied from A.M. to P.M., amount of education varied from freshmen to seniors, and sex of student varied from males to females. In effect, we would not know which of these variables to relate to math scores.

With respect to internal validity, the ideal is to have *no* confounding variables present. If we looked at the relation between marijuana smoking and math scores, examined the research carefully, and could find *no other* variables changing along with marijuana smoking, the marijuana–math relation would have maximum internal validity. Note that "no confounding" is an ideal, a goal that researchers seek to attain. Often this goal is impossible to achieve. For example, try to figure out a way of finding

Table 1.1   Description of a Study with Very Low Internal Validity

Group A	Group B
Smoked marijuana	No marijuana
Tested in A.M.	Tested in P.M.
Seniors	Freshmen
Males	Females

NOTE: Suppose that math test scores for Group A were observed to be higher than those for Group B.

neurotics and normals who differ *only* in that some are neurotic while others are "normal"—nobody has yet done so.

One reason why researchers prefer to do experiments—to manipulate a variable—is that manipulation gives them the opportunity to minimize or avoid confounding of relations. If I controlled marijuana smoking, deciding who would and wouldn't smoke (as opposed to just finding smokers and nonsmokers), I might be able to arrange things such that this variable would not be confounded with time of testing, amount of education, or sex. As mentioned earlier, manipulation does not guarantee success, but it does improve a researcher's chances of minimizing confounding. We will examine some techniques used to avoid confounding in Chapter 2.

Concern over confounding depends on plausibility. For example, if I had added "number 2 pencils" to the description of group A and "ball point pens" to the description of group B, "type of writing instrument" would be confounded with all the other variables. Yet this confounding would probably generate little concern because "type of writing instrument" is not a plausible explanation of differences in math scores. With respect to both external and internal validity, the key is to see whether *plausible* threats to validity are present. When evaluating the external validity, internal validity, or general theoretical contribution of a research finding, it is necessary to engage in thorough analysis and to use sensible judgment.

SUMMARY

Research methodology is a collection of procedures that scientists use to obtain and evaluate facts. Scientists assume that nature is knowable and orderly, and their goal is to construct a coherent account of the regularities in nature that have been and might be observed. Scientific knowledge concerns many but not all aspects of our existence, and changes over time. It is not clear whether scientific laws should be viewed as completely deterministic or fundamentally probabilistic, but in either case scientists can and do seek to identify and explain relations among variables as best they can. While the prediction and control of events might often be part of science, the primary goal of science is understanding.

Scientific explanations vary in scope, with formal theories usually characterized as relatively broad, abstract explanations. To judge how useful an explanation might be, scientists compare it to a number of criteria. An explanation is expected to involve clear terminology, to be internally consistent or logical, and to show agreement with the facts of observation. Other things being equal, scientists prefer general explanations that cover a broader range of observations, and they desire simple explanations rather than more complicated accounts. Explanations that involve the identification of causes and effects can be helpful for understanding the likely outcomes of intervening in nature.

Researchers are expected to follow a set of general rules when making observations. The procedures used to collect data must be specified in considerable detail and in rather ordinary terms different from those used in explanations. Observations need to be systematic and public, so that, in principle, anyone could repeat the observations. To warrant scientific concern, observations need to be related to questions of importance. Consequently researchers pay careful attention to the existing state of knowledge when choosing questions to study. Data might be collected to fill a gap in knowledge, to resolve apparently contradictory findings, or to test theoretical predictions. A single research study provides but a small amount of information, and many researchers conduct organized programs of research that extend over long periods. Societal needs and public pressures also affect the choice of a research question, with uncertain effects on the quality of research that results.

The outcome of a research project might be a description of some characteristics of a single variable, an important but preliminary step in scientific work. Most research deals with relations among variables and is concerned either with deciding whether a systematic relation exists or describing a relation with some precision. In studying relations among variables it is important to distinguish between variation that occurs naturally and variation that is a result of manipulation by the researcher. The term *experiment* refers to a study that is concerned with the relation between a manipulated variable and a natural one (in contrast to a relation between two natural variables). Experiments give researchers an opportunity to identify relations among variables that will be easier to understand or explain.

Research findings are not just accepted at face value but are evaluated in light of the procedures used to collect data and the current state of scientific knowledge. A general criterion concerns the extent to which the finding advances theoretical understanding; a finding might be judged as lacking because a poor question was asked, because flawed methods were used, or simply because the data are not clear. The procedures used to collect the data affect the external and internal validity of a finding. *External validity* refers to generality, or the range of conditions to which the observations are relevant; this criterion applies to all research findings. *Internal validity* applies to findings dealing with relations among variables and concerns the extent to which the relation can be clearly interpreted. Judging the quality of a research finding depends on the number of threats to validity that are identified and on the plausibility or likely importance of those threats.

SUGGESTED READINGS

If you are interested in gaining more information about the nature of science, you may wish to read the books listed here. Each presents a different view of science and research. The books are fairly short and thought provoking without being excessively abstract.

BRAGINSKY, B. M., and BRAGINSKY, D. D. *Mainstream Psychology: A Critique*. New York: Holt, Rinehart and Winston, 1974. (The authors argue that psychology has been based on inappropriate ideologies and raise questions about what psychology might become.)

DEESE, J. *Psychology as Science and Art*. New York: Harcourt Brace Jovanovich, 1972. (The author argues that psychological knowledge is a mixture of science, intuition, and myth.)

DETHIER, V. G. *To Know a Fly*. San Francisco: Holden-Day, 1962. (The author uses the example of studying "the humble fly" to explore scientific methods, with considerable wry humor.)

SIU, R. G. H. *The Tao of Science*. Cambridge Mass.: MIT Press, 1957. (The author compares and integrates Western science and Eastern philosophy.)

2

FUNDAMENTALS
OF
RESEARCH

Any research project involves making observations in some systematic fashion. Let me use this sentence to draw your attention to two basic aspects of research. The idea of "making observations," when applied to psychology, means that a researcher will always *measure* one or more aspects of behavior. The notion of being "systematic" implies that a researcher will in some way exercise *control* when making observations; more precisely, a researcher will control certain *variables.* Research projects take on many different forms, ranging from simple observational studies to complex experiments, but considerations of measurement and control are relevant to all forms of research.

In this chapter we will consider several different kinds of measures found in psychological research, concentrating on the type of information that each form of measurement provides. We will also consider the control procedures commonly used in research and how the different procedures affect the findings of a research study. In a sense this chapter is just a beginning; later chapters will cover more detailed topics such as the organization of sets of measurements and the particular variables that psychological researchers need to attend to when deciding what to control. Our focus here will be on the fundamental characteristics of the measurement and control procedures used in research.

Measurement and control are rather technical aspects of research. There is a third, less technical but still important aspect of research projects, namely, the issue of ethical considerations. Questions of ethics arise, sometimes quite forcefully, in research projects. We will consider this topic at the end of this chapter.

FUNDAMENTALS OF MEASUREMENT

In Chapter 1 we saw that at least one variable in a study will vary naturally—the researcher will not determine the values of the variable but, rather, will just observe and record the values that happen to occur. In simpler terms, a psychological researcher will always obtain some *scores* that represent different values of some naturally varying aspect of behavior. We are concerned here with what the scores might be like, viewed from several perspectives.

It is important to realize that a researcher's interest in an aspect of behavior is likely to be at a conceptual level, whereas the data (scores) stem from a particular measure of variation. It is useful to distinguish between a variable at the conceptual or theoretical level and at the empirical or measurement level. For example, a researcher might be interested in variation in level of anxiety among humans. It is possible to conceive of differences in anxiety in a rather abstract, conceptual sense; having done so, it then becomes apparent that "anxiety" might be measured in a variety of ways, some better than others. The question of the strength of the connection between a variable *as it is conceptualized* and *as it is measured* is of great importance in evaluating psychological research.

In general terms, the extent to which a measure accurately represents a variable as conceptualized is often called the *validity* of the measure. Two other important characteristics of a measure are reliability and sensitivity. *Reliability* refers to the stability or consistency of the values that are obtained. For example, if I measured a person's weight five times and obtained the values of 161, 170, 158, 165, and 157 pounds, my measurement would be less reliable than if the five values were 161, 163, 161, 162, and 163. As you can see, the values are more consistent in the second case. *Sensitivity* basically reflects the number of values that might occur; it is one way of talking about precision of measurement. For example, one might grade exams with either a "pass" or a "fail" or with an A, B, C, D, or E. The latter measurement is potentially more sensitive because it can reflect some differences that the simpler pass–fail measure cannot. We will return to the concepts of reliability, validity, and sensitivity throughout this chapter.

Verbal Versus Numerical Description

Measurement is generally defined as the assignment of numbers to objects or events in accordance with a set of rules. Of course we often use verbal descriptions. For example, the question "How anxious is Bill?" might elicit answers such as "cool as a cucumber," "extremely nervous," or "18 on the Taylor Manifest Anxiety Scale," among others. The first two descriptions are verbal while the third is numerical. Actually, verbal descriptions can be translated into numerical form. For example, a set of verbal descriptions like "strongly disagree, moderately disagree, moderately agree, strongly agree" could be translated into a set of numbers such as "1, 2, 3, 4" or "−3, −1, +1, +3." As you will see shortly, what the numbers mean is a critical consideration. Researchers commonly prefer to work with numerical descriptions, for several reasons.

First of all, numbers have clearer meanings than words, which can be vague. Suppose you want information about how frequently various words occur in ordinary language. The description of "frequency of occurrence" could be verbal or numerical in its original form. As a simple example, the values could consist of the numbers 1 through 10. Without saying exactly how the numbers would be used, we can still see that the numerical labels are virtually certain to represent order in a clear fashion—2 more than 1, 5 more than 4, and so on. In contrast, if the labels were words like *often, seldom, rarely, hardly ever,* or *frequently,* you might well find people disagreeing about whether *frequently* represents a greater frequency than *often.* Of course you wouldn't expect any disagreement over the statement that "45 occurrences is more than 39 occurrences" (a different numerical system). The clarity of the labels used can affect the reliability of measurement; vague, confusable labels can lead to less consistency when the measurement system is used. Numerical descriptions tend to have an advantage in this regard.

A second reason for preferring numerical descriptions is that there is usually a greater chance of having a more sensitive measure with numbers than with verbal labels. In simple terms, sensitivity or precision increases with the number of possible values that can be recorded. There are obviously a great many numbers, but it is often hard to think of very many verbal labels for describing something. Having said this, let me clarify and expand it in a very important way: Sensitivity increases with the number of possible values that can be *reliably* used. For example, suppose you want to measure a person's degree of agreement or disagreement with a particular statement, as is often done in public-opinion surveys and attitude research. One possibility would be to use a verbal scale, asking the person to select from "very strongly disagree," "strongly disagree," "disagree," "agree," "strongly agree," and "very strongly agree." This measurement scale would allow you to distinguish among six different values of agreement–disagreement. Another alternative would be to give the person a 100-point numerical scale, indicating that one end represents maximum disagreement and the other end maximum agreement, and asking the person to select the number that best represents his opinion. Clearly 100 values is many more than 6, and it would seem that the numerical scale should be far more sensitive. However, this will be true *only if* people can actually use the 100 points reliably, with consistency. Suppose you ask a person on two occasions to indicate her opinion regarding the *same* statement (we will assume both that the person's opinion doesn't change and that on each occasion she tries to indicate that opinion, rather than trying to reproduce her first response). You might find that, for example, a person who checked "strongly agree" on one occasion also checked "strongly agree" on the other occasion, indicating reliable measurement. But you might find that a person checks, say, 65 the first time and 72 the second (if her opinion has not changed, then you are getting inconsistent values for the same thing), indicating that the values are not being used reliably. The point should be clear—one increases the sensitivity of a measurement scale only by increasing the number of *reliable* values.

While it is clear that a researcher cannot casually use measurement scales with many numbers, it is also true that many times the number of reliable values will be greater than the number of verbal labels available. In some situations the use of numerical descriptions seems so appropriate that using verbal labels would appear foolish. Suppose you wish to measure "how long it takes various people to solve a problem." This interest virtually demands numerical description because it is so familiar and because it is easy to observe the number of seconds, minutes, hours, and so forth that someone requires to complete a task. It would seem pointless even to attempt to construct a verbal scale using such terms as "a very short time," "a long time," and so on. Furthermore, it would be quite easy, using a stopwatch, to measure solution times in seconds from 0 to 300 (providing a 301-point scale), whereas it would be impossible to construct 301 verbal labels without producing some rather strange (and thus probably unreliable) terms.

Using such devices as clocks and rulers to obtain numerical descriptions is so familiar that the alternative of verbal description does not seem realistic. However, when the measurements are "judgments" for which convenient "rulers" are not available, it is perhaps not intuitively obvious that numerical descriptions should be preferred. Perhaps the thought has occurred to you that if you had to respond to the question "What is your attitude toward the public financing of political campaigns?" the alternatives "strongly in favor," "opposed," and the like might be more meaningful than the numbers 1 through 15 (pick one), and thus easier to use. What you are suspecting is that the numerical descriptions might be hard to use reliably. The essential answer to this issue is empirical—can people use a 10 or 15 numerical point scale as reliably as a scale consisting of perhaps six verbal labels? Suffice it to say that for a fair number of judgments the answer is yes. While judges sometimes have difficulty discriminating reliably among more than five or seven values of a characteristic (which means that they could not reliably use a 10-value scale, whether verbal or numerical), there are other characteristics for which judges can discriminate a larger number of values, for which there may not be convenient verbal labels.

For example, suppose you were asked to judge the "quality" of paintings and were given a truly wide range of paintings to examine; it would not be surprising if you could reliably discriminate among, say, 10 or 12 values of quality. It might be quite difficult to think of 12 verbal labels, but 12 numbers are readily available.

A third reason for preferring numerical descriptions is an important one: If you have data in numerical form, you have *potential* access to powerful statistical techniques that can be of great help in understanding the observations. Think of the things we have all learned to do with numbers—to add, subtract, multiply, and divide them, for example. If one has numerical data *for which it makes sense to add scores together,* there is no real problem in doing the addition. In contrast, it is rather difficult to say what would be the outcome of adding together a "seldom," a "frequently," and an "often." The next section deals with *when* it makes sense to perform various arithmetic operations on numerical descriptions. For the moment let me emphasize that numerical data provide a researcher with the opportunity to perform certain operations whereas purely verbal descriptions essentially do not allow such treatment.

PROBLEM

Suppose a researcher has people judge the sweetness of various foods, using a 20-point scale (pick a number from 1 to 20) and finds that they do not use the 20 points with sufficient consistency for his purposes. What should he probably do?

If your answer is that he should reduce the number of values to match the number of levels of sweetness that people can reliably discriminate, you have the right idea. A 20-point sweetness scale might look good and appear very sensitive, but one does not have a useful 20-point scale unless the values can be used reliably.

Types of Scales

There are many things we know about numbers *as numbers.* For example, we know that 17 is greater than 14, that 45 is 9 times as large as 5, that the difference between 69 and 45 is half as large as the difference between 48 and 96, and so on. The issue we will consider in this section is the extent to which we can *sensibly* apply what we know about numbers as numbers when the numbers we are dealing with represent values of some psychological variable. To state the issue in a different way, there are many situations in which, say, one person is assigned the value 70 and another person is assigned the value 35, but it would be nonsense to say that the person with 70 has more (of something) than the person with 35, or that she has 35 units more, or that she has twice as much. Scales of measurement differ in terms of what one can reasonably do with the numbers used to describe things. The stronger the measurement scale, the more you can say about the numbers it contains. We will now consider various scales used in psychological research, beginning with the weakest one.

(1) *Nominal Scales.* A *nominal* scale consists simply of a set of mutually exclusive categories. "Mutually exclusive" means that the categories are so defined that, having placed something in one of the categories, it cannot be put into any other category at the same time. The categories of a nominal scale can have either verbal or numerical labels. The important point is that if the categories have numerical labels you cannot sensibly apply any of your knowledge of numbers to them, except to say that different numbers are different. Another way of stating this is that with nominal scales you don't really need numerical values.

A familiar example of a nominal scale is the set of numbers on the uniforms of the players on a baseball team. One player wears the uniform with the number 12 on it; another wears the number 55; and so forth. The only "rule" that has been followed in assigning the numbers is to give different players different numbers. You couldn't identify the players with a scorecard if there were three different players wearing uniforms with "8" on them. While in a strict sense you could add up the numbers on the uniforms of your favorite team or subtract Bob's number from Bill's, the answers you would get wouldn't mean much. The practice adopted by many professional sports teams of printing both a player's number and name on the back of his jersey really tells you something about the numbers—they aren't really necessary.

Despite the fact that nominal scales represent the weakest form of measurement, they are often used in psychological research. For example, one might categorize people as Lutherans, Baptists, Episcopalians, and so forth; college students as psychology majors, sociology majors, chemistry majors, and so forth; or subjects in a study of esthetic preferences as choosing the Picasso, the van Gogh, or the Rembrandt as their favorite painting. The researcher might decide to code Lutheran as 1, Baptist as 2, Roman Catholic as 7, but it should be abundantly clear that the numbers are assigned arbitrarily and could be reassigned without altering the nature of the scale (the researcher could just as easily choose to code Lutheran as 9). Consequently it makes no sense to interpret the magnitudes of the numbers assigned, to add or subtract, multiply or divide them.

(2) *Ordinal Scales.* To the requirements of a nominal scale (mutually exclusive categories, different numbers for different categories) let us add the property of *order.* If the categories of a scale are ordered, they constitute an *ordinal* scale. If numbers are used for the categories, the order of the numbers must correspond to the order of the categories. The most familiar example of an ordinal scale is ranking. In noting the outcome of a race we record who finished first, second, third, and so on. Or a person might be

given a set of paintings and asked to indicate which he or she likes best, next best, and so on.

In general, we would expect the larger numbers of an ordinal scale to represent more of the characteristic being indicated, but this is often not done when ranking. It is quite common to assign the rank of 1 to the largest, fastest, or prettiest item, and this is perfectly acceptable as long as we take into account the manner in which the numbers were assigned. An ordinal scale consists of any set of numbers whose order corresponds to the order of items in terms of the characteristic being measured. For example, having arranged five paintings from most liked to least liked, we could assign them the numbers 104, 65, 45, 17, and 2 as long as the order of the numbers represented the order of likability. Ordinarily this is not done; instead, consecutive numbers (1, 2, 3, 4, etc.) are used. The important point is that when consecutive numbers are used, the fact that the numbers themselves are equally spaced does *not* mean that the items are equally spaced in terms of the characteristic being assessed. Consider again the example of a race—the order of finishing is in effect an ordering based on time taken to complete the distance, but telling you that Jane, Mary, and Anne finished first, second, and third tells you nothing about how far apart they were.

(3) *Interval Scales.* If the magnitudes of the numbers on a scale represent the order among the items in terms of the characteristic being measured *and* the *distances* between items, one has an *interval* scale. In other words, an interval scale has a constant unit that makes the differences between values meaningful. The most familiar example of an interval scale is the Fahrenheit temperature scale—the difference between 70 degrees and 65 degrees is larger than the difference between 70 degrees and 68 degrees and exactly the same as the difference between 40 and 35 degrees, and so forth.

The step up from an ordinal scale to an interval scale is very important because an interval scale allows a number of arithmetic operations to be applied in a meaningful way. As already noted, an interval scale by definition allows the interpretation of differences between values. With an interval scale it makes sense to add and subtract values, which makes possible the application of a variety of useful statistical procedures. For example, calculating averages such as a grade point average, average income, and so on involves adding together the values of the individual entries and dividing by the number of entries. Adding the values together makes sense only if the distances between values are interpretable, that is, only if one has at least an interval scale.

In psychological research and in everyday life, people frequently add and subtract scale values for measures that, strictly speaking, might not yield interval scales. In certain areas of psychological research where measurement is taken quite seriously, there has been and probably always will be a debate over when adding and subtracting are appropriate, with both conservative and liberal views offered. Most people, including most psychological researchers, seem to be liberals with respect to this issue, and this does not seem to have led to serious errors.

Consider the familiar example of the grade point average. Grades are typically assigned in terms of A, B, C, D, and F; these letter grades are then translated into numerical values, usually A = 4, B = 3, C = 2, D = 1, and F = 0. If a student takes four courses and achieves grades of A, A, B, and C, his grade point average is determined by adding 4 + 4 + 3 + 2 and dividing by 4 (the number of courses) to yield the value 3.25. Many important decisions about a student are made at least in part by interpreting such averages—honors lists, probation, entry into graduate school, and so on. The relevant question is whether or not, in terms of amount learned or quality of performance or whatever grades presumably indicate, the difference between A and B is equal to the difference between B and C, C and D, or D and F. When they stop and think about it, many people decide that these differences are probably not equal. To a conservative this means that one should not add the numerical values associated with the letter grades, that is, that one should not calculate grade point averages in the usual manner. The liberal viewpoint is roughly as follows: "Well, the grades are probably not exactly equally spaced, but they're roughly equally spaced. Besides, calculating grade point averages seems to make sense to a lot of people; averages calculated in this way enter into a number of sensible relations; and there *is* a difference between a student with a grade point average of 2.14 and one with an average of 2.97!"

This issue has considerable importance for psychological research. Interval scales allow more powerful statements than ordinal scales do and are to be preferred on this basis. Again using the example of grade point average, consider the problem of deciding which of the following students has the higher average. Bob has earned grades of A, B, B, B, B, B, C, C, D, D, and F while Carol has earned grades of A, A, A, B, B, B, B, B, C, C, and C. If one assumes that grades represent only an ordinal scale (A > B > C > D > F but nothing more), then about all that can be done to determine the average grade for each student is to identify the middle score in the ordering of grades, which is B for both students. If one assumes that grades represent an interval scale and calculates the grade point average as described earlier, Bob's average is 2.26 while Carol's is 3.00, clearly higher. The assumption of an interval scale allows a distinction to be made that the assumption of an ordinal scale does not permit.

Perhaps it has occurred to you that attempting to determine an average grade is a waste of time, that Bob's grades are generally not as good as Carol's. This is a quite reasonable statement in this case. However, it would not be difficult to construct examples for which it would be very difficult to reach a decision by comparing one whole set with the other whole set in a general way. To put it another way, it is often advantageous to perform operations like calculating averages in reaching decisions about what observations mean. Clearly, an interval scale is better in such circumstances than an ordinal scale. The question is, When is it sensible to assume that one is dealing with measurements on an interval scale? There is no easy answer to this question. What generally happens is that a researcher assumes one or the other kind of scale; while he or she often has plausible reasons for this assumption, it is most commonly true that the researcher cannot rigorously demonstrate the truth of the assumption. You should realize that the question of whether or not one has an interval scale is by no means limited to the matter of grade point averages. When a person takes an intelligence test, he or she earns points by answering various questions correctly, and test scores commonly involve adding up points. It is reasonable to ask whether the point earned for getting one question correct represents the same amount of knowledge or intelligence as the point earned on another question, and the answer is "Probably not." Determining how much a person has learned about a list of words or how well someone has done in solving problems typically involves adding up points of some kind. It is usually hard to argue that the words or problems, the basis of the "points" that are summed, are strictly equal. As mentioned earlier, most researchers seem not to be disturbed by the lack of strict interval scales, and they commonly perform operations that assume interval scales.

Ratio Scales. A *ratio* scale has all of the properties of an interval scale *plus* a true zero point. On a ratio scale a value of zero indicates the complete absence of the characteristic indexed by the scale values—it means "none of _____." The importance of having a true zero point is that ratios of values on the scale can be meaningfully constructed—hence the name of the scale. On a ratio scale a value of 40 indicates twice as much of the characteristic being measured as a value of 20. For example, an object that is 800 cm long is twice as long as one with a length of 400 cm, four times as long as one 200 cm long, and so on. Except in a few areas of psychology such as psychophysics, psychologists do not ordinarily deal with ratio scales. Even if a researcher is willing to assume that the interval on a scale of measurement can be trusted, it is usually obvious that the scale does not have a true zero point. To date no one has identified zero intelligence, zero neuroticism, or zero knowledge of a college course. What this means is that quite often ratio comparisons of scale values are inappropriate—one cannot meaningfully say that a person with an IQ of 140 has twice as much intelligence as a person with an IQ of 70 because the IQ scale does not have a true zero point (zero IQ = no intelligence whatsover).

A researcher has people judge the beauty of a set of paintings using a rating scale ranging from 1 = least beautiful to 9 = most beautiful. One judge rates painting A as 7, painting B as 2, and painting C as 1. Would it be appropriate to infer that for this judge painting A is 3½ times as beautiful as painting B and 7 times as beautiful as painting C? Would it be reasonable to conclude that the difference in beauty between paintings A and B is greater than the difference between paintings B and C?

In the case of this rating scale it is clear that ratio comparisons about scale values are not meaningful, since a true zero point has not been established. The question about comparing distances between scale values is more difficult to answer—this question involves the issue of whether one has an ordinal scale or an interval scale (or something approximating an interval scale). If the rating categories are assumed to represent nothing more than an ordinal scale, then nothing can be said about $(7 - 2)$ versus $(2 - 1)$. If the values on the rating scale can reasonably be assumed to be separated by equal amounts of beauty, then comparisons of distances are quite appropriate. To choose between these answers we might want some further information, such as the instructions that the judges were given (Were they told to use scale values to represent equal unit distances with respect to beauty?) or some other information indicating that distance information is interpretable.

The four types of scales that we have considered are not the only kinds of scales that might be used in research, but they represent those that are most commonly used in psychological research. Furthermore, comparing types of scales clearly illustrates the importance of the kind of measurement a researcher employs. As the strength of the scale of measurement increases, the researcher is able to make more precise statements about the behavior in question. As a general rule, the danger in using weak scales is that one might "miss something." Measurements on a nominal scale provide less information than those on a ratio scale, and it is quite possible that the additional information that is obtained when a more powerful scale is used might be crucial to discovering an important fact or relation. Indeed, it has been argued that scientific progress depends as much on the development of more precise measures as on any other aspect of scientific activity.

Index Numbers

Special measurement problems sometimes arise when comparisons are made between groups or sets. The question is whether or not one can sensibly use "raw" numbers to make the comparison. Suppose you want to determine whether there is more car ownership in a large city than in a small town. You could simply count the number of cars in the city and in the town to see which is larger, but this comparison seems a little silly. The city has more people, which means that there are more opportunities for car ownership. To sensibly compare the city and the town, it would be better to adjust the number of cars for the number of people (number of opportunities to own a car). The *relative* measure is the more appropriate index number to use because of the difference in size between the city and the town. In many circumstances relative measures provide better comparison values than raw or absolute numbers. The task of developing the best index number usually involves choosing between raw and relative numbers.

Consider an example from everyday life. The National Safety Council frequently reminds us that most accidents occur in the home. The implication is that it is more dangerous to be at home than to be away from home. However, this implication might be incorrect. We need to know how much time people spend at home versus how much time they spend away from home. Suppose that 60 percent of personal accidents occur "at home" but that people spend 75 percent of their time at home. Such figures would indicate that being at home resulted in less than a "fair share" of accidents. If being at home and being away from home were equally likely to involve accidents, we would expect that the percentage of accidents occurring at home would be equivalent to the percentage of time spent at home. If the percentage of accidents at home were substantially lower than the percentage of time spent at home, this would indicate that being at home is actually safer (less *likely* to involve an accident).

PROBLEM

Two candidates for public office had a debate. One stated that "U.S. economic growth in the past year was less than that for Spain." The other stated that "U.S. economic growth last year was greater than Spain's." Indicate how both candidates, using exactly the same source material, could be at least technically correct.

The solution to this problem rests on the recognition that the economic base for the United States is considerably larger than that for Spain. Using arbitrary figures, suppose that the gross national product (GNP) at the beginning of the year in question was $400 billion for the United States but only $20 billion for Spain. Assume that during the year Spain's GNP increased by $2 billion whereas the U.S. GNP increased by $4 billion. One candidate, referring to the absolute amount of the increase, could state that the United States' growth was greater than Spain's ($4 billion is greater than $2 billion). The other candidate, using relative growth, could state that Spain's growth was greater—10 percent growth for Spain is greater than 1 percent growth for the United States. Generally, index numbers that adjust for different bases (different opportunities) are the most appropriate measures. However, if the bases are extremely different, comparing relative measures can itself present problems. A country with a GNP of $30 (to make up a ridiculous example) would have a far easier chance of doubling its GNP than a country with a GNP as large as that of the United States. In effect there is no good way to compare statistics when radically different bases are involved—both absolute and relative measures are likely to be misleading.

PROBLEM

A researcher gave a concept-learning task to a number of people. The task required a person to figure out how objects varying in several ways (e.g., size, shape, and color) were being sorted into two categories. Each trial of the task consisted of the following events: The person was shown an object, asked to indicate which category he or she thought it belonged to, and was then told which category was correct for that object. After receiving this feedback, the person could offer a hypothesis (roughly, a guess about how objects were being categorized) but was not told whether his or her hypothesis was correct or not. Each person received trial after trial until he or she correctly categorized (before feedback) ten objects in succession. The researcher hypothesized that one reason why people have difficulty learning concepts is that they form (incorrect) hypotheses too quickly (and too often) and thus fail to pay attention to the information that is potentially available. This idea translates into the prediction that people who take many trials to learn the concept are more likely to offer incorrect hypotheses than those who take fewer trials to learn. To test his idea the researcher divided the people into two groups, those who took more than the average number of trials to learn and those who took less than the average number of trials to learn. He then compared the number of incorrect hypotheses made by "slow learners" to the number of incorrect hypotheses made by "fast learners." He found that slow learners offered more incorrect hypotheses than fast learners, and concluded that his idea was correct—people take many trials to learn because they are more likely to develop incorrect hypotheses. Indicate why his conclusion might be incorrect.

The key to understanding the possible problem here is to realize that, by definition, slow learners had more trials and, thus, more opportunities to offer hypotheses (right or wrong). It is not appropriate to compare the sheer number of wrong hypotheses offered by fast and slow learners. Rather, the researcher should compare the percentage of wrong hypotheses offered by the two groups of people. That is, he needs to correct the *number* of wrong hypotheses for the total number of hypotheses offered. Because fast learners took fewer trials, it is very likely that they offered fewer hypotheses (right or wrong) than slow learners. A proper test of the researcher's idea requires that the percentage of wrong hypotheses (relative to the total number of hypotheses) is higher for slower learners. As this example indicates, correcting for "number of opportunities" does not always involve differences in the sizes of the groups. What one needs to do is to compare the number of occurrences to the number of opportunities, taking the context into account when evaluating the measure.

CONTROLLING VARIABLES

In order to make systematic observations a researcher will inevitably exercise some form of control in a research project. In Chapter 1, I pointed out that an experiment is the study of the relation between two (or more) variables, one of which is manipulated or controlled by the researcher. Thus experiments obviously involve control of variables. Yet control procedures of one sort or another are used even in nonexperimental research. There are two, basically separate reasons why a researcher might want to control a variable: to reduce the amount of "noise" in the data or to make the relation between two variables easier to interpret (to reduce confounding). Furthermore, there are different ways in which variables are controlled. The general context in which we will look at control procedures is one in which a researcher studies the relation between two variables. There are two basic questions to be considered: (1) How does a researcher decide that two variables are related? (2) What can a researcher do to make the relation easier to interpret?

Evaluating Treatment Differences

In a study of the relation between two variables one variable is always a natural one—a measure of some aspect of behavior. In other words, a researcher always obtains scores of some sort, and the purpose of the study is to see whether or how these scores are related to the levels of the second variable. For example, a researcher studying the relation between sex and arithmetic performance might compare the arithmetic test scores of males and females. The second variable involved in a relation might be either a natural one (such as sex in the preceding example) or a manipulated one directly under the control of the researcher, in which case the study is an experiment. As mentioned in Chapter 1, a relation between a manipulated variable and a natural variable is usually easier to interpret than a relation between two natural variables (a point we'll return to shortly). However, in either case the first decision that needs to be made concerns whether or not the data indicate that there is a relation to be explained. Whether she is comparing the arithmetic scores of males and females or comparing the trials-to-learn scores of rats given different amounts of reward (i.e., manipulated by the experimenter), the researcher needs to decide whether the scores differ enough from males to females, or from one reward level to another, to justify the conclusion that a systematic relation exists.

I will use the general term *treatments* to refer to the levels of the variable for which scores are compared. In the preceding examples the treatments would be males versus females or the different amounts of reward. Thus in general terms a researcher needs to evaluate how much the scores differ or change between treatments. An important point is that the change in score from one treatment to another must be examined in relation to the amount of random or uncontrolled variation in the scores. Let me clarify this statement with an example, using the hypothetical data in Table 2.1.

As you can see from the table, there is some change in score from one treatment to the other—the females' scores are somewhat higher. However, the scores also vary within the group of males and within the group of females—this score variation is random or uncontrolled. The amount of random score variation affects the comparison of the treatments. In later chapters we will deal in detail with the procedures researchers use to assess treatment differences. At this point the general principle will be enough, as illustrated in the following nonmathematical formula:

$$\text{Critical ratio} = \frac{\text{Differences in scores between treatments}}{\text{Amount of random variation in scores}}$$

The larger this "critical ratio" is, the more likely it is that there is really a difference in scores between the treatments. The amount of random variation in scores—in the example, the extent to which males' scores differ from each other and females' scores differ from each other—represents "noise." The scores vary, but not for any known, specified reasons. The essential question is whether the difference in scores *between* treatments (males vs. females) is just more noise or represents a real difference. For the researcher to conclude that a real difference between treatments exists, the observed score difference between treatments must be large relative to the amount of random variation in scores.

Table 2.1   Hypothetical Data: Number of Correct Answers on an Arithmetic Test

Males	Females
19	21
25	33
31	28
18	36
29	30
27	24
33	39
26	28
29	31
Average score 26	Average score 30

Note: Each entry is the score for an individual.

This concept of relating the score difference between treatments to the amount of random score variation has clear implications for research methods. Researchers can do things to increase the chances of finding a relatively large difference between treatments, and they can do things to decrease the amount of random variation in scores. In short, researchers can choose methods that increase the chances of obtaining a larger "critical ratio"—methods that make it easier to decide whether a relation between variables really exists. These methods involve controlling variables in different ways. As we will see shortly, some control procedures have two effects, both reducing the amount of random variation in scores and making the relation between variables easier to interpret by reducing confounding. But first let's consider what a researcher might do to maximize differences among treatments.

Manipulation: The Independent Variable

An experiment involves the relation between a manipulated variable and a natural variable (a measure of some aspect of behavior). The manipulated variable is often called the *independent variable*, while the behavioral measure is called the *dependent variable*. Because the experimenter has control over the independent variable, he can exercise considerable influence over the chances of finding score differences among treatments. We will consider three issues: the consistency with which the treatments are administered, the choice of values, and the number of values of the independent variable.

Once an experimenter has decided on the values of the independent variable to use in the study, it is important that he try to apply those values as consistently as possible. For example, suppose a researcher who is interested in the effects of reward magnitude on learning decides to give rats either 1 milliliter (ml) or 5 ml (the different treatments) of milk for each correct response. It is important that each "1-ml" reward be as close to 1 ml and each "5-ml" reward as close to 5 ml as possible. Compare these two situations: (1) The 5-ml rewards are approximately 5 ml but actually vary between 4 and 6 ml. (2) The 5-ml rewards are approximately 5 ml but actually vary between 4.9 and 5.1 ml. In the latter case the reward amounts would be administered with greater consistency; doing so obviously requires care and may require specialized equipment. The reason for desiring maximum consistency is simply this: The more consistently the treatments are applied, the less chance there is of random variation in scores. In other words, consistent administration of treatments reduces "noise" in the data and makes the evaluation of treatment differences more sensitive.

Choice of Values. Suppose a researcher wants to find out whether the amount of time between successive trials of a learning task influences the number of trials needed to learn. She plans to have a number of subjects learn some task and will manipulate the amount of time they are given between successive learning trials. She will measure the number of trials each subject requires to learn the task (to some criterion such as 100 percent correct responses) and compare the mean scores for different intertrial intervals. The question is, How should the experimenter choose the intertrial intervals she wishes to compare? One answer is that she should choose values of the independent variable that are reasonably far apart. Suppose an experimenter gave some subjects 1.0 seconds between successive trials while giving others 1.1 seconds between trials. The difference between 1.0 seconds and 1.1 seconds is a very small difference *in time*. Perhaps this slight difference in intertrial intervals will result in different mean trials-to-learn, but it not likely to result in a large difference in average performance—it will be hard to obtain a large critical ratio! If the researcher had compared 1.0 second and, say, 5.0 seconds, she would at least be giving "time between trials" a better chance to show that it makes a difference in trials-to-learn. Choosing the proper values of the independent variable always depends on the particular behavior being studied; a researcher must use knowledge of the area to select reasonably separate values. What can be said is that if the experimenter chooses values of the independent variable that are too close together, she runs the risk of failing to find out that the independent variable is important.

PROBLEM

A researcher was interested in the effects of giving hints on problem solving. In her study she used three different hints (we'll just call them hints A, B, and C) that all seemed to apply to the problem the subjects were given to solve. Each hint was given to a different group of randomly assigned subjects. When the three groups were compared in terms of average solution time, the analysis indicated that there were no significant differences among the groups. The researcher therefore concluded that giving a hint does not affect problem solving. What is wrong with her conclusion?

The major problem with this conclusion is that all that the researcher found was that the three hints resulted in equivalent levels of performance on the problem. What the researcher does *not* know is how the performance of the hint groups would compare with the performance of subjects who are given no hint at all. Because she did not include a no-hint treatment, she does not know whether giving a hint (vs. not giving one) helps, hinders, or has no effect on problem solving.

Number of Values. The issue we have just considered leads experimenters to use widely separated values of the independent variable. While this practice is generally reasonable, it can lead to problems if only two values are used. Suppose a researcher wants to determine whether "level of illumination" influences "reading speed." He will have people read something as fast as they can and will control the level of illumination they are exposed to while reading. Each person's reading speed will be measured and the average scores for the different levels of illumination compared. Suppose the researcher, realizing that there are dangers in comparing illumination levels that are "too close together," decides to use a very low illumination level (for some subjects) and a very high level (for others). To make the contrast (unrealistically) strong, imagine that some subjects will read under very dim light while others will read under extremely bright light. The possible problem that might arise here is that if the researcher finds that reading speeds are not significantly different for his two illumination levels he might be led to conclude that illumination level makes no difference. It is possible (indeed, likely) that reading speed is *not* linearly related to illumination level *over the full range of illumination levels.* That is, reading speeds might rise as one goes from very dim illumination to moderate levels, but decline as one goes from moderate to extremely high illumination levels. By choosing two extreme values of the independent variable, the experimenter might wind up comparing two values that yield equivalent speeds but fail to discover the changes in reading speed that occur between these two illumination levels.

The issue can be stated more generally. If a researcher wants to determine the relation between an independent variable and a dependent variable, he or she will not get much information about this relation by using just two values of the independent variable. Therefore an experimenter is well advised to use at least three (and perhaps more) values of the independent variable.

Figure 2.1 illustrates several plausible relations between an independent variable and dependent variable. Notice that including a third, intermediate value of the independent variable can help considerably in distinguishing between linear and nonlinear relations. For other possible relations, more than three values might be needed. Clearly, the more values of the independent variable that are used, the more confidence one can have that the data will accurately reflect the correct relation between the two variables.

PROBLEM

Suppose you have done an experiment comparing the running speeds of two groups of rats, one group being under 1 hour of food deprivation, the other under 72 hours of food deprivation. You find that running speeds do not differ for these two conditions. Of course the results are consistent with the hypothesis that running speed is not related to deprivation level. However, there are other possible hypotheses. First, state a different hypothesis about the relation between running speed and deprivation level that is also consistent with the results (no difference) for 1 and 72 hours of deprivation. Second, indicate how a modification of the experiment would enable you to choose between the hypothesis of no relation and your hypothesis.

There are several alternative hypotheses that could be proposed. Here is a common alternative: Between 1 and 72 hours of deprivation running

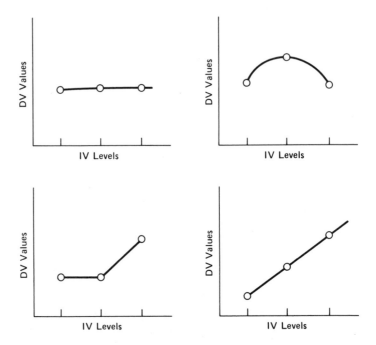

Figure 2.1. Examples of possible relations between an independent variable (IV) and a dependent variable (DV). In the upper-left panel, the IV does not influence the DV.

speed first increases, then decreases. In other words, running speed has a curvilinear relation to deprivation level. If the experiment were modified to include one or more intermediate values of deprivation level, the results would provide a basis for choosing between hypotheses. If, say, a condition of 36 hours of deprivation were included (a minimum modification), we could examine running speeds for the three deprivation levels, looking for one of two possible relations. If running speeds were the same for 1, 36, and 72 hours of deprivation, the results would support the "no-relation" hypothesis while contradicting the hypothesis of a curvilinear relation (at least the most plausible, simple version). If, however, we found that running speeds were equal for 1 and 72 hours of deprivation but that running speeds for 36 hours of deprivation were higher (or lower), we would have evidence favoring a curvilinear relation between running speed and deprivation level.

Application to Natural Variables. Many studies of relations between variables do not include a manipulated variable; rather, two natural variables are involved. In the "sex and arithmetic performance" example given earlier, neither variable would be manipulated by the researcher. The people would simply be grouped according to sex—males versus females—

and the arithmetic scores of the two groups would be compared. Let me give you two warnings about such studies: (1) In referring to a study like "sex and arithmetic performance," people sometimes call sex the independent variable and arithmetic scores the dependent variable. You should be aware that sex is *not* a true independent variable because the researcher has no control over which "treatment" (male or female) any person receives. When you encounter references to independent and dependent variables you should check carefully to see whether in fact the researcher had control over the values of the "independent variable." (2) Checking to see whether a manipulated variable is actually involved in the relation is important because, as mentioned in Chapter 1, a relation between two natural variables is extremely difficult to interpret. Basically, it is very hard to avoid confounding when two natural variables are involved, which makes interpreting the relation quite troublesome.

Accepting the fact that relations between two natural variables are difficult to interpret, let's consider what a researcher might do to get accurate information about what the relation is. We have seen that when an experimenter manipulates a variable it is advantageous to administer the treatment values consistently, to choose values carefully, and to use more than two values in most cases. Similar notions sometimes apply even when a researcher does not actually manipulate an independent variable. There are circumstances in which a researcher has few options; if "sex" has just two categories, male and female, there is little a researcher can do other than group people into males and females and compare their scores on some other variable. Similarly, a researcher who wants to compare the attitudes (say, toward abortion) of Catholics and Baptists has little choice. There are, however, natural variables for which choices do exist.

Quite commonly in psychological research some characteristic of people is measured using a test that yields a fairly wide range of scores. For example, a number of people might be given a "test of anxiety" with scores ranging from 1 to 40. Suppose a researcher wants to determine whether anxiety is related to arithmetic performance. Frequently, researchers form two groups—high anxiety and low anxiety—by dividing the test scale roughly at the middle. A researcher might consider scores from 1 to 20 as "low anxiety" and scores from 21 to 40 as "high anxiety." Having formed the two anxiety groups, the researcher then compares the arithmetic scores of the two groups. However, this practice can result in the researcher's getting an inaccurate picture of the relation between anxiety and arithmetic performance. Let's see why.

First, notice that the two values of anxiety being compared, high and low, are not very precise. All the "high-anxiety" people are not equally "high" and all the "low-anxiety" people are not equally "low." The situation is analogous to having inconsistent administration of an independent variable. The differences among the high-anxiety people (and among the low-anxiety people), which are being ignored when the "high" and "low" groups are formed, will add to the random variation in arithmetic scores and thus decrease the sensitivity of the comparison of the two groups.

Second, notice that, although the anxiety scores range from 1 to 40, the researcher is comparing only two values. It is very unlikely that two imprecise "high" and "low" values will adequately represent the full range of variation in anxiety. In addition to a sheer reduction in the number of values, the two values are in a sense not very far apart. Some of the people placed in the "high" group actually have anxiety scores that are rather close to those of some of the people placed in the "low" group (scores of 21–24 are included in "high" while scores of 17–20 are put in "low"). The result, in part, is that "high" and "low" are not clearly separated levels of anxiety. Furthermore, as we have seen, using just two values provides little information about the nature of the relation between the variables.

The situation would be considerably improved if the researcher made a small change, namely, grouping people into three groups, high, medium, and low, perhaps using cutoff scores such as 1–13 (low), 14–26 (medium), and 27–40 (high). Notice that with three values (high, medium, low) the values are more precisely defined; each value includes a smaller range of anxiety scores. For example, with just two groups "high" included scores from 21 to 40, while with three groups "high" includes scores from 27 to 40. Also, because three values of anxiety are compared, more information about the nature of the relation between anxiety and arithmetic performance will be obtained (our previous discussion centered on Figure 2.1 applies here).

Another problem can arise when "high" and "low" groups are compared. Sometimes researchers define "high" and "low" in terms of the particular scores they have rather than in terms of the possible range of scores on the test. For example, a researcher might have anxiety scores for 40 people and want to divide them into 20 high scorers and 20 low scorers. Although the test allows scores between 1 and 40, it might be the case that for these 40 people the scores range from 8 to 26. To divide them into 20 "highs" and 20 "lows," the division might have to be made at, say, 16 (because there were 20 scores below 16 and 20 scores above 16). As a consequence, in this study "high" would mean scores of 16–26 and "low" would mean scores of 8–15. Another researcher might use the same test and the same procedure for his subjects (say he has 30). His 30 scores might range from 14 to 35, and when the people are divided into 15 "highs" and 15 "lows," in this study "high" might mean scores from 25 to 35 while "low" means scores from 14 to 24. Both researchers would appear to be comparing high and low anxiety, yet they would not in fact be comparing the same values of anxiety. The lesson should be clear: When you encounter comparisons of "high" and "low" (or high, medium, and low), check to see how these values were defined in a particular study.

Let me close this discussion by considering a question that you may already have thought of: If a researcher starts out with scores covering a wide range (e.g., 1–40), why bother forming groups of highs and lows or highs, mediums, and lows? Why not just use the original values when studying the relation between two natural variables? There can be sensible reasons for forming groups on one natural variable and then comparing the scores of the groups on another variable. A researcher might question the reliability of the 40 points on a 40-point scale or believe that comparing high, medium, and low groups will provide adequate information about the relation between the two variables. Forming groups on one natural variable and then comparing them in terms of their scores on a second natural variable makes the study similar to one involving a manipulated variable and a natural one. For example, a researcher might manipulate "anxiety" by delivering treatments (in an experiment) designed to make people high or low in anxiety and then compare the arithmetic scores for the two treatments. She might wish to see whether the anxiety–arithmetic relation is similar when anxiety varies naturally and, to make the comparison easier, might compare the arithmetic scores of high- and low-anxiety groups (based on naturally varying test scores). There are, however, researchers who argue that relations between natural variables are best studied with different methods from those used to study the relation between a manipulated variable and a natural variable. We will consider some of these methods in Chapter 7.

Control Procedures and Confounding

An experimenter's goal when looking at the relation between an independent variable and a dependent variable is to have no other variables "cluttering up" the data. If one or more *other* variables might be involved, the relation between the independent and dependent variables is said to be *confounded*. For example, if an experimenter wants to compare the learning scores for two treatments, one treatment having 2 seconds between successive trials and the other 10 seconds between trials, she wants the treatments to differ only in terms of the intertrial interval. If (unwittingly) she had assigned only females to the 2-second treatment and only males to the 10-second treatment, the relation between intertrial interval and learning score would be confounded by the (possible) relation between sex of subject and learning scores. This example is of course extreme and is used only to give you a clear example of what is meant by confounding. In actual research confounding is usually not so obvious. The researcher's task is quite difficult because eliminating a confounding variable requires that he or she check, and check, and check again the treatments to be as sure as possible that the treatments differ only in the desired way. Since confounding variables do not sit up and say "Here I am," there is always the possibility that a researcher might miss one and thus obtain confounded data.

Experimenters employ a variety of techniques to avoid confounding. Three widely used techniques are constancy, balancing, and randomization. These control procedures avoid confounding in different ways, and the particular technique a researcher might use often depends on the particular question being studied as well as on the resources available.

Constancy. The simplest way to avoid confounding by some "other" variable is to keep that variable from varying in the experiment. As an example, suppose an experimenter has several rooms available in which he might collect his data, and suppose that the rooms are somewhat different—one room has windows while another does not, the rooms differ somewhat in brightness; perhaps one room is in a noisier part of the building than another. If the researcher has some subjects participate in the experiment in one room while others participate in another, he might face the problem that subjects' scores (on the dependent variable) might depend partly on which room they were in (perhaps the windows create distraction, which might affect performance). To avoid the possibility of confounding his treatments (whatever they might be) with "room differences," he might simply use the same room for all subjects. That is, he will hold "room" constant. If all subjects, no matter what treatment they are in, participate in the same room, then "room differences" cannot possibly be an explanation of differences in their scores.

The amount of concern generated by a particular, potentially confounding variable clearly depends on what is being studied. Minor fluctuations in room illumination might be unimportant if, say, subjects are filling out a questionnaire, but extremely critical if subjects must try to identify visual stimuli flashed briefly on a screen. A major reason why soundproof rooms, special pieces of apparatus, and laboratories in general are used in research is that such special facilities give researchers control over variables that might confound their experiments. If the behavior being studied might be affected by small fluctuations in room temperature, illumination, and noise level, a researcher would sensibly want a soundproof room with precise temperature and illumination controls in order to hold these features constant.

Constancy is extremely difficult to achieve (in the very strictest sense it is impossible). One frequent, practical reason for the difficulty is money—special facilities typically cost a considerable amount of money, which often is not available. More fundamentally, constancy is, strictly speaking, an ideal that can be approached but not attained. For example, the researcher who decides to avoid "room differences" by using the same room for all subjects still faces the possibility that illumination and noise level vary in that room from time to time. A researcher who wants to hold temperature constant can achieve only approximate constancy with the finest possible equipment—there is inevitably some variation. The goal is to exercise enough control so that the remaining variation is very small and unimportant. I do not want to overemphasize the impossibility of achieving constancy. Strictly speaking there is no way to, say, hold temperature precisely at 85°, but it is possible to make the variations in temperature around 85° so slight that they are of no consequence—temperature might reasonably be said to be constant.

Balancing. Achieving constancy is a very good way to avoid confounding, but it can be too expensive or inefficient in some circumstances. A different control technique involves letting a (potentially confounding) variable vary in the experiment but ensuring that its variation is balanced with variation of the independent variable. The idea is to have scores in all treatment conditions be *equally* affected by differences in the "other" variable. Consider the example of the researcher who has two rooms in which data might be collected and his worry about possible "room differences." If he used balancing, he would use both rooms but make sure that the data for each treatment were collected half in one room and half in the other.

Suppose the researcher wishes to compare two treatments, which I'll call A and B (precisely what they might be is not important here), and will have 10 subjects participate under each treatment. Table 2.2 illustrates how he could balance "rooms" with treatments. By using the balancing technique shown in the table the researcher can use both rooms but avoid having room differences confounded with treatment differences. When comparing treatments A and B the researcher will have 10 scores for each treatment, 5 of which will come from room 1 and 5 from room 2. Even if room differences lead to different scores, this effect will be equally present in both sets of scores. Suppose that, compared to participating in room 1, participating in room 2 raises scores by 4 units on the measurement scale—in effect, participating in room 2 adds 4 to a subject's score on the dependent variable. Table 2.3 illustrates such a "room" effect. As you can see, the room effect changes scores equally for the two treatments. When the researcher compares the 10 scores for treatment A with the 10 scores for Treatment B, any difference in scores between treatments cannot be due to room differences.

Table 2.2   Balancing "Room Differences" with Treatments

	TREATMENT A	TREATMENT B
Room 1	5 subjects	5 subjects
Room 2	5 subjects	5 subjects

Compared to using the technique of constancy, using balancing has one clear advantage. Researchers often control a variable not because they are sure it's important but only because they suspect that it might be important and want to avoid the possibility of obtaining seriously confounded data. If a researcher suspects that room differences *might* be important, it is only sensible for her to control room differences and avoid confounding them with treatment differences. Both constancy and balancing will achieve this goal, but balancing will allow the researcher to see whether the variable she has controlled is important and does influence scores. In the balanced arrangment shown in Table 2.2, notice that balancing works both ways—scores for treatments A and B come equally from rooms 1 and 2, and scores for rooms 1 and 2 come equally from treatments A and B. Thus the researcher could compare the 10 scores from room 1 with the 10 scores from room 2 to see whether there are room differences in scores, and any room difference would not be confounded with treatment differences. Balancing thus gives a researcher not only control over a variable (in order to avoid confounding) but also information about the relation between the controlled variable and the dependent variable. In

Table 2.3   Illustration of a "Room Difference" That Has No Influence on Treatment Differences Because of Balancing

	TREATMENT A	TREATMENT B
Room 1	17 13 10 6 9 $\left(\bar{X}_{A1} = \dfrac{55}{5} = 11\right)$	19 11 24 12 14 $\left(\bar{X}_{B1} = \dfrac{80}{5} = 16\right)$ Difference $= -5$
Room 2 (scores are 4 units higher than in room 1)	$17 + 4 = 21$ $13 + 4 = 17$ $10 + 4 = 14$ $6 + 4 = 10$ $9 + 4 = 13$ $\left(\bar{X}_{A2} = \dfrac{75}{5} = 15\right)$	$19 + 4 = 23$ $11 + 4 = 15$ $24 + 4 = 28$ $12 + 4 = 16$ $14 + 4 = 18$ $\left(\bar{X}_{B2} = \dfrac{100}{5} = 20\right)$ Difference $= -5$
Overall means	$\left(\bar{X}_A = \dfrac{130}{10} = 13\right)$	$\left(\bar{X}_B = \dfrac{180}{10} = 18\right)$ Difference $= -5$

contrast, when constancy is used the experimenter does not obtain any information about whether the variable he has held constant is important.

PROBLEM

A graduate student is working on a thesis project and must schedule subjects for her experiment when she has no classes. The experiment includes two treatments, an "experimental" condition and a "control" condition, and the student must collect data for 20 subjects under each condition, for a total of 40 subjects. Since the procedure requires that each subject participate for two hours, the student finds that she can schedule subjects only at 8 A.M. and 2 P.M. each day, Monday through Friday. How should the experiment be arranged?

This example illustrates a very real problem in conducting research—temporal restrictions on when data can be collected (in this case because the student/researcher must personally collect the data and is constrained by classes and the length of time each subject must participate). The student can collect data for 2 subjects a day, one in the morning and one in the afternoon, for 10 subjects a week, which means that 4 weeks would be necessary to complete data collection. The experiment could be arranged in a variety of ways, depending on how plausible it seems that whatever will be measured might change during a day, from day to day, or from week to week. On general grounds it would be rather foolish of the student to always collect data for the experimental condition in the afternoon while always collecting control condition data in the morning. If she did so, she would be running the risk of confounding "time of day" with treatments, a confounding that can be avoided. Similar notions apply to "days of the week" and "weeks"; each of these would have to be evaluated with respect to the extent of concern they warrant. The student could construct a random sequence of 20 E's and 20 C's and schedule subjects according to this sequence, counting on randomization to "control" the possibly confounding factors. If, however, she believed that one or more of these temporal factors might seriously affect the results, it would be better to balance that factor with treatments to make sure that no bias will occur.

At the end of this paragraph I outline an arrangement based on taking "time of day," "day of the week," and "week" very seriously and balancing each of these factors with the two treatments. The plan was arrived at by deciding to make sure that 5 subjects would be assigned to each condition each week and that one subject would be assigned to each condition each day. For week 1, a coin flip was used to decide which treatment would be given in the morning of each day; this schedule was then "flipped over" (between A.M. and P.M.) for week 2. Another set of coin flips produced the schedule for week 3, and this schedule was flipped over for week 4. The result is a schedule in which each treatment (experimental and control) occurs equally often in the morning and in the afternoon, on every day of the week, and in weeks 1–4 of data collection. Here is the plan:

		MON.	TUE.	WED.	THU.	FRI.
Week 1	8 A.M.	E	C	C	E	E
	2 P.M.	C	E	E	C	C
Week 2	8 A.M.	C	E	E	C	C
	2 P.M.	E	C	C	E	E
Week 3	8 A.M.	E	E	C	E	C
	2 P.M.	C	C	E	C	E
Week 4	8 A.M.	C	C	E	C	E
	2 P.M.	E	E	C	E	C

Randomization. Both constancy and balancing give an experimenter rather direct, clear-cut control over a variable. The technique of *randomization* provides statistical control and is based, roughly, on the idea that in the long run "things will balance out." In different terms, the idea is that if a variable takes on different values in a random, unsystematic fashion it is unlikely (but not impossible) that it will be confounded with the independent variable. An example of randomization (dealing once again with "room differences") is a case in which a researcher using two different rooms flips a coin to decide which room each subject should be assigned to, arguing that in the long run half the subjects in each treatment condition will be assigned to each room.

Randomization allows statistical or probabilistic control over a variable, and a key to understanding the technique is the phrase "in the long run." It is true that in the long run a fair coin will show heads and tails equally often. It is true that if a variable is controlled by randomization it is unlikely that it will be seriously confounded with the independent variable. However, problems can arise when randomization is used in the "short run." Table 2.4 shows the outcome of using a coin flip to assign 10 subjects in treatment A to either room 1 or room 2, and likewise for 10 subjects in treatment B. (I actually did flip the coin, using heads = room 1 and tails = room 2) As you can see, the outcome was not too bad: For treatment A, subjects did get assigned equally often to the two rooms, while room 1 was assigned to a slight majority of the subjects in treatment B. This technique would result in scores for treatment B coming from room 1 slightly more often than scores for treatment A. In other words, room differences would be slightly confounded with treatment differences. This example, while illustrating how randomization works, is a little extreme. A researcher who was concerned about the possibility of confounding room differences with treatment differences would be foolish to use randomization when he could *guarantee* that confounding would be avoided by using constancy (one room) or balancing.

Table 2.4   Actual Results of Using a Coin Flip to Assign Subjects to Rooms

	TREATMENT A	TREATMENT B
Room 1	5 subjects	6 subjects
Room 2	5 subjects	4 subjects

Randomization is involved in all research, at least as an assumption. A researcher who "holds temperature constant at 85°" assumes that the minor fluctuations in temperature that will occur over time will be random and will "balance out" over his treatment conditions. A researcher who uses just one room to collect data assumes that fluctuations in noise and illumination levels over time in that room will be random and will "balance out" over her treatment conditions. In a sense there is no way for a researcher to avoid assuming that randomization is providing control over possible confounding variables—it is impossible to control everything by balancing or constancy!

The most frequent use of deliberate randomization concerns all of the characteristics of subjects that might influence scores on the dependent variable. In most psychological experiments the researcher needs to measure some dependent variable for a number of subjects under each treatment condition (their behavior is of course the most important aspect of the study!). Quite obviously, the researcher does not want differences between treatments to be confounded with "basic" differences among subjects. In trying to control subject differences in order to avoid confounding them with treatments, the researcher faces serious problems because there are usually so many subject characteristics that might affect scores on the dependent variable. Trying to find subjects (people, monkeys, rats, etc.) who are "equal" with respect to all the characteristics that might influence performance is basically an impossible task. Consequently experimenters typically assign subjects to conditions randomly, thereby gaining control over *all* the subject characteristics that might affect scores on the dependent variable.

The nice aspect of randomization is that it allows control over potentially confounding variables whether or not the researcher is directly aware of their existence. If a researcher "randomly" distributes his treatments over time, he is randomizing the influence of any variable that fluctuates over time. Similarly, when a researcher randomly assigns subjects to treatments, she is randomizing the influence of any and all "subject differences" that might influence scores on the dependent variable. In contrast, a researcher can hold constant or carefully balance a potentially confounding variable only if he is aware of it and can directly control it.

Compared to constancy and balancing, randomization has both a clear disadvantage and a clear advantage. The disadvantage is that randomization does not guarantee perfect control over a potentially confounding variable. The advantage is that the technique provides its own form of probabilistic, statistical control over all variables that are randomized (even if the researcher can't really identify them). A variable that is held constant or completely balanced cannot logically confound the relation between the independent variable and the dependent variable. A variable that is randomized might possibly confound the independent-variable–dependent-variable relation, but the probability of such confounding can be made small and can be taken into account when the data are analyzed (we'll consider the details in Chapter 6).

Experimenters often use a mixture of control techniques, even with respect to subject differences. For example, a researcher might employ only female subjects, thereby holding "sex of subject" constant. In addition, subjects might be classified into "high" and "low" intelligence levels, with "intelligence level" balanced over treatments. Even if "sex of subject" has been held constant and "intelligence level" balanced, a careful experimenter would randomly assign subjects within a category to the various treatments. If there were 10 high-intelligence females and 10 low-intelligence females, the experimenter would randomly assign 5 high-intelligence females to treatment A and 5 high-intelligence females to treatment B (likewise for the 10 low-intelligence females). Holding "sex of subject" constant eliminates this variable as a possibly confounding variable; balancing "intelligence level" across treatments avoids confounding treatment differences with differences in this variable. Randomly assigning 5 high-intelligence subjects and 5 low-intelligence subjects to treatment A (and the same for treatment B) provides probabilistic, statistical control over all other subject characteristics that might influence scores on the dependent variable.

In an attempt to avoid confounding the relation between an independent variable and a dependent variable, an experimenter will try to use constancy or balancing whenever these techniques are feasible. Since these techniques cannot be used for all potentially confounding variables, experimenters use randomization to gain control over the other variables. Of course should a researcher fail to control a variable by means of one of these techniques, there is a clear risk that the relation between the independent and dependent variables will be seriously confounded.

Control, Treatment Evaluation, and External Validity

We have discussed control procedures with respect to the goal of reducing or eliminating confounding, and we have seen that in this regard randomization provides less control than balancing or constancy. Control procedures also affect two other important aspects of a research study, namely, the evaluation of treatment differences and the external validity or generality of the findings. We'll consider these issues separately.

Effects on Treatment Evaluation. Recall that to decide whether a relation exists between two variables a researcher compares the differences in scores between treatments to the amount of random variation in scores. The manner in which potentially confounding variables are controlled affects the amount of random variation in scores and, thus, the evaluation of treatment differences. The reference point for this analysis is randomization. To the extent that variables that might affect the scores obtained in each treatment are allowed to vary randomly, they will produce random variation in scores. The basic rule is quite simple: The more variables are allowed to vary randomly, the more random variation in scores there will be. The consequence is also simple: The more random variation in scores there is, the harder it will be to conclude that real score differences between treatments exist. In other words, when a researcher does *not* let a potentially important variable vary randomly by using either balancing or constancy, there will be less random variation in scores and the comparison of the treatments will be more sensitive.

First let's consider how balancing affects the amount of random variation in scores. In Table 2.2 I described a study in which a researcher wants to compare two treatments (A and B) and collect data in two rooms (1 and 2). If the researcher used two rooms but randomly assigned the subjects in treatments A and B to those rooms, then any differences between rooms (which would affect the scores) would contribute to random variation in scores. In contrast, if the researcher balances rooms with treatments (as in Table 2.2), room differences would no longer contribute to random score variation. Notice that if rooms are balanced with treatments, data will be collected in four different conditions (treatment A, room 1; treatment A, room 2; treatment B, room 1; treatment B, room 2). The index of random variation in scores would now depend on how much the scores varied in a particular room–treatment combination. The amount of random score variation is likely to be less with treatment–room combinations than if subjects had been assigned to rooms at random.

Constancy works in a similar fashion. Using the same example, holding "room" constant would mean that data would be collected in only one room. Obviously, when only one room is used, "room differences" cannot affect the scores obtained. Both constancy and balancing will probably reduce the amount of random score variation if the variable held constant or balanced is actually important. If "room differences" do affect the scores obtained and only one room is used (constancy), then there must be less random variation in scores. Because when balancing is used the index of random variation depends on differences among scores for each particular treatment–room combination, balancing will also reduce the amount of random variation.

To summarize, using balancing or constancy to control a variable will reduce the amount of random variation in scores if the variable held constant or balanced is actually important. The net effect is to make the comparison of score differences between treatments more sensitive. If the variable that is held constant or balanced does not affect the scores that will be obtained (i.e., it is an unimportant variable), then nothing will have been gained (or, really, lost) by using constancy or balancing.

Effects on External Validity. With respect to either avoiding confounding or reducing random score variation, it is clear that balancing and constancy are superior to randomization. Let's compare randomization and constancy. If a researcher randomizes a potentially confounding variable, the result is less control with respect to confounding and more random score variation than if constancy were used. It would appear that researchers should use constancy whenever possible. There is, however, another consideration, namely, the external validity or generality of the results that are obtained. The basic rule is this: Holding a variable constant limits the external validity of the results (in principle). Suppose, for example, that a researcher compares the reaction times to two different kinds of visual stimuli while holding sex of subject, level of illumination, and room temperature constant. *Strictly speaking,* the results might not tell us anything about the difference in reaction times for the two stimulus types that would result if subjects of a different sex, different illumination levels, or different room temperatures were used. If, on the other hand, the researcher had let sex, illumination level, and room temperature vary randomly, any difference between reaction times for the two stimulus types could reasonably be generalized to a wider range of conditions. There is, in effect, a trade-off; Randomization provides less control with respect to confounding and random variation in scores, but allows more general statements to be made. Constancy provides excellent control over confounding and random score variation but yields results that *might* be severely limited.

The most reasonable view is that holding variables constant leads to results of *uncertain* external validity. If a researcher uses only males or holds temperature constant at 70°, we don't know whether the difference between treatments would or wouldn't change if females, or people of both sexes, or other room temperatures were involved. It would be incorrect to state that surely the score difference between treatments would change if, say, females were the subjects, and it would be just as incorrect to state that the difference between treatments would not change if females were the subjects. The essential point is that we just would not know. Because we do need to know the generality of a relation between variables, the uncertainty resulting from holding variables constant is worth some concern.

In a sense, balancing offers "the best of both worlds." Rather than using just males, a researcher could use both males and females but carefully balance sex of subject with treatments. Rather than using just one temperature, a researcher could use a number of temperatures but carefully balance temperature across treatments. By averaging the score difference between treatments across the levels of the balanced variables, the researcher can obtain information about the treatment differences that has reasonable generality. In principle, balancing provides just as much control over confounding and random score variation as constancy but allows results of greater external validity to be obtained. In fact many modern researchers conduct studies in which extensive balancing is used. Such research becomes quite complicated (and often expensive); we will consider some of these techniques in Chapter 8.

PROBLEM

Two researchers studied the effects of delayed reinforcement on learning by monkeys. In researcher A's experiment the monkeys saw one of two different shapes on each trial and were reinforced with a peanut if they pressed a lever when the "correct" shape was shown. Researcher A found that monkeys who received immediate reinforcement (no delay) made more correct responses than those whose reinforcement was delayed for 5 seconds. Researcher B conducted a similar experiment in which monkeys heard one of two tones on each trial and received a peanut if they pushed a lever when the "correct" tone was sounded. However, researcher B found that monkeys whose reinforcement was delayed for 5 seconds made just as many correct responses as those who received immediate reinforcement. These findings appear to be contradictory, researcher A finding that delaying reinforcement hurts performance while researcher B found that delaying reinforcement did not affect performance. Your task: Construct a specific hypothesis about the effect of delayed reinforcement that agrees with the results of both studies.

The main point is that the two researchers did not use the same task. The monkeys in researcher A's experiment had to make a visual discrimination while those in researcher B's experiment had to make an auditory discrimination. Therefore a possible hypothesis is that delaying reinforcement (for 5 seconds) lowers performance on a visual discrimination but doesn't affect performance on an auditory discrimination. If it should turn out that delay of reinforcement has different effects for visual and auditory tasks, this would be an example of how holding a variable constant (in this case, kind of task) yields results of limited generality.

ETHICAL CONSIDERATIONS

The general goal of science is to increase understanding, and collecting data is an essential part of the process of advancing scientific knowledge. When doing research, investigators are virtually forced to make choices about the kinds of measures to be used, the variables to be controlled, and the control procedures to be used. The choices they make affect the quality of the information stemming from the research. In addition to confronting choices regarding such knowledge-related, "technical" issues, researchers also face questions of ethics. In Chapter 1, I pointed out that some people consider certain kinds of knowledge to be so dangerous that they believe we are better off being ignorant, and that scientists generally feel that knowledge is superior to ignorance. Even if we assume that knowledge for its own sake is good, there are still more concrete ethical issues that researchers often confront. Let's consider some of these ethical issues with respect to psychological research.

In psychological research there are always some organisms (usually referred to as "subjects") whose behavior is in some way studied or observed. Investigators must be concerned about protecting the rights, health, and well-being of the subjects who are studied, and sometimes this concern seems to be in conflict with the goal of gaining knowledge. Many ethical questions arise. For example, if it is important to know how people behave under extreme physical discomfort, does this justify subjecting people to extreme physical discomfort? Is it ethical to make lesions in the brains of rats to determine how certain brain abnormalities affect behavior? To gain understanding about how people respond to a person in distress, is it ethical to have a research assistant pretend to have a heart attack on a crowded bus? Is it ethical for a researcher to give people a problem that some of them might not solve and therefore feel bad about themselves for a short while? This is but a small sample of the ethical questions that can arise in psychological research. As you can see, the issues seem to range from major to minor, and answering such questions is not particularly easy.

Let me emphasize that ethical considerations are not limited to research in which human behavior is studied; such issues also arise when rats, cats, monkeys, or fish are the subjects. Let me also point out that there are rules and guidelines that apply to research activities. Researchers who study animal behavior are subject to rules imposed by local health departments and other agencies, such as the Department of Health, Education and Welfare. The American Psychological Association has published a set of principles governing research in which human behavior is studied. Although laws, rules, and guidelines might clearly ban some practices, many "gray areas" of uncertainty remain.

In research on human behavior the ethical issues that arise most frequently concern such matters as invasion of privacy, deception, stress, and informed consent. For example, it is considered desirable for the people who will participate as subjects in a study to agree to participate after they have been fully informed about the research project. But what must a person know in order to be "fully informed" about the study? Does a subject need to know the purpose of the study, the scientific hypothesis being investigated, the treatments that other people will receive, or the previous findings that led to this particular study? Or is it enough if subjects are given a general idea of the purpose of the study, what they will be asked to do, and the circumstances under which they will be asked to perform? The notion of obtaining "informed consent" is not quite as clear as it might seem. Giving people information (so that they can be informed before agreeing to participate) can lead to conflicts. For example, if a researcher wants to give some people large rewards for doing something and to give others small rewards (to see how reward magnitude is related to performance), should he tell someone who will receive a small reward that others will get large rewards? The researcher might want to analyze the effects of reward magnitude in situations in which people do not know that others are getting different rewards for the same task performance, and it will be impossible to study this question if all subjects are informed about others' rewards. Suppose a person has been asked to participate in a study because the researcher has information suggesting that that person is highly anxious. Should the researcher tell the person why she has been asked to participate (thus making her better informed, but probably also inducing some stress), or should this information be withheld?

A fair amount of psychological research involves stress of some sort, and it is indeed possible that some people will feel stress no matter what happens. While it seems obvious that receiving a painful but not harmful electric shock would be stressful, there are other, less obvious procedures that can involve stress. For example, college students, who are the subjects in many psychological studies, rated "giving a five-minute speech to a group of other students" as moderately stressful, and at least some students felt that "crossing out the *e*'s on the pages of a booklet" involved mild discomfort. A researcher might wish to compare the difficulty of different kinds of problems (stress having nothing to do with the purpose of the study), yet college students indicated that failing to solve a problem can be moderately stressful (Farr & Seaver, 1975). Researchers have no desire to induce stress or discomfort in their subjects. Yet it can reasonably be argued that it is important to understand how people behave under stressful conditions. Furthermore, as some of the preceding examples illustrate, a number of apparently innocuous procedures can produce at least mild discomfort in some subjects. Researchers often have to decide whether gaining potentially important information justifies inducing (how much?) stress in (how many?) subjects.

Some psychological research involves deception. In a review of nearly 1000 studies published in the early 1970s, Menges (1973) found that approximately 20 percent involved some kind of deception, where deception was defined as giving subjects inaccurate information about some aspect of the study. Deception can occur in many ways. For example, in a study of how people react to negative feedback some subjects might be told that they have performed very poorly on some task (regardless of how well they had actually performed), or a subject might be led to believe that he is delivering painful shocks to another person (actually a stooge of the experimenter, with no real shocks involved) to see whether people will follow instructions to punish others in this way. Interestingly, professional psychologists seem to be more likely to view deception as unethical and unjustified than college students, who might well be the subjects in such experiments (Sullivan & Deiker, 1973).

When deception is involved in psychological research, it is common practice to "debrief" subjects after the data have been collected. Debriefing means that subjects are told that some information they were given was inaccurate. The fact that experimenters debrief subjects suggests that researchers realize that deception might have some undesirable effects, at least temporarily. The question that arises is whether debriefing works. To give an example, if a person has been told that her performance on some task indicates that she is uncreative or poorly adjusted (as an experimental manipulation to see how people react to such information) and is later told that this information was inaccurate, does the debriefing (1) lead the subject to have an accurate understanding of the study and (2) eliminate subsequent undesirable effects on the subject? The available evidence (Holmes, 1976a, b) suggests that debriefing tends to work, although there is really not a great deal of information about the effectiveness of debriefing.

The need to protect an individual's privacy creates important and sensitive issues. One of the reasons for obtaining "informed consent" is to eliminate questions about invasion of privacy. If a person understands what the research involves and agrees to provide information, it is hard to argue that his or her privacy has been violated. In research involving children, parental consent is obtained. In many studies data are collected "anonymously"—the researcher literally does not know who provided a particular item of information. For example, if a researcher has a group of thirty people complete a questionnaire and carefully instructs them to avoid identifying themselves in any way on their answer sheets, the researcher really will not know who gave what answers. In general, researchers are not interested in information about specific individuals. A researcher might be interested in the information that "the ten high-anxiety subjects were more likely to endorse striking back at people who offend you," but he would not be interested in knowing that a particular person, John Doe, agreed that it was acceptable to "cut off" a driver who has cut in front of you.

Nevertheless researchers do have information about individuals in many research studies (even though the researcher may not need or want such information). Questions arise about who might have access to such information. Researchers typically guard the privacy of their subjects with great care; indeed, many researchers recode their data in such a way that shortly after the information has been obtained they themselves do not know the identity of the person associated with a particular item of information. For example, suppose a researcher had a number of people complete a questionnaire and originally knew everyone's name (in other words, knew who had given what answers). He might give each person an arbitrary number and recode the data by "subject number," discarding the original forms. At this point the researcher would know that "subject number 14 gave the following answers," but he would not know who was "subject number 14."

Quite obviously, having people identify themselves (e.g., by signing their names to questionnaires) raises questions of invasion of privacy that do not exist when data are collected anonymously. Researchers typically try to collect data anonymously in order to avoid such potential problems. Somewhat surprisingly, college students do not generally consider signing their names to questionnaires about drug use, feelings toward parents, or sexual practices to be a serious invasion of privacy (Farr & Seaver, 1975). At the same time, at least some students do object to providing certain kinds of information.

We have just touched on some of the ethical considerations that researchers face. These questions cannot be satisfactorily answered by adopting an "absolutist" position. Nobody has seriously suggested that gaining knowledge justifies anything a researcher might do. Conversely, if one argues that data should not be collected if just one subject might feel stress or believe that his or her privacy has been invaded, virtually no research would be done (and it is doubtful that people would desire a complete lack of information from research).

Many people and organizations have suggested that ethical issues be examined in terms of a "risk–benefit ratio." The idea is that researchers should compare the risks to the subject (and to society) with the benefits that are likely to result from the information obtained (to society, and perhaps to the individual subject). If the benefits outweigh the risks by a "sufficient amount," the research should be conducted. While in a general sense the idea of comparing potential risks to potential benefits is reasonable, we should not be misled into thinking that there is some formula that can be used to calculate the risk–benefit ratio and, thus, dictate the decision. People will differ with respect to the weights to be assigned to various risks and benefits. Furthermore, there are undoubtedly some "risks" that are so unacceptable that no potential benefit could possibly outweigh them. For example, no matter how important it might be to understand how people react to a death in the family, sensible people would simply never agree to killing a person to see how that person's family members react, and most would not endorse deceiving family members into thinking that someone has died.

I have raised the issue of ethical considerations because this issue should be recognized. However, it is impossible to propose a general solution or set of rules that will solve such problems. In practice, attempts are made to achieve some kind of consensus. In many universities and research organizations research proposals are subject to review by ethics committees. Research projects funded by various agencies are subjected to further reviews, and legal considerations provide another form of review. Such reviews, combined with the investigator's own assessment, provide some consensus about the value of a research project. Any number of reviews will not prevent someone from claiming that the wrong people conducted the reviews or that a wrong decision was made.

Let me close this discussion with two additional comments. First, ethical considerations apply to all research, although with varying degrees of importance, and decisions on these questions are difficult to make. Second, it is easier to make comparative judgments than to make absolute judgments. If a researcher can use either of two methods to obtain information, choosing the one with less negative ethical attributes should be relatively easy. However, it might be hard to decide whether the research should be conducted if the "best available" method is used.

SUMMARY

Psychological research always involves the measurement of one or more aspects of behavior. Three desirable measurement characteristics are validity, reliability, and sensitivity. *Validity* refers to the strength of the connection between a variable as measured and the same variable as conceptualized in psychological theory. *Reliability* depends on the stability of the values that are obtained with a given measure, while *sensitivity* or *precision* refers to the number of possible values that can be recorded. Measures can involve either verbal or numerical labels for values; in many circumstances numerical values are preferred because they are likely to be clearer and more precise and because they allow the use of powerful statistical techniques.

Different kinds of scales are used in research. A *nominal* scale is just a set of mutually exclusive categories; if the categories are ordered, the result is an *ordinal* scale. Adding a constant unit to the scale yields an *interval* scale, while further adding a true zero point yields a *ratio* scale. As the type of scale changes, the meanings of the numbers on the scale change in important ways. In some situations choosing the most appropriate index number is critical for making comparisons of the measures obtained for two or more cases. It is sometimes necessary to use relative measures that correct for opportunities in order to make appropriate comparisons.

Researchers control variables in various ways and for different purposes. When studying the relation between two variables, researchers often compare the scores for two or more treatments. The difference in scores between treatments is examined in relation to the amount of random variation in scores in order to decide whether the treatments are associated with really different scores. Variables can be controlled to increase the score difference between treatments, to reduce the amount of random score variation, or to accomplish both goals simultaneously.

An *independent* variable is one whose values are directly under the control of the researcher; an experiment involves the relation between an independent variable and a natural variable (usually called the *dependent* variable). The different treatments that are administered are the values of the independent variable chosen by the experimenter. It is important for the experimenter to administer the treatments consistently, to choose values of the independent variable that are reasonably different from each other, and to use enough values to adequately represent the full range of the independent variable. Similar notions apply when a researcher studies the relation between two natural variables; for example, grouping cases into "highs" and "lows" on one variable provides a minimum amount of information about the relation between the grouped variable and another variable.

Control procedures are often used to avoid the confounding that can occur when treatments differ in more than one way. Holding a variable constant in a research study is the most direct way of avoiding confounding, since something that does not vary cannot possibly confound treatment differences. *Balancing* is a control technique in which different values of a potentially confounding variable occur equally often with every value of the independent variable. *Randomization* provides statistical control and is based on the idea that in the long run things will even out. *Randomization* is typically used when constancy or balancing are not feasible as control procedures; in psychological research randomization is frequently used to control the many characteristics of subjects that might influence performance. With respect to evaluating treatment differences, constancy and balancing work better than randomization, since these two techniques reduce the amount of random score variation and thus make the treatment comparison more sensitive. However, constancy places constraints on the external validity of the findings; extensive balancing of many variables can be the best technique but does lead to complicated research designs.

All researchers face ethical issues to some extent. There can be conflicts between the goal of obtaining desired knowledge and the goal of protecting the health and well-being of the subjects who are studied. In research involving human subjects ethical issues tend to center on obtaining informed consent, inducing stress, using deception, and invasion of privacy. In a general sense, the potential benefits stemming from the research must be compared to the potential risks that the research involves. It is usually easier to decide that one method is ethically preferable to another than to decide whether a particular study should or should not be conducted on ethical grounds. Research projects are subjected to various forms of review in an attempt to reach a form of consensus about the justification for the research.

3

CHARACTERISTICS OF PSYCHOLOGICAL RESEARCH

In the preceding chapter we examined the techniques that researchers use to control and manipulate variables, and considered some of the ways in which control (or the lack thereof) affects the information gained from a research project. We will now take a closer look at research in psychology and related fields in order to identify more concretely the kinds of variables that attract the attention of researchers.

Any research study has many characteristics that might deserve attention. Because psychological research covers so many topics, it is impossible to list the "important" ones and hope to be complete. In addition, the importance of any particular characteristic depends on what is being studied; for example, temperature might be critical if one kind of behavior is studied but of no importance if a different kind of behavior is studied. However, we can consider several *classes* of characteristics that are often important in psychological research.

Whether you are planning a study or evaluating the results of a completed research project, your task is basically the same. You must examine the methods to see if you can identify any problems. In the case of planning research you examine the plan and have a chance of improving the plan if problems are identified. The quality of such examinations depends on how carefully and thoroughly you check the various characteristics of the study, and it is always possible to miss something. If you are planning a study, you might check the plan on Monday and find no problems, only to check it again on Friday and identify a potential difficulty. Several people might examine the same study and identify different potential problems. For these reasons careful researchers ask their colleagues for evaluations of research plans before collecting data. Journal editors have the important task of evaluating the results of completed research and deciding whether the findings warrant publication.

What should you look for in examining research? As already indicated, there is no simple, foolproof method. To help you with this task I will give you a mnemonic device, namely, the word *estimate*. The letters in *estimate* stand for eight general characteristics of psychological research. The *estimate* mnemonic is by no means complete, but it can provide you with a partial checklist of characteristics to examine. Here is what the letters stand for:

Experimenters
Subjects
Time
Instructions
Measurement
Apparatus
Task
Environment

A separate section of this chapter will be devoted to each of these characteristics.

QUESTIONS TO ASK

The characteristics of a research project can be examined from several different perspectives. In this chapter I will concentrate on research dealing with the relations between variables, in which case there are three perspectives to consider. Research characteristics can be examined with respect to (1) the evaluation of treatment differences, (2) internal validity, and (3) external validity. Let me summarize our earlier discussions of these issues as they apply to the examination of research characteristics.

A researcher will compare the score difference *between* treatments to an index of the amount of random variation in scores in order to decide whether the various treatments are really associated with different scores. In Chapter 2 we discussed the importance of using treatments that differ from each other in a sensible fashion. Let me now direct your attention to the amount of random score variation. Roughly speaking, as more characteristics are allowed to vary randomly in a study there will be more random variation in scores, and it will be harder for the researcher to conclude that the treatments are really associated with different scores (that there really is a relation between the two variables). In short, excessive random variation can lead to "missing relations."

From the perspective of *internal* validity, the issue is whether the relation between variables can be interpreted clearly. In other words, can you identify any characteristics that confound the relation between the two variables that are of interest to the researcher? Here is a simple example. If treatments A and B differ in the kinds of instructions given to subjects but also differ in the kinds of subjects assigned to each treatment condition, any differences in scores between treatments A and B are ambiguous. Perhaps the score differences are due to differences in instructions; perhaps they are due to differences in the subjects assigned to the two treatments; or perhaps both instruction and subject differences are producing score differences. We would simply not know how to interpret the score differences between treatments, a classic case of low internal validity.

From the perspective of *external* validity, the question concerns the generality of the findings. Any research finding is limited, in the strictest sense, to the particular circumstances under which the data were obtained. For example, finding that treatments A and B are associated with real score differences for 25-year-old males does not, strictly speaking, tell us what would happen if the subjects were females, younger or older males, and so on. If trustworthy treatment differences are found when anxiety is measured with a paper-and-pencil test, this result does not tell us what would happen if anxiety were measured in some other way, say, by assessing changes in heart rate. The key idea here is that characteristics that are held constant in a study might place important restrictions on the external validity of the results.

As you examine each characteristic of a research project, it is best to proceed in the following manner. The first question to ask about a characteristic is whether it varied *in the study*. If it was held constant in the study, it cannot be a source of confounding and is likely to lead to a more sensitive comparison of score differences between treatments. If it was held constant, the characteristic is a fixture of the study that must be considered in evaluating the generality of the results. If a characteristic did vary in the study, the next question to ask is, How did it vary? Was the variation random or systematic? If the variation was random, confounding is unlikely (though not impossible), and you should be most concerned if the researcher reports that "there were no real score differences between treatments"—perhaps there was too much random variation. If the characteristic varies systematically, the question is whether or not it is balanced with treatments. If the characteristic is *not* balanced, then it will confound the relation between treatments (i.e., values of one variable) and the "dependent" (other) variable.

Any of the various characteristics of psychological research might be the independent variable that is of interest, a variable that was held constant, or a source of potential confounding. As we discuss these characteristics I will not repeatedly consider all the possible ways in which each characteristic might influence the results. Rather, I will concentrate on the more likely ways in which each characteristic might be important and on what researchers might do to improve the quality of their findings.

EXPERIMENTERS

The first *e* in *estimate* refers to the people who are involved in the collection of data. In a large research project there might be a research director who plans the study; one or more experimenters who deal directly with the subjects, delivering the treatments; and observers who are part of the measurement process. Although the research planner has a great deal of influence over what a study will be like, we will concentrate on experimenters and observers who are more directly involved with the subjects. Note that a particular individual might serve as both an experimenter delivering treatments and an observer recording what subjects do.

The first question to ask is whether there is an experimenter/observer present in the research situation, interacting with the subjects participating in the study or observing and recording their behavior. Data might be collected with or without an experimenter present while the subject does whatever is requested, and the presence of an experimenter might influence subjects' behavior. For example, some subjects might be distracted or "nervous" when another person is in the room, and this might influence their scores (this influence is likely to lead to greater random variation in scores). If there is just one experimenter/observer, what are the potentially important characteristics of that person? For example, it has been suggested that *in some cases* male and female experimenters, or black and white experimenters, obtain different results. If so, a study employing only a male experimenter might yield findings that differ from the results of a study employing only a female experimenter. Overall, it does not seem that this kind of concern is often warranted—but it might be important for the topic you are studying!

Experimenter Bias

It is important to train experimenters to do their jobs consistently. Consistent experimenters (and observers) reduce the amount of random variation in a study and thus minimize the "noise" in the data. Of perhaps greater importance is the possibility that inconsistent experimenters might introduce bias into an experiment. In order to avoid confounding by experimenter bias, it is often desirable to have an experimenter know his or her specific job very well but know little else about the study. It has been reported, for example, that poorly trained experimenters handle rats who "are supposed to perform poorly" in a manner different from their handling of rats who "are supposed to perform well." (Barber, 1976, discusses a number of such problems.) Clearly experimenters and observers need to practice their jobs before collecting data for a study. Let me give you an example of how possible experimenter bias might be minimized.

The general technique for minimizing possible experimenter bias is to keep the experimenter from knowing which treatment group any particular subject belongs to. Of course this cannot always be done—in many instances an experimenter would certainly know which treatment was being used. However, sometimes it is possible to keep the experimenter "blind." For example, if a researcher wants to compare performance on two different kinds of mathematics problems that differ in a theoretically meaningful but *subtle* fashion he need not inform the experimenter who will be actually giving the problems to subjects about this difference. If a study includes a comparison of subjects with different scores on, say, some ability test, the experimenter can be kept "blind" regarding the test score of all subjects while collecting data. Obviously, using this technique requires at least two people working on the research project—one person has the information but doesn't interact with the subjects, while "the experimenter" interacts with the subjects but is not given possibly biasing information.

The kind of experimenter bias I have been discussing would result from the same experimenter's doing something differently for subjects in different treatments when he or she is supposed to be doing the same thing. Training experimenters to do their jobs consistently helps avoid such bias. Keeping experimenters from knowing possibly biasing information will also minimize the possibility of such bias. Notice that minimizing possible experimenter bias is one reason why researchers would want someone other than themselves to actually collect the data. The researcher who plans a study obviously knows what the different treatments are and what kinds of performance differences might be expected, but another person serving as experimenter need not have such information.

It should be clear that the experimenter bias we are considering is *not* deliberate "cheating" but, rather, a form of bias resulting from an experimenter's unconsciously doing something differently that should be done consistently. It is reasonable to ask how much we should be concerned about the possibility of such bias. The proper answer is "It depends." One must ask what the subjects are doing and how much interaction the experimenter has with a subject—what might an experimenter do to influence subjects' performance? Roughly speaking, the more the experimenter interacts with the subject, the more opportunities there are for some kind of unconscious bias to occur (provided that the experimenter has knowledge that could produce bias). If the subject's attention is strongly directed toward the task (and, thus, not toward the experimenter) and the experimenter has little interaction with the subject, the possibility of bias is obviously reduced. Although each situation must be evaluated on its own merits, Barber (1976) suggests that unconscious experimenter bias is really unlikely, especially if experimenters are well trained.

The issues I have discussed in regard to experimenters also apply to observers—people who are present in the situation to record subjects' behavior. One can ask whether or not an observer was present, what the important characteristics of an observer are, whether the observer is well trained, and so on. These issues also apply whether data are to be collected by one experimenter or several experimenters. Obviously, when more than one experimenter is involved it is important to balance experimenters across treatments.

PROBLEM

A researcher had the idea that punishing incorrect responses will aid learning. To test this idea she randomly assigned college students to either a "control" condition or one in which subjects received a mild electric shock for each incorrect response. Subjects sat in front of a panel with ten different buttons and were shown, one at a time, ten different words. Each button had been arbitrarily chosen as the correct response for a different word. When a word was shown, the subject pushed a button; if the subject was correct, a light labeled "right" was illuminated. For incorrect responses a light labeled "wrong" was illuminated for subjects in the control condition; for those in the punishment condition a mild shock was delivered in addition to illuminating the "wrong" light. The data were collected by two research assistants, one collecting data for subjects in the punishment condition (because she was experienced at operating the shock apparatus) and the other collecting data for the control condition. The results showed that learning to criterion was slightly but reliably better for the punishment condition (an average of 14 incorrect responses) than for the control condition (an average of 19 incorrect responses). The researcher therefore concluded that punishment did aid learning. What problem might exist in this experiment?

In this example there is no doubt that treatment differences (punishment vs. control) are confounded with differences between experimenters. The possibility exists that the lower number of incorrect responses for the "punishment condition" was due to the fact that data for this condition were collected by the experienced experimenter. To judge the plausibility of this alternate conclusion we would have to examine the study more closely—just what did the experimenters have to do? In general, it is dangerous to assume that all experimenters are equally good at their jobs and to run the risk of confounding results with experimenter differences. The researcher would have been much better off training both experimenters to use the apparatus and then having each experimenter collect half the data for each condition.

SUBJECTS

Psychology is concerned with behavior. Therefore research necessarily involves the assessment of some organism's behavior. The organisms whose behavior is studied are commonly referred to as *subjects*. (Some people prefer the term *participants* where human beings are concerned.) In evaluating research we need to ask what the subjects are like and how they are assigned to various treatments. Individual differences among people, monkeys, rats, or what have you are a fact of life and are often quite large. Consequently concern over the characteristics of subjects is quite justified.

At the outset let me point out that "subject differences" cannot truly be considered an *independent* variable. A researcher might compare males with females, older people with younger people, psychology majors with sociology majors, children raised in orphanages with those raised at home, and so on, but in so doing he or she would not have *manipulated* those variables. Rather, the researcher finds organisms who already differ in some way and compares their scores on some measure (often called the dependent variable). Notice that some of the contrasts just listed could *in principle* be a result of manipulation. In principle, but *not* in practice, a researcher could decide who will be raised in an orphanage and who will be raised at home. In contrast, it is difficult to imagine how a researcher could make some subjects old and some subjects young.

This point may be summarized as follows: A researcher may find some organisms who already differ in some stated way, and the scores of these different kinds of subjects on some measure may be compared. However, because the researcher has not controlled the assignment of subjects to different kinds of subjects there will be clear limitations on what the researcher can say about the meaning of the comparison. Recall that randomization is used to avoid confounding treatment differences with subject differences. If the researcher has *not* randomly assigned subjects to different treatments or groups, then confounding must be considered likely. For example, psychology and sociology majors obviously differ in that some are in fact psychology majors and others are in fact sociology majors. The question is, Might these two groups of people also differ in other ways that might influence or bias the comparison of psychology and sociology majors? Since the researcher has not randomly assigned subjects to the "psychology major" and "sociology major" treatments, clearly it is possible that confounding is present. Indeed, many researchers would say that in such a situation confounding is inevitable. Is it reasonable to assume that "choice of major" is the only way in which people who have chosen to become psychology majors differ from people who have chosen to become sociology majors? The implied answer is no. The same argument can be applied whenever a researcher compares groups of subjects who have been chosen because they already differ in some fashion.

Let's now consider situations in which researchers do manipulate some variable, that is, situations in which researchers can control the assignment of subjects to treatments. The first question to ask is, What are the subjects like? We need to know what is common to all of the subjects participating in the study, or what has been held constant. The reason for asking this question is that "kinds of subjects" is a fixture of any study that must be considered in evaluating the potential generality of the findings. What we should know about the subjects will depend on many things. Obviously, no researcher can tell us everything about the subjects (the job would never end), but we should be told about the potentially important characteristics of the subjects. Consider some examples of the descriptions that are found in research reports published in psychological journals:

> The subjects were 24 naive, male albino rats obtained from the Holtzman Company at 90 days of age. All subjects were deprived of food for 12 hours when data were collected.
>
> The subjects were 80 students from an introductory psychology class who volunteered to participate in the study. All subjects were right-handed and had normal, uncorrected visual acuity.
>
> The subjects were 160 students from an educational psychology course (80 males and 80 females) who participated to fulfill a course requirement.
>
> The subjects were 60 students from a middle-class, suburban school district with 10 males and 10 females in each of the following age groups: 4-, 7-, and 10-year-olds. All subjects had IQs within the normal range for the Otis-Lennon Test of Mental Ability, which had been administered by school personnel as part of normal school procedure.

As these examples illustrate, the kinds of characteristics described vary considerably from one situation to another. This practice makes sense. The kinds of characteristics that distinguish some rats from others are likely to be different from those that distinguish some human children or human adults from others. Generally, researchers describe the characteristics they consider important—it is these characteristics that they take the trouble to control. In describing a characteristic that applies to all the subjects in an experiment, the researcher is both indicating that this variable was held constant in the experiment and alerting other researchers to the particular value that was used. The importance of a characteristic also depends on what subjects will be doing. In the second example the researcher went to the trouble of ensuring that all subjects were right-handed and had normal vision. These are not generally important human characteristics but presumably were important for the particular task that subjects would be doing in that experiment.

Researchers hold subject characteristics constant primarily to reduce the amount of random variation in their experiments. This is likely to result in a more sensitive comparison of the treatments they employ. Of course holding a variable constant also limits the generality of the findings. For example, findings based on employing only "naive, 90-day-old, male albino rats" do not directly tell us what results would be obtained if the subjects were changed to "practiced" or "female" or "hooded" rats, monkeys, or what have you.

Although I believe that experimenters should pay much more attention to the generality of their findings, which includes consideration of the kinds of subjects they employ, it is important to understand what kinds of generalizations are involved. It is too easy to dismiss the results of an experiment simply because "the experimenter used only educational-psychology students and such people are certainly different from, say, high school students." Experimenters are interested in comparing treatments, and the question of external validity is whether *the comparison of the treatments* would be different if different subjects were employed. If an experimenter finds that treatment A is associated with higher scores (on some measure) than treatment B when using, say, introductory-psychology students as subjects, the question is *not* simply whether high school students (or any other kind of subject) would generally score higher or lower than the subjects employed, but whether treatment A would lead to higher scores than treatment B if other subjects were involved. There are numerous instances in which treatment differences are not the same for different kinds of subjects, but you should understand that it is the generality of the treatment differences that is at issue.

Once the kind of subjects has been determined, there remains the question of how they shall be assigned to the various treatments. There are three basic methods that might be used: independent groups, matched subjects, or repeated measures. Each method has both advantages and disadvantages. The three methods can be grouped in two different ways. With respect to evaluating treatment score differences, matched-subject designs and repeated-measures designs are similar and can be contrasted with the use of independent groups. Compared with using independent groups, the use of matched subjects or repeated measures is likely to *reduce* the index of random score variation and thus provide a more sensitive evaluation of treatment differences. From a procedural viewpoint, independent groups and matched-subject designs are similar and may be contrasted with repeated measures. With either matched subjects or independent groups, each subject receives *only one treatment*, while when repeated measures are used each subject receives *all* treatments. These similarities and differences are summarized in Table 3.1. I will have much more to say about these comparisons as we consider each method.

Table 3.1   Similarities and Differences Among Three Methods of Assigning Subjects to Treatments

With Respect to:	METHOD		
	Independent Groups	Matched Subjects	Repeated Measures
Evaluating treatment differences	Different	⟨Similar⟩	
Procedure	⟨Similar⟩		Different

Independent Groups

The use of independent groups serves as a kind of baseline to which the other methods can be compared. Forming independent groups is basically rather simple. Having decided that, say, forty students will participate as subjects in an experiment comparing treatments A and B, the researcher would use some random method to assign each subject to one of the two treatments. Usually researchers assign equal numbers of subjects to each treatment. The idea is that each treatment is equally important to the comparison and that equal amounts of data should be collected for each treatment. The use of equal-sized groups is *not* required, but merely preferred most of the time.

Let me give you some examples of how independent groups might be formed in actual practice. Suppose a researcher wants to compare two versions of a story. In one version (call it A) the sentence providing the theme for the story is placed at the beginning of the story, while in the other version (B) this sentence occurs last. Each subject will read one version of the story and then attempt to recall it, the question being whether recall differs for the two versions. An experiment like this was conducted by Thorndyke (1977) to see whether the location of information about the theme affects recall of the story (in Thorndyke's study it did—recall was better when the "theme" sentence came first). The researcher will collect data (recall scores) for 30 students who are all in the same classroom at one time. To form independent groups he might take 15 copies of version A and 15 copies of version B, mix them up in an unsystematic (random) fashion, and then simply distribute them to the 30 students. In this way he would have two independent groups of 15 subjects each in the experiment.

Here is another example. Suppose a researcher wants to compare learning scores for rats under three different conditions of "amount of reward"—one, two, or three pellets of standard "rat chow" for each correct response. Each rat will be given a number of trials involving a choice between two stimuli (e.g., a black door and a white door) and will receive a food reward each time the correct choice is made (e.g., the white door is arbitrarily designated as the "correct," or rewarded, choice). The experimenter will compare the number-of-correct-choices scores for the three amount-of-reward treatments. The procedure requires that each rat be run individually; the experimenter decides that a total of 45 rats will be used, 15 for each treatment. Notice that the 45 subjects will participate one at a time over some period of time; one rat will be the first to participate, another the second, and so on. All the rats will come from the rat colony maintained in the researcher's laboratory. To form three independent groups of 15 rats each, the researcher might devise a random order of 15 "ones," 15 "twos," 15 "threes," and then use this order to determine the treatment for each rat. Here is one such random order (which I obtained by consulting a table of random numbers):

133233121112311231213312322223311221231312332

Using this order, the first rat taken from the colony would receive the one-pellet treatment, the second the three-pellet treatment, and so on. In this way the researcher would form three independent groups of 15 rats.

As discussed previously, a researcher must compare the score difference between treatments to an index of the amount of random score variation in order to decide whether the treatments are associated with really different scores. When independent groups of subjects are used, random score variation depends on how much the scores *within a treatment* differ from each other. The more the scores *within each treatment* differ from each other, the harder it will be for the researcher to conclude that the score difference *between treatments* represents a real difference. To illustrate how score differences *within* treatments affect the evaluation of treatment differences, I have constructed the two artificial sets of data shown in Table 3.2.

Let me describe this hypothetical situation. The researcher wants to compare two treatments (A and B) and randomly assigns 10 subjects to

Table 3.2   Artificial Data Illustrating the Effect of Random Score Variation Within Treatments on the Comparison of Treatments

Data Set 1: Higher Random Score Variation Within Treatments

TREATMENT	INDIVIDUAL SCORES	AVERAGE SCORE	RANGE OF SCORES
A	68, 44, 63, 59, 45, 55, 47, 49, 50, 52	53.2	24
B	39, 63, 58, 54, 32, 50, 44, 46, 44, 41	47.1	21

Data Set 2: Lower Random Score Variation Within Treatments

TREATMENT	INDIVIDUAL SCORES	AVERAGE SCORE	RANGE OF SCORES
A	57, 50, 56, 49, 56, 55, 51, 52, 54, 52	53.2	8
B	43, 51, 52, 38, 51, 45, 47, 50, 46, 48	47.1	14

Note: The difference between the average score for treatment A and the average score for treatment B is the same in data set 1 and data set 2. However, because the scores within treatments vary more in data set 1, it is less likely that a researcher would decide that the score difference between treatments A and B represents a real difference.

treatment A and 10 to treatment B (thus she obtains 10 scores for each treatment). To decide whether treatments A and B are associated with *really different scores,* she will look at the difference between the average score for treatment A and the average score for treatment B, comparing this difference between treatments to the amount of random score variation in the data. The specific statistical formulas that researchers use to make such comparisons are presented much later in this book. At this point all we need to do is consider the basic ideas underlying the evaluation of treatment score differences.

Look first at data set 1. The average score for treatment A is 53.2, while the average score for treatment B is 47.1; the difference between the average scores for the two treatments is about 6 points. Notice further that the scores for the 10 subjects who received treatment A range from a low of 44 to a high of 68, a range of 24 points. Similarly, the scores for the 10 subjects who received treatment B range from a low of 32 to a high of 63, a range of 21 points. The differences among the 10 scores *within* treatment A and among the 10 scores *within* treatment B represent random score variation. As you can see, while there is a roughly 6-point difference between treatments, there is a lot of variation in scores within treatments. The set of 10 scores for treatment A overlaps considerably with the set of 10 scores for treatment B. It would be hard for the researcher to conclude that there is a real score difference between treatments A and B.

Look now at data set 2. As in data set 1, the average score for treatment A is 53.2, the average score for treatment B is 47.1, and the difference between treatments is roughly 6 points. However, the scores within each treatment are more similar to each other. In treatment A the scores range from 49 to 57, a range of 8 points; in treatment B the scores range from 38 to 52, a range of 14 points. Because there is less random score variation within each treatment, there is less overlap between the two sets of scores; and there is a clearer suggestion that treatments A and B are associated with really different scores.

The same two data sets are also shown in Figure 3.1, where you can see that when there is lower random score variation within treatments (as in data set 2) it is easier to detect a score difference between treatments.

It is clearly to the researcher's advantage to minimize the amount of random score variation within treatments. One thing a researcher can do to hold down score variation within treatments is to use subjects who are likely to get similar scores. For example, suppose an experiment will require that each subject try to solve a number of mathematical problems. Under treatment A the problems are presented as "word problems," while for treatment B the problems are presented in terms of formulas and mathematical symbols. The researcher wants to see whether the way in which the problems are presented affects performance on the problems; in order to do so he will form two independent groups, each consisting of twenty

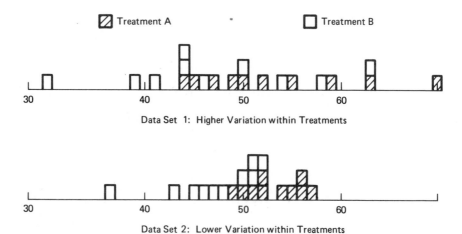

Figure 3.1. Effect of random score variation within treatments on the evaluation of treatment differences.

subjects. Suppose the subjects will come from a population of college students; the point is that college students differ in mathematical ability. To the extent that students differ in their ability to do the problems, the scores *within* treatment A and *within* treatment B will vary. The researcher could reduce the within-treatment score variation by using subjects with similar mathematical ability. Rather than using "college students in general," he could have all subjects be math majors or use as subjects only students whose scores on the math part of the college entrance examination were in a narrow range. By choosing more similar subjects (subjects who are likely to get fairly similar scores) in the first place, he can reduce the amount of random score variation within treatments and thus make the comparison of treatments more sensitive. Of course using a special type of subject (e.g., math majors) does have a possible disadvantage as well, namely, that the results will be limited, strictly speaking, to the particular type of subject used. When deciding whether to use carefully selected, similar subjects in a study, the researcher must compare the likely advantages (lower score variation within treatments) to the possible disadvantages (less general results).

The independent-groups design is rather neat. The researcher randomly assigns subjects to the various treatments, and each subject receives only one treatment. To make the comparison of treatments more sensitive, a researcher can use subjects who are likely to get similar scores. (It is also to the researcher's advantage to use larger groups of subjects, a matter we'll discuss in a later chapter.) Compared to using independent groups, the use of matched subjects or repeated measures represents an attempt to make the comparison of treatments more sensitive in a different manner.

However, these two designs can create special problems of their own, as we will see shortly.

PROBLEM

A researcher wanted to demonstrate that there is a difference between the speed of learning nonsense syllables and the speed of learning words. Her prediction was that learning a list of 15 words would require fewer study trials than learning a list of 15 nonsense syllables. The procedure called for each subject to learn only one list (words or nonsense syllables) and to alternate between 30-second study trials and recall tests until all 15 items on the list were correctly recalled. If a subject did not achieve 100 percent recall after 20 trials, he or she was dropped from the experiment and replaced by another subject. This occurred 10 times in the nonsense-syllable group and 2 times in the word group. In all, 20 subjects eventually learned each list. Comparison of the two groups on mean number of study trials to master their respective lists led to the surprising finding of no significant difference. Although she was puzzled, the researcher felt forced to conclude that the speed of learning nonsense syllables appeared to be the same as that of learning words. Criticize this conclusion.

We can accept the fact that there was no significant difference between the 20 word-learning scores and the 20 nonsense-syllable-learning scores without accepting the conclusion. The difficulty is that the scores that were compared came from only some of the subjects who tried to learn each list. A total of 30 subjects tried to learn the nonsense syllables, but 10 were unable to do so in 20 trials; 2 out of 22 subjects who tried to learn the word list were unable to do so in 20 trials. The score (number of study trials needed to learn) for any subject who was dropped from the experiment is unknown, was not included in the analysis, and would have to be at least 21. If the scores for the 12 subjects who were dropped were known and were included, the mean scores for the two groups would certainly increase. Since more subjects were dropped from the nonsense-syllable group, the mean for this group would increase more than that for the word group. In summary, the scores that were compared do not accurately reflect the relative difficulty of the two lists. Because of the differential loss of subjects (more from the nonsense-syllable group), we can reasonably propose that the "true" mean score for the nonsense-syllable group has been underestimated by a larger amount.

You might wonder how such a situation could actually arise. One possibility is that the researcher could have subjects participate for a limited amount of time. Perhaps each subject could participate for just a short time and it was "impossible" to give anyone more than 20 trials. If a subject doesn't finish the task before the time is up, what can a researcher do? The clear choices are to drop the subject's data from the experiment (as in the problem) or to estimate what the subject's score might have been had the task been continued. There is usually no good way to make such an estimate, but we could use a minimum estimate of 21 trials; such an estimate would obviously be at least somewhat incorrect. Perhaps, however, the comparison of the two groups would be a little more accurate if such artificial scores were included; the comparison would not be really accurate, but it would be more accurate than dropping the subjects from the analysis. When a researcher fails to get scores from some subjects there is really no very sound way of "saving the data." The seriousness of the problem depends on how many subjects are lost and on how unequal the losses from different treatments are. Forming independent groups by randomly assigning subjects to the different treatments usually results in a clean study with no special problems. To keep things "clean," however, it is important for the researcher not to "lose" any subjects from the study.

Matched Subjects

Like the independent-groups design, each subject in a matched-subjects design receives only one treatment. With matched subjects, however, the subjects are first matched on some basis before being assigned to treatments. The idea is that if a researcher can match each subject in one treatment with a "similar" subject in the other treatment the comparison of the treatments will be more sensitive. Rather than being limited to comparing the group of scores for one treatment with the group of scores for the other treatment, a researcher using matched subjects can compare each subject's score in one treatment to the score of the matched subject who received the other treatment. If subjects are well matched, the treatment comparison will be more sensitive.

Let's first consider how a matched-subjects design is constructed. Suppose a researcher wants to see whether performance on a reading comprehension test (read a passage, then answer questions about it) is affected by giving people money for correct answers (compared to just telling them when they are correct). There will be two treatments, a "control" treatment (subjects just receive feedback) and a "money" treatment (subjects receive feedback plus money for correct answers). The subjects will be high school students; let's say there are 20 subjects available. To use a matched-subjects design the researcher would want to find a way to form *pairs* of subjects such that within each pair the two subjects have similar reading comprehension ability. With 20 subjects he could form 10 pairs. One member of each pair will be randomly assigned to the control condition and the other member will be assigned to the money condition. Notice that it does not matter how much one pair differs from another pair; what does matter is how well the two subjects in each pair are matched.

If the researcher had vocabulary test scores for the 20 students (knowing that vocabulary scores are a pretty good indicator of reading ability), he could match subjects on the basis of these scores. He could rank order the 20 students in terms of vocabulary scores, from highest to lowest. The two students with the highest scores would become the first matched pair, the two with the next-highest scores the second pair, and so on until 10 pairs have been formed. Then some random method, perhaps a coin flip, could be used to determine which person in each pair will receive the control treatment and which will receive the money treatment. Table 3.3 illustrates the outcome.

The matched-subjects design does involve an element of randomization, although it is randomization within matched sets. In our example, after the researcher forms the matched pairs of subjects on the basis of their vocabulary scores, a random method, such as a coin flip, is used to determine which member of each pair will receive each treatment. In this way the researcher ensures that any remaining differences between subjects in a matched pair (which, it is hoped, are slight) will be randomized across treatments.

In a matched-subject design each subject in one treatment must be matched with a subject in the other treatment; thus the treatment groups must be equal in size. Table 3.4 presents some hypothetical data from a matched-subjects design. You will notice that there is a new entry: D, the

Table 3.3   Construction of a Matched-Subjects Design

Initial Information: Vocabulary Scores for 20 Students

George 45	Bob 44	Shirley 42	Tom 41	Nancy 40
Stan 39	Betty 37	Carol 36	Herb 33	Tracy 31
Sam 29	Phil 28	Peter 25	Paul 24	John 23
Sarah 22	Wendy 21	Hal 19	Bill 16	Bert 14

Outcome

10 pairs of subjects; the two students in each pair have similar vocabulary scores; a random method is used to determine which pair member will receive treatment

Treatments

PAIR NUMBER	CONTROL	MONEY
1	George	Bob
2	Tom	Shirley
3	Stan	Nancy
4	Carol	Betty
5	Herb	Tracy
6	Sam	Phil
7	Peter	Paul
8	Sarah	John
9	Hal	Wendy
10	Bill	Bert

Table 3.4   Hypothetical Data Illustrating Good and Poor Matched-Subjects Designs

Good Matching

Individual Scores

PAIR NUMBER	TREATMENT A	TREATMENT B	D
1	65	67	−2
2	75	80	−5
3	62	66	−4
4	54	59	−5
5	48	50	−2
6	43	45	−2
7	37	37	0
8	34	39	−5
Average score	52.2	55.4	
Range	41	43	
Average difference (D)			−3.2
Range of differences (D's)			5

Poor Matching

Individual Scores

PAIR NUMBER	TREATMENT A	TREATMENT B	D
1	65	80	−15
2	75	67	+8
3	62	59	+3
4	54	50	+4
5	48	66	−18
6	43	37	+6
7	37	39	−2
8	34	45	−11
Average score	52.2	55.4	
Range	41	43	
Average difference (D)			−3.2
Range of differences (D's)			26

difference between the scores of matched subjects. Since each pair of matched subjects yields one D, there are as many D's as there are pairs.

Look first at the data labeled "Good Matching." Notice that the scores *within* treatment A vary (from 34 to 75) and that the scores *within* treatment B vary (from 37 to 80). However, in a matched-subjects design it is not the variation in scores within treatments that is most important. Rather, it is the variability of the D's, the differences between the scores of matched subjects, that indicates how much random score variation exists in the data. That is, the researcher would compare the difference between treatments to the amount of variation in the differences (D's) from pair to pair. As you can see for the "Good Matching" data, the D's don't vary much from pair to pair; almost all the differences are negative (i.e., in almost all the pairs the score for treatment A is lower than the score for treatment B), and the size of the difference is fairly constant across pairs.

Let me describe these data in a slightly different way. In a matched-subjects design each pair provides information about the difference between treatments. If the difference (D) is rather stable from one pair to another, that is a pretty good indication that there really is a difference between the treatments. However, a matched-subjects design will provide a relatively clear and sensitive comparison of the treatments only if the subjects in each pair are well matched. How can you tell if the subjects have been matched well? Look again at the "Good Matching" data. Look at the scores for treatment A; identify the highest score, the next-highest score, and so on down to the lowest score. Do the same thing for treatment B. Now ask the question, To what extent is the subject who got the highest score in treatment A matched with the subject who got the highest score in treatment B, the subject who got the second-highest score in treatment A with the subject who got the second-highest score in treatment B, and so on? For the "Good Matching" data the matching is quite good. In general, the subjects who got the highest scores in treatment A were matched with the subjects who got the highest scores in treatment B; the "middles" in A were matched with the "middles" in B; and the "lows" in A were matched with the "lows" in B. It is because the matching is good that the differences (D's) are so consistent from one pair to another, even though the scores within treatment A and the scores within treatment B vary over a considerable range. This set of data illustrates precisely what researchers are trying to do when they use matched subjects—match the subjects well such that the D's are consistent from pair to pair.

Now look at the "Poor Matching" data. First, notice that the scores within treatment A and within treatment B vary over a wide range, just as they do in the "Good Matching" data. As mentioned earlier, the variation in scores within treatments is not as important as how much the D's vary from pair to pair. For the "Poor Matching" data you can see that the D's vary quite a bit, from −18 (for pair number 5) to +8 (for pair number 2).

Because the D's vary so much from one pair to another, it would be hard for a researcher to conclude that there was a real score difference between treatments A and B.

The lesson is clear. The reason for using matched subjects is to make the comparison of treatments more sensitive. If the subjects in each pair are well matched, the difference (D) between scores for a pair will vary relatively little from pair to pair and it will be easier to decide if there is a real score difference between treatments. As indicated by the "poor matching" data in Table 3.4, a researcher doesn't gain anything by using a matched-subjects design if the subjects are poorly matched. In the "poor matching" data there is not a very good matching of "highest in A" with "highest in B," middle with middle, or lowest with lowest, and because of the poor matching the D's vary a lot from one pair to another.

It is important to understand that subjects must be matched *before* the data are analyzed. The researcher needs to find a way to match subjects such that they will be well matched in terms of their scores on the dependent variable. Poor matching (on the dependent variable) results when a researcher initially matches subjects on some irrelevant basis. Here's an outlandish example: Suppose a researcher matched subjects in terms of how many marshmallows they could eat in one minute but her experiment measured learning scores. There is no good reason to suppose that two people who are similar with respect to marshmallow eating will in fact be similar in terms of learning scores. When the researcher analyzed the subjects' learning scores she would have poorly matched subjects and an insensitive comparison of the treatments.

There are two basic ways in which a researcher can get information to use for matching subjects before data are collected. Sometimes potential matching information has been collected (usually for some other purpose); if such information is not readily available, the researcher can directly collect such information. Here is an example of using already existing information: If the subjects for an experiment were students and the researcher had access to their school records, subjects might be matched on the basis of their reading scores, grade point averages, or some other information in the records. The problem that can arise when using existing information is that it might not provide a good basis for matching subjects *with respect to what will be measured in the experiment.* For example, students with similar grade point averages don't necessarily perform similarly on a visual-perception task or have similar attitudes with respect to some issue. A researcher planning a perception experiment would probably be wasting time and effort if subjects were matched on the basis of grade point averages. If, on the other hand, the experiment involved reading a story in order to recall as much of it as possible, it might be very advantageous for the experimenter to match subjects on the basis of their reading scores.

In addition to the possibility that existing information might not provide good matches for the experiment, there is also the possibility that the experimenter simply will not have access to such information. If no useful information is available, the experimenter must collect matching information if a matched-subjects design is to be used. It is important to realize that when an experimenter actually collects the matching information this activity is a part of the experiment. Each subject will be seen not once but twice—first to collect the matching information and then to participate in the "experiment proper." The experimenter needs to ask whether the act of collecting matching information might seriously limit the *generality* of the results of the experiment. Let me give you an example of how such a problem could arise.

Suppose a researcher wants to see whether "exposure to a positive model leads to more positive attitudes toward an issue associated with the model." The issue is spending more money for cancer research; people's attitudes will be measured by having them indicate their position on a scale ranging from "strongly oppose" to "strongly favor" (increased spending). Two treatments will be compared; both involve reading a short biographical story. In the "positive-model" treatment the story is about a person who is a cancer researcher, while in the "control" treatment the story is about a person with no connection with cancer research (e.g., an athlete). In both stories a person's life is described, from childhood through adulthood, in very positive terms. The stories differ only in that in the positive-model treatment the person eventually becomes a cancer researcher while in the control treatment the person becomes a professional athlete. Suppose the researcher decides that it would be useful to match subjects beforehand in terms of their existing attitudes toward spending more money for cancer research. To do this he uses the following procedure: A group of subjects is seen in a large room, and each person completes a form that includes an assessment of "attitude toward spending more money for a cancer research." After a short delay (while attitude scores are checked and the matched pairs of subjects are formed), each person reads one of the two stories; then attitudes toward the cancer-spending issue are again measured.

Suppose the researcher finds that people who had read the story about the cancer researcher later showed more positive attitudes toward spending money for cancer research than those who had read the story about the athlete. The possibility exists that the two stories result in different attitudes *only if* people's attitudes toward the issue have been measured *before* reading a story. The first attitude measurement, which was done to match subjects, might have sensitized subjects to the issue and made them more responsive to the "positive-model" treatment. Because of the desire to match subjects on initial attitudes, the sequence of events for all subjects was as follows: attitude measurement (for matching), story reading (treatments), attitude measurement (dependent variable). The argument might be made that if the sequence had simply consisted of story reading (treatments) and attitude measurement (dependent variable), the difference between treatments on the dependent variable might have been different. The idea could be that if subjects are not sensitized to the issue by the first attitude measurement, then the two stories would not result in different "after-story" attitudes. I am not saying that the initial step of collecting matching information *always* affects the results of a study; the essential point is that the act of collecting matching information *might* limit the generality of the findings.

Let me summarize the comparison of matched-subjects designs with independent groups. Compared to using independent groups, using matched subjects can have the advantage of providing a more sensitive comparison of the treatments, *if* the subjects are well matched with respect to what will be measured in the study. Despite this potential advantage, researchers might not use matched subjects for either of two reasons. First, useful matching information might not be available from existing sources. Second, the researcher might be concerned that directly collecting the matching information, and thus adding a "pretest" step to the study, might have undesirable effects on the generality of the findings.

In discussing independent groups and matched subjects I have concentrated on experiments involving just two treatments because it is easiest to see the differences between the designs in a basic, two-treatment experiment. The same ideas apply when more than two treatments are involved. If, say, four treatments were being compared, independent groups would be formed by randomly assigning subjects to the four treatments. If matched subjects were desired, sets of four matched subjects would be formed, with one member of each matched set randomly assigned to each treatment. Regardless of the number of treatments, using matched subjects can lead to a more sensitive comparison of the treatments and might present problems regarding generality.

Repeated Measures

A researcher's third alternative is to have the scores for each treatment come from the same subjects. I prefer to use the term *repeated measures* for such "same-subjects" designs because it emphasizes the fact that measurements (of the dependent variable) must be made more than once for each subject. The use of repeated measurements leads to some special problems, which will be discussed shortly. First let's consider why a researcher would want to use a repeated-measures or "same-subjects" design. The reason is fairly obvious: If having well-matched subjects in the different treatments leads to a more sensitive comparison of the treatments, the best match one can think of is to match each subject with himself or herself! From a statistical viewpoint, having the scores in each treatment come from the same subjects represents "best possible matching" and is likely to lead to the most sensitive treatment comparison.

Now let's consider the special problems that arise when repeated-measures designs are used. Suppose that two treatments (A and B) are involved; clearly the researcher needs to get two scores (on the dependent variable) for each subject, one for treatment A and one for treatment B. The basic problem arises because one of these scores will be obtained *before* the other, and this can lead to confounding *practice effects* with *treatment differences*. For example, suppose a researcher wants to compare learning scores for concrete and abstract word lists. Each subject will learn both a list of concrete words and a list of abstract words. Suppose every subject learns the concrete-word list first and the abstract-word list second. Clearly "concrete versus abstract" would be confounded with "first list versus second list." If there is any systematic change in subjects' learning ability from the first list they learn to the second list, the comparison of concrete words with abstract words will be biased. In general, the researcher who uses a repeated-measures design must find some way to avoid confounding treatment differences with practice effects.

Counterbalancing. Two basic methods are used to control practice effects in repeated-measures designs. Notice that there is no way of avoiding the possibility of practice effects in such designs—something must come first, something second, and so on. The trick is to *balance* practice effects across treatments, and the control techniques are generally known as *counterbalancing* (which may be thought of as a special case of the balancing technique). The two techniques differ in how counterbalancing is achieved, that is, either *within subjects* or *across subjects*.

Within-subject counterbalancing can be used when two things are "true" for an experiment: (1) The treatments can be repeated, and (2) "practice" produces a *linear* change in performance by itself. The latter statement needs explaining. We must be concerned with how subjects' scores will change simply as a function of performing the task again and again. The question is, How would subjects' scores change from the first thing to the second, and so on, if we were not introducing different treatments? For example, suppose the task required a subject to respond as quickly as possible when a stimulus figure is presented visually. We would be measuring reaction times to visual stimuli. For the experiment, our treatments will be different kinds of visual stimuli, but the present concern is how subjects' reaction times would change over repeated tests separate from any effects of changing the kinds of stimuli. Do subjects tend to generally get faster or slower as they do this task again and again? If it is reasonable to assume that this *general* change is *linear* (or that there is no general change), within-subject counterbalancing will work. In Figure 3.2 I have illustrated a linear general practice effect, using reaction times as the measure (dependent variable). The label "Ordinal Position" refers

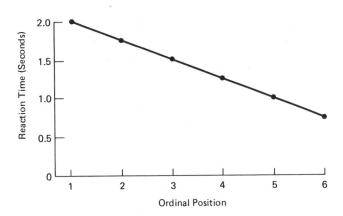

Figure 3.2. Example of a linear practice effect.

to successive stages of the experiment (i.e., "first thing," "second thing," etc.)

The particular numbers in the figure are arbitrary; the important point is the relation between reaction times and ordinal position. The relation shown in Figure 3.2 is linear and indicates that, other things being equal, subjects' reaction times can be expected to decrease linearly. Notice that the change from one ordinal position to the next is a constant decrease in reaction time of a quarter-second (.25 sec). It is important to realize that to use within-subject counterbalancing a researcher does not have to claim that the practice effect is *generally* linear but only that it is linear *within the experiment*.

Let's see how a researcher could avoid confounding a linear practice effect with treatment differences. Suppose we wanted to compare reaction times for three visual stimuli: pictures of faces, geometric forms (circles, squares, etc.), and "random" shapes (with no regular form). From Figure 3.2 we can see that reaction times can be expected to drop .25 second from one ordinal position to the next. In other words, compared to doing the task the first time, doing the task repeatedly subtracts a constant amount from reaction time. The reaction time for whatever stimulus is presented sixth can be expected to be 1.25 seconds faster than the reaction time for the stimulus presented first, *simply because of the general changes taking place as subjects repeat the task*. One way to counterbalance this practice effect would be to present each type of visual stimulus twice, in the following order: face, geometric form, random shape, random shape, geometric form, face. This is not the only order that would work; the following order would work just as well: geometric form, face, random shape, random shape, face, geometric form. The basic principle is to have one type of stimulus presented first and sixth, another type second and fifth, and the remaining type third and fourth. If this is done, and if each subject's score for each type of stimulus is the average of the reaction times for the two presentations of that stimulus, the practice effect will not confound the comparison of the treatments (types of stimuli).

Suppose the first order is used. The idea is that the six reaction times that would be measured can be considered to be made up of two components, one component for that type of stimulus and one component for the practice effect, as follows (using F for face, G for geometric form, and R for random shape):

$$\text{Reaction time}_{F, 1} = \text{Reaction time}_F + 0$$

$$\text{Reaction time}_{G, 2} = \text{Reaction time}_G - .25 \text{ seconds}$$

$$\text{Reaction time}_{R, 3} = \text{Reaction time}_R - .50 \text{ seconds}$$

$$\text{Reaction time}_{R, 4} = \text{Reaction time}_R - .75 \text{ seconds}$$

$$\text{Reaction time}_{G, 5} = \text{Reaction time}_G - 1.00 \text{ seconds}$$

$$\text{Reaction time}_{F, 6} = \text{Reaction time}_F - 1.25 \text{ seconds}$$

If we add together the two reaction times for each stimulus type, we will find that the influence of the practice effect is the same for each type. For faces, the total practice effect is -1.25 seconds ($0 + -1.25$ sec), as it is for geometric forms ($-.25$ sec $+ -1.00$ sec) and for random shapes ($-.50$ sec $+ -.75$ sec). Therefore if we compare reaction times for the three stimulus types by comparing the averages (or sums) of the two reaction times for each type, the comparison of stimulus types will not be confounded by the practice effect. Each type's average reaction time will be equally influenced by the practice effect.

It should be apparent that within-subject counterbalancing can be used only under special circumstances. The practice effect must be linear, and it must be possible or make sense to repeat the treatment conditions. Within-subject counterbalancing of this type is sometimes used in experiments on perception (rather like our example). However, counterbalancing *across* subjects is perhaps more common, either because it is not reasonable to repeat treatments or because it is not reasonable to assume that practice effects are linear.

Figure 3.3 illustrates a *nonlinear* practice effect. In this case it would be assumed that scores will *not* change by constant amounts from one ordinal position to the next. In this example there are successively smaller changes as practice continues. It would not be possible to use within-subject counterbalancing to equalize practice effects across treatments. However, it is possible to counterbalance practice effects across subjects. This technique results in a confounding of practice effects with treatment differences

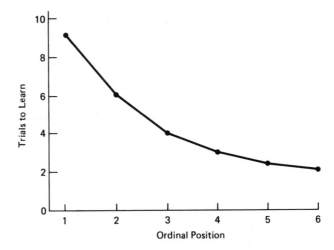

Figure 3.3. Example of a nonlinear practice effect.

for any individual subject but a counterbalancing of treatments and practice effect across subjects.

The basic idea is to have each treatment occur equally often in each ordinal position, across subjects. Suppose we have three treatments (A, B, C) and wish to use a repeated-measures design, but we cannot assume a linear practice effect and thus cannot use within-subject counterbalancing. A solution to this problem is to use different orders of the treatments for different subjects such that, across subjects, each treatment occurs equally often in each ordinal position. Table 3.5 illustrates a design of this kind. Notice that each subject will provide three scores for the analysis; for any single subject treatment differences are confounded with differences in

Table 3.5   Counterbalancing Treatments (A, B, C) with Ordinal Positions (1, 2, 3) in a Repeated-Measures Design

	Ordinal Positions		
SUBJECTS	**1**	**2**	**3**
No. 1	A	B	C
No. 2	B	C	A
No. 3	C	A	B
No. 4	A	C	B
No. 5	B	A	C
No. 6	C	B	A

ordinal position (practice effects). However, for the six subjects treatment differences are not confounded with practice effects, since each treatment occurs equally often (in this case twice) at each ordinal position.

Counterbalancing across subjects will avoid confounding treatment differences with practice effects no matter what the form of the general practice effect might be. The counterbalancing is achieved by using carefully arranged, different orders of the treatments for different subjects. The minimum number of different orders that must be used is always equal to the number of treatments. For example, with three treatments we could achieve counterbalancing with the following three orders: ABC, BCA, CAB (each order being used an equal number of times). With four treatments we would need a minimum of four orders, for example, ABCD, BDAC, CADB, DCBA. Clearly the number of subjects must be a multiple of the number of treatments so that each order is used equally often. Thus with three treatments a researcher would have to use 3, 6, 9, 12, 15, or 18 subjects (and so on by threes). With five treatments, a minimum of 5 subjects would be needed and multiples of 5 would be required (5, 10, 15, 20, and so on).

In repeated-measures designs the major problem facing the experimenter is the possibility of confounding practice effects with treatment differences. We have seen two techniques that may be used to avoid such confounding. Within-subject counterbalancing can be used when treatments can be repeated and the general practice effect is linear; in this case each subject's average treatment score is free of confounding by practice effects. Counterbalancing across subjects can be used to avoid confounding by general practice effects, whether linear or not, and this technique does not require repeating the treatments.

Here is an important point: Both kinds of counterbalancing require that there are *no special treatment-to-treatment transfer effects*. For example, suppose we have three treatments and counterbalance for *general* practice effects by using the following orders equally often: ACB, CBA, BAC. As long as there are only general practice effects to be concerned about, the counterbalancing will work. But suppose that whenever treatment B follows treatment C this *specific* sequence of events results in scores for treatment B being raised (or lowered). When we pool the A, B, and C scores to compare treatments, the scores for treatment B will contain a component that is not present in the scores for the other treatments. In part the scores for treatment B would reflect a special C-to-B transfer effect; notice that this is not a basic feature of treatment B but exists only because in the experiment B sometimes followed C. The comparison of the treatments would thus be biased by the presence of this special transfer effect.

At first glance, repeated-measures designs might look like an experimenter's delight. If each subject is matched with himself or herself, the comparison of the treatments will be very sensitive. As we have seen, however, using repeated measures requires the researcher to deal with problems of internal validity that are not present when the other designs are used. Steps must be taken to avoid confounding treatment differences with practice effects; counterbalancing of one type or another can accomplish this goal. In addition, the researcher needs to justify the assumption that there are no special treatment-to-treatment transfer effects (counterbalancing does not eliminate bias if such special effects exist). For these reasons repeated-measures designs must be used cautiously.

Contrast Effects. One additional point needs to be made about repeated measures, not about possible confounding but concerning generality. Because each subject receives each treatment, the *context* in which behavior is assessed is different for a repeated-measures design than for either independent groups or matched subjects. Basically, it is possible to have *contrast effects* with repeated-measures designs; the difference between treatments might be affected by the fact that each subject experiences the difference between treatments. With the other designs each subject receives only one treatment and thus does not know what other treatments might be like. Grice (1966) pointed out that the results of some animal learning experiments seem to vary depending on whether repeated measures or independent groups were used. For example, if each animal receives a large reward for performing one task and a small reward for performing another task, the "large versus small reward" difference in performance might be greater than it would be if each animal received only one reward level (some large, others small). Similar contrast effects that might occur with human subjects are discussed by Underwood (1966). Such contrast effects are themselves neither good or bad; the essential point is that results obtained from repeated-measures and independent-group designs might differ for this reason.

PROBLEM

An experimenter wanted to see whether words in different grammatical classes differed in learning ease. She had three lists of 20 words each, one of verbs, another of adjectives, and another of nouns. The procedure for each list was as follows: The subject was given one minute to study the list of 20 words and then had one minute to recall as many words as possible. The subject continued to alternate between study and recall until a perfect recall of all the words was produced. For each list a subject's score was the number of study periods needed before recalling the whole list. Since there were only 12 subjects available, each subject learned all three lists, the verb list followed by the adjective list and then the noun list. The results indicated that more study periods were needed to learn the verb list than to learn the noun and adjective lists, which did not differ significantly from each other. The experimenter therefore concluded that verbs are harder to learn than either nouns or adjectives, which are equally difficult to learn. What's wrong with the design of this experiment, and how should it be designed?

Since all the subjects learned the three lists in the same order, "verb versus adjective versus noun" is completely confounded, with "first list versus second list versus third list." If subjects tend to get better at learning word lists with practice, the design places the verb list at a distinct disadvantage and the noun list at an advantage. Of course some other change might occur, but in any case the results cannot be clearly interpreted. The experiment should be designed with the use of counterbalancing across subjects. For example, 4 subjects could learn the lists in the order verb–adjective–noun, another 4 in the order noun–verb–adjective, and the final 4 in the order adjective–noun–verb. Other schemes could be used, but the experimenter should make sure that each type of list occurs equally often as the first, second, or third list.

TIME

Time is one of the dimensions of our existence. Various kinds of temporal factors are characteristic of experiments. One can ask how much time was required to collect the data for an experiment (one day? six months?), how long each subject participated (2 minutes? 1 hour? 3 weeks?), or how much time a subject was given to perform a particular task. For example, suppose two researchers compare learning scores for concrete and abstract words. Both use the same kind of subject and the same list of words. However, one researcher decides to let subjects study each word for 2 seconds while the other allows subjects to study each word for 15 seconds. The results of the two studies might differ because of the difference in study time. Neither study would be "wrong"; rather, they would be different—the results obtained with a 2-second study time might not generalize to a 15-second study time, and vice versa.

Usually certain temporal factors are held constant in an experiment and are therefore fixtures of the study—it is reasonable to ask whether the results might change if different "times" were used. For this reason it is important to examine the temporal factors that characterize a study: How long were stimuli presented? How long did subjects have to respond? How much time elapsed between administering the treatments and measuring behavior? These are just some of the questions that might be important. Of course if some temporal factor is not controlled but is allowed to vary, there is the possibility of random noise or subtle confounding creeping into the results. For example, suppose a researcher wants to see whether giving students study questions helps them remember the content of a section of a textbook. Some students are given just the text while others are given the text plus the study questions. Suppose each student is allowed to study as long as he or she wants and then takes a test on the material. Imagine the following results: text only—average study time, 15 minutes, average percent correct on the test, 55; text plus study questions—average study time, 22 minutes, average percent correct, 70. You can see the problem: Did the study questions themselves result in higher test scores, or did the students who were given questions score higher because they studied longer? If the average study time for the "text only" students had been 22 minutes, would there have been a difference in test scores? Because we don't know the answers to these questions, the results are ambiguous. Further research would be needed.

Because we can't avoid "time," manipulating temporal intervals as the independent variable poses some special problems. If we change one time interval to create different treatments, some other time interval will also change. In other words, "time confounded with time" must be dealt with. For example, suppose we wish to investigate how recall of a list of words is related to study time. The list contains 20 words, and the basic procedure calls for presenting the 20 words one at a time, with the subject trying to recall as many words as possible immediately after the last word has been shown. We will compare three "presentation rates," with one word presented every 2, 5, or 10 seconds. Thus some subjects will see each of the 20 words for 2 seconds and then attempt recall, while others will attempt recall after seeing each of the words for either 5 seconds or 10 seconds.

The experiment seems straightforward: The independent variable is presentation (study) time. However, if we examine another temporal interval, the time between seeing a word and trying to recall it, we encounter a potential problem. Presenting 20 words for 2 seconds each means that 40 seconds will be required to present the whole list (after which the subject attempts recall). At 5 seconds per word, 100 seconds are required to present all 20 words, while 200 seconds are needed at the 10-second rate. As you can see, the slower the presentation rate, the longer the interval between seeing a word and trying to recall it (on the average). Consider the very first word shown (for which the confounding is greatest). As the presentation rate changes from 2 to 5 to 10 seconds per word, the interval between seeing the first word and having the opportunity to recall it changes from 38 to 95 to 190 seconds (similar relations hold for the other words in the list). Differences in presentation time (the desired independent variable) are confounded with differences in the length of the interval between presentation and recall. You might think that there is some way to unconfound the time intervals, but there really isn't; we might be able to change the nature of the confounding, but changes in one time interval will always be accompanied by changes in another interval.

What can a researcher do in such cases? There are two basic possibilities. First, it might be argued that the confounding time interval really isn't important. For example, if we could argue that the length of time between presentation and recall is unimportant, that it does not affect recall scores (which, in this example, we could not), then the confounding between this interval and presentation time would be considered unimportant. Such arguments are difficult to make in many circumstances. The second possibility is in a sense a modest variation of the first. The researcher can try to arrange things such that, without arguing that the confounding interval is *generally* unimportant, it can be argued that the differences in the particular experiment are unimportant. For example, suppose all the subjects in our experiment will attempt recall one week later. While there would still be differences in the interval between presentation and recall for the different presentation rates, we could argue that differences on the order of seconds are of no importance when considered in relation to a period of one week (a more believable argument). Since in a strict sense there is no way of completely avoiding confounding one interval with another, researchers must argue, one way or another, that the confounding is unimportant.

PROBLEM

A researcher believed that as people acquire more information that might be useful for solving a problem they pay less and less attention to additional information that is provided. To test this idea he had a number of people try to solve a problem after they had been given 20 items of information that might be helpful. Some of the items were in fact useless, others somewhat helpful; but there was one item that was absolutely crucial for solving the problem. Each person received the 20 items of information one at a time (one item every 30 seconds); each item was presented just once and did not remain in view, and subjects were not allowed to keep any records of the information they had received (in effect, the accumulating information had to be kept "in the head"). After the twentieth item had been presented, the subject was asked to try to solve the problem. The researcher manipulated the placement of the critical item in the series of 20 items. For different groups of subjects the critical item was presented either third, tenth, or seventeenth in the series of 20 items. The researcher's idea was that the later the critical item was presented, the less attention people would pay to it, with the result that performance on the problem would be worse. When the results were analyzed, however, he was shocked—the later in the series the critical item had been presented, the better people had performed when they had tried to solve the problem—the exact opposite of what he had expected. He went away quite puzzled and discouraged. Do you see any problem with the study?

An important feature of this experiment is that in all conditions people tried to solve the problem after the twentieth item was presented. As a consequence there was a confound between the number of items preceding the presentation of the critical items and the number of items (and amount of time) following presentation of the critical item. As the position of the critical item varied from 3 to 10 to 17, the number of items presented *after* the critical item varied from 17 to 10 to 3 and the time between seeing the critical item and trying to solve the problem varied from 510 seconds to 300 seconds to 90 seconds. To solve the problem a person not only had to pay attention to the critical item but also had to remember it until the twentieth item had been shown and the solution could be attempted. It is very reasonable to propose that the longer a person had to remember the critical information (and the more other items were presented afterward), the more likely it would be that the subject would forget the critical information and therefore perform poorly on the problem. The results suggest that "opportunity to forget" (more items and time after the critical item) had an important effect on problem-solving performance. The results do *not* really allow the conclusion that placement of the item in the series had no effect on attention to the information. It is quite possible that attention to the critical item did decrease as that item was presented later in the series but that the effect of decreased attention was "hidden" by a stronger effect of opportunity to forget. Because there was confounding between "number of items preceding the critical item" and "number of items following the critical item," the results are extremely difficult to interpret.

INSTRUCTIONS

When people participate as subjects in experiments, it is virtually inevitable that they will receive some instructions regarding their task. The purpose of giving instructions is to bring the subject to precisely the level of understanding that the experimenter desires. Perhaps this point seems obvious, but achieving this goal is not always easy. The experimenter must decide what it is that subjects should understand (for the experimenter's purposes) and then devise a means of providing that understanding. In everyday life we frequently try to explain to others what we would like them to do or how to do something—I am sure that you can think of an episode from your own life that illustrates the difficulty one may encounter in trying to "get the point across." It is quite common for experimenters to do preliminary "pilot work" to check their instructions, and the instructions may be modified several times as a result.

Poor instructions lead to noise in the data. If the instructions do not yield the desired understanding, then some subjects will understand the task better than others. This leads to increased variation among scores for a single treatment. Achieving the desired understanding sometimes seems to conflict with the general goal of keeping the instructions constant. A researcher might develop a set of instructions very carefully, wanting the same instructions to be given to all subjects (in all treatments). If the instructions are very well constructed, she might come very close to achieving this goal. A problem arises when a subject, after receiving the "standard" instructions, asks one or more questions, since the questions and perhaps the answers might vary from one subject to another (a lack of standardization in one sense). A researcher needs to decide which is more important, giving exactly the same instructions to all subjects (whether they all understand them equally or not) or modifying the instructions as needed to allow the subject to achieve the desired level of understanding. This is not a particularly easy choice, because while it might seem foolish to be "rigid" and run the risk of some subjects' not understanding, it is also dangerous to have the *actual* instructions deviate considerably from the prepared, standard instructions. A researcher needs to be able to describe the procedures of his or her study to other investigators, and the deviations might be difficult or impossible to describe adequately. In addition, experimenters who deviate from the standard instructions might unintentionally bias the experiment or otherwise produce undesirable effects. Pilot work is usually the solution; pretesting the instructions allows the researcher to learn what kinds of questions subjects might ask. The instructions might be modified such that subjects don't need to ask a question (because the instructions are clear), or "standard answers" to questions can be developed.

Because instructions have a strong influence on subjects' behavior, it is important to examine closely the instructions employed in an experiment. Ask yourself, "What did the subjects know (and not know) about the experiment?" Experiments that seem to be comparable might turn out to be quite different because different instructions were used, leading the subjects to have different understandings of the experiment. Here is an example from the field of concept identification. The task can be briefly described as follows: The stimuli are geometric forms (circle, square, etc.) varying in size and color as well as in shape. The experimenter decides on a basis for categorizing these stimuli (perhaps red things are called positive while blue and yellow things are called negative, with shape and size being unimportant). The subject, who is not told the basis for categorization, must figure it out by observing how stimuli are categorized by the experimenter.

Here are two different sets of instructions that subjects might be given about the task:

> You will be shown some stimuli, some of which will be called positive and some negative. As each stimulus is presented, indicate whether you think it is positive or negative; I will then tell you whether you are right or wrong. Try to get as many right as you can.

> This is an experiment on concept identification. The stimuli are geometric forms varying in color, size, and shape. Notice that there are three colors (red, blue, and yellow), three sizes (large, medium, and small), and three shapes (circles, squares, and triangles). As you can see, the colors, sizes, and shapes occur in many different combinations. We have picked one of these features as a basis for classifying the stimuli, and your task is to figure out how we are classifying them. The stimuli that belong to one category will be called positive, while those belonging to the other category will be called negative. As each stimulus is presented, indicate whether you think it is positive or negative; I will then tell you whether you are right or wrong. At first you'll probably have to guess, but if you can figure out which feature we are using to classify the stimuli you will be able to classify them without error.

If subjects were given the first, shorter set of instructions, they would have much less information about the stimulus features they should attend to, how the categories are formed, and how well they can do. You might well expect that people would perform differently depending on which set of instructions was used, and this has in fact been found to occur. For example, Erickson (1968) found that some treatment differences were not the same with more complete instructions as they were with shorter instructions. Thus the instructions that subjects receive, even if they are held constant within a study, can place important limitations on the generality of the findings.

Instructions are sometimes used as an independent variable, differing in some systematic way from one treatment to another. In many circumstances this manipulation is quite straightforward. However, sometimes instructions are manipulated in ways that can lead to problems. Let me give you an example. Suppose a researcher wants to determine whether increased anxiety affects performance on some task. To "manipulate" anxiety, he uses different instructions. In the "low-anxiety" condition the instructions simply describe the task; in the "high-anxiety" condition the instructions describe the task but also include the statement that "performance on this task is a very good indicator of personal adjustment—generally we find that people who do poorly on this task are poorly adjusted." The researcher would use such instructions in an attempt to increase subjects' anxiety. Quite obviously, ethical questions arise here. Is it ethical for a researcher to deliberately raise a person's anxiety level, however briefly, and however noble the purpose? Is it ethical for a researcher to lie to subjects (since the task is not in fact a good measure of personal adjustment)? As we saw in the preceding chapter, such questions can be difficult to answer with a simple yes.

Aside from ethical issues, another problem can arise. Suppose the researcher finds no real difference in performance between the two treatments. Does this mean that increasing anxiety does not affect performance on this task? Or does this mean that the "high-anxiety" instructions did *not* in fact raise anxiety? We really wouldn't know. This example illustrates a problem that must be considered whenever a researcher tries to use instructions to produce some theoretically defined state in subjects. The question is, Did the instructions in fact produce the desired state? Most researchers argue that when instructions are used in this way there should be some independent check on whether the instructions did produce the desired state.

PROBLEM

A psychologist believed that if people had more positive self-concepts they would perform better on many tasks. To test her idea she gave a number of people the task of making as many words as they could from a large set of letters, with ten minutes allowed for the task. Two treatments were compared, with subjects randomly assigned to the treatments. In the "control" condition the subject was told what the task was and then went to work on it. In the "positive self-concept" condition the person first engaged in a ten-minute conversation with the psychologist. In these conversations subjects were asked to tell about things they liked about themselves. The psychologist was encouraging, emphasizing whenever possible that a subject had some good quality. After the conversation the subject was given the task instructions and put to work on the task. When the results were analyzed, the psychologist found that people in the "positive self-concept" condition produced more words than those in the control condition. She therefore concluded that, at least for this task, her idea was correct: Giving people a more positive self-concept resulted in better task performance. What would you want to know before accepting this conclusion?

We can accept the fact that performance on the word-making task was better in the positive self-concept condition. But how do we know that the subjects in this treatment actually had more positive self-concepts before starting the task than those in the control condition? Basically, we don't know that this was the case. The study would have been better if the psychologist had measured self-concept for all subjects before they started the task (there are several techniques for making such assessments). The psychologist's conclusion would rest on firmer ground if she had found (1) that subjects in the positive self-concept condition had more positive self-concepts before starting the task and (2) that subjects in this condition performed better on the task. Just measuring task performance leaves the results a bit ambiguous. Suppose the psychologist found (if self-concept were assessed) that subjects in the PSC condition *did not* have more positive self-concepts before starting the task but *did* perform better on the task. Such results would radically change the interpretation of the findings.

MEASUREMENT

Since we discussed measurement in some detail in Chapter 2, I will be brief here. The measure (dependent variable) should be reliable and sensitive— it must allow a difference between treatments to "show itself" if one exists. With respect to generality, it is reasonable to ask (1) how well the measure indexes the construct that is of interest and (2) what other measures might be used. For example, some independent variable might have different effects on "anxiety," depending on whether "anxiety" is measured in terms of changes in heart rate or in terms of responses to a paper-and-pencil test. For many tasks efficiency of performance can be measured either in terms of speed of responding or in terms of accuracy (number of correct responses or number of errors). There is evidence showing different results depending on which measure is used. For example, Levis and Levin (1972) found that different stimulus presentation procedures did not affect the number of trials required to reach a criterion (for extinction of a response) but did influence the average speed of responding during extinction trials. In situations requiring people to make accurate but rapid responses, a "speed–accuracy trade-off" is frequently observed—treatments associated with faster responses are also associated with less accurate responding (e.g., Swensson, 1972). Because treatment effects can vary with the kind of measure used, many researchers employ multiple measures in order to gain more complete information about the issues they investigate.

When comparing treatments it is critical that the measurement process be unbiased. In many cases this presents no problem. When measurement involves judgments, however, it is wise to take precautions to avoid bias. Suppose a researcher wants to see whether a lecture on "being creative" leads people to write more creative stories. All subjects will write stories whose creativity will be judged; some subjects will write after receiving the lecture while others will write without receiving the lecture. When the stories are judged for creativity, the judges should not know which treatment any story represents. In this way biased measurement can be avoided.

PROBLEM

An experiment was conducted using Maier's Two-String Problem. The subject was brought into a room in which two strings hung from the ceiling, far enough apart to make it impossible to hold onto one string and walk over and grasp the other string. In the room the only object available was a pair of pliers. The subject was told to find a way to tie the strings together.

Two kinds of instructions were compared. With "new instructions" the subject was told that to solve the problem he would have to think of something new, a new way of using a familiar object. With "control instructions" the subject was simply told what the problem was and asked to solve it. By a random method 17 men were assigned to each instruction condition. Each subject was seen individually and given up to 15 minutes to solve the problem. The number of solvers was 17 for the new-instructions condition and 15 for the control instructions condition, a difference that was definitely not significant. The results are consistent with the conclusion that instructing subjects to think of new ways of using objects does not help solve the problem. However, there is a weakness in this experiment that should make you hesitate to accept this conclusion. What is the weakness?

The difficulty here concerns what is usually called a "ceiling effect," one kind of weakness that results from insensitive measurement. The score for each subject was either yes (solved the problem) or no (failed to solve). If you look carefully at the description of the experiment, you will see that nearly everybody solved the problem—just about all the scores were "as good as they could be." Under such circumstances it is virtually impossible to find a difference between conditions; there is simply not enough variation in scores to make a sensible comparison. There are two general techniques that could be used to improve the information. The researcher could use a shorter time limit; for example, if subjects were given just 5 minutes, perhaps only 50 percent of the "control" subjects would solve in this time, which would at least make it easier to see whether the percent of solvers is different with new instructions. As an alternative, the researcher could use a different score—the amount of time each subject needed to solve the problem; these scores would also yield more sensitive information about the possible difference between conditions.

APPARATUS

Various kinds of equipment or apparatus are used in research for control purposes. If visual materials need to be shown for carefully controlled, short time periods, a researcher might use a tachistoscope or programed slide projector; tape recorders (including very fancy models) are used for auditory presentations. Instructions might be tape recorded to avoid unwanted variation in instructions from one subject to another (although tape-recorded instructions are sometimes poorly understood, perhaps because subjects pay less attention and can't ask questions). Some researchers use on-line computers to conduct their studies; in effect the subject enters a room and interacts with a computer for the entire session.

Usually the kind of apparatus doesn't vary but is a constant, a fixture of the study. As such, the kind of apparatus used can be relevant to examining the generality of the results. There are at least a few suggestions in the literature that "automating" a study can affect the findings. Johnson and Mihal (1973) reported that differences between groups of schoolchildren that were observed when a test was administered "manually" (by an examiner) did not appear when the test was administered by computer. As the authors suggest, computerizing a testing session substitutes a person–machine interaction for an interpersonal interaction, and this could affect performance in some instances. Automating a study is not necessarily better or worse than other procedures; fundamentally, it changes the context of the research and *might* influence the results.

Sophisticated apparatus can be essential to conducting research, and substituting machines for people can lead to improved control or greater efficiency. There are no general objections to such practices. There is, however, a possibility that a subtle problem might result from extensive use of sophisticated equipment—a "reversal of priorities." The idea is that a researcher who wants to investigate an important question needs sophisticated apparatus to conduct the study. The equipment is purchased, often at great expense, and the researcher learns how to use it, often with considerable effort. The study is completed, but the equipment remains, "begging" to be used again. Because of the financial and personal investment he or she has already made in the apparatus, the researcher might be tempted to do research that requires the apparatus rather than choosing topics on the basis of their theoretical or practical importance. It is impossible to say how much merit this idea might have, but it seems worth some contemplation.

Materials

We ordinarily think of apparatus as "hardware"—slide projectors, tape recorders, Skinner boxes, computers, and the like. Let me broaden the term to include "software," which is usually referred to as *materials*. If a researcher wants to study reaction times to visual stimuli, he or she will need not only hardware but also materials—some stimuli to present. For example, a researcher who wants to see whether smoking marijuana affects learning will need something for subjects to learn, perhaps a list of words or the facts in a story.

If the materials are held constant in a study, their characteristics are one of the fixtures of the experiment and need to be considered with respect to generality. Here is an example. Many studies of human learning and memory involve arbitrary lists of nonsense syllables or words. Critics have argued that such studies tell us little about, say, school learning because the materials used in the experiments lack the organized structure of the material learned in school. Perhaps in response to such criticism, researchers began using more structured materials in their studies (and found that the critics were at least partly correct!).

Materials are often deliberately varied in an experiment; that is, a materials difference is the "independent variable." I put quotation marks around "independent variable" because often the materials difference is not manipulated in the ordinary sense—rather, the researcher finds materials that already differ in some describable fashion. Consider the example of comparing learning scores for concrete and abstract words. The researcher does not take some "neutral" words and make some of them concrete and others abstract. Rather, she tries to find words that are already concrete or abstract. In principle this is no different from comparing people who already happen to be either neurotic or normal, although words presumably have fewer attributes than people. Suppose we find that the concrete words are learned more readily than the abstract words. Is this learning difference due to "concreteness versus abstractness"? Perhaps not. Do the concrete and abstract words differ in other characteristics that might affect learning? They certainly could differ. It has been found that concrete words such as *bread, car,* or *chair* tend to be shorter and more familiar and have more associations with other words than abstract words (e.g., *honesty, justice,* or *progress*).

The problem is that materials that are selected because they differ in one way might well differ in other ways that could affect scores on the dependent variable. Researchers have employed a variety of techniques to handle such problems. One technique is to try to find materials that differ in the way the researcher desires but are equivalent with respect to the other known variables that might otherwise confound the results. For example, to compare concrete and abstract words, which on the average also differ in length, familiarity, and number of associations, a researcher would try to carefully select concrete and abstract words that are equal with respect to length, familiarity, and association value. In effect she tries to hold the other variables constant by careful selection of materials.

There are two problems with this technique. First, it might be nearly impossible to find items that are "equal" in all of the other variables that might be important; a researcher might miss one and later find it haunting the results. Thus the first weakness is that the desired matching on "other" variables might not be achieved. Nevertheless, researchers frequently use this method. When it is used, the second weakness needs to be considered: The careful selection of materials might result in the researcher's using very *unrepresentative* materials. That is, the results obtained with such carefully selected materials might not generalize (in our example) to concrete and abstract words in general. The idea is that if there is a strong tendency for concrete and abstract words to differ in, say, familiarity, finding and using concrete and abstract words of equal familiarity might mean that the words used are "peculiar." The concrete words used might not represent "concrete words" very well, and the abstract words might similarly be poor representatives of "abstract words." The extent to which this problem is serious depends on how difficult it is to locate "matched" materials—the harder it is to find items that are equal in terms of "other" variables, the more likely it is that the results will have poor generality.

An alternative technique is to let all the variables vary, preferably as much as possible. The researcher would let the words vary in concreteness–abstractness, length, familiarity, and association value. Learning scores would be obtained for all items. The researcher would then attempt to see which variables predict learning scores better than others; in this way the more and less important characteristics could be identified. The statistical methods used for such analyses are beyond the scope of this book, although we will touch on the basic concepts in Chapter 7.

TASK

In any experiment the subjects will do something, some task. We have of course been discussing many of the components of a task—instructions, materials, temporal factors, and the like. It is, however, useful to look at the task in its entirety. One reason is that some important feature of the task might not be captured by any of the other categories. I also believe it is important to focus on the task with respect to the generality of results. A large portion of psychology is concerned with topics such as learning, perception, problem solving, attitude change, bargaining, forgetting, and the like. The essential point is that a researcher inevitably investigates a topic like "learning" in a very specific way, by using a specific learning task. It is important to go beyond a general label like "learning" or "bargaining" and look very carefully at precisely what the subjects were doing. It is reasonable to ask how much the findings are limited to the specific task used and how much the findings generalize. Unfortunately we often lack such information.

To illustrate how one can "go beyond the general label," consider the example of results regarding a "curve of forgetting" (or remembering, if we focus on what remains rather than what is lost). The basic procedure is to have subjects learn something and then measure their retention after different temporal intervals. Suppose the results are like those shown in Figure 3.4.

The question is, To what extent does this finding represent *the* curve of forgetting (if there is one)? It would be theoretically easier if we had to deal with only one function relating amount retained to the length of the interval between learning and the test for retention. I will concentrate on the task in order to illustrate the kinds of questions we could ask about the generality of the finding. What was learned? What were the materials—a list of nonsense syllables, a list of words, a poem, the names of pictures, a series of unrelated sentences, a story, a set of facts about geology (and so on)? How much material was learned—20 words, 10 sentences, a chapter of a textbook? How much study time was given? Did subjects get repeated

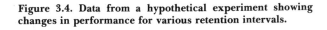

Figure 3.4. Data from a hypothetical experiment showing changes in performance for various retention intervals.

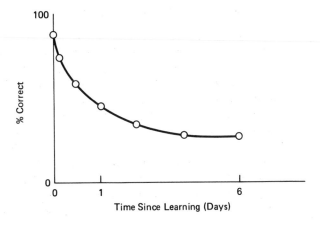

study periods? If so, how much time elapsed between study periods? What kind of test was given—recalling words (in order or not?), selecting the "old" picture from a set of three, summarizing the plot of a story, recalling the main facts from a textbook chapter, answering questions (short answer or multiple choice?) about political science? Were the subjects told that retention would be measured later, or did the test come as a surprise? These are just some of the questions that could be raised (and just some of the alternatives). I am not suggesting that there must be a different curve of forgetting for each answer to every question. Rather, I want to alert you to the possibility that results might be limited by the particular task employed.

ENVIRONMENT

In general terms, environmental factors refer to the conditions under which subjects perform whatever task they are given. We might ask whether data were collected in a classroom or in a soundproof room, and so on. When subjects participated, were they alone or were there other subjects or experimenters or observers present? Notice that the environment includes both physical and psychological–social factors. Usually these factors are held constant in an experiment and are relevant to examining the generality of the results. Of course, should they vary, it is important to ensure that environmental factors are not confounded with treatment differences.

Let's consider one environmental factor, namely, whether subjects are seen individually or in groups. There are two advantages to collecting data in group sessions (if it is possible to do so). One obvious advantage is that less experimenter time is needed to collect the data. For example, if I want to collect data for 60 subjects, each of whom will participate for one hour, 60 hours will be required if I see each subject individually whereas only one hour would be needed if I could collect data for all 60 subjects in one group session. The second advantage is related: Since group sessions shorten the total time required for data collection, there will be less variation in all of the things that vary over time (days, weeks, months) to be concerned about. The amount of random error should be less, and there is less chance of confounding by variables distributed over time.

There are, of course, disadvantages to collecting data in group sessions. It can be dangerous to associate a single treatment with a single session; if the data for treatment A are collected in one group session and the data for treatment B are collected in a different group session, there is the possibility of confounding session differences with treatment differences. The importance of this possibility depends on how the group sessions might differ and how such differences might affect the behavior being studied. If different treatments can be administered in a single group session, instructions must be very carefully prepared and might be difficult to give if different treatments require different instructions. Suppose that a group of subjects is given some task to perform and subjects are told that "if your booklet has a star on the cover, you will receive 10 cents for each correct answer." Because all the subjects would receive this information, they would be aware of the *contrast* between the money and no-money treatments, and this may have undesired effects on performance. The use of group sessions can also increase the amount of noise in the data if some subjects are distracted by others or become concerned because it seems that others are completing the task sooner. These potential problems can be solved in most cases, but they are problems that must be considered when group sessions are used. Finally, a researcher might get less information if group sessions are used. With groups, data collection is usually rather limited and automatic—subjects typically fill out forms of some sort, and only gross measures of "time to complete the task" are obtained. By seeing subjects individually, the researcher might be able to obtain more information (e.g., more precise time measurements, interview data, physiological measures such as heart rate). When considering the choice between seeing subjects individually and seeing them in groups, a researcher needs to evaluate what will be gained and what will be lost by each data collection method.

Throughout this chapter I have tried to show how the decisions made by a researcher can affect the results. I have emphasized the limitations and problems that can arise for a very deliberate reason: There is no "cookbook recipe" that guarantees good results. Rather, good research is a result of carefully considering various aspects of the study, looking for possible problems and taking steps to reduce or avoid them. If you adopt this approach when evaluating the research of others, you will have a better idea of what the results might and might not mean. If you use this approach in planning any research of your own, you will conduct better research.

PROBLEM

One theory of delinquency holds that lack of goal attainment (frustration) leads to aggression, which results in delinquency. Two hypotheses were tested: (1) that delinquents and nondelinquents will differ in perceived goal attainment and (2) that delinquents and nondelinquents will differ in aggressive tendencies. The first hypothesis was tested by using a special questionnaire designed to assess the extent to which an adolescent felt that personally important needs were being met. The second hypothesis was tested by rating the amount of aggression in stories written by adolescents based on thematic picture material (the adolescent was shown a picture depicting an interpersonal interaction and asked to write a story based on the picture). Both tests were given to 25 male delinquents from the county juvenile home (all had been "convicted" of misdemeanors) and to 25 male students from the local high school. All subjects were between 14 and 17 years of age and had IQs in the normal range. Both hypotheses were supported: Juvenile delinquents showed less goal attainment, particularly in the area of opposite-sex peer relationships. Delinquents' stories showed more aggression than those of nondelinquents. The results were interpreted as supporting the theory that lack of goal attainment (frustration) leads to aggression, which results in delinquency. Assuming that the measuring instruments were valid, indicate why this conclusion might not be correct.

There are several weaknesses in this example. The basic finding is that adolescents who are already juvenile delinquents and are incarcerated in a juvenile home show more frustration and aggression than nondelinquents who live in ordinary society. The results, of course, are consistent with the frustration–aggression–delinquency hypothesis, but there are alternatives.

We do not know whether the differences in goal attainment in fact preceded the differences in aggression that in fact preceded the delinquent (or nondelinquent) behavior. We would have to examine the plausibility of alternate explanations of the relations (e.g., is it plausible that differences in aggression would lead to differences in goal attainment?). What is noticeable here is that the environmental circumstances of the delinquent and nondelinquents are decidely different (as a consequence of the delinquent behavior). It does seem reasonable to propose that confinement to a juvenile home might lead to less goal attainment, particularly in the area of "opposite-sex peer relationships" (translation: with girls). Overall, it is plausible to propose that the differences in frustration and aggression are a result of the confinement of the delinquents—a sequence opposite to that contained in the researcher's conclusion.

SUMMARY

The characteristics of a research study can be examined from different perspectives. The comparison of treatments becomes less sensitive as more features are allowed to vary randomly. Characteristics that do not vary in a study can affect the external validity of the findings, whereas the results will be confounded if treatments differ in more than one way. If a characteristic varies in a study and is *not* the independent variable that is of interest, then it is important to determine whether the feature is balanced across treatments.

Experimenters can influence results in several ways. They need to administer treatments consistently to minimize the amount of noise in the data. To avoid experimenter bias, researchers who plan a study often employ other people to work as experimenters and keep the experimenters from having potentially biasing information.

Subject characteristics cannot truly be treated as independent variables.

Subjects who are selected because they already differ in one characteristic are virtually certain to also differ in other ways, making the comparison of groups of subjects difficult to interpret. To avoid confounding by subject characteristics, researchers need to control the assignment of subjects to treatments. Several methods of assignment may be used. A researcher may randomly assign subjects to treatments, forming independent groups. When independent groups of subjects receive each treatment, the sensitivity of the treatment comparison depends on how much the scores within each treatment differ from each other. To reduce score variation within treatments, researchers can use subjects who are likely to get similar scores, although doing so might limit the generality of the findings.

An alternate method is to form matched sets of subjects with the number of subjects in each set equal to the number of treatments; within each matched set subjects are randomly assigned to treatments. When matched subjects are used, the sensitivity of the treatment comparison depends on how much the difference between treatments varies from one matched set to another. If subjects are well matched, this design can provide a very sensitive treatment comparison. Finding a way to match subjects well can pose problems. Subjects must be matched before the data are analyzed. Useful matching information might be available in existing records; if not, the researcher can add a preliminary step to the study in order to collect information to use in matching. In some circumstances the preliminary data collection step limits the generality of the findings.

A third alternative is to have every subject receive all treatments, which results in repeated measurements (one per treatment). While this design usually yields the most sensitive data for deciding whether the treatments differ, interpretive problems can arise unless steps are taken to avoid confounding practice effects with treatment differences. If practice effects are linear in the study and treatments can be repeated, within-subject counterbalancing can be used to avoid confounding. If practice effects are nonlinear, or if treatments cannot be repeated, between-subjects counterbalancing can be used. In this case the data for an individual subject are confounded, but if the proper orders of treatments are used across subjects, treatment differences will not be confounded with practice effects when the data for all subjects are analyzed. Repeated-measures designs can yield results that differ from those found with independent groups or matched subjects because with repeated measures the subject experiences all treatments, and this can create a contrast effect that is not present with the other methods.

Using time intervals as independent variables poses special problems because when one time interval is manipulated some other time interval inevitably changes as well. Researchers must find some basis for arguing that the confounding time interval is not important in interpreting the results of the study.

Instructions have powerful effects on human behavior, and researchers who use "the same task" with different instructions can obtain quite different results. When researchers use instructions to induce a particular psychological state in subjects, it is important to obtain an independent check on whether the instructions actually produced the desired state. This check is kept separate from the comparison of treatments on the dependent variable.

To have a sensitive comparison of treatments, reliable and precise measurement is needed. When measurement involves judgments, it is important to keep judges from knowing the treatment associated with the behavior they are judging in order to avoid measurement bias. Sophisticated apparatus is often used to provide increased control in research; substituting machines for people in collecting data does change the research context and can lead to different results. The materials given to subjects represent a critical part of a study. Comparing materials chosen because they differ in one characteristic poses special problems because the materials are also likely to differ in other ways. Researchers must find a way to minimize confounding of one materials difference with another while at the same time avoiding the use of unrepresentative materials.

It is useful to take a broad look at the tasks that subjects are given. There are, for example, many different learning tasks, and it is reasonable to ask how well the results obtained with one such task generalize to others. The circumstances under which subjects perform a task also deserve attention. For example, collecting data in group sessions can be very efficient but can also lead to problems that are not encountered when subjects are seen individually.

4

TECHNIQUES FOR DESCRIBING DATA

Researchers commonly obtain many measurements by collecting a number of measures for the same organism, measuring some characteristic for a number of organisms, or both. The existence of a collection of measurements (scores) raises the question of how the mass of data shall be dealt with. In earlier chapters I have talked in general terms about the "average score" associated with a treatment and the amount of score variation within a treatment. We will now examine the specific techniques that can be used to organize and describe data. In Chapter 2, I stressed the importance of the kind of measurement scale a researcher uses; for example, scores on an ordinal scale do not provide the same information as scores on an interval scale. The techniques used to organize and describe collections of scores are also important. As you will see shortly, there are different kinds of "averages," and there are different ways of describing the variability of a set of scores. Each technique provides a different kind of information, and researchers need to choose the techniques that best suit their purposes. In this chapter we will consider some of the alternatives that are available.

FREQUENCY DISTRIBUTIONS

Suppose that you are the instructor of a class of 200 students, that you have just given an exam, and that someone asks you how the class did on the test. To answer this question you could recite the 200 test scores, but this would not be very useful. Not only would you bore your listener but you would probably fail to communicate the desired information. In general, understanding masses of data requires that they be organized and

Table 4.1   Distribution of Scores
on a Hypothetical Midterm Exam

SCORE	f
40	4
39	7
38	11
37	9
36	14
35	16
34	8
33	8
32	7
31	6
30	5
29	4
28	5
27	3
26	2
25	0
24	1
N =	$\overline{110}$

summarized in some fashion. The simplest way of doing this is to construct a *frequency distribution.*

The essential operation in constructing a frequency distribution is to tally or count the number of observations in each category of the measurement scale. To describe the set of scores one can then present the frequency distribution, which provides a more compact, organized, and understandable description of the data. Table 4.1 illustrates a frequency distribution for a hypothetical set of exam scores. The frequency distribution should be read as follows: Four students earned scores of 40, 7 students earned scores of 39, 11 achieved scores of 38, and so on. Notice the following about the frequency distribution: One column of numbers represents values on the scale of measurement (scores) while the other contains the number of observations obtained for each scale value. A frequency distribution expresses the relation between scale values and variation in the number of observations. It is important to clearly understand the two kinds of information contained in a frequency distribution in order to easily grasp the material to follow.

Look at the two symbols used in Table 4.1. The letter f at the top of the second column is the commonly used symbol for "number of observations in a category (frequency)." Notice that f varies from one category to another on the scale of measurement. The letter N is used to refer to

Table 4.2   Simple, Proportionate,
and Percentage Frequency Distributions

SCORE	f	p	%
40	4	.036	3.6
39	7	.064	6.4
38	11	.100	10.0
37	9	.082	8.2
36	14	.127	12.7
35	16	.146	14.6
34	8	.073	7.3
33	8	.073	7.3
32	7	.064	6.4
31	6	.055	5.5
30	5	.045	4.5
29	4	.036	3.6
28	5	.045	4.5
27	3	.027	2.7
26	2	.018	1.8
25	0	.000	0.0
24	1	.009	0.9
Σ	110	1.000	100.0

the total number of observations made; for any set of scores, N is some particular number. For any value on the scale of measurement (for any score), f answers the question "How many observations of that value were obtained?" For any complete set of scores, N answers the question "For all scale values combined, how many observations were obtained?" In other words, N is the sum of the f's for all of the categories.

A simple frequency distribution is just one way of describing a set of scores. In Table 4.2 I have reproduced the simple frequency (f) distribution and illustrated two alternate descriptions: proportionate frequency and percentage frequency.

The proportionate frequency (p) and percentage frequency (%) columns are closely related to each other. *Proportionate frequency* indicates the proportion of the total number of observations that is associated with any value on the scale of measurement. The proportionate frequency for any category is calculated by dividing its frequency (f) by the total number of observations (N); $p = f/N$. For example, the p value of .10 indicated for the score of 38 indicates that $^{11}/_{110} = ^{10}/_{100}$ of the total observations were scores of 38 (.10 is the fraction $^{10}/_{100}$ expressed in decimal form). The percentage frequency is simply the proportionate frequency multiplied by 100; $\% = 100 \times (f/N)$.

Proportionate or percentage frequency distributions are constructed when one wants to compare two or more frequency distributions that have very different N's. The reasoning is straightforward. If one set contains 250 scores and another set contains 50 scores, comparing the frequency (f) associated with any scale value will not be very meaningful. Suppose one wants to know whether some particular score was more popular in the large set than in the small set. Noting that this score has a larger frequency in the large set doesn't tell much, since any score had more opportunities for a large frequency in the large set simply because many more observations were obtained. The better comparison is in terms of proportionate or percentage frequency. If someone told you that 25 students in a class of 300 earned grades of A while 10 students in a class of 30 earned A's, you would be reluctant to conclude that the students in the larger class did better (even though 25 is greater than 10). It would be more correct to argue that the students in the smaller class did better because $^{10}/_{30}$, or 33 percent, of them earned grades of A while only $^{25}/_{300}$, or 8 percent, of the students in the larger class earned A's.

Another alternative to a simple frequency distribution is a cumulative frequency distribution. In Table 4.3 I have again reproduced the simple (f) distribution, which may be compared to the cumulative frequency distribution (cum f). The numbers in the "Cum f" column indicate the number of observations obtained up to and including each particular value on the scale of measurement. For example, this column indicates that 26 students earned scores of *31 or lower,* that 99 students earned scores of *38 or lower,*

Table 4.3 Simple Frequency, Cumulative Frequency, and Cumulative Percentage Distributions

SCORE	f	CUM f	CUM %
40	4	110	100.0
39	7	106	96.4
38	11	99	90.0
37	9	88	80.0
36	14	79	71.8
35	16	65	59.1
34	8	49	44.5
33	8	41	37.2
32	7	33	29.9
31	6	26	23.5
30	5	20	18.0
29	4	15	13.5
28	5	11	9.9
27	3	6	5.4
26	2	3	2.7
25	0	1	0.9
24	1	1	0.9

and so on. Notice that the number in the cumulative-frequency column associated with the highest score must equal N, the total number of observations. It is also possible to cumulate proportionate frequencies or percentage frequencies, as illustrated in the "Cum %" column in Table 4.3. This column indicates, for example, that 80 percent of the students earned scores of *37 or less*; when the highest score is reached, the cumulative percentage is, of course, 100 percent.

The various kinds of frequency distributions that we have discussed represent slightly different ways of describing a set of scores. Notice that they all present the same basic information in different forms; it is quite easy to translate from f to p to % to cum f, and so on. In some circumstances a simple frequency distribution might be modified to produce a different kind of distribution. When very many *scale values* are observed, the simple frequency distribution may have so many categories, each with its associated

Table 4.4   A Grouped Frequency Distribution of Scores on a Reading Test

SCORES	f
70–74	13
65–69	24
60–64	28
55–59	38
50–54	47
45–49	60
40–44	51
35–39	40
30–34	32
25–29	24
20–24	16
15–19	6
N =	379

Simple f Distribution		*Grouped f Distribution*	
SCORES	f	**SCORES**	f
29	8		
28	6		
27	4	25–29	24
26	3		
25	3		

frequency, that there is still too much information to be grasped. When this occurs, it is quite common to construct a *grouped frequency distribution* that uses fewer and larger categories. Table 4.4 illustrates a grouped frequency distribution.

This distribution is to be read as follows: Thirteen students earned test scores of 70 or 71 or 72 or 73 or 74; 51 students earned scores of 40 or 41 or 42 or 43 or 44; and so on. The purpose of a grouped frequency distribution is to reduce the amount of information a person has to process to get an overall impression of what a set of scores is like. Given this purpose, only rough rules apply to constructing grouped distributions. Typically it is suggested that between 10 and 20 categories be used and that the categories be of equal size (when the original data are scores on a numerical, preferably interval scale). Notice that in Table 4.4 each category or interval includes 5 values on the original scale of measurement and that 12 categories are used. These rules provide some consistency in the manner in which grouped frequency distributions are constructed.

Notice that the grouped distribution does not provide exactly the same information as a simple frequency distribution. Some information is lost when the larger categories are formed. As illustrated at the bottom of Table 4.4, the original information that 8 scores of 29, 6 scores of 28, and so on were obtained is reduced to the statement that 24 scores between 25 and 29 (inclusive) were obtained. The more specific information is not contained in the grouped frequency distribution. This loss of information is acceptable as long as the grouped distribution serves the purpose of providing a convenient, overall impression of a set of scores.

Researchers do more with their data than construct frequency distributions; for example, a researcher is likely to calculate an "average" and an index of the variability of the set of scores. If a researcher knows the actual value of each individual score (which is almost always the case), these original scores should be used for calculations. It would *not* be advisable to use a grouped frequency distribution for calculations; because some original information is lost in the grouped distribution, calculations based on the grouped distribution would be slightly in error. Therefore researchers typically use the original data for calculations while constructing a grouped frequency distribution to provide an overall impression of the set of scores.

PROBLEM

You have a set of 250 scores; the lowest score is 11 while the highest is 164. If you were going to construct a grouped frequency distribution for this set of scores, what would be the score limits of the highest interval you would use?

There is no single correct answer to this problem; the rough rules state that between 10 and 20 intervals of equal size should be used, and there are many ways of satisfying these rules. Here is one answer to this problem. We need to decide how large the intervals should be to have between 10 and 20 intervals in all. The set of scores covers a range of 153 points on the measurement scale (164 − 11 = 153). If we divide this range by 15 (halfway between 10 and 20, the number of intervals we would like), we get an answer near 10 (153 ÷ 15 = 10.2). This indicates that if each interval includes about 10 score values we will have between 10 and 20 intervals for the distribution. We could use intervals of 8, 9, 10, 11, or 12 and stay between 10 and 20 intervals overall, but 10 seems like a very good choice for an interval size. People are used to counting by 10s and thus will find it easy to "read" the grouped distribution if each interval includes 10 score values. Having chosen 10 as an interval size, we need to decide how to place the intervals. We could start with the lowest score, 11, and form successive intervals of 10 score values each; then the score limits of successive intervals should be 11–20, 21–30, 31–40, and so on, the highest interval being 161–170. This would be an acceptable solution. However, it will probably be easier for people to "read" the distribution if each interval starts with a multiple of 10. If we chose this solution, the score limits for successive intervals would be 10–19, 20–29, 30–39, and so on, the highest interval being 160–169. Notice that having each interval include 10 score values (rather than 8 or 9 or 11) and having each interval start with a multiple of 10 are matters of preference. The "rules" for constructing grouped frequency distributions are *not* rigid and may be satisfied by a number of slightly different grouped distributions.

PROBLEM

Assume that a "warm" day is defined as one on which the official temperature equals or exceeds 80°. Assume further that, looking at the records for a year, it is determined that Chicago has more warm days than San Francisco. How, then, could it also be true that for the same year the average daily temperature in Chicago is 44° while the average is 53° for San Francisco?

Arriving at the answer to this problem involves some good thinking about frequency distributions. What we are told is that the distribution of temperatures for Chicago has more entries at or above a value of 80° yet has a lower average temperature. There are many ways in which this situation could come about. One possibility is that, while Chicago has more days with temperatures of 80° or more, San Francisco's warm days are much warmer, thus raising San Francisco's average relative to Chicago's. Another possibility is that Chicago has more cold days, or colder days than San Francisco, thus lowering Chicago's average on a relative basis.

Graphing Frequency Distributions

An alternative to presenting frequency distributions in tabular form is to construct a graphic display of the distribution. We will consider two types of graphs that are frequently used, the bar graph and the frequency polygon (in rough terms, a line graph). Before discussing these two types of displays it will be necessary to consider a different distinction between types of scales because this distinction is related to the kind of graphic display that is appropriate.

Discrete Versus Continuous Scales. One distinction that can be made is between *discrete* and *continuous* scales. The notion of a discrete scale is that the scale consists of a finite set of values, with the consequence that the value associated with any observation is exact. For example, counting the number of things is considered to involve a discrete scale—there might be any number of people in a room, but there are no half-people or quarter-people; thus the values on the scale of number of people consist of whole numbers. When students are introduced to the concept of counting as a discrete scale, they sometimes think of a problem case—what if a person is standing right in the middle of the doorway to the room? Might this not be a "half-person" to be counted? The question is a good one, and it is handled in the following way: A discrete scale is one that is used in such a way that only certain values are possible. In the case of counting people in a room, some criteria would be established for including any individual in the set of people to be counted such that any individual is either to be counted or not to be counted. For example, one might use the following criterion: "Any individual with any part of his or her body on or inside of a line drawn through the middle of the doorway is defined as 'in the room' and thus is to be counted." While there is an element of arbitrariness to such definitions, it is nevertheless true that useful discrete scales can be defined in many circumstances.

The notion of a continous scale is best exemplified by an interval or ratio scale for which there is in principle an infinite number of possible values between the lower and upper limits of the scale; for a continuous scale the value associated with any observation is *approximate.* For example, consider the question "Exactly how long is the desk?" Length is defined in terms of a ratio scale and is considered to be continuous, which means that the exact length of the desk cannot be determined. One might measure the desk to the nearest foot and report its length as 4 feet, but quite obviously one could measure its length to the nearest inch or centimeter or millimeter, or some unit smaller than the smallest one used thus far (in principle—engineering creativity might be required in order to practicially accomplish more precise measurement). This idea can be looked at in a different manner: Between 1 foot and 3 feet is there some length that is theoretically impossible? For example, is it impossible for a length to be 2.4 feet or 1.888 feet or 1.00000001 feet? The answer is no—an infinite number of values is possible in principle.

Whereas a discrete scale has gaps in it, a continuous scale has no gaps between values. It is important to realize that the values obtained for a continuous scale will appear to have gaps, but this is only because one has chosen to measure to the nearest "unit of measurement" and has thus "rounded" the values. Suppose you have used a ruler to measure the lengths of various objects to the nearest inch, and assume that the smallest unit indicated on the ruler is one-eighth of an inch. The values or scores you would record would all be whole numbers of inches, such as 14 inches, 28 inches, and so on. You would not record any scores like 10¼ inches. However, it is clear that you were not limited to measuring to the nearest inch; in fact when you record a length of 11 inches for an object this would mean that when you applied the ruler to that object some length between 10.5 inches and 11.5 inches was observed. Thus the 11 represents an interval from 10.5 to 11.5 inches, and any other value recorded similarly represents an interval—there are no gaps or impossible values.

If you have the impression that whether one has a discrete scale or a continuous scale is a matter of assumption or theoretical predilection, you are largely correct. Indeed, many psychologists have argued that many scales that appear to be discrete "really" refer to essentially continuous characteristics. For example, the dichotomy "male–female" (discrete) has been translated into "degrees of masculinity–femininity" (continuous). A great deal of intellectual passion has been spent debating whether or not "dead–alive" is discrete or continuous. Such debates are unlikely to be settled soon, but it is useful to know that the distinction between discrete and continuous scales is not automatic. In psychological research it is generally true that values obtained by counting the number of objects or organisms in a particular category (usually on a nominal scale) are considered to be on a discrete scale, while values obtained by measuring some characteristic of organisms are considered to be on a continuous scale. With respect to the latter point, you should realize that quite often characteristics or performance levels are measured by counting the number of correct items (or incorrect answers, or answers of a particular sort), yielding scores consisting of whole numbers. However, in these cases it is assumed that the characteristic is *fundamentally continuous* and that the values consequently represent approximate measurement to the nearest whole number. Thus scores such as the number of points earned on a test or the number of words recalled correctly are usually treated as values on a continuous scale because it seems reasonable that knowledge of course content, intelligence, the difficulty of learning some task, or personality characteristics, and the like are continuous variables.

The relevance of the distinction between discrete and continuous scales to graphing frequency distributions is that constructing a frequency polygon or line graph makes sense only if one is dealing with a continuous scale and has obtained at least interval values. Otherwise a bar graph is appropriate. We will now consider some examples of these graphic displays.

Bar Graphs. Figure 4.1 shows a bar graph of the distribution of values on a nominal scale of political association. Several features of the graph deserve attention. The horizontal line (axis), also known as the X axis or *abscissa,* is used for values of the scale of measurement, in this case the categories of political association. The vertical axis (*ordinate* or Y axis) is

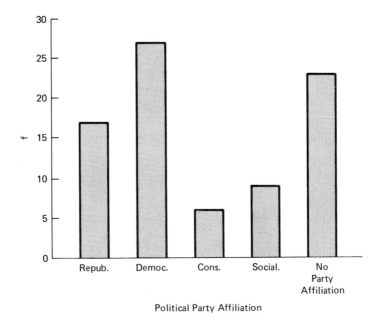

Figure 4.1. A bar graph of a distribution of political affiliations.

used for values of f (if a proportionate or percentage distribution were being displayed, the vertical axis would be used for the values of p or %). The bar graph is constructed by erecting a bar for each category of the measurement scale equal in height to the frequency for that category. This graph indicates that, for the set of observations obtained, 17 people were Republicans, 6 were Conservatives, 23 had no party affiliation, and so on.

There are several important points to attend to in inspecting this bar graph. First, the order of the categories of political affiliation is arbitrary because no claim is made for this scale other than that different affiliations could be identified. Second, the width of the bar is arbitrary because the categories do not have meaningful "distances" on the nominal scale. Third, the separation of categories is arbitrary because the nominal scale does not contain information about distances between categories.

Frequency Polygons. Figure 4.2 presents a frequency polygon based on the distribution of reading test scores shown in Table 4.4. The polygon is constructed by placing a point (dot) above the *midpoint* of each score interval used, at a height equal to the frequency for the category. To understand this procedure, refer back to Table 4.4, specifically the score interval 25–29. As illustrated at the bottom of the table, the interval 25–29 includes five scores. Keep in mind that because reading ability is considered to be a continuous variable, there are no gaps on the scale. What this means is that any score reported represents an interval; for example, a score of 25 represents 24.5–25.5 (since reading ability is being measured to the

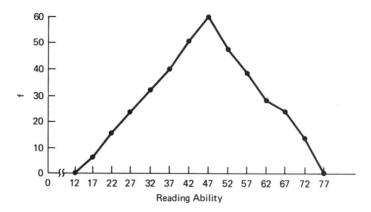

Figure 4.2. A frequency polygon depicting a set of scores on a continuous scale of reading ability.

nearest whole number of points on the test). Consequently the interval labeled "25–29" in principle extends from 24.5, the lower edge of the interval represented by 25, to 29.5, the upper edge of the interval represented by 29. Since a grouped frequency distribution was used, what is to be displayed for this interval is the information that 24 scores were observed between the points 24.5 and 29.5 on the continuous scale of reading ability. In the frequency polygon (Figure 4.2) this information is shown by locating a dot at a height equal to that for 24 on the f axis and directly above 27, which is the middle of that interval (27 is midway between 24.5 and 29.5 on the scale of reading ability). The points for the other intervals are similarly placed. For example, 67 is the midpoint of the interval labeled "65–69," which had a frequency of 24; thus a dot is located above 67 at a height equal to that of 24 on the vertical (f) axis.

Three additional features of Figure 4.2 are worthy of attention. Obviously, the dots located at appropriate heights above the midpoints of the score intervals have been connected by straight lines. In addition, the frequency polygon has been "closed off" by representing the midpoints of the intervals just below the lowest interval for which observations were obtained and just above the highest interval for which observations were obtained, locating a dot at zero frequency in each case, and extending lines to these points. Notice that there is a dot at zero frequency for 12 and a dot at zero frequency above 77, and that these dots have been connected by straight lines to the adjacent dots. Closing off the polygon in this way indicates the ends of the distribution and avoids leaving the line connecting dots for intervals for which observations were obtained "hanging in midair" in the graph. The third point is that a break is displayed for the horizontal axis, between 0 and 12 on the scale. The break is indicated because, for this continuous interval scale, distance is important; the break shows that, below 12, distance on the page does not correspond to distance on the scale.

The frequency polygon clearly gives the impression of variation in frequency on a continuous, uninterrupted basis over values of the scale of measurement. A viewer gains an impression not only of the frequency associated with various scale values but also of the rate of change in frequency on the basis of the slope depicted by the line graph. Such impressions are justified only when the measurement scale reflects a continuous variable on at least an interval scale. If one placed points above the various categories of political affiliation shown in Figure 4.1 and connected the points with straight lines, the impression given would be totally misleading. Drawing a line between "Republican" and "Democratic" would imply that frequencies could be obtained between these two categories, but there is no definition of what "between Republican and Democratic" means. Further, the slope of the line between categories would be uninterpretable because the spacing of the categories on the horizontal axis is completely arbitrary. While it is quite unlikely that anyone would contemplate constructing a frequency polygon for the data in Figure 4.1, there are other instances in which the decision is not so obvious.

PROBLEM

A researcher has a number of people rate a recording of rock music by having each person select one of seven ratings. The data (number of people choosing each rating) are as follows: dislike very much, 5; dislike, 17; dislike slightly, 24; neither dislike nor like, 37; like slightly, 39; like, 44; like very much, 52. For display purposes the various categories are given numerical values according to the following scheme: dislike very much = −3, dislike = − 2, and so on through like = +2 and like very much = +3. The question is whether or not the graph of the data shown in Figure 4.3 is appropriate.

Figure 4.3. Opinion of rock music.

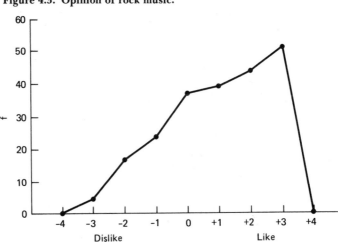

To develop the answer to this question, let's consider the issues related to the use of frequency polygons with respect to the data obtained. First, is "opinion of rock music" (recognizing that only one selection has been rated) a continuous variable? The most reasonable answer seems to be yes, since from the most positive opinion possible to the most negative opinion possible there appear to be no compelling reasons for suggesting that there is some intermediate position that is impossible to hold. Thus the first requirement for using a frequency polygon—namely, that the scale of measurement refer to a variable that is in principle continuous—is met.

A look at Figure 4.3 shows that nine values of "opinion of rock music" have been arranged with equal spaces between them on the horizontal axis. Two points are worth considering. Nine points are used on the X axis, whereas only seven rating categories were used; the two most extreme values (−4 and +4) have been used to close off the polygon with zero frequencies. One question is whether or not extending the scale in this fashion is justifiable—are opinions more extreme than "dislike very much" and "like very much" possible? Since it is not difficult to conceive of opinions such as "like (or dislike) very very much," it does not seem that extending the scale to include the more extreme points with zero frequency presents any fundamental problem with respect to the scale of opinions toward rock music. The more important point concerns the spacing of the values, and here we again face the question of whether one has an ordinal or an interval scale. In assigning numerical values differing from each other by one to the rating categories, it is being assumed that the difference between "dislike very much" and "dislike" is equal to the distance between "like" and "like very much" or to the distance between "neither like nor dislike" and "like slightly" or between any other pair of adjacent categories. If the assumption that the categories are equally spaced is reasonable, then using the frequency polygon is also reasonable. If, on the other hand, we assume that the rating categories constitute only an ordinal scale, then the frequency polygon in Figure 4.3 is misleading because the distance between adjacent points on the rating scale is unknown. As you can see, it is possible to argue for either a yes or no answer to the question. If I had to choose an answer, I think it would be safer to choose no unless some additional information that the points on the rating scale are reasonably equally spaced were given.

Describing Frequency Distributions

Frequency distributions can be described in several different ways, all of which convey information about the shape of the distribution. While these descriptions can be defined rigorously, they are typically used only as rough characterizations of distributions, and we will deal with them as general descriptions. Only rather stylized frequency polygons will be shown as examples.

Modality. One characteristic of a distribution is its *modality*, which refers to the number of categories or scale values that have especially high concentrations of frequencies. Strictly speaking, *the* mode is the scale value with the highest frequency, but this definition is relaxed such that people frequently describe a distribution as *bimodal* (having two modes) even though the frequency for one "mode" is less than that for the other. Remember, these descriptions are used in a rough manner.

Figure 4.4 displays distributions of varying modality. For most purposes one need consider only unimodal and bimodal distributions. Distributions with more than two "modes" like that in Figure 4.4(c) are rare; furthermore, they represent a problem because it becomes difficult to say that any category or scale value has especially high frequency when more than a couple of values have roughly equal frequencies. Let me also em-

Figure 4.4.

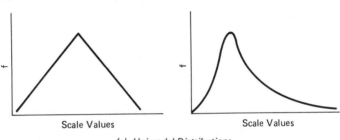

(a) Unimodal Distributions

(b) Bimodal Distributions

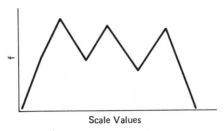

(c) A Trimodal Distribution

phasize that describing the modality of a distribution by looking at it is reasonable only when the distribution contains a rather large number of scores (i.e., a large N). If one has collected only 10 scores (three 8's, five 6's, and two 5's), it is very difficult to say anything about modality with confidence.

Most of the time psychologists measure characteristics in such a way that unimodal distributions are obtained. This statement has two aspects. First, it is commonly assumed that the characteristics we measure *should* yield unimodal distributions. Second, since the measurement process is largely under the control of the investigator, steps can be taken that are likely to yield unimodal distributions. These points can be understood by considering the standard interpretation of a bimodal distribution. When a bimodal distribution like those in Figure 4.4(b) is obtained, it is commonly assumed that the bimodality exists because one has put together into one distribution two separable unimodal distributions. The search then goes on for the characteristic that will allow the separation into two unimodal distributions. For example, suppose you measured the weights of a large number of adult human beings. It is likely that you would obtain a bimodal distribution because the set of observations is based on both males and females, who tend to have different weights. Thus you would obtain one mode at the highest concentration of males and another mode where the highest density of females occurs. The solution would be to plot separate distributions for males and females, each of which would be unimodal.

The male–female distinction can be used to illustrate another way in which unimodal distributions can be produced. It is known that among adult humans males and females tend to have different kinds of abilities (for a variety of reasons). Suppose you were constructing a "test of intellectual ability." The point is that the set of items you include in the test might have a large number in which males and females tend to differ, in which case a bimodal distribution would be obtained. One solution would be the one I have already described, namely, to construct separate distributions of test scores for males and females. When the test is used, any individual female's score will be compared to the "female" distribution, while any individual male's score will be compared to the "male" distribution; this procedure is followed for a number of standardized tests. A different solution would be to select the items for the test in such a way that no male–female difference in test scores will be obtained. When this procedure is used, just the single whole distribution needs to be used, and any individual's score (whether male or female) can be compared with this single distribution. This procedure has also been followed in constructing standardized tests.

To summarize this discussion, psychologists tend to prefer unimodal distributions, seek explanations for bimodal distributions, and to disbelieve distributions that appear to have more than two "modes." Unimodal distributions can be obtained "without really trying" or by subdividing the initial set of objects or organisms into separate groups, each of which will yield a unimodal distribution, or by constructing the measuring instrument in such a way that a possible bimodality is avoided. Let me stress one implication of this presentation: Measurement is not a passive activity! Especially with respect to measuring psychological characteristics for which rather complex measures must be constructed, the investigator can have considerable influence on what kinds of data are obtained. Since there is typically no obviously correct way of measuring such characteristcs, different investigators use different methods.

   Skewness. Another characteristic of a frequency distribution is its *skewness*. A distribution can be described as negatively skewed, symmetrical, or positively skewed; Figure 4.5 provides examples of the three types. In general, skewness refers to the manner in which frequencies are distributed on either side of the point of highest concentration. Note that skewness will be difficult to assess unless a distribution is unimodal. If, starting at the mode, the remaining frequencies are distributed to roughly equal extents on both sides, the distribution is described as symmetrical, as in Figure 4.5(a). If the remaining frequencies are extended farther on one side of the mode than on the other, the distribution is skewed. Since it is standard practice to locate negative numbers to the left of the X axis and positive numbers to the right (see Figure 4.3 for an example), a distribution for which the frequencies are extended more to the left is said to be

Figure 4.5. Examples of symmetrical and skewed frequency distributions.

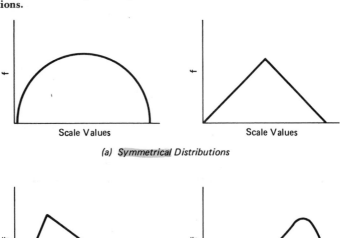

(a) *Symmetrical* Distributions

(b) *Positive Skewness*   (c) *Negative Skewness*

negatively skewed and a distribution with frequencies extended more to the right is said to be positively skewed.

Like unimodal distributions, investigators prefer symmetrical distributions. In part, symmetrical distributions are expected in many situations for theoretical reasons (which we'll discuss later in the chapter); in addition, many advanced statistical procedures require symmetrical distributions. A different reason for preferring symmetrical distributions can be illustrated by considering the situation of the test constructor (e.g., an instructor in a class or a psychologist preparing a standardized test for general use). If the test constructor desires to distinguish individuals from "much above average" through "average" to "much below average" (which is often the goal), the symmetrical distribution allows him or her to do this most easily. In a skewed distribution too many of the frequencies are too closely packed at either the upper or the lower end to allow reasonable discriminations to be made. For example, in a negatively skewed distribution the difference between "average" scores, or those near the mode, and scores that are "much above average," or the highest ones obtained, might be so small that one cannot have much confidence in the distinction; identifying someone as "above average" would be tenuous indeed.

The situations in which skewed distributions will be obtained can to some extent be predicted. Certain measures, such as reaction times or trials to learn some task, almost always yield positively skewed distributions, and for understandable reasons. If one is measuring reaction time, in principle the shortest reaction time is zero or something extremely close to it (responding "immediately" after the stimulus is presented). Most reaction times will be somewhat longer than this (perhaps $1/5$ to $1/2$ sec), but one will also obtain some relatively long reaction times for various reasons, such as inattention or confusion about the response. Suppose the modal reaction time is about $1/2$ second but there are also some scores of up to 5 seconds (4.5 sec above the mode); notice that it is impossible to obtain scores that are much below the mode. A positively skewed distribution will result. Similar reasoning applies to trials-to-learn: Nobody can learn in less than one trial; most will learn in a moderate number of trials; and some will take very many trials, again yielding a positively skewed distribution.

Skewed distributions will also result whenever most of the scores fall near one end of the scale of measurement. For example, if an instructor gives a class an extremely difficult test, most of the scores will be near zero, with only the better students earning scores away from the mode and then only in the positive direction. An extremely easy test will for analogous reasons yield a negatively skewed distribution. If a number of people are asked how much they like or dislike something and it turns out that most like it very much or most dislike it very much, the result would be a negatively or positively-skewed distribution of ratings. In many such situations the skewed distribution can be avoided by adjusting the system of measurement; for example, the instructor can adjust the difficulty of the test so that a more symmetrical distribution is obtained. Avoiding skewed distributions is a common goal because symmetrical distributions with modes roughly in the middle of the measurement scale are advantageous not only for distinguishing among individuals within the distribution but also for comparing distributions. For example, if an instructor wants to determine whether, say, requiring homework increases test scores, and gives an extremely easy test to both the "homework" and "no-homework" groups, *both* score distributions might be concentrated near the upper end of the scale, making it very difficult to tell whether the "homework" distribution is generally higher. A failure to find differences between distributions because too many of the scores in both distributions are near the *low* end of the scale is called *floor effect*. A failure to detect a difference between distributions because too many scores are near the *high* end of the scale is termed a *ceiling effect*. Floor and ceiling effects are consequences of insensitive measurement; although the scale used may have a sufficient number of possible values, a vast number of the observations are clustered in a relatively small area at one or the other end of the scale.

PROBLEM

Draw graphs fitting the following descriptions:

(1) A unimodal, positively skewed distribution.
(2) A bimodal, symmetrical distribution.
(3) A slightly bimodal, negatively skewed distribution.

Your graphs should resemble those in Figure 4.6. (see p. 142).

MEASURES OF CENTRAL TENDENCY

Constructing frequency distributions and drawing graphs of distributions are ways of organizing sets of data and describing them with some efficiency. This process can be continued by calculating numerical descriptions of data by methods that we will now consider. Two important features of a frequency distribution are the location of the distribution on the scale of measurement and the spread of scores within the distribution. First we will consider the location of a distribution. A measure of *central tendency* is a single value on the measurement scale that in some way represents the location of a set of scores. The common "average" is what is meant by a measure of central tendency. There are several popular measures of central tendency, each of which represents a distribution's location in a different fashion.

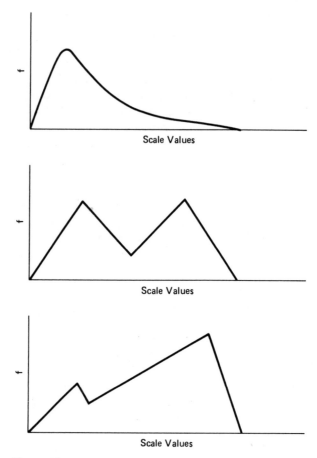

Figure 4.6.

The Mode

The *mode*, which we encountered in the preceding section, is defined as the category or scale value with the *highest* frequency. The logic of using the mode to represent the location of a distribution is that the mode is "the most popular value"—more observations of that value are made than any other. The mode can be used for observations on any scale of measurement, from nominal on up. For example, for the set of political affiliations shown in Figure 4.1 the mode would be "Democratic," since the distribution included more Democrats than any other category. If a grouped frequency distribution is used, the mode is the midpoint of the category with the greatest frequency. For example, for the distribution in Table 4.4 the mode is 47, since the interval 45–49 has the greatest frequency and 47 is the midpoint of that interval.

The weakness of the mode as a measure of central tendency is that it is relatively unstable or unreliable. The highest frequency (which will identify the mode) might not be particularly high or might not be much larger than the frequencies of several other values. Particularly for smaller sets of scores, the mode can seem quite capricious. As an extreme example, for a set of scores consisting of the values 1, 5, 7, 9, 19, 19 the mode would be 19 (the most frequent value). Notice that 19 does not describe the center of the distribution very well; it is not a very good index of where the set of scores is located. As we saw in the preceding section, a distribution might have two (or more) modes, which confuses matters considerably. Generally, a distribution must contain many scores for the mode to be reasonably distinct and representative of the distribution's location.

The Median

Provided that scores are obtained on at least an ordinal scale, the median can serve as a measure of central tendency. The *median* is defined as the value on the measurement scale that has half of the frequencies below it. Sometimes the median is called the "middle score." This is roughly correct, although the median does *not* have to be a score that was actually achieved by any individual. Fundamentally, the median is a scale value that divides the distribution of scores into two halves—one half above the median, one half below. Table 4.5 illustrates several small score distributions and the median for each distribution.

The examples in Table 4.5 were deliberately constructed to illustrate several properties of the median. First, the median is *not* sensitive to changes in the scores at the extremes of a distribution. Look at distributions (b), (c), and (d); in each case there are 9 scores and the median is 68. Compared to distribution (b), the scores below the median in distribution (c) are lower in value, and those above the median are also lower. Nonetheless, the median is 68 in both distributions—the value of the "middle

Table 4.5   Identification of the Median for Several Distributions

(a)	Scores: 11, 11, 12, 13, 14, 14, 15, 17, 17, 18, 19, 20, 21, 21, 22, 24
	N = 16; median = 17
(b)	Scores: 56, 59, 61, 65, 68, 71, 74, 77, 82
	N = 9; median = 68
(c)	Scores: 33, 42, 44, 45, 68, 69, 69, 69, 70
	N = 9; median = 68
(d)	Scores: 33, 42, 44, 45, 68, 69, 69, 69, 150
	N = 9; median = 68
(e)	Scores: 33, 42, 44, 45, 48, 69, 69, 69, 70
	N = 9; median = 48

score" is not affected by how high the highest scores are or by how low the lowest scores are. In distribution (d) I included as the highest score a value considerably higher than those in distributions (b) or (c), yet again the median is unchanged.

The median *is* sensitive to changes in scores near the middle of a distribution. Compare distributions (c) and (e); the only difference between these distributions is the value of the middle score, which of course makes the medians different. Finally, the median can sometimes only be approximated, as in distribution (a). Since there are 16 scores in this distribution, the median would have 8 scores below it (and 8 scores above it). Counting up from the lowest score, we find that both the eighth and ninth scores are 17s, which presents a problem: We cannot identify a precise value on the measurement scale that has exactly 8 scores below it. However, this is but a slight problem; the median is approximately 17, and reporting the median as 17 seems quite reasonable.

The fact that the median is not sensitive to changes in the values of extreme scores can be either a strength or a weakness, depending on the nature of the score distribution. For example, the scores in distribution (c) are generally lower than those in distribution (b), but the median does not reflect this change. On the other hand, the fact that the median is unaffected by the extremely high score of 150 in distribution (d) looks like a plus for the median—its value stays close to most of the scores despite the presence of an unusual score. Notice that distribution (d) is a small but severely skewed distribution; most of the scores lie between 33 and 69, with one extremely high score of 150 (and no corresponding extremely low score). In general, the median is not affected much by skewness, a property that leads many researchers to prefer the median as the measure of central tendency for skewed distributions. In effect the median "stays near the middle" despite skewness.

The Mean

A very precisely defined measure of central tendency is the *arithmetic mean*, usually referred to simply as the mean. The formula defining the mean is shown in Table 4.6. There are several symbols in this formula, which you should take the time to fully understand. Since the mean is used in other formulas of greater complexity, it is convenient to give it a symbol, namely, M. When you see other formulas in this book that include the symbol M, that M refers to the mean. The symbol N you already know—it is the total number of observations (scores) in a distribution. The symbol X is a general symbol for a variable; with respect to the distribution in Table 4.6, X refers to scores on the midterm exam. The scores of 8, 10, 14, and so on are X's, or values of X. The capital Greek sigma (Σ) is an instructional symbol indicating that you should *sum* whatever follows it; the

Table 4.6   Calculation of the Mean for a Set of Scores

Scores: 8, 10, 14, 16, 18, 20, 22, 25, 26

$$M = \frac{\Sigma X}{N}$$

$\Sigma X = 8 + 10 + 14 + 16 + 18 + 20 + 22 + 25 + 26 = 159$

$N = 9$ (the total number of scores)

$$M = \frac{159}{9} = 17.7$$

horizontal line between ΣX and N is one of the ways of indicating division. The formula for the mean (M) thus can be read as follows: Sum (add up) the values of all the X's and divide this sum by N (the total number of observations). Using this formula for the set of scores in Table 4.6, the mean is calculated to be 17.66666 (ad infinitum). Since the mean is commonly reported to one or two decimal places more than the original scores have (and the scores here are whole numbers), the mean would be reported as 17.67 or 17.7.

You are, of course, quite familiar with the mean, having encountered it in many situations, usually labeled "average." Grade point averages, athletes' scoring averages (total points scored divided by number of games), and many other "averages" are means. Notice that calculating the mean makes sense if it makes sense to sum the values of the scores. The mean is based on the actual values of all scores and reflects distance information; thus the scores should contain meaningful distance information. Strictly speaking, the mean is an appropriate measure of central tendency for scores on at least an interval scale. The formula for the mean could be applied to your social-security number, phone number, and zip code, but the calculation would be pointless.

The mean can be considered the "balance point" of a set of scores. That is, the deviations (distances) of the scores *below* the mean are balanced by the deviations of the scores *above* the mean. Another way of stating this is to say that the sum of the deviations from the mean (paying attention to whether the deviations are positive or negative) is always zero. In symbolic terms, $\Sigma(X - M) = 0$ for any set of scores. This property of the mean is illustrated in Table 4.7.

Of the three measures of central tendency that we have considered, the mean is the only one that directly reflects the value of each and every score. If one had scores on (at least) an interval scale, one could use either the mode, the median, or the mean as the measure of central tendency. Since the mean makes the greatest use of the information available in the

Table 4.7   Illustration of the Mean as "Balancing Point"

Scores: 16, 19, 21, 25, 29

$$M = \frac{\Sigma X}{N} = \frac{110}{5} = 22.0$$

Deviations of Individual Scores from the Mean $(X - M)$

Score	X − M
29	+7
25	+3
21	−1
19	−3
16	−6
$\Sigma(X - M)$	=0

Note: It is always true that the positive deviations from the mean are balanced by (numerically equal to) the negative deviations from the mean.

set of scores, it is generally to be preferred as the measure of central tendency whenever it can sensibly be calculated. A possible exception to this rule concerns skewed frequency distributions. For the small distribution in Table 4.7, notice that the median is 21; if the highest score in the set were changed from 29 to 70, the median would stay 21. However, the mean would change—ΣX would now be 151 and M would equal 30.2. As you can see, the mean is drawn toward an extreme score when it is not balanced by an extreme score in the opposite direction. Many people would argue that 21 is a better description of where "the center of the distribution" is than 30.2 in such an instance, and therefore would prefer to use the median for skewed distributions even though the mean could be calculated.

PROBLEM
_____

The heights (in inches) of the members of the local basketball team are as follows: 68, 70, 71, 74, 76, 79, 79, and 80. Determine the mode, median, and mean for this set of scores.

The mode is 79, the median 75, and the mean 74.6. In determining the median one finds that the scale value with half the frequencies below it is somewhere between 74 and 76; the common practice in such cases is to "split the difference"; thus 75 is reported as the median.

PROBLEM
_____

A check is made of the eye color of the students in a college class, with the following results: brown, 24; blue, 13; green, 4; gray, 2. What is the mean eye color?

The answer in this case is that the mean cannot be calculated because the scale of measurement is only nominal. The use of the names of the eye colors perhaps makes it rather obvious that a mean cannot be calculated. However, suppose the investigator employed the following coding scheme: brown = 1, blue = 2, green = 3, gray = 4. There would now be some numerical scale values to use; the data could be described as twenty-four 1's, thirteen 2's, four 3's, and two 4's. One could add up the values of these scores and divide by the number of observations to produce a calculated number, but that calculation would make no more sense than trying to sum browns, blues, greens, and grays.

PROBLEM

An experimenter has each of 20 judges rank order a set of paintings from "most artistic" to "least artistic," assigning rank 1 to the most artistic painting. He therefore has 20 ranks for each painting, one from each judge. In determining the "average" rank for each painting, should he calculate the median or the mean?

The simple, conservative answer to this problem is clear: Since ranking by definition requires only that a judge order the paintings, the ranks represent only ordinal measurement and the experimenter thus should use the median rank in characterizing each painting. However, even in this apparently simple case the situation is in fact more complicated than it seems. It has been argued that, even though each judge produces only an order of the paintings (or whatever else is being judged), the mean ranks will represent the distances among the paintings in terms of "artistic merit." This argument is based on the following reasoning: If in fact all of the objects to be ranked were identical in terms of the characteristic being judged, then the judges would not agree with each other more than chance and each object would have the same mean rank. In effect each judge would produce a random assignment of the ranks to the objects because there is no way they can be distinguished in terms of the characteristic being judged. In the long run every object should be ranked 1, 2, 3, and so on equally often, thus producing equal mean ranks for the objects. If, on the other hand, the objects were extraordinarily different from each other in terms of the characteristic being judged, ranking the objects would be very easy and the judges would agree with each other virtually perfectly. In this case one object should wind up with a mean rank of 1, another with a mean rank of 2, and so on. If the objects were moderately different from each other, the judges would show moderate agreement and the differences among mean ranks would be of moderate size.

This argument can be illustrated with the following example: Suppose you ask a number of people to rank order a set of sticks in terms of length. If the sticks differ in length, but by amounts so small that it is hard to tell which of two sticks is longer, the people will agree with each other only to a low degree and the mean ranks for the sticks will be similar. Now increase the differences in length among the sticks. The agreement among judges will increase, and so will the separation of the mean ranks. If you increase the differences in length still more, the judges will agree still more closely and the mean ranks will be further separated from each other. Empirical evidence supporting this argument has been obtained, making it reasonable to assume that, while each judge gives only ordinal information about a set of objects that he or she ranks, the pooled responses of many judges do provide information about the distances among objects if mean ranks are calculated. Needless to say, making decisions about how to describe data is not an automatic procedure.

MEASURES OF VARIABILITY

Whereas measures of central tendency provide information concerning the location of a distribution on a scale of measurement, measures of variability give an idea of the spread of a set of scores over the scale. Since measures of variability provide a kind of distance information, they achieve full meaning when the scores are based on at least an interval scale. Just as there are various measures of central tendency, there are several measures of variability, each of which describes the spread of scores in a different way. Each measure of variability provides a single numerical value (usually a distance on the measurement scale) to describe the spread of the set of scores. Any measure of variability *increases in numerical value* when the *spread* of scores (reflected by the measure) *increases.* We will examine five such measures.

The Total Range

The simplest and least reliable measure of variability is the *total range,* which is the difference between the highest and lowest scores in a distribution. For the distribution of scores in Table 4.8, the highest score is 28 and the lowest is 5; thus the total range is $28 - 5$, or 23. The reason the total range is rather unreliable is that it depends too heavily on the values of just two scores; for example, if the highest score were 38, the total range would be 33 rather than 23, a change of 10 units caused by changing one score (the spread of the other 15 scores remains the same). For this reason the total range is typically used for a "quick look" at the variability of a distribution and is not relied on too strongly.

Table 4.8   Measures of Variability

Scores	$X - M$	$(X - M)^2$
28	+ 7	49
27	+ 6	36
27	+ 6	36
26	+ 5	25
25	+ 4	16
25	+ 4	16
24	+ 3	9
24	+ 3	9
23	+ 2	4
21	0	0
20	− 1	1
18	− 3	9
16	− 5	25
14	− 7	49
13	− 8	64
5	−16	256
$\Sigma X =$ 336	$\Sigma =$ 0	$\Sigma =$ 604

$N = 16$ Median $= 23.5$ $Q_3 = 25.5$ $Q_1 = 17$

$$M = \frac{\Sigma X}{N} = \frac{336}{16} = 21.0 \qquad\qquad IQR = Q_3 - Q_1 = 25.5 - 17 = 8$$

$$\Sigma \mid X - M \mid = 80 \qquad\qquad A.D. = \frac{\Sigma \mid X - M \mid}{N} = \frac{80}{16} = 5.0$$

$$\sigma^2 = \frac{\Sigma(X - M)^2}{N} = \frac{604}{16} = 37.75$$

$$\sigma = \sqrt{\frac{\Sigma(X - M)^2}{N}} = \sqrt{\frac{604}{16}} = \sqrt{37.75} = 6.15$$

$$\text{Total range} = 28 - 5 = 23$$

The Interquartile Range

A measure of variability based on considerations similar to those involved in calculating the median is the *interquartile range*. For practice, let's find the median (the scale value with one-half of the frequencies below it). There are 16 scores in the distribution in Table 4.8; thus the median will be the scale value with $\frac{1}{2}(16)$, or 8, scores below it. Counting up from the lowest score, we find that the eighth score is 23 and the ninth is 24; thus the median is somewhere between 23 and 24. Splitting the difference, the median would be reported as 23.5. The interquartile range is based on two values that are similarly determined: the third quartile (Q_3), which is the scale value with three-fourths of the frequencies below it, and the first quartile (Q_1), which is the scale value with one-fourth of the frequencies below it. Since $N = 16$, Q_3 will have three-fourths of 16, or 12, frequencies below it while Q_1 will have one-fourth of 16, or 4, frequencies below it. Counting up the appropriate numbers of scores, we find that Q_1 is between 16 and 18 while Q_3 is between 25 and 26; splitting the difference in each case, $Q_1 = 17$ and $Q_3 = 25.5$. The interquartile range (IQR) is equal to $Q_3 - Q_1$, which in this case is $25.5 - 17$, or 8.5. The interquartile range indicates the distance on the measurement scale over which the middle 50 percent of the scores are spread. When the median is chosen as the measure of central tendency for a distribution, IQR is ordinarily used as the measure of variability.

PROBLEM

Suppose you are told that for a distribution of scores (on an interval scale) the median = 68 and IQR = 12. Assuming that the distribution is roughly symmetrical, what values would you expect for Q_3 and Q_1?

If the distribution is symmetrical, the median will be halfway between Q_1 and Q_3. Consequently Q_3 will be about ½IQR above the median [68 + ½(12), or 74] and Q_1 will be about ½IQR below the median [68 − ½(12), or 62]. Thus we would expect the middle 50 percent of the scores to be roughly between 62 and 74. This example illustrates how providing just two values, the median and IQR (plus the assumption of a symmetrical distribution), can give a considerable amount of information about a distribution.

The Average Deviation

Not only is the mean usually the best measure of central tendency to use; it is also the basis of a number of measures of variability that are themselves the better ones to use. Before considering some "mean-based" measures of variability, let's consider a calculation that *cannot* be used as a measure of variability. Basing a measure of variability on the mean involves indexing in some fashion how the scores are spread out from the mean. One idea that is fairly appealing on an intuitive basis is to consider the distance of each score from the mean. For example, 28 is 7 units above the mean; 5 is 16 units below it; and so on. The second column in Table 4.8 lists the deviation of each of the 16 scores from the mean, taking into account whether a score is above the mean (+ deviation) or below the mean (− deviation). It might seem reasonable to add up these deviations, the idea being that the larger the sum of these deviations, the more spread out from the mean the scores are. However, as we have already seen, $\Sigma(X - M)$ is always equal to zero for a set of scores; remember that the mean is the balance point of the distribution, and thus the negative deviations will always be perfectly balanced by the positive deviations. Therefore we cannot use the *algebraic* sum of the deviations from the mean as a measure of variability (the algebraic sum is the sum of the deviations taking into account their + and − signs). Something must be done with these deviations such that, as they get larger, the index we calculate gets larger and therefore reflects the increased spread of the scores.

One method of using deviations from the mean to index variability is to calculate the *average deviation*, which is the *average distance* of the scores from the mean. Rather than using the algebraic deviations (with + and − signs), the average deviation (AD) is based on the *absolute values* of the deviations. In other words, if a score is 7 units from the mean, that deviation is treated as 7 units whether the score is above or below the mean; symbolically, an absolute value is indicated by enclosing the value between vertical bars−$|5 − 7| = 2$. If the values in column 2 of Table 4.8 are summed (ignoring the + and − signs), the sum is 80, and the average deviation is this sum divided by N: $^{80}/_{16} = 5.0$. Notice that AD is a clear index of variability; as the scores get more distant from the mean the average deviation increases.

The Variance

A different way of using deviations from the mean to index the spread of a set of scores involves *squaring* the deviations. The third column in Table 4.8 lists the squared deviation $(X − M)^2$ for each of the 16 scores. Since any number, positive or negative, yields a positive product when multiplied by itself, all squared deviations are positive, and the sum of the squared deviations will increase as the deviations increase. The *variance*, symbolized by σ^2 (to be read "sigma squared"), equals the sum of squared deviations divided by N. For the data in Table 4.8, the sum of squared deviations from the mean is 604 and the variance equals $^{604}/_{16}$, or 37.75.

Keep in mind that we are looking for ways of using the deviations from the mean to devise a numerical index that will increase in value as the scores in a distribution spread out more. We cannot use the algebraic sum of the deviations because $\Sigma(X − M)$ always equals zero for a set of scores. The average deviation solves the problem by "ignoring" the signs of the deviations (using the absolute values of the deviations): $\Sigma|X − M|$ will increase as the scores spread out more from the mean. The AD is the average distance of the scores from the mean. Squaring the deviations also solves the problem because all squared deviations are positive; $\Sigma(X − M)^2$ will increase as the scores spread out. The variance is actually the average squared distance of the scores from the mean.

To illustrate how these measures work I have constructed the three small distributions shown in Table 4.9. All three distributions include five

Table 4.9   The Average Deviation and the Variance for Three Small Score Distributions

Distribution A

Scores	X − M	|X − M|	(X − M)²	
18	+2	2	4	$M = \dfrac{80}{5} = 16.0$
17	+1	1	1	
16	0	0	0	
15	−1	1	1	$A.D. = \dfrac{6}{5} = 1.2$
14	−2	2	4	
Σ 80	0	6	10	$\sigma^2 = \dfrac{10}{5} = 2.0$

Distribution B

Scores	X − M	|X − M|	(X − M)²	
20	+4	4	16	$M = \dfrac{80}{5} = 16.0$
18	+2	2	4	
16	0	0	0	
14	−2	2	4	$A.\,D. = \dfrac{12}{5} = 2.4$
12	−4	4	16	
Σ 80	0	12	40	$\sigma^2 = \dfrac{40}{5} = 8.0$

Distribution C

Scores	X − M	|X − M|	(X − M)²	
22	+6	6	36	$M = \dfrac{80}{5} = 16.0$
19	+3	3	9	
16	0	0	0	
13	−3	3	9	$A.D. = \dfrac{18}{5} = 3.6$
10	−6	6	36	
Σ 80	0	18	90	$\sigma^2 = \dfrac{90}{5} = 18.0$

scores and have the same mean (16.0); going from distribution A to B to C, the scores are spread out more and more. As you can see in the table, the algebraic sum of the deviations from the mean equals zero in every distribution, indicating that $\Sigma(X - M)$ does *not* reflect the spread of the scores. However, the sum of the *absolute values* of the deviations, $\Sigma|X - M|$, does increase from distribution A to B to C, and the average deviation (A.D.) increases from 1.2 to 2.4 to 3.6. Similarly, the sum of the *squared* deviations, $\Sigma(X - M)^2$, increases, and the variance (σ^2) increases from 2.0 to 8.0 to 18.0 across the distributions. Both the average deviation and the variance (the average squared deviation) reflect the spread of scores in a distribution.

The Standard Deviation

The last measure of variability that we will consider is also based on squared deviations from the mean and is in fact closely related to the variance. The *standard deviation*, symbolized by σ (read "sigma"), is simply the *square root of the variance*. The formula for the standard deviation is shown in Table 4.8; for that distribution of scores, $\sigma = \sqrt{37.75} = 6.15$.

Just to refresh your memory, the square root of a number is another number that, when multiplied by itself, yields the first number. For example, the square root of 16 is 4 because $4 \times 4 = 16$; the square root of 49 is 7 because $7 \times 7 = 49$; and so on. Since $6.15 \times 6.15 = 37.75$, 6.15 is the square root of 37.75. (Strictly speaking, any positive number has two square roots, one positive and one negative. For example, either $+4$ or -4 could be the square root of 16 because either $(+4 \times +4)$ or (-4×-4) equals 16. However, in calculating the standard deviation the *positive* square root is always used.)

Let's look at a few more examples of standard deviations. Keep in mind that the standard deviation is the square root of the variance. For the three distributions in Table 4.9, the variances were 2.0 (distribution A), 8.0 (distribution B), and 18.0 (distribution C). We can calculate the standard deviation of each distribution by calculating the square root of the variance in each case. For distribution A, $\sigma = \sqrt{2.0} = 1.41$; for distribution B, $\sigma = \sqrt{8.0} = 2.83$; for distribution C, $\sigma = \sqrt{18.0} = 4.24$. As you can see, the standard deviation increases (from 1.41 to 2.83 to 4.24) as the scores in a distribution are more spread out.

All of the measures of variability that we have considered have the property of getting numerically larger as the scores in a distribution spread out more on the measurement scale. Quite obviously, each measure of variability indexes spread in its own special way. The standard deviation is similar to the average deviation in that both use deviations of scores from the mean; the average deviation uses the absolute values of the deviations while the standard deviation is based on the squares of the deviations. For any set of scores, the standard deviation will be slightly larger than the average deviation. For the three distributions in Table 4.9, the standard deviations are 1.41, 2.83, and 4.24 while the average deviations are 1.2, 2.4, and 3.6. As you can see, the standard deviation is slightly larger in each case.

The total range, interquartile range, average deviation, and standard deviation all represent distances on the scale of measurement (in different ways). The variance does *not*; rather, the variance is a *squared* distance. Since the standard deviation is the square root of this "squared distance," the standard deviation itself is a distance on the measurement scale. With the exception of the variance, each measure of variability could be pictured as a line of a given length (the variance must be pictured as an area). For example, if the scores in Table 4.8 represented the heights of some plants (measured in inches), the total range, interquartile range, average deviation, and standard deviation could each be pictured as a line so many inches in length (the variance would be pictured as an area of so many square inches). Figure 4.7 illustrates the measures of variability in this way.

The average deviation, standard deviation, and variance are all based on deviations from the mean. These three measures thus use more of the information available in a set of scores (i.e., each score's deviation contributes), which tends to make them better, more reliable measures of variability than the total range (which depends only on the highest and lowest scores) or the interquartile range (which reflects only the spread of the middle percent of the scores). As we have seen, the average deviation and the standard deviation are numerically similar, the standard deviation being slightly larger for any set of scores. The average deviation is fairly easy to understand intuitively—it's the average distance of the scores from the mean. It is difficult to make a comparable statement about the standard deviation. Its formula is more complicated, involving squaring deviations from the mean, summing them, dividing by the number of scores, and then taking a square root. Indeed, you might wonder why we bother with

Figure 4.7. Illustration of measures of variability for the scores in Table 4.8 (heights of plants in inches).

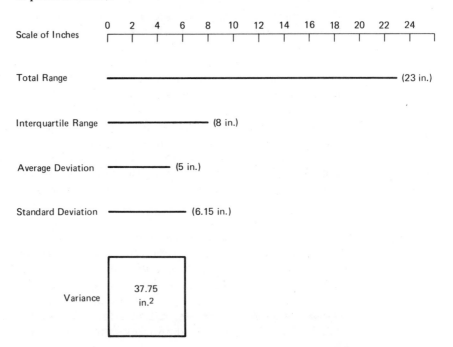

it! Why not just use the average deviation and forget the complications? The general answer is that the standard deviation is much more involved in formal statistical theory than the average deviation. What this means is that, if we want to use statistical theory to help us understand and describe data, the standard deviation is the measure of variability that we're likely to use. Let's now consider one use of the standard deviation in conjunction with statistical theory.

NORMAL DISTRIBUTIONS

Mathematicians have created many theoretical frequency distributions that, because they are theoretical creations, are described very precisely and are known to have certain properties. We will shortly examine one very useful type of theoretical distribution, but first, what is meant by a theoretical distribution? A set of scores or frequency distribution that is based on actually making observations is an *empirical* distribution; the examples we have used (heights, exam scores, etc.) would be empirical distributions. In contrast, a *theoretical* distribution is *not* based on actually making observations; rather, it is generated by an *equation* or formula. In effect theoretical distributions are *models.* If we go out and collect some scores, our empirical distribution will *not* be *exactly* like any theoretical distribution. However, if the empirical distribution is reasonably similar to some theoretical distribution, we can make use of what is known about the theoretical distribution and apply that knowledge to the measurements we are actually obtaining. We will consider one type of theoretical distribution and see how knowledge of the theoretical distribution can be applied to actual data.

One extremely useful kind of theoretical distribution is a *normal distribution.* A normal distribution is generated by a particular equation or formula (which will not be presented here). The equation can be used to generate many different normal distributions. To use the equation to generate a particular normal distribution, two numerical values must be inserted into the equation. Each time a different pair of numerical values is inserted, a different normal distribution is generated. All normal distributions are related to each other because all are generated by the same basic equation; they differ from each other because different numerical values are used.

Now we come to the heart of the matter. The two numerical values that must be inserted into the equation for a normal distribution are the *mean* and the *standard deviation.* In other words, select a value for the mean and a value for the standard deviation, insert these values into the equation, and a particular normal distribution will be generated. For each different pair of values (mean, standard deviation), a different normal distribution will be generated. However, all normal distributions share certain characteristics. For example, all normal distributions are perfectly *symmetrical* and perfectly *unimodal* (because of the nature of the generating equation). In addition, all normal distributions have the characteristics shown in Table 4.10.

To interpret this table, concentrate on the first and second columns. An example of the type of information contained in the table is that, for a value on the scale of measurement that is 3.5 standard deviations *above* the mean, 99.98 percent of the frequencies in the normal distribution will be below it. For a point that is 1.5 standard deviations *below* the mean, just 6.68 percent of the frequencies will be below it. The entries in Table 4.10 are just a sample; for a normal distribution one can determine the percent of frequencies below values that are any number of standard deviations above or below the mean.

PROBLEM
_____

In a normal distribution with M = 64 and σ = 5, what percent of the distribution will be below a value of 74 on the measurement scale?

Table 4.10   Characteristics of Normal Distributions

NUMBER OF σ's FROM MEAN	% TOTAL FREQUENCY BELOW	% TOTAL FREQUENCY BETWEEN VALUE AND MEAN
+3.5	99.98	49.98
+3.0	99.87	49.87
+2.5	99.38	49.38
+2.0	97.72	47.72
+1.5	93.32	43.32
+1.0	84.13	34.13
+0.7	75.80	25.80
+0.5	69.15	19.15
+0.3	61.79	11.79
0.0	50.00	0.00
−0.3	38.21	11.79
−0.5	30.85	19.15
−0.7	24.20	25.80
−1.0	15.87	34.13
−1.5	6.68	43.32
−2.0	2.28	47.72
−2.5	0.62	49.38
−3.0	0.13	49.87
−3.5	0.02	49.98

To solve this problem we must determine how many standard deviations above or below the mean a value of 74 is and then consult Table 4.10. First calculate (X − M), the algebraic deviation of 74 from the mean: 74 − 64 = +10. This tells us that 74 is 10 units on the scale of measurement above the mean of 64. However, we need to know how many standard deviations above the mean 74 is (remember, the standard deviation is a distance on the scale of measurement). To determine this we need to divide (X − M) by σ: +10/5 = +2.00, indicating that 74 is two standard deviations above the mean. Consulting Table 4.10, we see that 97.72 percent of the frequencies will fall below a value that is two standard deviations above the mean. Therefore, in a normal distribution with M = 64 and σ = 5, 97.72 percent of the scores will be below 74.

PROBLEM

In a normal distribution with M = 37, σ = 4, what percent of the distribution lies *above* a scale value of 33?

The answer to this problem is 84.13 percent, determined in the following manner: The deviation of 33 from the mean is (X − M) = 33 − 37 = −4; dividing this deviation by the value of the standard deviation indicates that 33 is one standard deviation below the mean; −4/4 = −1.00. The second column in Table 4.10 shows that 15.87 percent of a normal distribution falls *below* a scale value one standard deviation below the mean. Therefore the rest of the frequencies, 100% − 15.87% = 84.13%, must lie above that value.

z Scores

These problems illustrate how one can determine various kinds of information about normal distributions as well as stressing the importance of the mean as a measure of central tendency and the standard deviation as a measure of variability. Notice again that the useful item for solving a normal distribution problem is "the number of standard deviations above or below the mean." This quantity has a symbolic representation, the *z score* or simply *z*. Thus we can write the formula for *z* as follows:

$$z = \frac{X - M}{\sigma}$$

Using the term *z* or *z score* saves the trouble of always saying "number of standard deviations above or below the mean" and makes it convenient to employ this concept (*z*) in other formulas.

Look again at Table 4.10. Notice that column 2 indicates that 50 percent of a normal distribution lies below a z score of 0.0. Of course a scale value 0 from the mean is the mean itself; in a normal distribution half of the frequencies are above the mean and one half are below it. In other words, in a normal distribution the mean and the median are the same value because normal distributions are perfectly symmetrical. The symmetrical nature of normal distributions is also indicated by the entries in column 3, which gives the percent of the distribution that lies between any z value and the mean. For example, column three indicates that 43.32 percent of a normal distribution lies between $z = -1.5$ and the mean; another 43.32 percent lies between the mean and $z = +1.5$. You can see in column 3 that the percent frequency between a z value and the mean is the same for both the positive and negative versions of that z value because of the symmetrical nature of normal distributions.

The Assumption of Normality

Both Table 4.10 and Figure 4.8 illustrate other properties of normal distributions. Most of a normal distribution is concentrated fairly close to the mean—more than two-thirds of the total frequencies are within one standard deviation of the mean (34.13% between M and $z = +1.00$, and 34.13% between M and $z = -1.00$). Nearly all of the frequencies lie within three standard deviations of the mean. Whenever it is reasonable to assume that what one is measuring yields a roughly normal distribution, all of these

Figure 4.8. Schematic representation of a normal distribution showing relative frequencies within given standard deviation distances from the mean.

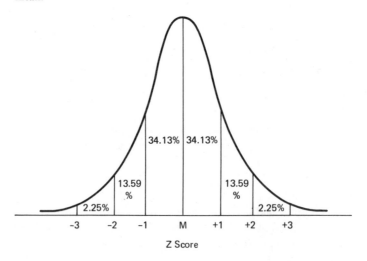

facts about normal distributions can be fairly accurately applied to the empirical distribution. Telling someone the mean and standard deviation of your distribution is really telling a great deal if it is reasonable to assume that your distribution is approximately normal in form.

PROBLEM

A paper-and-pencil personality test is given to a large number of people. The mean score is 50 and the standard deviation of the distribution is 10. Assuming that the distribution of test scores is (roughly) normal, answer the following questions: (1) Between what two test scores would you expect to find the middle two-thirds of the scores? (2) What would you expect to be the highest and lowest scores achieved? (3) What value would you predict for Q_3?

The answers to these questions are determined as follows: (1) Since about two thirds of the frequencies in a normal distribution lie between $z = +1.00$ and $z = -1.00$, we would expect about two thirds of the test scores to be between $50 + 10 = 60$ and $50 - 10 = 40$. (2) Since virtually all of the frequencies in a normal distribution lie within three standard deviations above and below the mean, we might expect the highest score to be about $z = +3.00$, or $M + 3\sigma = 50 + 3(10) = 50 + 30 = 80$, and the lowest score to be $z = -3.00$, or $M - 3\sigma = 50 - 3(10) = 50 - 30 = 20$. (3) Since about 75 percent of the frequencies fall below $z = +0.7$ in a normal distribution ($75\% = \frac{3}{4}$), we would expect Q_3 to be about $M + 0.7\sigma = 50 + 0.7(10) = 50 + 7 = 57$.

We have covered considerable ground in discussing the organization and description of data. Starting with an unorganized set of scores, we have considered various methods of summarizing information about the scores. The general purpose of these methods is to make the data more intelligible, and doing so usually involves ignoring some of the information available in the original set of scores. For example, constructing a grouped frequency distribution involves the loss of information concerning the frequencies of the individual scores that are grouped together into a larger interval. The mode or median provides some information about where a distribution is located on the scale of measurement, but a measure of central tendency alone obviously provides only partial information about the distribution. In the preceding section we saw that the combination of the mean, the standard deviation, and the assumption that one has a normal distribution is indeed a powerful one, enabling a person to reconstruct the distribution with considerable detail.

Earlier we discussed reasons why psychologists might prefer to measure characteristics in such a manner that they obtain unimodal and symmetrical frequency distributions—such distributions make it easier to distinguish individuals within a distribution and to compare distributions with each other. Now we can see another reason for this preference: A unimodal and symmetrical distribution might well resemble a normal distribution, enabling the researcher to apply knowledge of normal distributions to the data. We have covered a few of these applications and will encounter further uses of "the assumption of normality" in later chapters.

Another point may be made about the "assumption of normality." It is clearly useful for a researcher to obtain measurements that are approximately normally distributed, for the reasons we have just discussed. But can we go beyond this practical approach? Is it possible to develop an argument that normal distributions *should* be obtained? Such an argument exists, and it takes the following form: Assume that a characteristic is subject to a large number of influences. For example, there is not just one reason for a person's achieving a particular score on an intelligence test; rather, there are many reasons. Assume further that each contributing influence has a relatively small effect on the characteristic and that each influence operates independently of the others. If one assumes that the characteristic being measured is influenced by many different factors, that each factor has a small effect by itself, and that the factors operate independently of each other, then one might reasonably expect that the measurements of that characteristic will have a normal distribution.

To make this argument a little less abstract, consider the following illustration: Suppose we have 40 coins, each of course having a "head" side and a "tail" side. Each coin represents a factor influencing some characteristic; thus the characteristic is influenced by 40 factors. The "head" side of each coin indicates that an individual's score when the characteristic is measured will be a little higher than the mean, while the "tail" side results in a score a little lower than the mean. Any individual's score is determined by dropping the 40 coins on the floor and counting the number of heads and tails. Each head pushes the score a little above the mean, while each tail pushes the score a little below the mean; the person's score will depend on the numbers of heads and tails. Notice that each coin lands heads or tails without regard for what the other coins are doing (independent factors).

The idea is that each person's score is a result of one outcome of dropping the 40 coins. Most of the time we would expect the 40 coins to land heads and tails in about equal numbers, which means that the positive and negative influences will fairly well cancel each other out; thus we would expect most scores to be near the mean. Sometimes, by chance, the 40 coins will land with noticeably more heads than tails, resulting in a score somewhat higher than the mean. Just as often we would expect to see noticeably more tails than heads, resulting in a score somewhat lower than the mean. Only rarely would we expect the 40 coins to almost all land heads or almost all land tails, resulting in either a very high or a very low score. To summarize, we would expect most of the scores to be near the mean, smaller percentages of the scores to be moderately above or below the mean, and very few of the scores to be very much above or below the mean. I'm sure you recognize the characteristics of a normal distribution in this description. The coin-dropping analogy illustrates the essential features of the argument that psychological characteristics that are influenced by a large number of independent, small-effect factors should have normal distributions.

This argument is quite plausible and is a reason why many psychologists expect the measurements they obtain to have (roughly) normal distributions. However, two cautions need to be given. First, there are many psychological and biological characteristics for which it is fairly easy to argue that this model does not apply. For example, what if some factors have larger influences than others, or what if the factors don't operate independently? In such cases the expected distribution would be quite different from a normal distribution. Consequently the notion that normal distributions ought to be found might apply to only some characteristics. The second caution is that the researcher has considerable influence on how a characteristic will be measured and therefore on the kind of distribution that will be obtained. It is possible that one might obtain a roughly normal distribution if one *chooses* to measure a characteristic one way but a very different distribution if an alternate measurement technique is chosen. In general, the notion that measures are largely created by the researcher makes it hard to accept an argument that there is some "natural" form of measurement that is simply discovered by the investigator. As you might expect, it is easy to find people who will debate this issue with great energy.

SUMMARY

Beginning with an unorganized collection of scores, researchers employ a variety of techniques to organize and describe their data. A frequency distribution shows the actual number of cases, the proportion of the total number of cases, or the percentage of the total number of cases that is associated with each score value. A *cumulative* frequency distribution indicates, for each score value, the number of cases having that score or a lower one. When a large number of score values is obtained, a grouped frequency distribution is often constructed. In a *grouped* frequency distribution the original score values are grouped into fewer but larger categories and the frequency for each larger category is presented. A grouped frequency distribution can make it easier to get an overall impression of a set of scores, but some information is lost when the larger categories are formed.

Graphic displays of frequency distributions are often used. When the scale of measurement is discrete (only a limited number of values is possible), bar graphs are used. In a bar graph a bar is drawn for each category, with the length of the bar representing the frequency in that category. For continuous measurement scales (an infinite number of values is possible in principle), frequency polygons are typically used. A *frequency polygon* is a form of line graph showing how frequencies change from one category to another and giving the impression of continuity across categories.

Frequency distributions can be described in terms of modality and skewness. *Modality* refers to the number of categories with exceptionally high frequencies; if just one category stands out as having the highest frequency, the distribution is *unimodal;* if two categories stand out, the distribution is *bimodal. Skewness* refers to the manner in which frequencies are distributed at various distances away from the point of highest frequency. In *symmetrical* distributions, the remaining frequencies are distributed to equal extents on both sides of the maximum-frequency point. In a *positively skewed* distribution, the frequencies are extended more to the right than to the left, while in a *negatively skewed* distribution the frequencies are extended more to the left than to the right.

A measure of central tendency is a number intended to indicate the location of a distribution on the scale of measurement; in simple terms, it represents the "average" score. Several different measures are used. The *mode* is the most frequently occurring score, while the *median* is the "middle score" or the value on the measurement scale that has half of the frequencies below it and half above it. The *arithmetic mean* is calculated by summing the values of all scores in a distribution and dividing that sum by N, the number of scores. In strict terms, scores on an interval scale are needed to justify calculating the mean; the median is appropriate for sets of scores on at least an ordinal scale, while the mode may be used with any kind of scale. Where all three measures of central tendency may reasonably be calculated, the mean is generally preferred because only the mean directly reflects the value of every score in a distribution. However, some people prefer to use the median for severely skewed distributions.

Measures of variability are numbers that reflect the spread of a set of scores over the scale of measurement. All measures of variability are designed to increase in numerical value as the spread of scores increases. The *total range* is the distance between the highest and lowest scores, while the *interquartile range* is the distance covered by the middle 50 percent of a distribution. Several measures are based on the deviations of individual scores (X's) from the mean (M) of the distribution. The *average deviation* is the average distance of the scores from the mean. The *variance* (σ^2) is the average squared distance of the scores from the mean, while the *standard deviation* (σ) is the square root of the variance. The total range, interquartile range, average deviation, and standard deviation all represent distances on the scale of measurement, reflecting in different ways the spread of a set of scores.

The mean and the standard deviation are especially useful descriptions of a distribution because they can be used to relate an empirical frequency distribution to theoretical frequency distributions called *normal distributions*. *Empirical distributions* result from actually collecting scores, while *theoretical distributions*, such as normal distributions, are generated from mathematical equations. Theoretical distributions serve as abstract models; because they are generated from equations they have specifically defined properties. All normal distributions (which are all theoretical distributions) are perfectly symmetrical and perfectly unimodal, and have relative frequencies distributed in a precise fashion. For example, in any normal distribution 34.13 percent of the frequencies lie between the mean and a point one standard deviation from the mean. In general, in a normal distribution the distribution of relative frequencies is precisely related to "number of standard deviations from the mean." A *z score* indicates "number of standard deviations above or below the mean" for any value in a frequency distribution. Knowing about normal distributions can be useful if it is reasonable to assume that a distribution of scores actually collected is similar to a normal distribution. If one knows the mean and the standard deviation of an actual set of scores and can reasonably assume that the scores follow a normal distribution, one knows a great deal about the distribution of scores.

In some circumstances it can be argued that a set of measurements should be expected to resemble a normal distribution. If it is assumed that the trait being measured is influenced by many factors, that each factor has a small influence, and that each factor operates independently, then a normal distribution of scores might reasonably be expected. Although this argument seems plausible for some traits, it is important to remember that a researcher can choose to measure a trait any of several ways and can thus influence the form of score distribution that will be obtained.

5

OBSERVATION AND GENERALIZATION

It is very rare for researchers to limit their interest to the observations they have made; rather, they usually want to generalize their findings to some larger context. In Chapter 1, I stressed the importance of the external validity of research findings for scientific purposes. Scientists seek general statements and, in any case, need to know how a particular finding fits into the overall pattern of results, how a finding is relevant to one or another topic we seek to understand. In Chapters 2 and 3, while discussing the control of variables and the characteristics of psychological research, we encountered some of the factors that can affect the generality of research findings. This chapter is devoted to the topic of external validity or generality. To simplify the discussion I will concentrate on relatively simple forms of research—those that do not involve intricate experimental procedures. However, you should keep in mind that external validity is important for all kinds of research, from simple observation to complex experiment.

We will address the topic of generalizing results from two perspectives. First we will consider how formal statistical theory can be used to make precise generalizations from what might seem to be rather limited information. In this section you will see that the "assumption of normality" (introduced in the preceding chapter) is an important part of this process. Then we will discuss the broader aspects of making generalizations, which include questions about the setting in which data are collected and the particular procedures used to make observations. A large part of this section will focus on issues that arise when researchers collect data by taking surveys or making observations in natural settings.

STATISTICAL CONSIDERATIONS

Statistical theory provides a rigorous, formal system for making generalizations. If a researcher conforms to the conditions imposed by the theory, he or she is in a position to make generalizations of considerable accuracy. We will discuss only a few points of the relevant statistical theory, just enough to enable you to understand the process that researchers frequently follow in making generalizations.

Populations and Samples

A *population* is nothing more than a defined set of cases; from a statistical viewpoint the issue is "Name your population." For example, I could define as my population of interest "all the boxes in the warehouse at 174 Main Street" or "all the cars in Cleveland" or "all the people in the opera house tonight." Of course populations like these are unlikely to be used in psychological research. Here are some examples of populations that better characterize the groups that are of interest in psychological research: "all the voters in the United States," "all the rats that could be placed in my Skinner box," "all 3-year-old children," "all the people who could be asked to learn the task I have constructed," "all arbitrarily formed groups of three college students." As these examples indicate, the populations that are of interest to psychological researchers vary considerably, but they tend to be large, rather abstractly defined sets. Because it *is* a problem, let me point out that the populations just described are incompletely defined. Take the example of "all 3-year-old children." Does this mean "all 3-year-olds currently alive in the entire world," "all normal 3-year-olds in Western cultures," "all 3-year-olds who are currently alive or who might be born in the next ten years," or what? In principle it is necessary to thoroughly specify a population, and we should not ignore the fact that it is difficult for most psychological research to accomplish this goal. However, for the moment let us assume that a population is adequately defined.

Once one has defined a population, a *sample* is defined as any subset from that population. For example, having defined a population as "the 48 students in this classroom," any group of students (2, 3, 4, 12, 18, 34, etc.) would be a sample from this population (strictly speaking, one student would be a sample of one, but ordinarily samples are thought of as containing at least two members of the population.

PROBLEM

There are 27 children in the second grade at Lincoln School. Does this group of 27 children constitute a sample or a population?

The answer to this problem can be nothing but "it depends." Since populations are a matter of definition, one needs to know what population has been defined. It would be possible to define these 27 children as a population. However, if the population had been defined as "all children in Lincoln School" or "all second-graders" or any larger group, then this group of 27 children would be a sample.

Populations and samples are not defined just for the exercise. Some characteristic of the population is of interest; that is, one is not interested in "U.S. voters" as such but in "the voting preferences of U.S. voters." The set of measurements for a population is called a *population distribution*, and it is the population distribution that is really of interest. Thus what is of interest might be "the voting preferences of U.S. voters" or "the attitudes toward morality of 3-year-olds" or "the learning scores of people who could be given the task I have constructed." It is important to realize that it is the set of some *measurements for a population* that researchers are interested in, that the population distribution is what one wishes to make generalizations about.

Once one takes into account that interest lies in the characteristics of some population distribution, it becomes possible to distinguish among better and worse samples. What is desired is a *representative sample*, one whose measurements will adequately represent the measurements in the population. By contrast, a *biased sample* is one whose measurements do not accurately represent the measurements in the population. There are many ways of obtaining a representative sample, including "dumb luck." That is, one might obtain a sample of measurements in the sloppiest possible manner but wind up with a set of measurements that accurately represent the population distribution. However, statistical theory deals with samples drawn in accordance with certain rules; if the rules are followed, it is possible to make statements about the representativeness of the sample information.

In essence, statistical theory rests on the concept of random sampling (there are more complex versions than the one we will discuss, but we will cover the basic idea). For our purposes a *random sample* can be defined as a sample obtained by a procedure that gives every member of the population an equal chance to be included. Here is an example of one (not necessarily perfect) method of selecting a random sample: The population is defined as all students in a particular school. The name of each student is written on a slip of paper and the slips of paper are placed in a box and thoroughly mixed. Then a sample of 10 students is selected by having someone reach into the box without looking, move his or her hand around in the box in an unsystematic fashion, and pick out 10 slips of paper. Roughly speaking, this procedure will yield a random sample. Notice what is needed for a random sample to be drawn: The population must be defined and the sample drawn such that each population member has an equal chance of being selected. Realistically, drawing a truly random sample is an ideal that a researcher can try to accomplish rather than something that is regularly done. To use the example just given, if the slips were not thoroughly mixed, or if the person picking the slips tended to pick slips from the right half of the box, one could argue that the sample drawn would not be truly random. Perhaps this argument strikes you as tedious or nitpicking. I mention it to emphasize that it is usually impossible for a researcher to demonstrate that he or she has really followed procedures that strictly conform to the conditions imposed by statistical theory. In practice, the relevant question is whether one can identify reasons why the sample should be considered biased—if not, it seems reasonable to consider the sample randomly drawn if one has tried to draw it in this fashion.

PROBLEM

A critic believed that the editors of a newspaper selected "letters to the editor" for publication to ensure that the majority of the letters published support the paper's editorial position, rather than simply publishing a random sample of the letters received. To check his view he selected a controversial issue, proposal X (what the issue was doesn't matter), which the paper had supported. He found that 75 percent of the letters to the editor about Proposal X which were published in the paper were in agreement with the paper's position, while a national poll of the population had shown that only 34 percent of the population favored the position endorsed by the paper. Since these percentages are clearly different, the critic concluded that his point had been demonstrated, at least for this issue—the editors did not publish a random sample of the letters received. Indicate why the critic's conclusion is not justified by the data.

The major difficulty is that the critic has mixed up samples and populations. The question is whether or not the editors publish a "random" sample of the letters they receive—that is, whether the letters published adequately represent the population of letters received. The national population has fundamentally nothing to do with the question; the national population is *not* the population that is of interest. In effect the critic is comparing the percentages in samples from two populations, the poll percentage coming from a sample of national population and the published-letter percentage coming from a sample of letters received. Comparing the percentages in the two samples tells him nothing about whether the published-letter sample is a random or otherwise representative sample of letters received. This is the essential point. We can speculate further that it might happen that letters sent to the editor tend to agree with editorial positions, assuming that people tend to read papers whose opinions they agree with and that a representative sample of readers send letters to the editor. However, this speculation is not necessary in order to criticize the critic—he has made an inappropriate comparison.

Sampling Distributions

A population distribution is a kind of theoretical distribution; that is, while one can imagine its existence (and it does exist), nobody is ever actually going to see the entire distribution. People can easily agree that there is a "distribution of heights of U.S. males over 21 years of age," but no person will ever see that whole distribution. While you can sensibly imagine various population distributions, neither you nor anyone else could sensibly imagine obtaining the measurements for the entire distribution. I emphasize that it is reasonable to imagine the existence of distributions that you will never actually see because you will need to use your imagination in this way to understand what researchers are doing when they make generalizations from samples to populations.

To understand making generalizations via statistical theory it is necessary to understand the concept of a sampling distribution. Set your imagination at full power. First imagine some population distribution; while it really makes no difference what that distribution is like, perhaps it will be easier to imagine "the distribution of heights of U.S. males over 21 years of age." This distribution exists (though we can't show it to anyone on a sheet of paper), and furthermore, this distribution has some shape, some mean, some standard deviation, some median, and so forth. If there is a distribution of heights, then there is a median height, a mean height, a highest and a lowest height, a standard deviation of the set of heights, and so on.

If you have this population distribution firmly in mind, we can proceed further. Now imagine drawing a sample of 10 heights from this population distribution, using a random sampling method, and calculating the *mean height of the sample*. Imagine recording the value of the sample mean. Now imagine drawing another sample of 10 heights and calculating and recording the value of this second sample mean. Go further and imagine drawing sample after sample of 10 cases each, calculating and recording the mean of each sample. (We can draw any number of samples we like without exhausting or changing the population, simply by placing any value we sample back into the population before sampling the next value.) It is important to realize that we could draw a very large number of samples of the same size from the population, calculating and recording the value of the mean for each sample. The record we would be producing would be the mean heights for a number of samples of size 10; this set of values of "mean heights for samples of size 10" would be a *sampling distribution*. It might be useful at this point to go back over this material to be sure that you understand how a sampling distribution is created.

Let's look again at what we have done. We started out with a distribution of individual heights—a population distribution. By repeatedly drawing random samples of size 10 from the population distribution we have created a new distribution—a sampling distribution. Each value in the sampling distribution is the mean height of a sample of 10 cases. We can now ask questions about the sampling distribution: What is the mean of the distribution of sample means? What is the standard deviation of the distribution of sample means? What is the shape of the distribution of sample means? Fortunately for us (just how fortunately you will see shortly), mathematical statisticians have worked out the answers to these questions. But before considering these answers it will be helpful to define some terms:

M = the mean of the population distribution
σ = the standard deviation of the population distribution
$\bar{X}$ = the mean of a single sample (a sample mean)
$M_{\bar{X}}$ = the mean of the distribution of sample means
$\sigma_{\bar{X}}$ = the standard deviation of the distribution of sample means (called "the standard error of the mean")
n = the size of a sample

Let's "plug in" these symbols. The population distribution is a set of individual scores, and this distribution has some mean (M), some standard deviation (σ), and some shape (which is not known). Perhaps the population distribution is a normal distribution; perhaps it has some other shape. By repeatedly drawing random samples of size n and calculating and recording the mean of each sample ($\bar{X}$), we could create a distribution of sample means ($\bar{X}$'s); this distribution has some mean ($M_{\bar{X}}$), some standard deviation ($\sigma_{\bar{X}}$), and some shape. What we would like to know is what, if anything, can be said about $M_{\bar{X}}$, $\sigma_{\bar{X}}$, and the shape of the distribution of sample means ($\bar{X}$'s). If the samples have been drawn in accordance with the requirements of statistical theory, here are the answers:

(1) $M_{\bar{X}} = M$

(2) $\sigma_{\bar{X}} = \dfrac{\sigma}{\sqrt{n}}$

(3) Even if the population distribution is *not* a normal distribution, the distribution of $\bar{X}$'s will resemble a normal distribution if the sample size (n) is large enough.

Answer (1) states that the mean of the distribution of sample means will be equal to the mean of the population from which the samples were drawn. This makes intuitive sense. If, for example, we were drawing samples from a population with M = 65, we would of course get sample means ($\bar{X}$'s) both above and below 65, but we would expect the average of the sample means—that is, $M_{\bar{X}}$—to be equal to 65 in the long run.

Answer (2) requires a preliminary comment. Just as we can imagine drawing a large number of samples of size 10 to create a distribution of sample means, we can also imagine drawing a large number of samples all of size 2, or of size 5, or of size 88, or of any size we'd like. For each sample size that we might select, we would create a different distribution of sample means. Answer (1) implies that, no matter what the sample size, the mean of the distribution of sample means ($M_{\bar{X}}$) will always be equal to the mean (M) of the population distribution. Answer (2) states, in general terms, that the variability among the sample means will decrease as the sample size increases (the equation states the precise relation between $\sigma_{\bar{X}}$ and n, the size of the samples). Answer (2) also makes intuitive sense. If we were drawing very small samples, say, $n = 2$, it wouldn't be too surprising to get a value for $\bar{X}$ that is some distance from M. On the other hand, if we were drawing larger samples, say, $n = 200$, we would expect the sample means to stay somewhat closer to M. In other words, compared to the chances of randomly selecting 2 scores considerably higher than M (thus producing a value for $\bar{X}$ considerably above M), we would expect the chances of randomly sampling 200 scores that far from M to be much smaller. As sample size increases, we expect more of the sample means to cluster closer to M.

Answer (3) is important for making generalizations, as you will see very soon. What it says is that even if we don't know the shape of the population distribution we can say something about the shape of the distribution of sample means—namely, that it's close to a normal distribution—if the sample size is large enough. This statement obviously raises the question, How large is large enough? The answer depends on how different from a normal distribution the population distribution is. If the population distribution is itself a normal distribution, then any distribution of sample means for any size (n) will be a normal distribution. If the population distribution isn't too different from a normal distribution, then the distribution of sample means for fairly small samples, say, $n = 10$, will closely resemble a normal distribution. If the population distribution is radically different from a normal distribution, then a larger value of n will be required before the distribution of sample means will approximate a normal distribution. For most of the measurements used in psychological research (few of which deviate radically from a normal distribution), a sample size of 30 might be sufficient to make it reasonable to assume that the distribution of sample means resembles a normal distribution.

Figure 5.1 illustrates the relation between sample size and the characteristics of a sampling distribution, starting with a population distribution that was deliberately chosen to be somewhat different from a normal distribution. The graphs of the various distributions are schematically drawn and are intended only to give a general impression of what the distributions would look like. As you can see, the variability of the distributions of $\bar{X}$'s decreases noticeably with an increase in sample size, and the

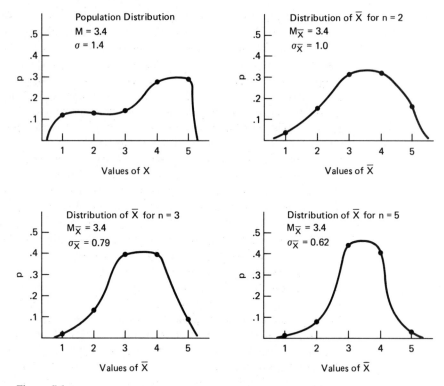

Figure 5.1.

sampling distributions rather quickly take on the general characteristics of normal distributions.

Inferences About the Population Mean

The discussion of sampling distributions might well make you think, "Well, that's fine and dandy, but so what? What is this good for?" We will now consider this issue. First let's take another look at sampling distributions. The distribution of sample means ($\bar{X}$'s) has the same mean as the population distribution ($M_{\bar{x}} = M$). What this means is that if we can say something about the mean of the sampling distribution ($M_{\bar{x}}$) we are simultaneously saying something about the population mean (M). The variability among sample means decreases as sample size increases, which means that, with large enough samples, it is likely that most sample means will be fairly close to M. In addition, the distribution of sample means is reasonably likely to resemble a normal distribution in most circumstances. Putting this all together, a distribution of sample means is likely to resemble a normal distribution whose mean is the same as the population's and whose standard deviation can be controlled by controlling sample size.

Consider what we know about normal distributions—all normal distributions, whether they are distributions of individual scores or distributions of sample means. The information about normal distributions in Table 4.10 allows us to make statements like "95.44 percent of the values in a normal distribution lie within 2 standard deviations of the mean." Keeping in mind that the standard error of the mean ($\sigma_{\bar{x}}$) is the standard deviation of a distribution of sample means, we can say that "if a distribution of sample means is approximately normal, then about 95 percent of the $\bar{X}$'s will be no more than 2 standard errors ($\sigma_{\bar{x}}$'s) from M." Suppose we are talking about a distribution of sample means based on $n = 40$ for which $M_{\bar{x}} = 38$ and $\sigma_{\bar{x}} = 2$. Assuming this to be a normal distribution, we can say that about 95 percent of the $\bar{X}$'s will be between 34 ($M_{\bar{x}} - 2\ \sigma_{\bar{x}}$) and 42 ($M_{\bar{x}} + 2\ \sigma_{\bar{x}}$). What this means is that if we randomly select one sample mean from this distribution there is a 95 percent chance that it will be between 34 and 42 (there is a 95 percent chance that it will be no more than 2 $\sigma_{\bar{x}}$ from $M_{\bar{x}}$). In practice, a researcher makes use of this fact but works "in the opposite direction."

Suppose a researcher has measured the mathematical ability (using some test) of 36 fourth-graders who can reasonably be considered a random sample from the population of fourth-graders in a city. She calculates the mean score of her sample, obtaining the value of 85.4. What can she say about the mean score for fourth-graders in the city? Her sample mean of 85.4 belongs to a sampling distribution for which the mean is the mean score for the population. Furthermore, this sampling distribution can reasonably be assumed to be a normal distribution. If so, the sample mean of 85.4 is very likely (95% chance) to be within 2 standard errors of the population mean. If the researcher knew the value of σ, the population standard deviation, she could calculate $\sigma_{\bar{x}}, = \sigma/\sqrt{n}$, and then make a rather precise statement about the value of the population mean.

Of course the researcher doesn't know the value of the population standard deviation, but she can *estimate* its value *by using the scores in her sample*.[1] Suppose she uses the 36 scores in the sample, calculates an estimate of σ, and obtains the value of 7.2. She can then calculate an estimate of $\sigma_{\bar{x}}, = 7.2/\sqrt{36} = 7.2/6 = 1.2$. At this point the researcher has the value of her sample mean ($\bar{X} = 85.4$) and an estimate of the value of the standard error of the mean (1.2). If she assumes that her sample mean belongs to a normal distribution of sample means, she can use this information to estimate the value of the population mean (M).

---

[1] The precise formula used to estimate the population standard deviation from sample data is presented in Appendix B.3. At this point, the formula is unimportant; the logic of the procedure is most important.

We know, for example, that in any normal distribution 95.44 percent of the frequencies lie within two standard deviations of the mean. Applying this knowledge to a sampling distribution of $\bar{X}$ (assuming it to be normal), we can state that about 95 percent of the $\bar{X}$'s lie within two standard errors of the mean from $M_{\bar{X}}$ (which is of course equal to M, the population mean). Applying this knowledge to this particular sample, we can state that there is about a 95 percent chance that the sample mean of 85.4 is no more than 2.4 points (2 × 1.2) from the population mean. This sample mean might be either above or below the population mean—the population mean might be lower or higher than the sample mean of 85.4. If the researcher's sample mean (85.4) is below M, it should be no more than 2.4 points below M, which means that the highest value she would expect for M is 85.4 + 2.4 = 87.8. If her sample mean is above M, it should be no more than 2.4 points above M, which means that the lowest value she would expect for M is 85.4 − 2.4 = 83.0. Thus the researcher can state that she expects the population mean to be somewhere between 83.0 and 87.8. Using the procedure we have outlined, she would be correct about 95 percent of the time.

The procedure of setting numerical limits for the value of the population mean is known as establishing a *confidence interval* for M. The "percent confidence" refers to the chances that the stated interval will include the actual value of the population mean (M). For example, a "95 percent confidence interval" for M is based on a procedure that will, 95 percent of the time, yield an interval that will include the actual value of M. Clearly the goal is to maintain a high level of confidence while establishing a confidence interval that includes a small range of values. A straightforward way of accomplishing this goal is to use larger samples. Keep in mind that the value of the standard error of the mean ($\sigma_{\bar{X}}$) is a critical factor in determining the size of the interval, and that sample size affects the value of $\sigma_{\bar{X}}$ ($\sigma_{\bar{X}} = \sigma/\sqrt{n}$). For example, if the researcher's sample mean (85.4) and estimate of the population standard deviation (7.2) had been based on a sample of $n = 100$, the estimated value of $\sigma_{\bar{X}}$ would be $7.2/\sqrt{100} = 7.2/10 = 0.72$. With the same 95 percent confidence, the researcher could estimate the population mean (M) to be somewhere between 84.0 [85.4 − 2(0.72)] and 86.8 [85.4 + 2(0.72)]. The interval is smaller (84.0–86.8 compared to 83.0–87.8) because of the larger sample size.

PROBLEM

Suppose a researcher gives an intelligence test to a sample of 25 psychology majors, obtaining a sample mean of 120. Using the 25 scores in his sample, he estimates the population standard deviation to be 15. What would be his "95 percent confidence interval" for the mean intelligence score for the population of psychology majors?

The first step in solving this problem is to calculate the value of the estimate of the standard error of the mean, $= 15/\sqrt{25} = 15/5 = 3$. A 95 percent confidence interval is based on the idea that there is a 95 percent chance that the researcher's sample mean is no more than 2 standard errors from the population mean. Thus his estimate of the highest value for M is $120 + 2(3) = 126$, and his estimate of the lowest possible value for M is $120 - 2(3) = 114$. He would therefore state that he is "95 percent confident" that the mean intelligence score for the population of psychology majors is between 114 and 126.

The procedure followed in constructing an interval estimate for the population mean can also be used to estimate other characteristics of population distributions. The details of the statistical formulas vary, but the logic of the procedure is the same. One commonly seen example of estimating population values from sample values concerns poll taking, often in connection with political elections. If a pollster found that 60 percent of the people in her sample of 1600 U.S. voters intend to vote for candidate A (rather than for candidate B) in a coming election, her 95 percent confidence interval for the percentage of the population who intend to vote for candidate A would be $58\% - 62\%$. This estimate has a 95 percent chance of being accurate, provided of course that the pollster obtained a random sample of the population. With respect to the procedure of estimating population values from sample values, two points are worth emphasizing. First, one does not usually need a particularly large sample to make a fairly accurate estimate of something like the population mean. Even if the population is extremely large, a sample of 100 is large from a statistical viewpoint, and samples of 1500 are "enormous." Second, the procedure for estimating population values works very well if one has a random sample of the population, but not otherwise. In practice, the problem that is likely to be faced by a researcher who wants to estimate a population value is obtaining a random sample; getting a large enough sample typically is not the major problem.

Sampling Problems

Statistical theory provides an excellent mechanism for making estimates of population values with considerable precision when all one has is information about a sample. However, as we have seen, the procedure is based on the requirement that one has a random sample from the target population. There are two general problems related to meeting this requirement that occur with noticeable frequency in psychological research, and they deserve our attention.

A researcher might be able to define his or her population with complete accuracy and to conceive of a method of obtaining a random sample. To strictly conform to the requirement of statistical theory, he or she must then actually obtain information for that sample, and this often proves extremely difficult in practice. To illustrate the difficulty, suppose we have defined our population as "all people whose names are in the phone book for Oak Park, Illinois." Clearly, since we can readily obtain the phone book, we know what our population is without any difficulty. Suppose further that we employ a random-sampling procedure to identify 80 people who will serve as our sample from this population. What we must now do is actually contact these 80 people and obtain measurements for them. It would not be surprising if we used the telephone to contact our sample, assuming that the information we want could be obtained in this way. We work diligently, making phone call after phone call, and after much effort we succeed in contacting 67 of the 80 people. The other 13 either do not answer or always give "busy signals," or they answer the phone but do not answer our questions. The problem is clear: Until we have obtained information from all 80 people, we have not obtained information from our random sample.

What about the data we do have for the 67 people who gave us information—what can we do with it? Would it be reasonable to consider the 67 people a random sample and to estimate population values as if we had data for a random sample of $n = 67$? Giving the right answer to this question is not easy. Strictly speaking, the answer is no—our random sample would be the 80 people and we obviously do not have data for that sample. However, if such strict answers were uniformly imposed, we would only rarely see a researcher making a generalization. Furthermore, we do have data for 67 out of 80 people, and it seems intuitively sensible that those data must be worth something. Keep in mind that the 67 people might be a representative sample even though they do not constitute a truly random sample. There are no hard-and-fast rules to follow in reaching a decision on this issue. The most common approach is to consider whether one can identify reasons why the sample actually obtained might be biased. If none can be found that seem compelling, that sample might reasonably be treated *as if* it were a random or representative sample. Looking at it in the opposite way, are there good reasons for us to susepct that the 13 people about whom we don't have information might well have given us data different from those we obtained from the 67 people we contacted?

Clearly one important question is how much of the intended random sample was contacted. If we had data for only 22 out of 80 people (or for 67 out of an intended 300), we should on this basis alone be suspicious about considering our obtained sample as representative. Obviously, if we had data for 79 people out of 80, it would be hard to get terribly concerned about bias, even though we do not have a truly random sample. Other considerations are likely to vary with the situation. Using our example, failing to contact people because of no answer or busy signals might not be a cause for concern, the idea being that some *randomly determined* percentage of the people we try to contact might be unavailable. If, however, we noticed that most of the 13 nonrespondents refused to answer or came from one part of the city (with it being reasonable to expect different data from different parts of the city), we should then be concerned about the representativeness of our obtained sample. It should be clear that making such judgments is difficult. Because actually getting data for a well-defined random sample is most often a problem, such judgments are regularly made by researchers in order to use the data they do have to make some generalization. It seems reasonable to treat an obtained sample as representative or random if, after careful analysis, one can find no strong reasons for suspecting bias. It is also true that in doing so one begins to "bend" statistical theory.

PROBLEM

In college courses, course ratings are typically obtained by having students complete a rating form during one of the class meetings near the end of the term. With this method it is likely that the ratings obtained present a "too favorable" picture of the course. One possible reason is that students might deliberately bias their ratings in the favorable direction in order to "put the instructor in a good mood" before final grades are determined (the validity of this argument is uncertain). There are two other reasons why the ratings obtained might give too favorable a picture, even if every student completing a rating form gives an accurate opinion. What are they?

The point at issue is that the students who complete rating forms might well represent a favorably biased sample of the students who have been exposed to the course. Students who have dropped the course, and therefore might plausibly be expected to have less favorable opinions, are not given a chance to offer their views. Of course it could be argued that the opinions of those who have dropped the course (and thus have not experienced all of it) should not be included. The second reason is that the students completing rating forms might be a biased sample of those who are still in the course when the ratings are obtained. Assuming that class attendance is optional, as it is at most colleges, the students who elect to attend class (and thus get to complete rating forms) might be expected to have more favorable opinions than those who choose not to attend. What these arguments illustrate is that in assessing the representativeness of the sample providing ratings it would be useful to know the percentage of the students still in the course who actually submitted ratings and the percentage of the students beginning the course who are still enrolled.

The second sampling problem that literally plagues psychological research concerns the fact that much research is based on what can be called "samples of convenience." The idea of a sample of convenience is that rather than having a well-defined population from which a sample is drawn by some random method the researcher employs a group of subjects who are available or accessible, thus obtaining information for a sample from an unknown population. That is, it is not clear what population the sample might represent. Much experimental research with human subjects employs college students who volunteer or who are fulfilling a course requirement, that is, students coming from a particular college and often from a particular course in a particular college. To what population may the results of the experiment be generalized? While one can imagine, in abstract statistical terms, that such samples come from some population—that is, that the sample means belong to some sampling distribution—describing the population might be an impossible task. Notice that the students have not been randomly selected from a list of student volunteers, a list of students in a particular course, a list of students at a particular college, or most obviously, a list of members of any larger group. While it is possible that the results obtained with subjects selected in this fashion *might* be generalizable to all the students in a course or in a college, to all college students in the country, to all adult humans, to all humans, or even to all organisms, the simple fact is that the generality of the results is unknown. This problem is not limited to research with college students; similar procedures are used in most research employing children, rats, monkeys, cats, and other organisms.

The problems of representativeness produced by using samples of convenience are by no means limited to experimental investigations conducted in "laboratories." A researcher interested in studying, say, psychotic patients is most likely to make use of psychotic patients who are located in some nearby facility. Clearly no population of psychotic patients has been defined from which the subjects have been randomly selected, except for the possibility of defining the population as "psychotic patients in this facility." Consequently one does not know whether the findings might be generalized to "all psychotic patients." Similar remarks can be made about research employing various patient groups or other noticeable segments of the general population.

Samples of convenience are used for several reasons. Experimenters are usually interested primarily in the internal validity of their results, in trying to ensure that they can accurately assess the effects of the variables they manipulate, with the issue of generality of secondary concern. However, practical limitations might be the major reason why samples of convenience are employed. Researchers have limited resources—manpower, money, and to varying extents, time. In terms of these resources, the cost of identifying the members of a well-defined and large population, selecting a random sample, and actually contacting that sample is frequently prohibitive. In addition, defining a population or contacting the members of a sample might require the cooperation of individuals or institutions, such as hospital administrators, school principals, or prison systems, who are not themselves engaged in research and might, for various reasons, fail to provide the necessary cooperation. A researcher can easily face the choice between employing subjects of unknown representativeness and doing nothing at all.

In assessing the generality of findings based on samples of convenience, the common approach seems to be, "If you are wondering whether my results can be generalized to _____, can you think of a reason why they might not apply? If not, they probably apply." This approach clearly lacks a theoretical basis such as statistical theory, yet it is not completely unreasonable. Information about the generality of such findings can be obtained by repeating investigations. If a number of different investigators, each employing his or her own sample of convenience, obtain comparable results, one's confidence in the generality of the findings would and should increase. Achieving statements of generality in this fashion is slow and unsystematic; the history of psychological research indicates that findings based on samples of convenience, while sometimes achieving generality through repeated investigations, frequently are found to be of very limited generality. An attitude of caution is therefore appropriate.

THE CONDITIONS OF OBSERVATION

Our discussion so far has concerned the statistical aspects of making generalizations, with emphasis on the definition of target populations and the collection of data from representative samples of subjects. We will now consider the issue of generality in broader terms. The idea is that in asking what, *in general,* we learn from the results of an investigation we must examine many aspects of the research that is conducted. To illustrate the extended scope of the discussion to follow, consider again the example of asking voters how they intend to vote in a coming election. In the first part of this chapter we were concerned with the basis on which one might make accurate statements about the percentage of voters in the population favoring a particular candidate by using the percentage obtained for a sample. Suppose that the kinds of issues discussed earlier were all handled satisfactorily—that, having found that 57 percent of the people in the sample intend to vote for candidate A, we could state with all the accuracy allowed by statistical theory that between 54 percent and 60 percent of the voting population intends to vote for candidate A. Having resolved these issues, numerous questions remain, including the following: While we might have a good idea of the percentage of voters who currently favor candidate A, what does this tell us about how they will actually vote in the election two weeks later? Is it possible that people might have had some tendency to avoid endorsing candidate B even though they are favorably disposed toward that candidate? Could we have asked the question in such a way as to bias the respondent's answers in one direction or the other?

Psychological research takes a number of different forms; different types of research usually have different primary goals, and each has its own strengths and weaknesses. Before discussing some specific issues related to the generality of research findings, it should be helpful to briefly consider several common forms of research and their general strengths and weaknesses. Methods of investigation vary in terms of the degree of control the researcher can exercise over the situation in which observations are made, the kinds of measurements obtained, and the time at which observations will be made. Methods also differ with respect to the possibilities for manipulating variables, controlling the influence of differences among subjects, and obtaining subjects of different types. Differences in these aspects influence the usefulness of the findings that are obtained.

Research in Natural Settings

The primary reason for conducting research in natural settings is to collect data while having the minimum possible influence on the situation. The extreme version would be to make observations of organisms who are doing nothing other than what they would be doing if the observations were not being made. For example, suppose you wanted to collect data concerning children's sandbox play. What you might do is select a sandbox on some basis, wait for children to show up to play in the sandbox, and make the desired observations while making the maximum effort to avoid influencing what the children do. Clearly a primary concern of the researcher electing to do research in this way is the generality of the results obtained. The researcher is trying to study organisms "doing the things they ordinarily do." If the behavior of interest is "sandbox play," that is in fact what the researcher is observing.

The possible gains in generality that can be made by studying behavior in natural settings are not necessarily easy to achieve, and certain losses also occur. For example, such research can be extremely inefficient—what if no children show up to play? Observing behavior in natural settings typically involves large amounts of time (and perhaps other expenses) relative to the amount of data collected. For example, a researcher who is interested in "reactions to aggression" might have to observe much behavior unrelated to that interest, having to wait until an aggressive act occurs in order to observe reactions to it.

Obtaining representative data in natural settings involves other problems. Notice that the investigator might have no control over who the subjects will be and usually has little information about them. The researcher chooses the setting (e.g., a sandbox) and gets information from subjects who, for whatever reason, happen to behave in that setting when observations are being made. Numerous questions arise: To what extent does the particular sandbox represent "sandboxes in general"? Are the children who play in the observed sandbox representative of "children who play in sandboxes"? Have the observations been made in such a way that an adequate sampling of "sandbox play" has been obtained? For the moment assume that it is true that children tend to be more aggressive just before lunch (11 A.M.–noon) than earlier or later in the day. A researcher who makes the majority of his or her observations late in the morning would then get a misleading impression of the amount of aggression occurring in sandboxes generally.

The hallmark of scientific observation is making observations systematically. There is a vast difference between, say, sitting in a park noticing "what catches the eye" and making systematic observations. Because there is in a natural setting so much uncertainty about who will do something, when they will do something, and what they will do, making systematic observations often requires special procedures. The observer in a natural setting must guard against having "what catches the eye" influence the data collected.

Observations are made systematically in several ways. For example, one would carefully select a number of sandboxes in which to make observations in order to have a broader and more representative sample of "sandbox behavior." For similar reasons, the investigator might plan to make observations equally often at various times of the day. To minimize the influence of extraneous factors on the observations recorded, two procedures are commonly employed. Typically something like an observational checklist is used—the observer is trained prior to being sent into the field and is instructed regarding how observations shall be recorded. The observer must have some idea of what to watch for and must have criteria for categorizing behavior so that reliable data can be collected. In addition to using observational checklists, researchers often employ a procedure called *time sampling*, which means that the observer, rather than continuously monitoring the situation, makes observations only during predetermined periods. A simple time-sampling scheme would be to make observations for two minutes, take two minutes off, observe for two minutes, take two minutes off, and so on. Time sampling is used to avoid fatigue and to reduce the influence of extraneous factors on the data; if an observer attempts to continuously monitor the situation, it is likely that his or her attention will fluctuate, in which case the observations are more likely to be affected by events that "catch the eye." Designing a good observational system is not an easy task; in addition, the fundamental data are usually no more than records of occurrences in various behavioral categories. Making more precise measurements is extremely difficult in natural settings.

Although the basic reason for doing research in natural settings is to observe ordinary behavior in ordinary circumstances, it is possible to do certain kinds of experiments in natural settings. Recall that an experiment is a study in which the investigator manipulates at least one variable. The trick to doing experiments in natural settings is to manipulate a variable without affecting the "naturalness" of the situation. Here are some examples of experiments that might be conducted in natural settings (these are not necessarily good experiments, but they do involve manipulation of a variable in a natural setting): From week to week a restaurant owner alternates between giving customers a free glass of wine and doing nothing, relating this manipulation to the amount of money that customers spend. A researcher sends a number of assistants to shop at various stores, instructing some assistants to "act belligerently" and others to "be very nice," and observe the reactions of store clerks. A teacher of two fifth-grade classes writes positive comments on the test papers in one class while only indicating the grade for the other class, and observes changes in test scores over a period of time.

While experiments can be done in natural settings, they are difficult to conduct in such conditions. One reason is that getting control over a variable in a natural setting can be close to impossible. For example, suppose a researcher wants to study the effect of supervisor behavior on worker productivity. To do an experiment the researcher would in effect have to find a company that will let him determine which type of supervisor is assigned to various worker groups; finding such a company might take forever. A second reason is that manipulating a variable might destroy the naturalness of the setting; the most common problem is that human subjects might discover or even suspect that they are being studied, in which case it can no longer be claimed that the setting is "natural."

To sum up, research in natural settings is intended to maximize the generality of the findings by observing behavior in ordinary situations. Achieving representative results requires adequate sampling of settings and the development of schemes for obtaining systematic observations. There is usually little control over variables operating in the situation, and manipulating variables is possible but difficult. In all cases the researcher faces the possibility of destroying the naturalness of the situation by making observations. Later in this chapter we will discuss the ethical issues that are raised by making observations of people who do not know that their behavior is being studied.

Surveys

Surveys are now commonplace in our lives. Taking a survey basically involves obtaining information from a sample of human subjects. Compared to research in natural settings, surveys differ in four major ways: (1) The person participating in a survey knows that he or she is a subject of study. (2) The subject must agree to participate if data are to be obtained. (3) Participating in a survey represents an interruption of "everyday life." (4) Typically, survey takers strongly limit the possible responses that a subject may give and rely heavily on verbal questions and answers.

Let's concentrate on the special properties of surveys as they relate to the issue of generality. While surveys are frequently intended to yield information about everyday behavior, the survey itself does not involve observations of such behavior. For example, a survey taker who is interested in how male workers react to having a female supervisor would in some way interview the workers rather than observe them at work. Because survey information about behavior comes from self-reports rather than from observations, there is the question of the extent to which self-reports accurately represent the behavior about which the report is made. A reasonable starting point is to assume that the report is accurate unless one can identify specific reasons why the self-report might be inaccurate. However, there are several reasons why a person's self-report might be inaccurate, including failures of memory, unwillingness to provide accurate information, biases due to the manner in which the survey is taken, and inadequate self-knowledge (the survey requires that the respondent be aware of his or her own tendencies, but the person might have no clear idea of his or her own behavior with respect to some particular question). We will consider some of these issues in greater detail later in the chapter. For the moment three comments can be made: (1) Problems concerning the accuracy of self-reports apply to any study using self-reports (including laboratory experiments). (2) Surveys rely heavily on self-reports and are thus especially subject to the problems imposed by using such reports. (3) An investigator can limit his or her statements to "reported behavior" and make no claim that the reports accurately represent the behavior in question; doing so places the investigator above criticism for overstating his or her conclusions, but still leaves the generality of the results in question.

Collection of survey data requires the cooperation of the respondents. To put it simply, the generality of survey data becomes more suspect as the number of people who choose not to respond increases. Earlier in the chapter we discussed the importance of actually obtaining data from the members of a randomly selected sample. However well an investigator might have chosen the sample from which he or she intends to get data, the important question concerns the sample from which data are actually obtained. When the entire sample is not measured, the relevant questions refer to the percentage of the intended sample for which data are not available and the reasons why data were not obtained. When the percentage of nonrespondents is small, the obtained data are likely to be subject to at most a small bias; as this percentage increases, the representativeness of the obtained data becomes more doubtful. When data are not obtained for some subjects, one should attempt to determine whether the missing data might differ from those obtained. The question is whether the people for whom data were not obtained might be expected to give different responses than those who did respond. For example, might the people who were not home when the interviewer called be expected to give different responses than those who were at home? There is no general answer to such questions; rather, the possibility of bias must be considered relative to the particular survey. However, one type of nonrespondent is always a source of concern: The person who has been contacted and asked to participate in the survey but refuses to participate might well yield different data (if only we could obtain them) than those who agreed to participate.

The fact that the person who responds to a survey is aware of being studied can be partly responsible for failures to obtain data and can lead to other difficulties as well. The issue is the extent to which a person will provide accurate information, which obviously varies with the nature of the survey. Generally, people are reluctant to give information about "personal" items, particularly if responding might involve giving "socially undesirable" responses. For example, one is likely to get more, or more accurate, responses to a question such as "How many children are there in the family?" than to a question like "How often do you use hallucinogenic drugs?" The accuracy of responses is also related to the person's perception of the source of the survey, its purpose, and the degree of anonymity involved. The same survey might well yield quite different findings when conducted by a university, the city government, or the Communist party. A survey whose results might be used for social action can yield different findings than one conducted simply to gain information; the former can encourage respondents to give answers that might lead to actions they consider desirable. Consider the possible differences between workers' answers to the question "Are you satisfied with your present salary?" when asked by company management and their answers to this question when asked by a university professor who has no connection with the company and no potential power to affect workers' incomes.

In addition to these factors, the degree of anonymity felt by the respondent is likely to affect his or her responses. It is generally believed that the more the respondent feels that his or her answers will be anonymous, the more accurate those responses will be. Obviously, this depends on the nature of the information sought; anonymity is more likely to affect the giving of personal information compared to giving relatively "impersonal" information such as whether one owns one's home or rents it. Studies have demonstrated differences when questionnaires are distributed such that respondents can readily see that the investigator will not be able to determine who filled out which form, compared to distributing and collecting questionnaires such that respondents are well aware that the investigator will know which person filled out which form. Surveys are taken by various methods, including mail surveys, telephone surveys, and the use of personal interviews. In rough terms, as one goes from mail (depending on possible coding of return envelopes or questionnaires) to telephone to personal interviews the respondent is placed in a less anonymous position and, further, is required to give responses more in the "presence" of another person. Choosing among these methods presents the investigator with a problem, however; while an obviously uncoded mail survey might produce the maximum anonymity, mail surveys tend to have low response rates (it is easier to discard a mailed questionnaire than it is to refuse to talk to someone who contacts you personally).

Surveys employ verbal statements or questions to which a person is asked to respond. Consequently the wording of the statements or questions is important, both because the respondent must understand what he or she is being asked to respond to and because one should avoid biasing answers by the way in which the question is asked. It is likely that one would obtain different percentages of "yes" answers to the questions "Do you favor reducing the budget for the Department of Defense even though the country's national security will be dangerously weakened?" and "Do you favor reducing the budget for the Department of Defense and thus reducing the tax burden on the ordinary citizen?" Notice that the simpler question "Do you favor reducing the budget for the Department of Defense?" might leave the respondent somewhat hesitant—he might be wondering what the consequences will be—but such a question is clearly preferable to a "loaded" question and probably better than attempting to point out a large number of possible consequences, both positive and negative (the added information can confuse the respondent).

Responses to surveys are typically simple in form. The person may be allowed a "free response" by asking an open-ended question such as "What do you think is the major problem facing the city?"; however, even in this case the answers are likely to be brief and readily categorized. A common procedure is to restrict the respondent to certain choices, such as "yes" or "no"; marking a rating scale ranging from "strongly agree" to "strongly disagree"; or asking the person to select among a number of alternatives ("Which of the following do you think is the city's major problem: crime or repairing the streets or honesty in government?"). All of these methods usually yield data that can be easily analyzed, and whether one gets gross or more refined information depends on the sophistication with which the survey is constructed.

Surveys can be used simply to estimate population characteristics (e.g., the percentage of the population favoring a particular candidate) or to study relations between variables, for example, "Is there any relation between a person's income level and his or her attitude toward reducing the defense budget?" When survey data are used to study relations, it is almost always true that the variables are "naturally varying" rather than under the control of the investigator. Consequently interpreting observed relations among naturally varying variables that stem from survey research always poses problems because one does not know what other variables (which might not have been included in the survey) covary with those involved in the relationship. For example, if it is found that Catholics and Protestants differ with respect to their attitudes toward women's liberation, it is not clear whether people with different attitudes toward women's liberation tend to join different religious groups, whether there is something about being a Catholic or Protestant that is responsible for the differing attitudes, or whether some other, unstudied variable might provide the best explanation of the observed relation between religious affiliation and attitude toward women's liberation. While variables can be manipulated in surveys, the manipulations tend to concern the survey method itself rather than the variables that form the focus of the survey. It is possible to compare two versions of a question, or two kinds of interviews, and thus obtain information about the survey method, but one cannot "make" people Catholic or Protestant.

The survey method can be characterized as the indirect study of behavior because surveys rely on reports of behavior rather than observations of that behavior. However, this characterization is not completely accurate because the focus of a study is often a general trait rather than a behavioral act as such. It is important to understand the difference between a focus on behavior and a focus on a trait. An example of a behavioral focus would be a study concerned with "how a person reacts to someone of another race in a social setting." Given this focus, it should be clear that asking a black person "How would you react to a white person who sat down next to you at a party and began a conversation?" represents an indirect method compared to observing such an interaction in a party setting. In contrast, a researcher with a trait focus might be interested in "a person's attitude toward people of other races." Although there is some debate about just what *attitude* means, it seems plausible to most people that an attitude can be expressed in various ways. One can gain information about a person's attitude by asking her a question (as in a survey) or by observing certain behavior of that person (as in research in natural settings); in principle neither method can be considered "more direct" than the other. Each method has its strengths and weaknesses with respect to gaining information about the trait that is the focus of study. What can be said is that the investigator who relies on one method runs the risk of getting incomplete and possibly misleading information.

Compared to making observations in natural settings, the survey method is efficient—it is certainly easier to interview 100 people by telephone about various aspects of their jobs than to observe those 100 people at work. The survey method draws the researcher's attention to the issue of getting a representative sample of subjects, and because of the relative ease of contacting many people via a survey, the survey has certain advantages in this respect. As we have seen, the special problems of surveys concern their reliance on verbal questions and answers, which raises questions about possible biases in the information obtained. In addition, the survey allows only limited opportunities for manipulating variables.

PROBLEM

Which of the following is *not* a reasonable criticism of public-opinion polls?
(1) Respondents' behavior in the survey might differ from their behavior at other times. (2) The samples used are too small to make sensible generalizations. (3) The results obtained might be due in part to the manner in which questions are phrased. (4) The actual respondents are not always those initially selected, which can lead to biased samples.

The best answer here is (2). Most poll-taking organizations use samples of hundreds or even thousands of respondents; such samples are easily large enough to make rather precise generalizations. All of the other criticisms are much more plausible. In fact the more respected polling organizations make strong efforts to avoid asking biased questions (see alternative 3) and to contact the people who were initially selected as part of a random sample (by making repeated efforts to contact them—see alternative 4). In some circumstances there is little a pollster can do regarding alternative (1); for example, no matter how accurately one might estimate voters' opinions two weeks before an election, actual opinions at the time of the election might differ. In addition, there is an obvious difference between telling someone else whom you will vote for (as in a survey) and casting the vote in privacy (in the actual election), which might lead some people to give inaccurate information. Nonetheless, of all the problems that pollsters must face, the possibility that their samples are numerically too small for sensible generalizations is seldom a serious criticism.

Laboratory Experiments

One does not need to work in a laboratory full of fancy equipment and wear a white coat in order to do an experiment. Fundamentally, an experiment exists whenever the researcher manipulates a variable, and as we have seen, experiments can be done in natural settings and in the context of surveys. However, a great deal of psychological research does involve conducting experiments in special places (laboratories), and it is worth considering the general characteristics of such research.

The argument for conducting laboratory experiments can be described partly as the "test tube" or "vacuum chamber" argument. Experiments are done to study relations between variables, and the general argument is that important relations might be difficult to find by means of observations in natural environments because such relations might be masked by the "noise" of the environment. By controlling variables and simplifying the situation, relations between variables might be identified more readily. The laboratory experiment also shares with any experiment the characteristic that one or more variables are manipulated by the researcher; gaining such control is likely to be more feasible in the laboratory setting. Thus the laboratory experiment is characterized by manipulation of certain variables in a simplified, highly controlled situation.

Researchers conducting laboratory experiments are most likely to concentrate attention on the internal validity of their results. The primary goal is to determine the effects of manipulations as clearly as possible. To a large extent the question of interest is, Do the manipulations have clear, measurable effects? The question of the generality of the results is often of secondary interest.

In psychology, laboratory experiments typically involve observations of behavior (as does research in natural settings), although self-reports might also be used (as in surveys). The setting in which behavior occurs is *not* a natural one but one that has been specially created. Consequently there is the question of the extent to which the behavior exhibited in laboratory settings is representative of behavior in other (natural) settings. In addition, the human subject is aware of being a participant in a research study, and this raises some of the questions that apply to survey research. Finally, most psychological laboratory experiments involve "samples of convenience," making statistical generalizations somewhat questionable. Overall, laboratory experiments in psychology are strong with respect to internal validity but weak with respect to external validity or generality.

The laboratory experiment is, of course, a method borrowed from the physical sciences, where it has served extremely well. Critics have argued that in psychology, laboratory experiments have fundamental flaws, particularly when human behavior is studied (Lachenmeyer, 1970). Others have argued that laboratory experiments need to be supplemented or to some extent replaced by research in natural settings (Bronfenbrenner, 1977; Miller, 1977). Two criticisms have been made with some frequency. First, it has been argued that, more than other methods, laboratory experiments in psychology involve unrepresentative subjects and unrepresentative tasks. Second, it has been argued that human behavior depends on the person's perception or interpretation of the situation, and that since laboratory situations are perceived as different from natural settings, unrepresentative behavior occurs.

This controversy cannot be readily resolved. While some investigators have found laboratory findings to be useful sources of generalizations (e.g., Clark, 1971), others have stressed the difficulty of generalizing findings to natural settings (e.g., Repucci & Saunders, 1974). While it is proper to require criticisms of the generality of laboratory findings to be based on *plausible, well-articulated* arguments, it is also true that the typical laboratory experiment offers a weak base for making general statements. Information about the generality of laboratory findings has accumulated very slowly. The "track record" is decidedly mixed—some effects seem to hold up over variations in procedure, but there are also indications that the effects of manipulations change considerably from one situation to another. I offer three comments: First, criticisms of laboratory experiments should be separated from criticisms of the experimental method itself, since the method can be used in a variety of settings. Second, the question of the generality of laboratory findings should be considered in the context of the topic under investigation, since in psychology the evidence varies greatly from one area to another. Third, the laboratory experiment is *not* a fixed entity—it is quite possible for experimenters to create laboratory situations that resemble in important respects the natural settings to which they might wish to generalize their results.

REACTIVE AND NONREACTIVE MEASUREMENT

In discussing the various kinds of psychological research a number of problems related to the generality of findings could be mentioned. In this section several well-known problems will be described. This discussion is based on an interesting and informative book by Webb, Campbell, Schwartz, and Sechrest (1966), which is highly recommended to the interested reader. These authors identified a number of *reactive measurement* effects, most of which are biases that can occur because human subjects are aware of being observed. In contrast, *nonreactive* measurement involves the use of methods that are less obvious to the subject (in effect data are collected without people knowing that they are subjects). At the outset several comments must be made. First, the biases we will consider might occur in any kind of research, be it a survey, a laboratory experiment, or observations in natural settings. Second, biased data can be obtained for a number of different reasons, not just because of what appears to be an obviously poor measurement procedure. Third, you should not get the impression that nonreactive measures are "perfect"; as we will see shortly, these techniques pose their own problems.

Factors Decreasing External Validity

External validity concerns the extent to which the data obtained in a research study adequately represent what the investigator intends to study. I have mentioned that researchers often employ a method of criticism based on the question, Is there any reason why the generality of these findings should be questioned? What follows is a list of several specific reasons for doubting the external validity of findings obtained in certain ways.

The Guinea Pig Effect. The general idea of the guinea pig effect is that subjects behave *unrepresentatively* because intrusive, obvious data collection methods are used. Human subjects might well be expected to react to being watched. Actually, biases can be introduced even in rather subtle ways. Here are some examples of the sorts of things that can cause concern: A person responding to a survey question might be inclined to withhold "socially undesirable" responses. The children in a sandbox might play quite differently because of the presence of an adult nearby (should the adult be holding a clipboard and making notes, the effect is likely to be stronger). The monkeys on an island might interact quite unrepresentatively owing to the introduction of a strange organism (the human observer) into their life space. Children might be less adventuresome and their parents more accepting of a child's misbehavior in the presence of a non-family member.

As these examples illustrate, biases can be introduced in many ways. Furthermore, it is rather difficult to make general statements about the kind of bias that might result—each situation requires consideration on its own merits. What is clear is that as observation and measurement become more obvious or intrusive the possibility of biased data increases.

Role Selection. People and their behavior are complex entities, and an individual varies according to the time and the situation. In effect each of us has a number of different "selves," each of which is "true" but no one of which is totally representative. The possibility exists that a person might select (knowingly or otherwise) one of those "selves" in a research study and respond on that basis. Which "self" or role is chosen can depend on the expectations suggested by the researcher. Notice that whenever a person has agreed to participate in a study he or she has in effect agreed to play the role of subject, a role that carries certain expectations. It has been argued, and to some extent demonstrated, that subjects are inclined to give a researcher the data that they believe he or she wants ("subjects" are expected to be cooperative). Bias is introduced to the extent that the role adopted by the subject does not represent the role that he or she adopts when not being studied. The problem of role selection has been addressed in slightly different terms as "demand characteristics" (Orne, 1962), the idea being that certain responses might be suggested to the subject by the manner in which the study is conducted.

For example, a worker might have mixed feelings about his pay and job conditions, sometimes feeling underpaid and overworked in undesirable conditions, sometimes feeling adequately compensated and satisfied, and agreeing with the company's need to hold down costs. When he views himself as a loyal union member he emphasizes a certain selection of these feelings; a different selection is emphasized when he views himself as a loyal employee. Surveys taken by different agencies (for example, the union vs. management) might well elicit different responses from this person. Consider a different example. Suppose a subject, after completing a verbal learning task, is asked whether she used imaginal mediation or associative mediation or just memorized the list of words. Although the problems involved here might not be as serious as those in the first example, there are potential difficulties. The request suggests to the subject that she must have used one of these strategies (there is a "demand" that she indicate one of these strategies, making it difficult for her to give a different answer or say "I don't know"); furthermore, the request might suggest that indicating one of the mediational strategies is more appropriate (for the "good subject") than "just memorizing." There is evidence in the literature suggesting that the kinds of answers subjects give to such questions vary with the degree of "direction" associated with the request.

One kind of demand characteristic or role selection problem has been responsible for much concern among social psychologists. Suppose a person is asked his opinion (positive–negative) toward drinking alcoholic beverages, then shown a film depicting harmful effects of alcohol, and then again asked his opinion. It has been argued that such a procedure indicates quite clearly to the subject what is "expected" of him, making a finding that the film affects opinions toward alcohol of doubtful generality. Notice that the idea that the film changes opinions *with this procedure* is not necessarily questioned; rather, the criticism is that the effect of the film on opinions might be quite different if less obvious procedures were used.

Response Sets. Research on the way people respond to questions and use rating scales has resulted in the identification of systematic response tendencies that can lead to biased data. For example, people show a tendency to agree with statements that are presented to them. The idea is that the percentage of people agreeing with a given statement will be greater than the percentage disagreeing with the opposite of the statement. If people were, for example, asked to agree or disagree with the statement "The President is doing a good job," the data would be likely to give a more favorable impression of people's opinions than if they had been given the statement "The President is doing a poor job." Another response set is a "position set," which refers to the tendency to stay on the same side of a rating scale when making a series of ratings. Students in college classes are frequently asked to rate various aspects of an instructor's performance (e.g., how well the instructor organized the material, explained concepts, exhibited interest in the subject matter, and so on). The point is that if all the rating scales are arranged such that, say, the positive end of each scale is to the right, this arrangement might lead to stereotyped responses.

Response sets can usually be avoided by asking nondirective questions

("What kind of job do you think the President is doing?" rather than "Do you think the President is doing a good job?") and by varying the positions of the positive and negative ends of rating scales. For such procedures to work, it is clearly necessary that the respondent be encouraged to attend closely to the content of each item. Arranging the majority of rating scales with the positive end to the right and a few with the positive end to the left can lead to "odd" results if the subject does not attend to the orientation of each scale.

Population Restrictions. We have already discussed the importance of obtaining data for a representative sample of the target population. The method used to collect data needs to be assessed for its possible biases, some of which can be rather subtle. The basic question is whether a particular method is likely to result in various segments of the population being under- or overrepresented. For example, a survey of voting intentions was made by telephone prior to a presidential election in the 1930s, with the results showing a strong preference for the Republican candidate. However, the survey result proved to be considerably in error, the reason being that a large segment of the population, too poor to own telephones and tending to vote Democratic, was not accessible by telephone.

Here are some additional examples of population restrictions that are likely to be associated with particular data collection methods. Keep in mind that whether or not such restrictions will lead to biased data will depend on the nature of the observations being made. A telephone or household survey taken during the daytime hours will underrepresent males and working women. Observations made in airports are likely to overrepresent higher-income and professional groups. Selecting a random sample from a list of homeowners will underrepresent young adults and unmarried people. A sidewalk survey will tap quite different segments of the population, depending on whether it is taken in a supermarket, outside the opera house, or at the entrance to the boxing arena. It would be easy to extend this list; obviously, it is important to consider the population restrictions that might be associated with a given data collection method. Let me emphasize again that the seriousness of a restriction will depend on the nature of the restriction and its relation to the topic being studied. Men and women, or high-income and low-income groups, do not differ on *everything!* Consequently overrepresenting women or underrepresenting low-income people might be a critical flaw in one study but of little importance in another.

Unobtrusive Measurement

While the generality of research results can be reduced by a number of factors regardless of the manner in which the research is conducted, it is clear that special problems can occur when subjects are aware of being studied. A solution to these problems is to obtain data without placing the organism in the position of "obviously" being a subject in an investigation. Such methods are termed *unobtrusive measurement* by Webb and his associates (1966), who provide numerous examples of unobtrusive techniques. The idea of unobtrusive measurement may be illustrated by contrasting some obvious, potentially reactive techniques with alternate, unobtrusive methods. Rather than asking people which of two paintings they like more, one could place a device under the carpet to record the amounts of time people spend looking at the two paintings (the assumption being that more time means greater liking). Rather than having an adult sitting on a bench next to a sandbox making notes, one could hide a television camera in a nearby tree or bush to record children's play. Rather than asking people how much alcohol they consume at home, one could examine the empty bottles in their garbage. Rather than asking a person who runs a telephone order business how much business she does, one could tap her telephone line. Rather than asking students in various classes how much anxiety they feel during exams, one could count the number of cigarette butts left on the floor after the exam (the assumption being that more cigarettes means more anxiety).

The purpose of unobtrusive methods is easy to understand: To avoid possible biases due to the subject's being aware of being studied, don't let him or her know! It is important to realize that there aren't really two classes of methods, obvious and unobtrusive, but that data collection techniques can be more or less obvious. For example, anthropologists studying the people of a village in a foreign country typically do not begin recording observations until they have been in the village for some time, the idea being that as the villagers become accustomed to the presence of the outsiders their behavior will return to "normal." Similarly, a psychologist who visits a home to observe preschool children's language development attempts to become "a familiar person" before recording observations. For a slightly different example, a researcher who approaches people in a bus station, announces that he is taking a survey, and asks questions about political preferences is being more obvious than one who mingles with the crowd and "casually" engages in conversations about politics.

While unobtrusive methods have obvious advantages over more straightforward data collection techniques, they also have relative disadvantages. Generally, an unobtrusive measure contains a lot of "noise" and can have low validity. For example, the amount of time people spend looking at a painting is influenced by many factors in addition to how much they like the painting (perhaps they are tired and want to rest a bit), and it is possible that people might spend considerable time looking at a painting they don't like (e.g., wondering why it's in the museum or criticizing it). As mentioned earlier, the problems of noise and possible lack of validity apply to any measure. For example, the tendency to agree with statements and the tendency to develop response sets are sources of difficulty for ordinary, "direct" measurement techniques (a response of "strongly agree" reflects more than the person's opinion on the issue). However, it is fair to say that unobtrusive measures tend to have more noise in them than other techniques, and this represents a relative disadvantage.

Using Existing Records. The unobtrusive methods that we have considered so far have involved deliberate efforts by the investigator to make observations, admittedly in rather unusual ways. Webb and his associates (1966) emphasize that a relatively unobtrusive method of gathering data is to make use of the information contained in existing records. Various agencies accumulate records for many different purposes, and it is always possible that such records might contain information relevant to a particular research question. Since such records are ordinarily obtained "in the normal course of events," using them minimizes the problems of reactivity associated with people knowing that they are subjects in an investigation. The general idea is that a researcher can employ analyses of existing records to supplement or substitute for other data collection techniques. For example, over time a psychological clinic will amass records that are likely to allow an investigator to relate various personal characteristics to the incidence of psychological disorders or to perform at least a preliminary analysis of the effectiveness of therapy.

Because existing records are maintained for purposes other than research, their use does involve special problems. It is of course possible for an investigator to find that the records do not contain the information he or she desires in the appropriate form. Perhaps some information that the researcher would like to have has not been recorded, or the categories used in creating the records are not quite those that would provide the best information. Using existing records might require the researcher to depend on a different index of the concept that he or she is interested in. For example, if a researcher were interested in relating several variables to job satisfaction, she might have to rely on measures such as "average length of time people stay on the job," "number of days off the job," and "frequency of complaints" if she used existing personnel records, whereas she might ask workers "how satisfied they are" if she engaged in direct data collection. Another problem faced by the user of existing records is that the method of record keeping might change over time, making comparisons dubious. Of most serious concern is the possibility that those who keep the records might become aware that the records are used for investigative purposes and thus alter the content of the records. In general, the difficulties associated with using existing records stem from the fact that the investigator does not have direct control over the keeping of the records. Nevertheless existing records can provide useful and relatively nonreactive information.

One year after the new, reform-minded police chief had taken over the department, an alderman called for his dismissal, stating that police department records showed that crime had increased by 25 percent during the year. Assuming that his statement about the records is correct, give a good reason why they might not indicate an actual increase in the crime rate.

The most obvious reason why the increase in recorded crime might not reflect an actual increase in crime is that the record-keeping method might have changed. With the change in administration of the department, it is possible (even likely) that different procedures were adopted. Thus it is possible that the increase shown in the records reflects nothing more than the fact that the records now index the number of crimes more accurately. Even without arguing that the records are more accurate, it is possible that the record-keeping system was changed in such a way that counts are higher.

There is another possible, though unlikely, reason why the increase in recorded crime might not reflect an increase in actual crime rate. Suppose the population had also increased by 25 percent during the year; in this case the crime *rate* (number of crimes relative to population) would be the same. For a large city this large a change in population in one year is rather farfetched, but such an "index number" consideration might be more reasonable for a small suburb that was experiencing a dramatic increase in population.

Throughout this discussion I have tried to illustrate the advantages and disadvantages of various data collection methods. To fully understand the issues involved, remember what was said in the preceding chapter: Any variable considered at the conceptual level might be measured in a variety of ways. Any single measure reflects the variable that is of interest as well as various kinds of noise, and has its own biases. In comparing unobtrusive measures with other, more obvious data collection methods, the idea is *not* "Which one should be used?" Each method has its own advantages and disadvantages. For example, "anxiety" is reflected in subjects' answers to the question "How anxious are you?"; in other, less obvious verbal responses; in the frequency of use of presumably anxiety-reducing drugs; and in various physiological measures; among other things. Each measure in part indexes variation in anxiety as well as noise, and each is subject to peculiar biases. To comprehensively understand a concept, multiple measures should be used. When only a single method is used, the generality of the findings may justifiably be criticized. For example, studies of attitude change that rely solely on responses to rating scales can reasonably be cricitized as not fully representing the possible ways in which attitudes might be assessed. As Webb and his associates (1966) argue, a considerable amount of research has relied on a small selection of possible methods, thus leaving the generality of the findings in some doubt.

Ethical Considerations. A number of unobtrusive methods involve the deliberate collection of observations without the knowledge of the subject. The use of hidden cameras, tape recorders, or a data collector who plays the role of an ordinary person clearly raises ethical (and legal) questions. Is it ethical to film a person's behavior in a public place without that person's knowledge? Is it ethical to tape record a person's conversation with a research assistant who plays the role of "ordinary person"? Is it ethical to send a research assistant into a store pretending to be a shopper but intending to observe a clerk's behavior?

In Chapter 2, I pointed out that when human behavior is studied, ethical issues usually center on such matters as invasion of privacy, deception, and stress. Obtaining subjects' informed consent before collecting data is an obvious way of avoiding or reducing ethical problems. By definition, unobtrusive methods do not allow for informed consent, since the person is not aware of being studied. Consequently ethical issues are likely to be much more salient when unobtrusive methods are used. In Chapter 2 debriefing was described as a means of reducing any negative effects of deception; yet debriefing is not likely to be used when unobtrusive methods are employed.

In addition to raising sharper ethical issues, unobtrusive methods might involve legal problems as well. Silverman (1975) asked several legal authorities for their opinions of a variety of unobtrusive methods, several of which involved deception—pretending to be a shopper to observe behavior of store personnel, phoning randomly selected people and pretending to be a motorist in distress, pretending to have an attack of a physical illness in a public place. The legal issues that were considered included such matters as invasion of privacy, trespass, fraud, harassment, and disorderly conduct. The legal opinions were quite varied; while there was no agreement that obvious legal transgressions were involved, there were some suggestions that some procedures *could* possibly lead to criminal action (misdemeanor) or civil suits.

Unobtrusive methods have some clear advantages over more reactive procedures with respect to the generality of the findings. However, unobtrusive methods raise more salient ethical issues and might involve legal problems. At present, there is no clear indication that the ethical and legal complications are especially serious (and of course they vary widely across unobtrusive methods). Nonetheless, I am sure you can understand why researchers might choose not to use such methods. Because unobtrusive methods have advantages for knowledge-gathering purposes, it seems likely that they will continue to be used, perhaps quite selectively. We can expect that over time the special issues that they raise will gradually be resolved.

SUMMARY

Statistical theory provides a formal system for making generalizations from samples to populations. A *population* is a defined set of cases, while a *sample* is a subset of a population. In making generalizations a critical question is whether the sample is representative of the population. Statistical theory bases generalizations on the assumption that samples are drawn in a random fashion. The theory allows very precise statements to be made about characteristics of the population distribution of values (on some measurement scale) on the basis of the scores in a random sample.

Having defined a population distribution, one can then conceive of creating a sampling distribution of means by repeatedly drawing random samples of the same size and calculating the mean ($\bar{X}$) of each sample. Many different sampling distributions can be generated from the same population distribution by varying the size of the samples. For example, one could generate sampling distributions of ($\bar{X}$) based on sample sizes (n) of 2, 5, 10, 20, 50, 100, and so on. The mean of a sampling distribution ($M_{\bar{X}}$) will be equal to the mean (M) of the population distribution, regardless of sample size. However, the variability of the sample means ($\bar{X}$'s) decreases as sample size increases. In addition, the distribution of sample means ($\bar{X}$'s) tends to resemble a normal distribution more and more closely as sample size increases (regardless of the shape of the population distribution).

Statistical theory is relevant to making generalizations in the following manner. If a researcher has scores for a single sample, the mean of that sample must belong to some sampling distribution of $\bar{X}$'s. By making use of what is known about such sampling distributions and about normal distributions, the researcher can construct a confidence interval for the population mean (M) based on the known value of a single sample mean ($\bar{X}$). A confidence interval for M is a stated range of values within which M is expected to lie; the procedure allows a researcher to associate a level of confidence with the interval. For example, a "95 percent confidence interval for M" is a statement of a range of possible values for M based on a procedure that will be correct 95 percent of the time. A researcher can reduce the size of the confidence interval (i.e., specify a smaller range of values for M) while maintaining a high level of confidence by increasing the size of the sample.

While statistical theory allows researchers to make quite accurate generalizations about population values (such as M), the procedure rests on obtaining scores for a random sample. It is often difficult to obtain a truly random sample of scores, for a variety of reasons. Therefore researchers frequently must judge whether the sample values they have are reasonably representative of the population. In psychological research special problems arise from using "samples of convenience"—subjects who are readily available but not systematically drawn from a well-defined population. Rigorous generalizations are virtually impossible when such samples are used.

Research is done in natural settings to maximize the chances of observing representative behavior. Such research is often inefficient, is not conducive to studying the effects of manipulations, and can pose special problems regarding systematic observations. Surveys tend to rely on self-reports rather than on behavioral observations. While surveys can be very efficient, they can pose special problems because of questions about the validity of self-reports. Laboratory experiments involve observations made in highly controlled, "artificial" situations. Such settings are ideal for studying the effects of manipulations, but the generality of laboratory findings has been questioned. Critics have argued that laboratory experiments tend to involve unrepresentative subjects and tasks, and that human subjects behave unrepresentatively because they perceive the difference between the laboratory and ordinary, natural settings. Information about the generality of laboratory findings varies from one area of psychology to another.

Reactive measurement effects refer to biases that can occur because subjects are aware of being studied. Sources of bias include the "guinea pig effect," role selection, response sets, and population restrictions. Unobtrusive methods involve collecting data without the subject being aware of being observed. The use of unobtrusive measures can eliminate some reactive measurement biases, but unobtrusive measures tend to be "noisier"—more difficult to interpret theoretically. A special unobtrusive method involves the use of existing records, which can yield useful information but can also be inefficient or incomplete (primarily because the records are kept by agencies that are not concerned with the research project). Some unobtrusive methods involve special ethical and possibly legal problems, which can make them relatively undesirable even though they yield good information for knowledge-gathering purposes.

6

USING DATA
TO MAKE
DECISIONS

Researchers collect data to get answers to questions, and those questions may take many different forms. Here are some examples: "Does the prestige of a speaker affect the degree of acceptance of an argument?" "Do males and females have different levels of anxiety?" "Does giving a hint make problem solving easier?" "Do Republicans and Democrats have different attitudes toward gun control?" Researchers use the data obtained to decide on the most reasonable answers to the questions they pose.

In Chapter 2 I discussed the evaluation of treatment differences, pointing out that researchers compare the *score difference between treatments* to an *index of random score variation* to decide whether *real* treatment differences exist. In this chapter we will go beyond this general idea and consider more closely the procedures used to make decisions. We will not consider specific statistical tests (several of which are described in Appendix B). Rather, we will concentrate on the *fundamental concepts* and the *logic* of the procedures that are used. After we have considered the procedures themselves, we will discuss several issues related to their use. To begin, however, I will present an ordinary, nonresearch example to illustrate how data are used to make decisions.

An Example: Is This A Fair Coin?

Suppose we wish to decide whether or not a particular coin is "fair," that is, equally likely to land "heads" or "tails." Let's begin by considering the *hypothesis that the coin is fair* (notice that the idea of a "fair coin" is a model or hypothesis that *may or may not* be correct for this coin). To test this hypothesis we decide to flip the coin 8 times and count the number of times "heads" occurs. In 8 flips we could get anything from 0 to 8 heads. The first question is, What does the fair-coin hypothesis predict for these possible outcomes? Table 6.1 shows the *probabilities* for all possible outcomes based on the fair-coin hypothesis (I will not present the formula by which these probabilities were calculated).

To understand Table 6.1 you need to know a few things about probabilities. Probabilities are numbers ranging between 0.00 and 1.00; a probability of 1.00 indicates that something is *certain* to occur, while a probability of 0.00 indicates that something is *impossible*. Probabilities between these two end points indicate greater and lesser likelihoods. Something that has a probability of occurrence of .109 has 109 chances out of 1000 or about 1 chance in 10 of occurring; something with a probability of .004 has only 4 chances in 1000 of occurring, and so on. In Table 6.1 you can see that, *if* the coin is fair, it is most likely that one would get about 4 heads when a coin is flipped 8 times; the probability of getting 3, 4, or 5 heads in 8 flips is .711 (.219 + .273 + .219 = .711)—the chances are about 7 out of 10 that 3, 4, or 5 heads will be obtained in 8 flips *if* the coin is fair. In contrast, under the assumption that the coin is fair, it is rather unlikely that one would get 0, 1, 7, or 8 heads in 8 flips. With a fair coin, the chances of getting either no heads or all heads in 8 flips are extremely low, and the chances of getting either just one head or all but one (7) heads are low as well.

Table 6.1 indicates the probabilities for all possible observations (numbers of heads) when a coin is flipped 8 times, *according to the hypothesis that the coin is fair*. To test this hypothesis we need to decide which possible outcomes would be reasonable evidence against this hypothesis. That is, which possible outcomes would be reasonable grounds for deciding that

Table 6.1   Probabilities for All Possible Outcomes When Flipping a Coin Eight Times Under the Hypothesis That a Coin is Fair

NUMBER OF HEADS	PROBABILITY
0	.004
1	.031
2	.109
3	.219
4	.273
5	.219
6	.109
7	.031
8	.004

the fair-coin hypothesis is wrong? The set of outcomes that will lead to *rejecting* the hypothesis is called the *critical region*. Thus we need to specify the critical region for this test. To do this we need to consider the *logical alternative* to the fair-coin hypothesis. Of course the logical alternative to the fair-coin hypothesis is the hypothesis that the coin is *biased*. Notice that if the coin is *not* fair it might be biased either in favor of "heads" or against "heads." Therefore in testing the fair-coin hypothesis we need to allow for evidence of bias in either direction. What this means is that we would be willing to reject the fair-coin hypothesis *if* we obtained either too few or too many heads in 8 coin flips.

We could establish a critical region for testing the fair-coin hypothesis by deciding that we would reject the hypothesis if we obtained either zero (0) heads or all (8) heads in 8 flips of the coin. This would be reasonable because 0 heads or 8 heads represent deviant and unlikely observations *if the coin is fair*. Under the fair-coin hypothesis the probability of getting either 0 heads or 8 heads in 8 flips is just .008 (.004 + .004 = .008)—there would be less than 1 chance in 100 of getting 0 or 8 heads *if the coin is fair*. By defining the critical region to include 0 heads or 8 heads, we have set up a test of the fair-coin hypothesis. We could now make the 8 flips of the coin, knowing that if we get either 0 heads or 8 heads we will reject the idea that the coin is fair, and that if we get 1, 2, 3, 4, 5, 6, or 7 heads we will *not* reject the fair-coin hypothesis.

The test that I have just described would be a perfectly reasonable test of the hypothesis that a coin is fair. A person who would reject the fair-coin hypothesis if either 0 heads or 8 heads were obtained in 8 flips would have reasonable grounds for rejecting the hypothesis as accurate. Notice, however, that the test is somewhat "conservative." Defining the critical region to include only 0 heads and 8 heads means that the hypothesis will be rejected only if the evidence against it is quite strong. A more liberal test could be set up by expanding the critical region to include more possible values. For example, suppose we decided to reject the hypothesis that the coin is fair if we obtained any of the following outcomes: 0, 1, 7, or 8 heads in 8 flips. In Table 6.1 you can see that according to the fair-coin hypothesis the probability of getting 0, 1, 7, or 8 heads is .070 (.004 + .031 + .031 + .004 = .070). If we decided to define the critical region as including these four possible outcomes, we would be requiring less serious evidence against the fair-coin hypothesis to reject it. This "more liberal" test would be reasonable—after all, *if* the coin is fair, the chances of getting 0, 1, 7, or 8 heads in 8 flips are only 7 in 100. These four outcomes do represent a set of reasonably unlikely outcomes according to the fair-coin hypothesis.

Let me summarize the test described in this example. We began with the hypothesis that the coin is fair. We decided how we would collect data to test this hypothesis (flip the coin 8 times). We examined the probabilities assigned by the fair-coin hypothesis to all possible outcomes of our experiment. We then chose a set of extreme outcomes that are unlikely to occur according to the fair-coin hypothesis; these outcomes make up the critical region. Taking into account the fact that if the fair-coin hypothesis is wrong the coin might be biased in either direction, we included outcomes representing "too many heads" and outcomes representing "too few heads" in the critical region. I pointed out that "unlikely" could be defined in terms of slightly different probability levels. For the conservative test of the fair-coin hypothesis, the critical region included just 0 heads and 8 heads, and "unlikely" meant "$p = .008$ according to the fair-coin hypothesis." For the more liberal test, the critical region included 0, 1, 7, or 8 heads, and "unlikely" meant "$p = .07$ according to the fair-coin hypothesis." Both tests can be viewed as reasonable.

This example illustrates the essential features of the procedures researchers use to make decisions on the basis of data. Notice that the test of the fair-coin hypothesis was completely set up before the coin was actually flipped. In fact I have not mentioned any actual data; you can now take a coin and, after deciding whether you want to make a conservative test or a liberal one, actually test the fair-coin hypothesis for your coin by flipping it 8 times. This corresponds to what researchers do: decide on the hypothesis to be tested, set up the test, and then collect the data and see what decision should be made.

We will now consider hypothesis-testing procedures in more formal terms and in greater detail. At several points in the following discussion I will refer to the fair-coin example in order to provide a concrete illustration.

THE LOGIC OF HYPOTHESIS TESTING

The hypothesis-testing procedures commonly used in psychological research involve a choice between two mutually exclusive answers to a question. The hypotheses are stated in statistical terms and are set up such that one or the other hypothesis must be correct (the two hypotheses in some way cover all the possible answers to the question). For example, if the question is whether or not there is a difference between the "true" mean scores for males and females on a vocabulary test, the two hypotheses are virtually certain to be (1) $M_m = M_f$ and (2) $M_m \neq M_f$. The two hypotheses state that the means for males and females are either "really the same" or "really different." One of these hypotheses has to be correct because there aren't any other possibilities. Notice that the two hypotheses are set up such that rejecting one hypothesis is equivalent to adopting the other—if you reject the hypothesis that $M_m = M_f$, you must be adopting the position that $M_m \neq M_f$. As you will see shortly, however, the two hypotheses have quite different status with respect to the decision-making process.

The Null Hypothesis

One of the hypotheses is taken as a starting point and is directly tested; the hypothesis that plays this role in the test is called the *null hypothesis*. In our example the hypothesis that the coin is fair served as the null hypothesis. There are two criteria that a hypothesis must satisfy to be used as a null hypothesis. First, the hypothesis must be *specific* and *complete* enough to allow the *calculation of probabilities for all possible observations* that might be made. Second, there must be sufficient theoretical *justification* for taking the hypothesis as the starting point. Let's examine these criteria.

We will first examine the *specificity* criterion. A null hypothesis is *directly tested* and either rejected or not rejected. Consequently a null hypothesis *must* specify which possible observations are more likely to occur, which are unlikely to occur, and so on. Strictly speaking, a null hypothesis must specify the *probability of occurrence* for every *possible* observation. Only then can a researcher determine whether the data *actually obtained* belong to "things that are relatively likely to occur" or to "things that are unlikely to occur" *if the null hypothesis is correct*. In our example the fair-coin hypothesis satisfied this criterion. The idea of a fair coin translates into the following statement: "On any flip of the coin, the true probability of getting 'heads' is equal to the probability of getting 'tails'—the true probability of getting 'heads' equals precisely 0.5." It was on the basis of the statement that "p(heads) = .5" that I calculated the probabilities shown in Table 6.1. To make those calculations it was necessary to have a precise numerical value for "p(heads)."

Here are two examples of hypotheses that are *not* specific enough to serve as null hypotheses: (1) "For a measure of anxiety, the true mean score for males is *higher than* the true mean score for females." (2) "The coin is *more likely* to fall 'heads' than 'tails.'" "Higher than" and "more likely" just aren't good enough; to be directly testable the hypothesis must state *exactly* how much higher or *precisely* how much more likely. For example, the hypothesis that "p(heads) = 0.7" is *specific* enough to serve as a null hypothesis—the numerical value can be inserted into the appropriate formula to generate probabilities for all possible outcomes. But without a precise value, probabilities can't be calculated. If probabilities can't be calculated, there is no way to decide which possible outcomes are the "more likely" or "unlikely" outcomes. In other words, a vague hypothesis can't be properly tested; therefore a null hypothesis, which is directly tested, must be precise.

The second criterion for a null hypothesis is that there must be good reasons for taking the hypothesis as a starting point. To see why, consider how a null hypothesis is treated. A null hypothesis is formulated in advance of data collection; it is directly tested, and it is *rejected only if* the data actually obtained seriously *contradict* its predictions (about which outcomes are more and less likely). In effect a null hypothesis is taken as the most reasonable hypothesis *prior to* data collection, and it will continue to have "most reasonable" status *after* data collection *unless* the data seriously contradict its predictions. A null hypothesis does *not* really have to prove itself; rather, it just has to *survive the test* to maintain its "most reasonable" status. For this reason a null hypothesis must be extremely acceptable *before* data collection.

Consider our "fair-coin" example. We *started with* the hypothesis that the coin is fair. We did *not* then require that this hypothesis prove that it makes the best possible predictions for the outcomes of a set of coin flips. Rather, the fair-coin hypothesis would be *rejected only if* its predictions were *seriously* contradicted. To maintain the fair-coin hypothesis it was *not* necessary to actually observe exactly half "heads" and half "tails" when the coin was flipped. Rather, the fair-coin hypothesis would be maintained *unless* "too many" or "too few" heads were obtained when the coin was flipped. To state this in general terms: Since we are willing to maintain a null hypothesis unless the data seriously contradict it, we ought to have a lot of confidence in it before the data are collected.

PROBLEM

None of the following hypotheses would be used as a null hypothesis by a psychological researcher. For each hypothesis, indicate why it fails to meet the criteria for a null hypothesis.
(1) "The mean IQ for males is lower than the mean IQ for females."
(2) "The percentage of people who prefer Pepsi-Cola is higher than the percentage of people who prefer Coca-Cola."
(3) "Rats given one food pellet for each correct response will take fewer trials to learn a task than rats given two food pellets for each correct response."
(4) "People will learn a list of 20 concrete words in exactly 4.5 trials less than it will take them to learn a list of 20 abstract words."

For hypotheses (1), (2), and (3) we don't even have to consider whether they are the "most reasonable" statements that might be made because they are just not specific enough to be directly tested. It is impossible to test a hypothesis unless it is numerically precise, and none of these three hypotheses meets this criterion. Hypothesis (4) is specific enough to be tested, but it would not satisfy the "sufficient-justification" criterion. Why should we believe that the difference in trials to learn is exactly 4.5 trials, rather than 4.6 trials or 5 trials or some other specific number of trials? It is extremely unlikely that we could find sufficient grounds for proposing a difference of exactly 4.5 trials *before* data have been collected. Consequently it wouldn't make sense to use hypothesis (4) as a null hypothesis.

Because a null hypothesis must be quantitatively specific *and* a very plausible starting point, it can be difficult to formulate null hypotheses. Many ideas that are generally plausible are *not* specific enough to serve as null hypotheses. Most specific hypotheses lack the general acceptance to be taken as reasonable starting points. There are exceptions. For example, Mendel's theory of genetics has been around a long time and is widely accepted as a reasonable theory; it is also quantitatively specific. Consequently, Mendel's theory has been used as the null hypothesis for experiments in genetics. In most areas of psychology the theoretical ideas that have been proposed lack the specificity or the long-term acceptance (or both) required of null hypotheses.

Most null hypotheses actually used in research turn out to be rather simple statements. They are statements like "There is no difference between population means," "There is no relation between the variables," "The person is just guessing," or, in the case of our example, "There is no bias" (i.e., the coin is fair). There are two reasons why such null hypotheses are used. First, ideas like those just listed translate into quantitatively specific hypotheses. For example, stating that there is no difference between two population means specifies a particular value, namely zero, for the difference ($M_1 - M_2 = 0$). If a person is trying to select the correct response from four alternatives, the statement that the person is guessing means that the chance of a correct response is $\frac{1}{4}$. As we have already seen, the idea of a fair coin translates into the hypothesis that on any flip the probability of getting "heads" is exactly .5. Such ideas meet the specificity criterion for null hypotheses.

Such statements are also reasonable starting points. Notice that if we conclude that some difference or relation exists, that conclusion generates a need to find an explanation, to develop a theory. For example, if we conclude that neurotics do have higher anxiety levels than normals, the question that quite reasonably arises is "Why?" If, on the other hand, we state that there is no real difference, there is no urgent need to develop an explanation—basically, there is nothing to explain. The "catalog of facts" for which explanations must be developed contains the differences and relations that are judged to exist on the basis of research. It is reasonable for science to adopt a policy requiring that the hypothesis of "no difference or relation" be rejected on reasonable grounds before "entering another fact in the catalog." This policy provides sensible control over the "facts" for which explanations must be developed. What this means is that before science must pay any attention to my claim that "concrete words are easier to learn than abstract words" I must demonstrate that the hypothesis that "there is no difference in learning difficulty between concrete and abstract words" can be reasonably rejected on the basis of the data that I have collected.

PROBLEM

A researcher plans to compare the arithmetic scores of samples of males and females. The researcher believes that the true mean score for males is higher than that for females. When the researcher analyzes the data, what would be the null hypothesis?

The answer is that the null hypothesis would state that there is no real difference between the mean scores of males and females, that $M_m - M_f = 0$. The researcher's belief that males should score higher is not sufficient to serve as a null hypothesis. First of all, if the researcher is unwilling to state a precise value for the difference between means, it is impossible to directly test his idea. Second, the researcher's belief that males should score higher is *not* sufficient justification for a null hypothesis (perhaps someone else believes that females should score higher). The researcher would have to collect data that lead to a reasonable rejection of the hypothesis of *no* mean difference.

The Alternate Hypothesis

Whereas the null hypothesis is specific and is directly tested, the alternate hypothesis is nonspecific and is not directly tested. In effect the alternate hypothesis is nothing more than the logical alternative to the null hypothesis. If one rejects the null hypothesis, one in effect adopts the alternate hypothesis. In other words, the test is set up such that if the null hypothesis is judged "wrong," the alternate hypothesis must be "right." To satisfy this requirement the alternate hypothesis ordinarily contradicts or denies some part of the null hypothesis. If the null hypothesis were "$M_1 - M_2 = 0$," the alternate hypothesis would be "$M_1 - M_2 \neq 0$." If the null hypothesis is "$p(\text{heads}) = .5$," the alternate hypothesis is "$p(\text{heads}) \neq .5$." As you can see in these examples, rejecting the null hypothesis "forces" one to adopt the alternate hypothesis. One or the other of the two hypotheses must be correct.

The form of alternate hypothesis just described, in which an equality stated in the null hypothesis is changed to an inequality in the alternate, is called a *nondirectional* alternate hypothesis. A test set up in this way is based on the sensible notion that if the null hypothesis is wrong, then the correct value might be either higher or lower than the value stated in the null hypothesis. Occasionally researchers set up a test differently, using a *directional* alternate hypothesis. For example, if the null hypothesis stated that "$M = 60$" the alternate might state that "$M < 60$"; if the null stated that $p(\text{heads}) = .5$, the alternate might state that $p(\text{heads}) > .5$. A nondirectional alternate hypothesis replaces an "equals" sign ($=$) in the null hypothesis with a "does not equal" ($\neq$) sign, while a directional alternate hypothesis substitutes a "greater than" ($>$) or "less than" ($<$) sign.

The null and alternate hypotheses together are supposed to be exhaustive such that if one of them is wrong the other must be correct. When a nondirectional alternate hypothesis is used, there is no problem since either "$=$" or "$\neq$" must be correct. However, when a directional alternate hypothesis is employed ("$=$" vs. "$<$" or "$=$" vs. "$>$"), it is obvious that the pair of hypotheses is not all-inclusive, at least in a logical sense. A researcher who uses a directional alternate hypothesis therefore must adopt one of two positions: (1) It is really impossible that the true value could fall in the direction opposite to that stated in the alternate hypothesis. (2) The researcher does not care to distinguish between "equality" and a difference in the direction opposite to that stated in the alternate hypothesis. For example, if a researcher tests the null hypothesis $M_1 - M_2 = 0$ against the alternate $M_1 - M_2 < 0$, he must either argue that it is impossible that $M_1 - M_2$ could be >0.00 or that he does not care to distinguish between "$M_1 - M_2 = 0.00$" and "$M_1 - M_2 > 0.00$." It is extremely difficult to imagine circumstances in which argument (1) could be asserted strongly. In some practical situations argument (2) makes sense, but it is not generally appropriate for scientific purposes.

Consider the following practical example. Suppose a manufacturer wishes to compare the average quality of products made by the current method (call this M_c) with the average quality when a proposed new method is used (call this M_n). The manufacturer could sensibly argue that the only two possibilities she wishes to consider are "$M_c = M_n$" and "$M_c < M_n$." The reasoning is easy to understand. If the average quality with the new method is higher ($M_c < M_n$), then she will have to consider changing production methods to the new method. If the average quality is the same ($M_c = M_n$), there is no obvious need to change. Obviously, there would also be no need to change if the average quality with the new method were lower ($M_c > M_n$). In other words, there are just two possible actions that might be taken: switching to the new method (if $M_c < M_n$) or keeping the current method (if $M_c = M_n$ *or* $M_c > M_n$). Thus the manufacturer could argue that she should test "$M_c = M_n$" against the alternate "$M_c < M_n$" and that she has no sensible need to distinguish between $M_c = M_n$ and $M_c > M_n$.

A researcher might make a similar argument. Suppose the research question concerns the difference between theoretical means (call them M_1 and M_2). The null hypothesis is "$M_1 = M_2$." The researcher might argue that since his theory predicts that M_1 should be less than M_2, he should use the alternate hypothesis "$M_1 < M_2$" and ignore the possibility that $M_1 > M_2$. In essence the researcher is arguing that using a directional alternate hypothesis is appropriate because his theory predicts a difference in a particular direction. With respect to his theory a directional alternate hypothesis makes sense. A problem might arise, however, because other scientists, perhaps with less faith in his theory, could argue that *both* the null hypothesis *and* his theory could be wrong, that it would be important to find out that $M_1 > M_2$ even though *no* existing theory predicts a difference in that direction. The point is that for scientific, knowledge-gathering purposes (in contrast to practical situations) we should always consider all the possibilities—we should use nondirectional ($\neq$) alternate hypotheses. As you might imagine, scientists do not all agree on this issue; some argue that directional alternate hypotheses are sometimes appropriate. The most widely held opinion, however, is that nondirectional alternate hypotheses should be used in research.

Consider our "fair-coin" example. We tested the null hypothesis that the coin is fair, that p(heads) = .5. There are two logical possibilities: Either the coin is fair or it is biased. It is hard to imagine arguing that if the coin is biased it could be biased only in favor of heads. It seems much more reasonable to state that if the coin is biased it might be biased either in favor of heads or against heads. Therefore the most reasonable alternate hypothesis is the statement that "p(heads) $\neq$ .5."

The Nature of the Test

From this point on I will assume that all tests involve a null hypothesis including some "equals" sign and a nondirectional ($\neq$) alternate hypothesis. As you know, the null hypothesis is directly tested. The null hypothesis must be specific and must predict probabilities of occurrence for all possible observations. The null hypothesis is rejected *only* if the observation *actually made* is *deviant* and belongs to a set of observations that are *unlikely according to the null hypothesis*. Let's consider what is meant by "deviant, unlikely" observations.

The null hypothesis, by predicting probabilities for all possible observations, predicts that some observations are more likely than others. In testing a null hypothesis attention is focused on the *possible* observations that the null hypothesis states are *unlikely* to happen. The reason is that, should one of these supposedly unlikely observations actually occur, there would be reasonable grounds for deciding that the null hypothesis is wrong. What a researcher needs to do is decide what "unlikely" should mean. That is, *how unlikely* does something have to be *according to the null hypothesis* in order to be good evidence *against* the null hypothesis if it *actually* occurs? There is no simple, general answer to this question. There is, however, fair agreement among researchers that "unlikely" should ordinarily be defined as a probability no greater than about .05 (1 chance in 20). In other words, actual observations that are predicted by a null hypothesis to have about 1 chance in 20 of occurring (or less) are generally considered to be good evidence against the null hypothesis. This criterion is not (and need not be) always used by researchers, but to keep things uncomplicated I will use this criterion throughout the remainder of this discussion.

Once a researcher has decided on a reasonable definition of "unlikely," he or she needs to identify the *possible* observations that are deviant and unlikely *according to the null hypothesis*. These possible outcomes constitute the *critical region*—if any of them actually occurs, the null hypothesis will be rejected.

Let's apply these notions to our "fair-coin" example. We tested the null hypothesis that the coin is fair, that p(heads) = .5. According to the null hypothesis, we should obtain about half "heads" when the coin is flipped a number of times. We decided to flip the coin 8 times. Obviously, if we obtained about half "heads" in the 8 flips, this would not be good evidence against the null hypothesis. We needed to observe "too many heads" or "too few heads" to sensibly reject the null hypothesis ("too many" or "too few" heads are *extreme, deviant* outcomes). I described two different tests of the null hypothesis, a conservative test and a more liberal test. For the conservative test, the null hypothesis [p(heads) = .5] would be rejected *only if* we obtained 0 or 8 heads in 8 flips; "unlikely" was defined as p = .008 according to the null hypothesis (much less than 1 chance in 20). For the more liberal test, the null hypothesis would be rejected if we obtained 0, 1, 7, or 8 heads in 8 flips; "unlikely" was defined as p = .07 according to the null hypothesis. Both tests were described as reasonable (because both tests conform to the generally accepted rule of defining "unlikely" as a probability of about .05 or less). If the conservative test were made, we would reject the hypothesis that "p(heads) = .5" if we actually obtained 0 or 8 heads in 8 flips, and we would *not* reject the null hypothesis if we actually obtained 1–7 heads in 8 flips. If the more liberal test were made, we would reject the null hypothesis if we obtained 0, 1, 7, or 8 heads in 8 flips, and we would *not* reject the null hypothesis if we obtained 2–6 heads in 8 flips.

Both tests are reasonable, yet they could lead to different decisions. If we actually obtained, say, 7 heads in 8 flips, we would *not* reject the null hypothesis that "p(heads) = .5" under the conservative test, but we *would* reject the hypothesis that "p(heads) = .5" under the liberal test. We would reach completely opposite decisions depending on which test we used, yet both tests are reasonable. You should be wondering how researchers decide what kind of test to use. To understand how such decisions are made we need to consider the kinds of errors that might be made in making decisions about null hypotheses.

Decision Errors and Their Probabilities

The outcome of a test of a null hypothesis is a decision by the researcher to reject or not to reject the null hypothesis on the basis of the evidence. The simple fact of the matter is that the researcher's decision, no matter which it is, could be wrong. There is always some risk of making a decision error when testing a null hypothesis. The situation facing the researcher is outlined in Table 6.2.

As you can see, a researcher might reach either of two decisions, each of which might be correct or in error, depending on "the state of the world." Suppose (unknown to the researcher) the null hypothesis is *true*; if so, deciding to reject the null hypothesis would be a mistake while

Table 6.2 Possible Outcomes of Decisions When Testing Null Hypotheses

"STATE OF THE WORLD"	Researcher's Decision	
	REJECT	**DON'T REJECT**
Null hypothesis true	Type I error	Correct
Null hypothesis false	Correct	Type II error

deciding not to reject it would be a correct decision. If, on the other hand, the null hypothesis is really *false*, rejecting it is the correct decision and failing to reject it would be an error. There are two important ideas that you must understand in order to understand why researchers face such risky situations. First, the researcher *does not know* whether or not the null hypothesis is true; if you knew the null hypothesis was true (or false), there would be absolutely no reason to make observations to test it! Second, no evidence can be collected that will logically allow a researcher to be *certain* that his or her decision is correct. We will now explore this idea in regard to the two kinds of errors that might be made.

Type I Errors. The error of rejecting a true null hypothesis is called a type I error. Look again at Table 6.1. Notice that when flipping a coin 8 times there is *no* outcome that is *impossible* (assigned probability = .000) according to the null hypothesis [p(heads) = p(tails)]. Getting zero heads in 8 flips, or 8 heads in 8 flips, is surely unlikely *if* the coin is fair, but neither outcome is *impossible* if p(heads) = p(tails). In 8 flips we could get from 0 to 8 heads, and all of these outcomes are possible if the null hypothesis is true. What this means is that we *cannot* identify a possible outcome that will definitely prove that the null hypothesis is wrong. All we can do is identify a set of outcomes that are unlikely according to the null hypothesis—we can be reasonable but we can never be sure!

Suppose a researcher decides to conduct the "conservative" test of the hypothesis that p(heads) = p(tails), defining the critical region to include 0 heads and 8 heads. Suppose further that when the observations are made the outcome is 8 heads in 8 flips. The researcher would, according to the test set up, reject the null hypothesis. Here is the critical question: Is it possible that the coin is really fair and that the researcher just happened to get 8 heads in 8 flips from a fair coin? The answer is an unambiguous *yes*. As you can see in Table 6.1, it is possible to get 8 heads in 8 flips of a fair coin. *If* the null hypothesis is true—if the 8 heads in 8 flips just happened to come from a fair coin, and *if* the researcher decided to reject the null hypothesis (which he would), he would make a type I error.

I hope that I have driven home the essential point: A researcher cannot eliminate the possibility of making a type I error. What a researcher can do is control the risk of making a type I error, in a relatively direct fashion. Consider again the conservative test of our "fair-coin" example. The critical region includes 0 heads and 8 heads. Should either of these outcomes actually occur, the researcher would reject the null hypothesis. Question: *If* the null hypothesis is true, what is the probability that the researcher will reject it? The answer is .008, which is not that much of a risk. Realize that *if* "p(heads) = p(tails)" *is true*, the probabilities in Table 6.1 are the correct probabilities. The researcher will reject the null hypothesis only if he or she observes 0 heads or 8 heads. We can simply ask, "If the null hypothesis is really true, what are the chances that the researcher will get an outcome that will lead him or her to reject the null hypothesis?" The answer, gleaned from Table 6.1, is .008.

Controlling the risk of a type I error is one basis for deciding how to test a null hypothesis. We have just seen that a researcher who chooses to reject the null hypothesis if she obtains 0 heads or 8 heads runs a ".008 risk" of making a type I error. *If* the null hypothesis is true, the probability of her observing 0 heads or 8 heads is .008, and that is the risk. Compare this to the more liberal test in which the critical region is defined to include 0, 1, 7, or 8 heads in 8 flips. With this test a researcher would run a ".07 risk" of making a type I error because *if* the null hypothesis is true, the probability of getting 0, 1, 7, or 8 heads in 8 flips is .07.

Let me restate these points. A researcher can make a type I error only if the null hypothesis is true and he or she decides to reject it. A researcher can control the risk of making a type I error when deciding what the critical region will include, that is, when deciding what "unlikely" will mean. A researcher who defines "unlikely" to be (p = .07 according to the null hypothesis) runs a higher risk of making a type I error than one who defines unlikely to be (p = .008 according to the null hypothesis), *if the null hypothesis is true.* This is the reasoning behind a tendency to be "conservative." Researchers who want to guard against the risk of making a type I error will define "unlikely" in terms of small probabilities (according to the null hypothesis), establish relatively small critical regions, and require rather strong evidence against the null hypothesis before they reject it. Perhaps the solution to the problem seems obvious—make the most conservative test you can of the null hypothesis and thus run the smallest possible risk of making a type I error. However, the matter is not so simple. There is another possible decision error, called a type II error, which we will now consider.

Type II Errors. What if the null hypothesis is really false? If so, rejecting it is the correct decision and the only error one could make is to fail to reject it. Failing to reject a *false* null hypothesis is called a type II error. It is crucial to keep in mind that the researcher does *not* know whether the null hypothesis is true or false. Concern over the risk of making a type I error is based on the following reasoning: "Well, the null hypothesis could be true, and, *if it is true,* I'd better guard against the mistake of rejecting it." But the researcher must also consider the possibility that the null hypothesis is really false, in which case he or she must guard against making the mistake of *failing* to reject it! Consider our example. Suppose a researcher makes the conservative test of "p(heads) = p(tails)" and will thus reject the null hypothesis if he observes 0 or 8 heads—he will not reject this hypothesis if he observes 1–7 heads in 8 flips. Suppose he actually gets 5 heads in the 8 flips. Does this mean the null hypothesis is true? No. Could he get 5 heads in 8 flips if the coin were biased [p(heads) ≠ p(tails)]? Sure. Look at Table 6.3 and you will see why.

In Table 6.3 I have reproduced the probabilities based on p(heads) = .5, which may be compared to the probabilities based on two degrees of bias, p(heads) = .6 and p(heads) = .8. If a coin is fair (the null hypothesis being tested), it will in the long run fall heads 50 percent of the time and tails 50 percent of the time [p(heads) = .5]. An example of a slightly biased coin is one that in the long run falls heads 60 percent of the time and tails only 40 percent of the time [p(heads) = .6]. An example of a strongly biased coin is one that in the long run falls heads 80 percent of the time and tails just 20 percent of the time [p(heads) = .8].

As you can see in Table 6.3, it is clearly possible to get a "modest" number of heads, such as 3, 4, or 5, in 8 flips even if a coin is strongly biased. The importance of this fact is that a researcher testing the hypothesis that p(heads) = .5, using our conservative test, would reject that hypothesis if 0 or 8 heads were obtained but would not reject that hypothesis if 1–7 heads were obtained. Obviously, the researcher could get an outcome (anything between 1 and 7 heads, inclusive) that would lead to *not* rejecting the null hypothesis [p(heads) = .5] even though the coin is biased. *If* the coin is biased, and if the researcher fails to reject the null hypothesis of a

Table 6.3   Outcome Probabilities When Flipping a Coin Eight Times for Different Values of the Probability of "Heads"

NUMBER OF HEADS	p(HEADS) = .5	p(HEADS) = .6	p(HEADS) = .8
0	.004	.001	.000[a]
1	.031	.008	.000[a]
2	.109	.041	.001
3	.219	.124	.009
4	.273	.232	.046
5	.219	.279	.147
6	.109	.209	.294
7	.031	.090	.336
8	.004	.017	.168

[a] These probabilities are not exactly .000; they are very small (much less than 1 chance in 1000).

fair coin on the basis of the evidence, a type II error has been made. The probability of making a type II error is simply the probability of getting an outcome that will lead to *not* rejecting the null hypothesis when (in our example) the coin is really biased. The probability of a type II error depends on how biased the coin is. If the coin were slightly biased [p(heads) = .6], the probability of a type II error, equal to the probability of getting 1–7 heads when p(heads) = .6, would be .983 (.008 + .041 + .124 + .232 + .279 + .209 + .090 = .983). If the coin were strongly biased [p(heads) = .8], the probability of making a type II error would be .833 (.00 + .001 + .009 + .046 + .147 + .294 + .336 = .833).

PROBLEM

Suppose a researcher tests the fair-coin null hypothesis [p(heads) = .5] using the more liberal test that we have discussed. That is, the researcher will make 8 coin flips and will reject the null hypothesis [p(heads) = .5] if she obtains 0, 1, 7, or 8 heads. Suppose that, unknown to the researcher, the coin is slightly biased—p(heads) is actually .6 for this coin. What is the probability that the researcher will make a type II error? (Use Table 6.3.)

The researcher will make a type II error if she does *not* reject the null hypothesis [p(heads) = .5]. As the test is set up, she will make this decision [don't reject p(heads) = .5] if 2, 3, 4, 5, or 6 heads are obtained when the coin is flipped 8 times. The probability of making a type II error is simply the probability of obtaining 2, 3, 4, 5, or 6 heads when p(heads) = .6. Using the information in Table 6.3, the probability of getting 2–6 heads when p(heads) = .6 can be calculated as .885 (.041 + .124 + .232 + .279 + .209). Thus the probability of making a type II error is .885.

We have now discussed the two types of decision errors that a researcher must guard against when testing a null hypothesis. It is essential to remember that a researcher does *not* know whether the null hypothesis is really true or false. *If* the null hypothesis is *true*, there is a possibility of making the error of *rejecting* it (a type I error). *If* the null hypothesis is *false*, there is a possibility of making the error of *not rejecting* it (a type II error). The test cannot be set up such that there is absolutely no chance of making one error or the other. Rather, researchers must try to hold down the probability of making a type I error *and* the probability of making a type II error.

Here is some terminology that applies to these concepts. The probability of making a type I error (rejecting a true hypothesis) is called *alpha* (Greek α). Researchers often use the term *significance level*, which refers to the same concept as alpha. For example, "5 percent significance level" or "significant at the 5 percent level" means that alpha = p(type I error) = .05. Each of these means that the test was set up such that *if* the null hypothesis was really true there was a 5 percent chance (p = .05) of making the mistake of rejecting it. The probability of making a type II error (not rejecting a false hypothesis) is called *beta* (Greek β). In the problem just presented, the probability of making a type II error was calculated to be .885; we could simply say that beta was .885.

The Power of a Test. We have considered the two kinds of errors that might occur and their respective probabilities (alpha and beta). Let's now turn to a concept reflecting the more positive side of testing null hypotheses. The *power of a test* refers to the probability of *rejecting* a *false* null hypothesis, which is of course a correct decision. Numerically, the power of a test is equal to (1 − beta). For example, if beta, the probability of a type II error, is .70, the power of the test is (1 − .70) or .30; if beta is .40, the power of the test is .60, and so on. Quite simply, the power of a test and beta are inversely related—as one goes up, the other goes down.

When a null hypothesis is tested, one of two decisions will be made— reject or don't reject the null hypothesis. If the null hypothesis is *wrong*, the researcher will make either a mistake (not rejecting the false null hypothesis) or a correct decision (rejecting the false null hypothesis). Beta refers to the probability of making a mistake when the null hypothesis is false, while the power of the test refers to the probability of making the correct decision (reject) when the null hypothesis is false. We could say that researchers would like beta to be small, or we could say that they would like the power of the test to be high. These are two alternate ways of talking about the same basic aspect of the test.

PROBLEM

Suppose a researcher tests the fair-coin null hypothesis [p(heads) = .5] using the conservative test described previously. That is, he will make 8 coin flips and will reject the null hypothesis [p(heads) = .5] if he obtains 0 or 8 heads. Suppose that, unknown to the researcher, the null hypothesis is false—p(heads) is actually .6 for the coin. What is the power of this test? (Use Table 6.3.)

First, note that for this problem I have stated that the null hypothesis is false—p(heads) is actually .6. Therefore (unknown to the researcher making the test) the correct probabilities are those listed under p(heads) = .6 in Table 6.3. Second, the researcher will make the correct decision of rejecting the null hypothesis if 0 or 8 heads are obtained when the coin is flipped 8 times. Therefore the power of the test is the probability of getting 0 or 8 heads when p(heads) = .6. From Table 6.3 we can see that this probability equals .018 (.001 + .017). In other words, the researcher has very little chance of finding out that the coin is actually slightly biased (less than 2 chances in 100). The test has very little power.

Factors Affecting Error Probabilities. Obviously, researchers would like to minimize the risks of making decision errors. The task is to arrange the test of a null hypothesis such that risks of errors are reasonably small (which would mean that chances of correct decisions are reasonably high).

Several factors affect the risks involved in the test, some of which we will consider briefly.

Alpha, the probability of a type I error (rejecting a correct null hypothesis), is *completely under the control of the researcher.* The researcher decides how unlikely outcomes must be (according to the null hypothesis) to lead to rejecting the null hypothesis. In making that decision he or she is choosing the level of risk of a type I error. For example, a researcher making the conservative test of the fair-coin hypothesis would reject the null hypothesis if 0 or 8 heads were obtained. *If* the coin *is* fair [p(heads) = .5], the probability of getting 0 or 8 heads is .008 (see Table 6.3), and that is exactly the risk the researcher runs of making a type I error. If a researcher chose to make the more liberal test of the fair-coin hypothesis, he or she would reject the null hypothesis if 0, 1, 7, or 8 heads were obtained. *If* the coin *is* fair, the probability of getting 0, 1, 7, or 8 heads is .07, and this is exactly the risk of a type I error for this test.

Beta, the probability of a type II error (not rejecting a false null hypothesis), is a more complex matter. Notice that we are concerned here with what might happen when the null hypothesis is *false.* Quite clearly, if the null hypothesis is false, then some other hypothesis is actually correct. It is not possible to state the precise value of beta for a test of a null hypothesis (for reasons I'll mention in a moment). We can, however, identify factors that tend to increase or decrease the value of beta. Three factors that affect beta are (1) the alpha level chosen by the researcher, (2) which specific alternate hypothesis is correct when the null hypothesis is false, and (3) the number of observations involved in making the test. Let's consider each of these.

As already mentioned, the α level is chosen by the researcher. Using our fair-coin example, a researcher might choose to make the conservative test (reject the null hypothesis if 0 or 8 heads are obtained; thus alpha = .008) or the more liberal test (reject the null hypothesis if 0, 1, 7, or 8 heads are obtained; thus alpha = .07). Compare these two tests: With the conservative test, the null hypothesis [p(heads) = .5] will be rejected if 0 or 8 heads are obtained, but it will not be rejected if 1–7 heads are obtained. With the more liberal test, the null hypothesis will be rejected if 0, 1, 7, or 8 heads are obtained, but it will not be rejected if 2–6 heads are obtained. Choosing the more liberal test makes it "easier" to reject the null hypothesis (which is why the more liberal test runs a greater risk of a type I error). Conversely, the conservative test makes it "easier" to *not* reject the null hypothesis, and that is important. Choosing to make the conservative test makes it more likely that the null hypothesis will *not* be rejected, whether the null hypothesis is correct or wrong. Choosing to run *less* risk of a type I error results in running a *greater* risk of a type II error (other things being equal). There is *not* a precise numerical trade-off between the two risks; for example, choosing to lower alpha by .05 does *not* mean that beta will be raised by .05 (the relation is more complex). However, the general tendency does apply—choosing to use a lower alpha level does raise the probability of a type II error (by an unspecified amount).

The situation might seem hopeless. If you want to run less risk of a type I error, you have to run greater risk of a type II error—it looks as if you can't win. However, the situation is neither that simple nor that hopeless. Beta is affected by a number of factors, and the alpha level is only one of them. Consider the second factor—which alternative hypothesis is correct when the null hypothesis is wrong? In discussing the fair-coin example I have consistently shown you two different, specific alternate hypotheses (degrees of bias): slight bias [p(heads) = .6] and strong bias [p(heads) = .8]. With respect to testing the null hypothesis [p(heads) = .5], beta would be *less* if the correct value were p(heads) = .8 than if the correct value were p(heads) = .6. In more general terms, the *greater* the difference between the correct hypothesis and the null hypothesis being tested, the *smaller* the risk of making a type II error (failing to reject the false null hypothesis). The influence on beta of both the alpha level and the difference between the correct and null hypotheses is illustrated in Table 6.4 (using the fair-coin example).

The first row in Table 6.4 simply shows the difference between the conservative and more liberal tests regarding type I errors. If the null hypothesis is true, the probability of making a type I error is .008 for the conservative test but .07 for the more liberal test. The bottom two rows show beta values; notice that beta is always larger for the conservative test than for the more liberal test (.983 vs. .885 and .833 vs. .497). This illustrates the alpha–beta relation—lower alpha means higher beta, other things being equal. Notice also that regardless of which test is used, beta is smaller for the more different alternate hypothesis [p(heads) = .8]. If

Table 6.4   Comparison of Conservative and More Liberal Tests of the Hypothesis That p(heads) = p(tails) = .5

	CONSERVATIVE TEST (Reject if 0 or 8; Don't Reject if 1–7)	MORE LIBERAL TEST (Reject if 0, 1, 7, or 8; Don't Reject if 2–6)
If null hypothesis true, then p(type I error) is:	.008	.070
If null hypothesis false and p(heads) = .6, then p(type II error) is:	.983	.885
If null hypothesis false and p(heads) = .8, then p(type II error) is:	.833	.497

the conservative test was used and the fair-coin null hypothesis was wrong, the probability of *not* rejecting this false null hypothesis would be .983 if the coin was actually slightly biased but just .833 if the coin was actually strongly biased. The same relation holds for the more liberal test; if the coin was only slightly biased, the probability of failing to reject the false null hypothesis would be .885, while it would be only .497 if the coin was strongly biased. In somewhat oversimplified terms, what this means is that if you are testing a null hypothesis that is false (unknown to you, of course), you will be better off (less likely to make a type II error) if the correct hypothesis is very different from the null hypothesis.

Beta is also influenced by the number of observations used to test a null hypothesis. The basic rule is this: The *larger* the number of observations used in the test, the *smaller* the risk of a type II error. This relation can also be stated in "power" terms: As the number of observations *increases*, the power of the test *increases*. If the null hypothesis is *false*, then as more observations are used in the test, the risk of making the mistake of *not* rejecting the false null hypothesis goes down and the chances of making the correct decision (i.e., rejecting the null hypothesis) go up. I will not give a detailed explanation of how and why increasing the number of observations reduces beta (increases power); I will make some remarks on this topic in a later section. I will, however, give you an intuitive feel for this important concept, again using the fair-coin example.

A person testing the fair-coin hypothesis is basically trying to decide whether a coin is fair or biased (starting, of course, with the hypothesis that it is fair). Suppose the coin is in fact biased. Flipping the coin just once will hardly provide clear evidence. As we have seen, making 8 flips does not provide a very powerful test—a biased coin does not behave very differently from a fair coin over just 8 flips. But suppose we flipped the coin 100 times or 500 times or 1000 times. The more flips we make, the less likely it is that a biased coin will "look like" a fair coin—the bias will become more and more apparent, and thus it will be less and less likely that we would fail to reject the fair-coin hypothesis.

To sum up, the probability of a type II error (not rejecting a false null hypothesis) goes *up* as the chosen alpha level goes down, goes *down* as the correct hypothesis differs more from the (false) null hypothesis being tested, and goes *down* with an increase in the number of observations used in the test. In setting up a test of a null hypothesis, a researcher needs to be concerned about the possibility that the null hypothesis is correct and about the possibility that the null hypothesis is wrong. One way to set up a good test is to do the following: First, choose a low level of alpha to hold down the probability of a type I error in case the null hypothesis is correct. Second, use a large enough number of observations to bring beta down to an acceptable level (in case the null hypothesis is false). By choosing a low alpha level and making enough observations, researchers can conduct tests of null hypotheses with low risks of both type I and type II errors.

COMMONLY TESTED HYPOTHESES

Although we cannot possibly hope to discuss a large number of the hypotheses that researchers test, we can consider some types of null hypotheses that are tested with some regularity. Doing so will give you an idea of the kinds of data analysis that researchers employ. We will consider tests of two kinds of null hypotheses—those concerned with frequencies and those concerned with differences between means.

Hypotheses About Frequencies

Throughout this chapter I have been using the example of testing the hypothesis that a coin is fair. While researchers obviously do not occupy themselves testing this hypothesis, they often test hypotheses that are formally equivalent to the fair-coin hypothesis. The coin-flipping example can be described as follows: On each trial (flip) there are two possible outcomes: heads or tails. By observing the outcomes for a number of independent trials, we can test a hypothesis about the probability of getting each of the two outcomes. There are many situations that fit this description.

For example, suppose I ask a number of people, separately and independently, to make a binary choice, such as "Are you for or against gun control?" A likely null hypothesis is that, in general, people are as likely to be "for" as they are to be "against"; that is, $p(\text{for}) = p(\text{against}) = .5$. By asking, say, 30 people and counting the number of "fors" I get, I can test this null hypothesis against the alternate hypothesis that $p(\text{for}) \neq .5$. Notice that this test is formally the same as testing the fair-coin hypothesis by making 30 coin flips.

The actual method used to test such hypotheses involves a statistical test called *chi square* analysis. I will not describe this statistical test here (it is summarized in Appendix B), but I will outline the general procedures used to test null hypotheses about frequencies.

Let's use the example of testing "$p(\text{for}) = .5$" by asking 30 people. A central question is this: If 30 observations will be made, what would be the ideal or expected frequencies according to the null hypothesis? The answer is straightforward. If "for" is just as likely as "against," it follows that for 30 observations the ideal or expected frequencies are 15 "fors" and 15 "againsts." We can then test to see whether the actual, obtained frequencies differ enough from the expected frequencies to warrant rejecting the null hypothesis. A diagram of the test looked at in this way is shown in Table 6.5, together with some hypothetical observed frequencies.

Of course, to conduct the test, we would have to choose an alpha level (a precise definition of "differs enough"). Suppose we chose alpha = .05, meaning that we would reject the null hypothesis [p(for) = .5] if the obtained frequencies belonged to the most extreme 5 percent of possible outcomes according to the null hypothesis. To complete the test we would calculate a chi square statistic that would indicate whether the obtained frequencies (20 "fors," 10 "againsts") differ "enough" from the expected frequencies (whether 10 "fors," 20 "againsts" is among the most extreme 5 percent of outcomes when the ideal frequencies are 15 "fors," 15 "againsts"). In this particular case chi square analysis would indicate that we could *not* reject the null hypothesis on the basis of the data. This result is not that important for our present purposes. I want you to concentrate on the logic of the test. Thus, as this example shows, one first determines what the ideal or expected frequencies should be according to the null hypothesis and then determines whether the obtained frequencies differ enough from the expected frequencies to justify rejecting the null hypothesis.

This method can be used when more than two categories are involved; the logic remains the same. For example, suppose a number of people had learned a list of words and were each asked afterward to indicate which of three learning strategies they had used: memorizing, making up sentences with the words, or making up images to represent the words. The null hypothesis would be that each method is equally likely to be used; that is, p(memorization) = p(sentences) = p(images). If a total of 60 people had learned the list and had been asked what strategy they had used, the expected (ideal) frequencies (on the basis of the null hypothesis) would be memorization 20, sentences 20, images 20. Of course if the three methods are *in principle* equally likely to be used, this does not mean that the 60 observations must be exactly evenly distributed among the three categories (no more than a fair coin *must* yield equal numbers of heads and tails in

Table 6.5   Expected and Observed Frequencies for a Test[a] of the Null Hypothesis That p(for) = p(against)

	FOR	AGAINST	TOTAL OBSERVATIONS
Expected frequencies (based on null hypothesis)	15	15	30
Observed frequencies	20	10	30

[a] The test: Do the observed frequencies differ enough from the expected frequencies to warrant rejecting the null hypothesis?

a given number of flips). According to the null hypothesis, some arrangements of frequencies are more likely than others. In general, the more uneven the frequencies are, the less likely the null hypothesis predicts them to be. To test the null hypothesis we would have to choose an alpha level, say, .05, and then determine whether the actual, obtained frequencies are among the least likely 5 percent according to the null hypothesis. If so, we would reject the null hypothesis.

It is usually difficult to tell just by "looking at" the data whether the obtained frequencies differ enough from the expected frequencies to justify rejecting the null hypothesis (which is, of course, the reason for statistical tests such as chi square). Table 6.6 presents the expected frequencies [based on the null hypothesis that p(memorization) = p(sentences) = p(images)] and seven different patterns of possible observed frequencies. Try your hand at "eyeball" analysis—for each of the seven patterns of observed frequencies, try to decide whether the frequencies differ enough to justify rejecting the null hypothesis with alpha = .05.

The answers (based on chi square analysis) are that data sets B, D, and F are sufficiently different from the expected frequencies to justify rejecting the null hypothesis; the patterns of frequencies shown in data sets A, C, E, and G do not differ enough from the expected frequencies to warrant rejecting the null hypothesis.

Let me use Table 6.6 to point out a feature of such tests. I have not yet stated what the form of the alternate hypothesis would be for this test.

Table 6.6   Which Observed Frequencies Would Lead to Rejecting the Null Hypothesis? [Null Hypothesis: p(memorization) = p(sentences) = p(images)]

	Methods			
	MEMORIZA-TION	SENTENCES	IMAGES	TOTAL OBSERVATIONS
Expected Frequencies (based on null hypothesis)	20	20	20	60
Possible Observed Frequencies				
A	25	18	17	60
B	15	33	12	60
C	18	18	24	60
D	40	8	12	60
E	17	28	15	60
F	21	10	29	60
G	14	22	24	60

Notice that the null hypothesis includes two "equals" signs (because three categories are involved). The alternate hypothesis would be that "at least one unequals sign exists." The alternate hypothesis is quite nonspecific; to deny the equalities stated in the null hypothesis means that perhaps p(memorization) $\neq$ p(imagery) or p(memorization) $\neq$ p(sentences) or p(sentences) $\neq$ p(images), or that all three differ—p(memorization) $\neq$ p(sentences) $\neq$ p(images). A practical consequence of the nature of the alternate hypothesis is that it really makes no difference (for the test) which category has which frequency. For example, the frequencies in data set B would justify rejecting the null hypothesis; if the frequencies were memorization 12, sentences 15, images 33, the null hypothesis would also be rejected. For a test of a multicategory null hypothesis, which category has especially high or especially low obtained frequencies is *not* important; what *is* important is how unevenly the frequencies are distributed over the categories.

Tests of Independence. Thus far we have considered relatively simple, although useful, null hypotheses about frequencies. Whether two or more categories are involved, the null hypothesis has been that "everything is equally likely." A more complex and more interesting situation concerns tests of independence. The basic feature of such situations is that the frequencies can be classified in two (or more) different ways. For example, suppose 30 men and 30 women had each been asked to choose their favorite kind of movie from a list of four alternatives: "westerns," "musicals," "love stories," and "thrillers." One question that we might like to have answered is whether the preferences of the men and women are different. We would test the null hypothesis that men's and women's preferences are the same, which is equivalent to saying that there is just one set of preferences that applies equally well to men and women.

In statistical terminology the null hypothesis is somewhat cumbersome, but you should know what it would be. Using m and w to identify probabilities, the null hypothesis would be p_m(western) $= p_f$(western) and p_m(musical) $= p_f$(musical) and p_m(love story) $= p_f$(love story) and p_m(thriller) $= p_f$(thriller). The null hypothesis would state these four equalities, while the alternate hypothesis (as you might suspect) would state that *there is at least one inequality*. It is important to notice what the null hypothesis does *not* say—it does not say anything about what the probability of choosing a western, musical, love story, or thriller is, and it says nothing about these probabilities being equal or differing in some particular way. In effect the null hypothesis states that whatever p(western) is, it is the same for men and women; whatever p(musical) is, it is the same for men and women; and so on. It is important to understand the precise nature of the null hypothesis for this test in order to understand how the expected frequencies are figured out. Table 6.7 shows the derivation of the expected fre-

Table 6.7   Developing Expected Frequencies for the Test of Independence Between Gender and Movie Preference

| | | | Accepted as Given | | |
	WESTERN	MUSICAL	LOVE STORY	THRILLER	TOTAL
Women					30
Men					30
Totals	12	8	14	26	60

Null Hypothesis

p_m(western) = p_f(western) and p_m(musical) = p_f(musical) and p_m(love story) = p_f(love story) and p_m(thriller) = p_f(thriller)

Logic of Developing Expected Frequencies

"Given that the total group of 60 people is half women and half men, and given that 12 people chose westerns, according to the null hypothesis the 12 'western choosers' should be half women and half men" (and likewise for the other movie choices).

| | | | Expected Frequencies (According to the Null Hypothesis) | | |
	WESTERN	MUSICAL	LOVE STORY	THRILLER	TOTAL
Women	6	4	7	13	30
Men	6	4	7	13	30
Totals	12	8	14	26	60

quencies for this test (i.e., a test of whether movie preferences are *independent* of gender).

As you can see, the null hypothesis "doesn't care" how many men and women there are in the total group, nor does it care how many people chose westerns or musicals or other types of movies. These facts are accepted as given. What the null hypothesis does assert is that if the total group is half women, then each group choosing a particular type of movie should be half women (ideally, of course). The test of this null hypothesis therefore involves comparing the actual, obtained frequencies in the "inside" cells (women choosing westerns, women choosing musicals, men choosing love stories, etc.) with the expected frequencies developed on the basis of the null hypothesis. Suppose the obtained frequencies looked like those shown in Table 6.8. Starting in the upper left-hand cell, we would be concerned with the difference of 2 between the number of women who

Table 6.8   Observed Frequencies for the Test of Independence Between Gender and Movie Preference

	WESTERN	MUSICAL	LOVE STORY	THRILLER	TOTAL
Women	4	6	11	9	30
Men	8	2	3	17	30
Totals	12	8	14	26	60

actually chose westerns (4) and the number predicted to make that choice (6) by the null hypothesis, with the difference between 6(obtained) and 4(expected) for "women choosing musicals," and so on for the other "inside" cells. Here's a chance to try another "eyeball analysis": Do you think the data in Table 6.8 differ enough from the expected frequencies in Table 6.7 to warrant rejecting the null hypothesis with, say, alpha = .01? (Alpha = .01 suggests that we're requiring rather strong evidence against the null hypothesis to reject it). If you feel that the right answer is no, you are correct—the arrangement of frequencies in the "inside" cells in Table 6.8 does not warrant rejecting the null hypothesis with alpha = .01.

These examples should give you an idea of the kinds of null hypotheses about frequencies that are tested in psychological research. In general, the null hypothesis (which must be examined quite carefully) leads to the development of ideal or expected frequencies for the various categories. The test then involves determining whether the actual, obtained frequencies differ enough from the expected frequencies to justify rejecting the null hypothesis (at a chosen level of significance, of course).

Hypotheses About Mean Differences

Researchers often test null hypotheses about differences between population means. Although these tests have several different forms and involve statistical techniques such as t ratio and F ratio (summarized in Appendix B), we can cover the essentials of such tests by considering just two means and using what we know about normal distributions.

As far back as Chapter 2, I mentioned that researchers evaluate treatments by comparing the "score difference between treatments" to "an index of random score variation." We can now consider a much more precise meaning of this statement. Suppose a researcher obtains scores on an arithmetic test for a sample of males and a sample of females and wants to determine whether the average scores for males and females are "really different." Let's begin by considering the null hypothesis, which would be (in words) the statement that the true or population mean for males does *not* differ from the population mean for females. In symbolic terms, the null hypothesis is $M_m - M_f = 0$. The researcher will have two *sample* means, one for the sample of males ($\bar{X}_m$) and one for the sample of females ($\bar{X}_f$). To test the null hypothesis ($M_m - M_f = 0$) the researcher must determine whether the observed difference between *sample means* ($\bar{X}_m - \bar{X}_f$) is "far enough" from zero to justify rejecting the null hypothesis. To understand how the test is conducted we need to consider another statistical concept.

Distributions of Sample Mean Differences. We have already discussed two kinds of normal distributions. In Chapter 4 we considered normal distributions of individual scores (X's), characterized by a mean (M) and a standard deviation (σ). We discussed sampling distributions of $\bar{X}$ in Chapter 5. These refer to the distribution of values of the mean ($\bar{X}$) calculated for samples of size n, all drawn from the same population. A distribution of $\bar{X}$ has a mean ($M_{\bar{x}}$) and a standard deviation ($\sigma_{\bar{x}}$), called the standard error of the mean. Remember that $M_{\bar{x}} = M$, that $\sigma_{\bar{x}} = \sigma/\sqrt{n}$, and that the distribution of $\bar{X}$ will be approximately normal if sample size (n) is fairly large. We will now consider another type of sampling distribution, namely, the distribution of differences between sample means.

Since I will be talking about two population distributions, I need some way to identify them. I will use the usual and simple technique of calling them populations 1 and 2. Thus population distribution 1 has mean M_1 and standard deviation σ_1 while population 2 has mean M_2 and standard deviation σ_2. To imagine how a sampling distribution of mean differences might be constructed, consider the following. Suppose we draw a sample of size n_1 from population 1 and calculate the mean of that sample ($\bar{X}_1$). At the same time, we draw a sample of size n_2 from population 2 and calculate its mean ($\bar{X}_2$). We then calculate the difference between the two sample means ($\bar{X}_1 - \bar{X}_2$). By repeating this procedure many times we would generate a distribution of values for ($\bar{X}_1 - \bar{X}_2$), and this would be a distribution of sample mean differences.

The following things are true of distributions of sample mean differences. First, the mean of the distribution ($M_{\bar{x}_1 - \bar{x}_2}$) is equal to the difference between the two population means ($M_1 - M_2$). Second, if the samples are fairly large, the distribution of sample mean differences will resemble a normal distribution. This means that the knowledge we have about normal distributions can be reasonably applied to distributions of sample mean differences, which is important for conducting tests about differences between population means. The third characteristic we need to consider is the standard deviation of a distribution of sample mean differences. Actually, the complete formula is rather complicated. The essential point is that a distribution of sample mean differences clearly has a standard deviation; it is called the *standard error of the difference* and symbolized by

$\sigma_{\bar{X}_1-\bar{X}_2}$. Furthermore, it is possible to estimate the value of $\sigma_{\bar{X}_1-\bar{X}_2}$ from the scores in the two samples that a researcher will actually have.

To sum up, a researcher has data for two samples, one from each population, and can calculate the difference between sample means ($\bar{X}_1 - \bar{X}_2$). This sample mean difference belongs to some distribution of ($\bar{X}_1 - \bar{X}_2$). That distribution has a mean ($M_{\bar{X}_1-\bar{X}_2}$), which is equal to the difference between the two population means ($M_1 - M_2$). Under most circumstances it is reasonable to assume that the distribution of sample mean differences resembles a normal distribution. Finally, the researcher can estimate the value of the standard error of the difference ($\sigma_{\bar{X}_1-\bar{X}_2}$). Let's now apply some normal-curve concepts to such distributions.

Consider what we know about normal distributions. For example, in a normal distribution less than 5 percent of the values lie more than two standard deviations from the mean (in either direction). Applying this knowledge to distributions of sample mean differences, we can state that less than 5 percent of the values of ($\bar{X}_1 - \bar{X}_2$) will lie more than $2 \times \sigma_{\bar{X}_1-\bar{X}_2}$ from $M_{\bar{X}_1-\bar{X}_2}$. Such facts form the basis of tests of null hypotheses about mean differences.

The null hypothesis states that $M_1 - M_2 = 0$, which is equivalent to stating that $M_{\bar{X}_1-\bar{X}_2} = 0$. To test this hypothesis (against the alternate hypothesis that $M_1 - M_2 \neq 0$) with alpha equal to .05, a researcher need only estimate the value of $\sigma_{\bar{X}_1-\bar{X}_2}$ and then determine whether the actual, obtained value of ($\bar{X}_1 - \bar{X}_2$) is more than $2 \times \sigma_{\bar{X}_1-\bar{X}_2}$ from zero. If it is, then the obtained value of ($\bar{X}_1 - \bar{X}_2$) is among the most extreme 5 percent of possible values according to the null hypothesis. Such an occurrence would be reasonable grounds for rejecting the null hypothesis that $M_1 - M_2 = 0$. If a researcher wants to use a different value of alpha, he or she can use information about normal curves (such as that in Table 4.10) to determine how far from zero an obtained value of ($\bar{X}_1 - \bar{X}_2$) must be to justify rejecting the null hypothesis. For example, to test the null hypothesis ($M_1 - M_2 = 0$) at the 1 percent significance level (alpha = .01), the obtained value of ($\bar{X}_1 - \bar{X}_2$) would have to differ from zero by at least $2.58 \times \sigma_{\bar{X}_1-\bar{X}_2}$ for the null hypothesis to be rejected.

Let's return to the example of comparing the arithmetic scores of males and females. The null hypothesis would state that $M_m - M_f = 0$. Suppose the researcher decides to test this hypothesis (against the alternate hypothesis that $M_m - M_f \neq 0$) with an alpha level of .05. This means that the critical question will be whether the obtained value of ($\bar{X}_m - \bar{X}_f$) is more than $2 \times \sigma_{\bar{X}_m-\bar{X}_f}$ from zero.

PROBLEM

Suppose a researcher obtains the following sample means: $\bar{X}_m = 41.4$, $\bar{X}_f = 37.2$. Suppose also that, using the scores in the two samples, $\sigma_{\bar{X}_m-\bar{X}_f}$ is estimated to be 3.2. With alpha = .05, would the null hypothesis be rejected?

The obtained sample mean difference is 4.2(41.4 − 37.2); dividing this by the value of $\sigma_{\bar{X}_m - \bar{X}_f}$ (3.2), we obtain the critical ratio of 1.31(4.2/3.2 = 1.31). The obtained sample mean difference is *less* than two standard errors of the difference from zero; it is *not* among the most extreme 5 percent of values according to the null hypothesis, and it is thus not sufficient evidence to reject the null hypothesis. In brief, the researcher could not reject the hypothesis that $M_m - M_f = 0$.

Increasing the Power of the Test. In testing null hypotheses about mean differences, researchers must of course be concerned about the risks of type I and type II errors. *If* the null hypothesis ($M_1 - M_2 = 0$) is correct, there is a risk of erring by rejecting it. The researcher controls this risk when choosing an alpha level for the test. *If* the null hypothesis is wrong, there is a possibility of erring by failing to reject it. Researchers want to keep beta (the probability of a type II error) small; in other words, they want to conduct a test with considerable power. If the null hypothesis is wrong, they want to have a very good chance of rejecting it. Beta is strongly influenced by the value of $\sigma_{\bar{X}_1 - \bar{X}_2}$; the smaller $\sigma_{\bar{X}_1 - \bar{X}_2}$ is, the smaller beta will be; the smaller $\sigma_{\bar{X}_1 - \bar{X}_2}$ is, the greater the power of the test will be.

The value of $\sigma_{\bar{X}_1 - \bar{X}_2}$ reflects the variability of a distribution of ($\bar{X}_1 - \bar{X}_2$). The smaller $\sigma_{\bar{X}_1 - \bar{X}_2}$ is, the greater the tendency for values of ($\bar{X}_1 - \bar{X}_2$) to cluster close to $M_{\bar{X}_1 - \bar{X}_2}$ ($M_1 - M_2$). To see why this is important, consider the following example. Suppose a researcher is testing the null hypothesis that $M_1 - M_2 = 0$. The alpha level he has chosen is .05, which means that he will reject the null hypothesis if the obtained value of ($\bar{X}_1 - \bar{X}_2$) is *more* than $2 \times \sigma_{\bar{X}_1 - \bar{X}_2}$ from zero. It also means that he will *not* reject the null hypothesis if the obtained value is *less* than $2 \times \sigma_{\bar{X}_1 - \bar{X}_2}$ from zero. Since we are concerned with the likelihood of a type II error (*not* rejecting a false null hypothesis), we must concentrate on what will lead him to "not reject" the null hypothesis. Suppose that, unknown to the researcher, the actual value of $M_1 - M_2$ is +6. The critical question is, What is the probability that he will err by failing to reject the null hypothesis? The answer depends on how variable the distribution of sample means is; that is, the answer depends on the value of $\sigma_{\bar{X}_1 - \bar{X}_2}$.

Suppose that $\sigma_{\bar{X}_1 - \bar{X}_2} = 4$. In setting up the test the researcher would *not* reject the null hypothesis if the obtained value of ($\bar{X}_1 - \bar{X}_2$) were between −8 and +8 [0 − 2(4) and 0 + 2(4)]. But in fact his obtained value of ($\bar{X}_1 - \bar{X}_2$) will come from a distribution centered on +6. What are the chances that he will obtain a value of ($\bar{X}_1 - \bar{X}_2$) that is between −8 and +8, which will lead him to err by *not* rejecting the null hypothesis? The situation is diagramed in panel (a) of Figure 6.1. You can see that the distribution of sample mean differences centered on +6 overlaps considerably with the range of observations that will lead to *not* rejecting the null hypothesis. There is a very good chance of making a type II error; beta would be quite high.

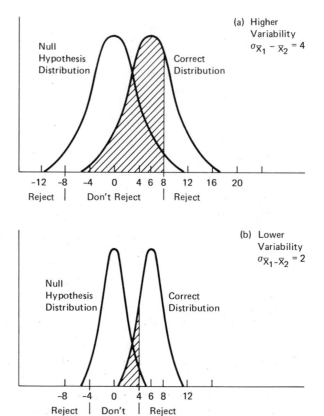

Figure 6.1. Illustration of the influence of the value of $\sigma_{\bar{x}_1-\bar{x}_2}$ on beta. The striped area represents the probability of making a Type II error.

Now let's change one important item. Suppose the value of $\sigma_{\bar{x}_1-\bar{x}_2}$ is 2 rather than 4. In this case the researcher would *not* reject the null hypothesis ($M_1 - M_2 = 0$) if the obtained value of ($\bar{X}_1 - \bar{X}_2$) falls between -4 and $+4$ [$0 - 2(2)$ and $0 + 2(2)$]. As before, the obtained value of ($\bar{X}_1 - \bar{X}_2$) will actually come from a distribution of sample mean differences centered on $+6$. However, we are now considering a distribution with less variability. This situation is diagramed in panel (b) of Figure 6.1. As you can see, there is much less overlap between the correct distribution (centered on $+6$) and the range of observations that will lead to *not* rejecting the null hypothesis. There is a much smaller probability of a type II error; beta is considerably reduced. In "power" terms, the power of the test increases as $\sigma_{\bar{x}_1-\bar{x}_2}$ gets smaller. Notice how much of the distribution centered on $+6$ lies in the region that will lead to (correctly) rejecting the null hypothesis in panel (b). If $M_1 - M_2$ is actually $+6$, the researcher is very likely to reject the null hypothesis ($M_1 - M_2 = 0$) when $\sigma_{\bar{X}_1 - \bar{X}_2}$ is small.

It is obviously to a researcher's advantage to have a small value for $\sigma_{\bar{X}_1 - \bar{X}_2}$. This doesn't affect the probability of a type I error (since that is chosen by the researcher), but small values of $\sigma_{\bar{X}_1 - \bar{X}_2}$ reduce the probability of making type II errors. A reasonable question is, How can the value of $\sigma_{\bar{X}_1 - \bar{X}_2}$ be made smaller? There are several ways. In Chapter 3 I pointed out that using matched subjects or repeated measures results in a "more sensitive" evaluation of treatment differences. More precisely, using well-matched subjects or repeated measures reduces the size of $\sigma_{\bar{X}_1 - \bar{X}_2}$. Reducing the value of $\sigma_{\bar{X}_1 - \bar{X}_2}$ reduces the chances of making a type II error—or, reducing the value of $\sigma_{\bar{X}_1 - \bar{X}_2}$ increases the power of the test. Compared to using independent groups of subjects for different treatments, using well-matched subjects or repeated measures reduces the value of $\sigma_{\bar{X}_1 - \bar{X}_2}$ and thus provides a more powerful test of the null hypothesis.

There are ways of reducing the value of $\sigma_{\bar{X}_1 - \bar{X}_2}$ even when independent groups of subjects are used. To illustrate how $\sigma_{\bar{X}_1 - \bar{X}_2}$ can be reduced when independent groups are used, here is the formula that applies to this situation:

$$\sigma_{\bar{X}_1 - \bar{X}_2} = \sqrt{\frac{\sigma_1^{\,2}}{n_1} + \frac{\sigma_2^{\,2}}{n_2}}$$

As you can see, the value of $\sigma_{\bar{X}_1 - \bar{X}_2}$ depends on the values of σ_1^2 and σ_2^2 and on the sample sizes (n_1 and n_2). To make $\sigma_{\bar{X}_1 - \bar{X}_2}$ smaller, one would like to reduce the size of σ_1^2 and σ_2^2 or increase the sizes of n_1 and n_2. In Chapter 3 I stated that researchers might want to use "homogeneous" groups of subjects to increase the sensitivity of the treatment comparison, for example, to use just females rather than a mixture of males and females (assuming that females will be more alike). The translation is that using "more homogeneous" subjects lowers the values of σ_1^2 and σ_2^2, which of course lowers the value of $\sigma_{\bar{X}_1 - \bar{X}_2}$. Earlier in this chapter I pointed out that beta, the probability of making a type II error, goes down as more observations are made. You can see this relation clearly in the formula for $\sigma_{\bar{X}_1 - \bar{X}_2}$ for independent groups. The larger the values of n_1 and n_2, the smaller the value of $\sigma_{\bar{X}_1 - \bar{X}_2}$.

To summarize, it is to a researcher's advantage to have a small value of $\sigma_{\bar{X}_1 - \bar{X}_2}$ when testing a null hypothesis about mean differences. The value of $\sigma_{\bar{X}_1 - \bar{X}_2}$ is not important *if* the null hypothesis ($M_1 - M_2 = 0$) is correct, because the probability of a type I error depends solely on the researcher's choice of an alpha level. The value of $\sigma_{\bar{X}_1 - \bar{X}_2}$ is extremely important if the null hypothesis is wrong, since the probability of a type II error goes down as the value of $\sigma_{\bar{X}_1 - \bar{X}_2}$ goes down. Since the researcher doesn't know beforehand whether the null hypothesis is right or wrong, he or she should try to have a small value for $\sigma_{\bar{x}_1 - \bar{x}_2}$. This can be accomplished by using well-matched subjects or repeated measures (rather than independent groups), by using more homogeneous subjects (and thereby reducing the values of $\sigma_1{}^2$ and $\sigma_2{}^2$), or by increasing sample sizes. By employing one or more of these procedures, a researcher can set up a test of a null hypothesis that is as sensitive as he or she would like.

PROBLEM

Following are several pairs of alternatives for conducting research. For each pair, decide which alternative (1) should result in a more powerful test of the null hypothesis and (2) should lead to results of greater generality. Note that the two alternatives might be equal with respect to either power or generality.

Pair A: 10 subjects per treatment in an independent-groups design versus 20 subjects per treatment in an independent-groups design.
Pair B: Using subjects of both sexes versus using subjects of only one sex.
Pair C: A matched-subjects design versus an independent-groups design.

Here are the answers. For pair A, increasing the number of subjects per treatment (20 vs. 10) will result in a more powerful test of the null hypothesis. *If* the null hypothesis is wrong, it is more likely that a researcher will reject it if there are 20 subjects per treatment than if there are only 10 subjects per treatment. With respect to the generality of the results, the two choices are fundamentally equal. For pair B, using subjects of just one sex is likely to result in a more powerful test of a null hypothesis (this will be true if there is any difference at all between sexes with respect to what is being measured). In contrast, any results based on both sexes would have greater generality than results based on only one sex. For pair C, using matched subjects will result in a more powerful test of the null hypothesis *if* the subjects are well matched. Comparing these alternatives with respect to generality is less clear. If we can assume that, most often, subjects are *not* deliberately matched, then the independent-groups design would yield more representative results.

INTERPRETING TEST OUTCOMES

The test of a null hypothesis is used by a researcher to guide the conclusions that will be reached on the basis of the data. We have now considered a number of the formal aspects of tests of null hypotheses. There are, however, several other issues that we must cover to help you understand how research decisions are made and where potential difficulties lie.

"Accept" Versus "Don't Reject"

Throughout this chapter I have described the two possible decisions as "rejecting" or "not rejecting" the null hypothesis. Some writers refer to "accepting" or "rejecting" the null hypothesis; obviously, they substitute "accept" for "don't reject." In a sense the difference between these two terms is slight, although thinking in terms of "accepting" the null hypothesis can have some dangers in it. A null hypothesis *is* given favored status and basically either survives or doesn't survive the test. If a null hypothesis is *not* rejected, it does maintain its status as a reasonable ("acceptable") hypothesis. This idea suggests that there is little difference between "don't reject" and "accept." However, it is important to recognize that a test of a null hypothesis *never* demonstrates that the null hypothesis is correct. The potential danger in using "accept" is that a person might be led to believe that the null hypothesis has been *proven* to be correct, which is *not* so. Basically, a researcher testing a null hypothesis decides what kind of evidence will lead to rejecting that hypothesis and then either gets such evidence or *fails to obtain sufficient evidence to reject the null hypothesis.* A careful researcher might be reluctant to say "I accept the null hypothesis," preferring to say "I did not get sufficient evidence to reject the null hypothesis." Thus "accept" is a somewhat stronger statement than "don't reject," and, strictly speaking, the test allows only "don't reject."

Statistical Versus Psychological Interpretation

I cannot emphasize too strongly the fact that the null and alternate hypotheses are statistical hypotheses. Of course researchers do not test null hypotheses just for practice—they have reasons, based on existing psychological theory, for testing particular null hypotheses. Suppose a researcher has devised a theory that leads to the prediction that large rewards will lead to faster learning than small rewards. Ordinarily the theory (and the prediction) will lack either the specificity or the general acceptance (or both) to justify using the prediction as a null hypothesis. Consequently to support her *psychological hypothesis* (that large rewards lead to faster learning) the researcher will have to obtain evidence *against* the null hypothesis that amount of reward has *no effect.* If she is measuring trials-to-learn for different amounts of reward, the null hypothesis will be $M_{small} = M_{large}$ and she will arrange two conditions, one called "large reward" and the other "small reward," and collect samples of data under each condition. Suppose the data allow her to reject the null hypothesis (at some level of significance). All the test establishes is that there are reasonable grounds for rejecting the hypothesis that the true population mean for the condition called "large reward" is equal to the true population mean for the condition called "small reward." The test does *not* demonstrate that the *reason* these two M's may reasonably be considered different is "large reward versus small reward." To justify the conclusion that "large reward versus small reward" is the most reasonable explanation of the difference between M's, the researcher would have to show that there are no other reasonable explanations for the difference.

To emphasize this point let me describe a hypothetical and thoroughly confounded experiment. Two conditions, labeled A and B, are compared. Here is a description of the two conditions:

	CONDITION A	CONDITION B
Amount of reward	Large	Small
Subjects	Female rats	Male rats
Time of learning	Morning	Evening

For this test the null hypothesis would be "$M_A - M_B = 0$" and the alternate hypothesis would be "$M_A - M_B \neq 0$." Suppose the evidence ($\bar{X}_A - \bar{X}_B$) warrants rejecting the null hypothesis. The test makes it reasonable to conclude that a difference between population means exists. Now, why does this difference exist? Clearly there is no way to tell. Perhaps the difference is due to the difference in amount of reward, or to the difference in sex of subjects, or to the difference in time of learning. The point is that rejecting a null hypothesis means that there are reasonable grounds for rejecting the null hypothesis *on statistical grounds,* but the test says nothing by itself about why that statistical hypothesis might (reasonably be considered to) be wrong. To justify any particular explanation of the difference, one must demonstrate that there are no other plausible explanations of the difference (which is not possible in this case).

Such interpretive problems plague comparisons of "existing groups." Earlier we used the example of testing the null hypothesis that "$M_{neur} = M_{norm}$" with respect to scores on an intelligence test. Suppose the evidence warranted rejecting this null hypothesis. Does this mean that the two M's differ because of the difference between neuroticism and normality? Not necessarily. What if the "neurotics" were less educated than the "normals"? It is plausible to argue that level of education might influence scores on an intelligence test, in which case it would be inappropriate to conclude that the difference between M's results from "neuroticism" versus "normality."

In short, a test of a null hypothesis is a statistical test that does not itself establish any particular psychological explanation. Comparisons of naturally existing groups (e.g., neurotics vs. normals, men vs. women, boy scouts vs. nonscouts) are particularly troublesome in this respect. Experiments, in which some variable is manipulated by the researcher, are generally easier to interpret, but researchers can conduct "poor" experiments!

In general, a test of a null hypothesis indicates no more than that there is (or isn't) something to be explained—it does not support any particular explanation.

PROBLEM

A psychology instructor studied the relation between exam scores and students' study techniques. He surveyed the class and found that each student could be placed into one of four categories defining "method of studying the textbook": underlining, outlining, making marginal notes, or "just reading." He then gave an exam based solely on the textbook material and obtained the following average scores: underliners, 58 percent correct; outliners, 55 percent; marginal-note makers, 76 percent; readers, 56 percent. Applying an appropriate statistical test, he found that the average score for marginal-note makers was significantly higher than the average for any other group. He therefore decided to tell the entire class to adopt the note-making technique because making marginal notes produces the highest exam scores. Why might this conclusion be incorrect?

There is no reason to question the statistical result, that marginal-note makers earn higher scores. The question concerns the interpretation of the result. Basically, both exam scores and study techniques were natural variables in this study; the instructor made no attempt to manipulate study techniques. Therefore he does not know whether other important variables might be confounded with study technique. In other words, the marginal-note makers might differ in some other characteristic(s) from the other students, and some other characteristic, not the study technique, might be responsible for their higher exam scores. For example, suppose we found that the note makers had higher general scholastic ability than the other students—if so, the instructor's conclusion would be considerably weakened. Suppose we found that note makers spend more time studying than the other students—if so, perhaps the proper conclusion is that spending more time studying (regardless of which technique one uses) results in higher exam scores. In general, we would look for plausible "other" characteristics that might be responsible for differences in exam scores. If we identify "other" characteristics that are confounded with study techniques, the instructor's conclusion is weakened.

Criticisms of Null-Hypothesis Tests

Although tests of null hypotheses are widely used in research, the use of such tests to guide research decisions has been criticized. We will consider two different criticisms, both of which have merit but neither of which makes it necessary to abandon null-hypothesis tests.

The first criticism is that tests of null hypotheses are too rigid and arbitrary. The standard procedure for testing a null hypothesis requires a researcher to specify ahead of time the criterion that will be used to reject the hypothesis and then either reject or not reject the hypothesis once the evidence has been obtained. The criticism is that the rejection criterion is rather arbitrary and that the choice between "reject" and "don't reject" is too limited. Consider a couple of examples.

Early in this chapter I described both a conservative and a liberal test of the fair-coin hypothesis. Under the conservative test (alpha = .008), the fair-coin hypothesis would be rejected only if 0 or 8 heads were obtained in 8 coin flips, while under the liberal test (alpha = .07) the fair-coin hypothesis would be rejected if 0, 1, 7, or 8 heads were obtained. Both tests were described as reasonable. Critics argue that choosing an alpha level is arbitrary, and they point out the peculiarities that can arise. For example, suppose that 7 heads were actually obtained—one person, using the liberal test, would conclude that the coin was biased while another, using the conservative test, would not reject the fair-coin hypothesis. On the basis of the same data, two different decisions would be made. Who made the better decision? How can both decisions be sensible? Doesn't this show that something is wrong with the procedure?

Here's another example. Suppose a researcher is testing a null hypothesis with alpha = .05. Suppose his data belong to the extreme 6 percent of possible outcomes under the null hypothesis but not to the extreme 5 percent. According to the rules of the test, he will not reject the null hypothesis. The criticism is that, by setting an arbitrary 5 percent significance level and simply "not rejecting" the null hypothesis because the data don't quite meet this criterion, the researcher is ignoring the fact that his data do belong to the most extreme 6 percent of possible outcomes under the null hypothesis. In other words, the criticism is that the simple "reject–don't reject" choice ignores information and might even misrepresent the situation.

Critics have suggested that it makes more sense to determine how likely (or unlikely) the obtained data are under the null hypothesis, recognizing that the lower their predicted likelihood, the stronger the argument against the validity of the null hypothesis. For example, perhaps data belonging to the most extreme 10 percent of possible outcomes under the null hypothesis should be considered "suggestive evidence against the null hypothesis." Data in the extreme 5 percent might be considered "solid evidence against," those in the extreme 1 percent "strong evidence against," and those in the extreme one-tenth of 1 percent "compelling evidence against" (or some similar scheme). The argument for replacing "reject–don't reject" with a graded series of decisions or "levels of confidence for or against the null hypothesis" has some advantages but does not completely eliminate the problem of establishing decision criteria. For example, how do we decide *how* unlikely evidence must be under the null hypothesis before it should be viewed as "compelling evidence against" the hypothesis? Isn't there going to be a point at which a researcher will "firmly believe" the null hypothesis is wrong, and shouldn't we try to agree on where this point lies?

In effect the argument for graded, multiple decisions substitutes a multiple-criterion problem for a single-criterion problem (reject vs. don't reject). However, the use of graded decisions also "softens" the problem because the difference between adjacent decisions is less severe (the difference between "suggestive evidence" and "solid evidence," for example, is not as great as that between "reject" and "don't reject"). In practice, researchers do use a vague form of a multiple-criterion scheme in testing null hypotheses. In journal articles one can find researchers using modifiers such as "suggestive," "strong," and "very strong" in referring to tests of null hypotheses. In part this issue will be resolved gradually, by the emergence of a consensus among researchers. Remember, "reject versus don't reject" and "don't use a significance level larger than 5 percent" did not come down from a mountain on stone tablets—these "standard" procedures became standard by virtue of their general acceptance among researchers. The simpler "reject versus don't reject" system is easier to describe and communicate, but there is nothing to prevent the general adoption of a different system (except perhaps the resistance of researchers who are happy with the simpler system).

A second criticism of null-hypothesis tests is based on a rather startling premise: All null hypotheses are probably false, so why do we bother deciding whether to reject or not reject them? The criticism is based on taking null hypotheses very literally. For example, the hypothesis that $M_1 - M_2 = 0$, strictly speaking, means exactly zero—0.0000000000000 ad infinitum. The critics argue that there is no particular reason to believe that any difference between M's is precisely zero in this sense. What if there is a 1 out there in the thirty-fifth decimal place? Why couldn't there be? In brief, the criticism is that if you take any null hypothesis seriously and really test it, you're likely to find good evidence against its accuracy. If so, what are we doing testing null hypotheses?

If you ponder these criticisms of null-hypothesis tests, you might get the feeling that the tests are part of some crazy game researchers play to amuse themselves. You might wonder why I bothered to write a chapter about these procedures. The answer is that the tests are not crazy even though the procedures, when pressed to their limits, show some weaknesses. In a sense the criticisms can be viewed as criticisms of poorly arranged tests. A thorough researcher can accept the points made by the critics and still use such tests sensibly.

We must remember that null-hypothesis tests are not an end in themselves. They exist to help researchers make decisions. A researcher's goal is to construct a coherent account of "the world around us." To construct an account a researcher will have to make decisions about "what the facts are." The goal is to make the most reasonable decisions we can, given our current knowledge. A set of procedures that helps make these decisions is useful even if it is not perfect. Decisions (about "the facts") *are* going to be made, and a generally agreed-upon, generally understood decision procedure is an advantage.

A null hypothesis is usually a theoretically simple hypothesis that is worth keeping unless there is serious evidence against it. In the context of a particular research issue, a researcher must consider what "serious" means. This is a judgment, but one that is guided by existing knowledge relevant to the issue. For example, if a null hypothesis states that "$M_1 - M_2 = 0$," perhaps it would not seem important (given current knowledge) to reject this hypothesis if $M_1 - M_2$ were .001 but it would be theoretically important to reject this hypothesis if $M_1 - M_2$ were 2 or more. If so, the researcher's job is to arrange the test such that there is a very good chance that he or she will reject the null hypothesis if it is "off" by two or more units on the scale of measurement. In brief, the researcher needs to maximize the *power* of the test with respect to *theoretically meaningful* alternatives.

Earlier in this chapter I pointed out that researchers can control the probabilities of type I and type II errors. To tie the test of a null hypothesis to theoretically meaningful decisions, a researcher could do the following: First, use a low alpha level so that if the null hypothesis is correct or off by a slight, "unimportant" amount it is unlikely to be rejected. Second, collect enough observations so that if the null hypothesis is off by an "important" amount it is likely to be rejected. Of course a researcher must know a great deal about the topic under investigation to adopt this procedure; for example, a researcher must have a sound basis for identifying an "importantly different" alternate hypothesis. However, the procedure can be used in many instances, and it represents a careful and sensible method of conducting research.

SUMMARY

To evaluate differences between treatments researchers conduct statistical tests of null hypotheses. A *null hypothesis* is a specific statement that predicts probabilities for the various outcomes that might be observed when data are collected. A null hypothesis is set up as a reasonable starting point and then tested directly by comparing the data actually obtained with the probabilities predicted by the null hypothesis. A null hypothesis is rejected only if the actual data belong to a predesignated set of possible outcomes that are extreme and unlikely according to the null hypothesis.

Most psychological hypotheses lack either the specificity or the general acceptance required of null hypotheses. Consequently the null hypotheses that are actually tested in research tend to be simple statements such as "There is no relation between two variables" or "There is no difference between population means." Typically, before a researcher can conclude that some relation or difference exists he or she must obtain data that justify rejecting the simple null hypothesis that no relation or difference exists.

The test of a null hypothesis is formally arranged in such a way that either the null hypothesis or an *alternate hypothesis* must be correct. That is, if the null hypothesis is rejected, one must logically be adopting an alternate hypothesis. Typically the formal alternate hypothesis merely denies some aspect of the null hypothesis; for example, if the null hypothesis is "$M_1 - M_2 = 0$," the formal alternate hypothesis will be "$M_1 - M_2 \neq 0$." Notice that either the null hypothesis (=) or the alternate hypothesis ($\neq$) must logically be correct; alternate hypotheses containing a simple inequality are known as *nondirectional* alternate hypotheses. On occasion a *directional* alternate hypothesis might be used; such hypotheses substitute a "greater than" or "less than" (> or <) for the equality (=) of the null hypothesis. For example, if the null hypothesis is "$M_1 - M_2 = 0$," a directional alternate hypothesis would be "$M_1 - M_2 < 0$." While tests involving directional alternate hypotheses have some advantages when used to guide practical decisions, they are not usually recommended for scientific purposes because it is not logically necessary for either (=) or (<) to be correct.

Since the researcher does not know whether the null hypothesis is right or wrong, there are two possible decision errors that might be made when the null hypothesis is tested. If the null hypothesis is correct, it would be an error to reject it; such errors are known as *type I errors*. If, however, the null hypothesis is wrong, it would be an error to fail to reject it; these decision errors are known as *type II errors*. In setting up the test the researcher must try to minimize the chances of making either kind of error. The probability of a type I error (called *alpha*) is directly under the control of the researcher because the researcher decides what the actual data must be like to reject the null hypothesis. For example, if a researcher decides to reject the null hypothesis if the actual data belong to the most extreme 5 percent of possible outcomes according to the null hypothesis, there is a 5 percent chance of making a type I error if the null hypothesis is correct. The probability of a type II error (called *beta*) is determined in a more complex way. The chances of failing to reject a false null hypothesis decrease when larger values of alpha are used, when the correct hypothesis differs more from the null hypothesis being tested, and when the number of observations is increased.

The *power* of a test is the complement of beta; while beta refers to the probability of failing to reject a false null hypothesis, the power of a test is the probability of rejecting a false null hypothesis. Researchers desire tests for which beta is low (i.e., power is high) and for which alpha is low. Such tests can be arranged by choosing a small value for alpha and by making enough observations to result in a low value for beta.

Many different forms of null hypotheses are used in research. Some null hypotheses concern the manner in which *frequencies* (of observations) will be distributed over two or more categories. The null hypothesis leads to the development of ideal or expected frequencies for the categories, and the test consists of determining whether the obtained frequencies differ enough from the expected frequencies to justify rejecting the null hypothesis.

Very often researchers test hypotheses about differences between population means. Typically the null hypothesis states that there is no difference between population means $(M_1 - M_2 = 0)$. The test consists of determining whether the obtained difference between sample means $(\bar{X}_1 - \bar{X}_2)$ differs enough from zero to justify rejecting the null hypothesis. The test is based on the concept of a distribution of sample mean differences; that is, differences between sample means $(\bar{X}_1 - \bar{X}_2)$ may be expected to vary around the value of the difference between population means $(M_1 - M_2)$. If sample sizes are fairly large, such distributions may reasonably be treated as normal distributions, allowing researchers to make use of normal-curve concepts to test the null hypothesis. The power of the test depends on the degree of variability that can be expected among differences between sample means. This variability is indexed by the standard error of the difference (symbolized $\sigma_{\bar{X}_1-\bar{X}_2}$). The less the sample mean differences $(\bar{X}_1 - \bar{X}_2)$ vary around the population mean difference $(M_1 - M_2)$, the more powerful the test of the null hypothesis will be. The value of $\sigma_{\bar{X}_1-\bar{X}_2}$ can be reduced by using matched-subjects or repeated-measures designs (compared to using independent groups) or by increasing the sample sizes. Reducing the size of $\sigma_{\bar{X}_1-\bar{X}_2}$ means that if the null hypothesis is wrong it is more likely that data will be obtained that will lead (correctly) to rejecting the null hypothesis. Since researchers can control the size of $\sigma_{\bar{X}_1-\bar{X}_2}$ (by using matched subjects, larger samples, etc.), it is possible to conduct very powerful tests of null hypotheses about population mean differences.

It is important to realize that in testing a null hypothesis one either does or does not obtain data that justify rejecting the hypothesis. If the data do not justify rejecting the null hypothesis, it can be dangerous to "accept" that hypothesis since obtaining "insufficient evidence to reject" does not mean that the null hypothesis is actually correct. It is also important to distinguish between statistical decision making regarding a null hypothesis and psychological interpretations of data. A test of a null hypothesis provides a reasonable basis for deciding whether a relation or difference exists, but the test does not support any particular explanation of the relation or difference. If, for example, a test allows the reasonable conclusion that two population means differ, determining why the difference exists depends on a careful examination of the methods used to collect data.

The use of null-hypothesis tests to guide research decisions has been criticized. Some have argued that the choice between "rejecting" and "not rejecting" a null hypothesis is too limited and arbitrary. They suggest that a graded series of conclusions be used—the smaller the probability predicted by a null hypothesis for the data actually obtained, the stronger the evidence against the null hypothesis. While this idea has merit and is actually sometimes used in research, it does not eliminate the need for researchers to agree on criteria for making decisions on the basis of data. Another criticism is that since all null hypotheses are probably false if taken literally, it makes little sense to test them. This criticism also has merit, but it need not lead to the abandonment of null-hypothesis tests. Researchers can arrange tests of null hypotheses in such a way that their statistical decisions are closely tied to theoretically meaningful alternatives. In this way null-hypothesis tests can be used to guide research decisions in a productive fashion.

7

CORRELATIONAL METHODS

Studying relations between variables is the hallmark of scientific work because understanding how variables are related to one another is the core of scientific understanding. We have seen how researchers study relations between variables by comparing treatments (which represent levels of one variable) in terms of the scores obtained (i.e., values of the other variable). When researchers test a null hypothesis and decide whether or not their data justify concluding that the treatments are associated with real score differences, they are making a decision about whether or not a relation exists between two variables. As mentioned in the last chapter, the treatments that are compared may stem from manipulation of a variable by an experimenter or may result from natural variation. For example, if a researcher compares the arithmetic scores of males and females, "male versus female" is *not* a result of an experimental manipulation. Usually, however, the treatments that researchers compare have been created by experimental manipulation. In this chapter we will concentrate on methods that are most commonly used to study relations between *natural* variables. In different terms, these methods are usually used to study the way in which (naturally occurring) individual differences on one variable are related to (naturally occurring) individual differences on another variable.

We will begin by considering the method itself, which involves computing a statistic called a *correlation coefficient*. Then we will discuss the uses of correlational methods and the interpretive issues they bring forth.

Let's start with a small example. Suppose I have given two tests to a small class of students and wonder whether performance on test 1 is systematically related to performance on test 2. The data might look like those in Table 7.1.

Table 7.1   Scores of Five Imaginary Students
on Two Exams

STUDENT	% CORRECT, TEST 1	% CORRECT, TEST 2
Bill	85	70
George	68	64
Sally	55	72
Wendy	47	66
Steve	50	53

Examine this table closely. It illustrates the fundamental kind of data to which correlational methods are applied. Notice the nature of the data: For each student I have two measurements, a score on test 1 and a score on test 2. In general, correlational methods can be used whenever one has two (or more) measures for each case or unit. In this example the cases or units are students, but they could just as well be cities, baseball teams, or therapy groups. The essential point is that, however a case is defined, two (or more) measurements have been obtained for each case.

My curiosity concerned the relation between performance on test 1 and performance on test 2. As you will see shortly, precisely what is meant by that relation can have different meanings. For now, let me point out that in conducting a correlational analysis I would *not* be interested in such questions as "Did the students do better on test 2 than on test 1?" Rather, my interest lies in finding out how variation in test-1 performance is related to variation in test-2 performance. This point is important. In conducting a correlational analysis of the data in Table 7.1, I would *not* be trying to compare average performance on test 1 with average performance on test 2. I would be interested in finding out how *individual differences* in performance on test 1 are related to *individual differences* in performance on test 2.

It is important to understand the basic nature of the question being asked. Looking at Table 7.1, it is obvious that the students differed in terms of the scores they achieved on test 1 and that they also differed in terms of the scores they achieved on test 2. Here is the basic question: Is there any systematic relation between variation (among students) on test 1 and variation (among students) on test 2? Is there a tendency for the students who got the higher scores on test 1 to also get the higher scores on test 2? Maybe the students who got the lower scores on test 2 tended to get the higher scores on test 1. On the other hand, perhaps there is no systematic relation between performance on test 1 and performance on test 2—knowing, say, that an individual scored relatively high on test 2 really wouldn't tell us much about whether that individual was a high, medium, or low scorer on test 1. Correlational methods are designed to provide information about issues like these. Let's consider how such data are analyzed.

SCATTER DIAGRAMS

The simplest kind of data that are suitable for correlational analysis consist of two measurements for each of some number of cases, as in Table 7.1. Rather than presenting the data in tabular form, they could be represented in a more pictorial fashion, called a *scatter diagram*. In Figure 7.1 the data from Table 7.1 have been reproduced as a scatter diagram. Notice that the horizontal axis in Figure 7.1 refers to scores on test 1 while the vertical axis refers to scores on test 2. Each point in the scatter diagram represents one case (student) and is located in the diagram by finding the intersection of a vertical line extended upward from a student's test 1 score with a horizontal line extended to the right from that same student's test 2 score. For example, the point that is closest to the upper right-hand corner represents Bill's pair of scores (85 on test 1, 70 on test 2). It is important to understand that each point in a scatter diagram represents a pair of scores for one case.

Ordinarily data are collected for many more than five cases and the scatter diagram contains a large number of points. Several examples of

Figure 7.1. Scatter diagram for the five students' scores on Test 1 and Test 2.

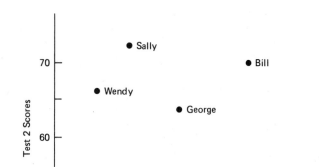

scatter diagrams are shown in Figure 7.2; the general shape of the distribution of points in each diagram provides information about the relation between the two variables (X and Y).

In panel (a) of Figure 7.2 the points are spread rather uniformly throughout the entire diagram. If we look at the scores on measure Y for the cases that have the lowest scores on X (looking up the left-hand side of the diagram), we see that just about the full range of scores on Y was obtained. In fact the distribution of Y scores is virtually the same no matter where on the X scale we look. Similarly, the cases with the highest scores on Y obtained X scores across the whole range of the X distribution, as did the cases with the lowest Y scores, or those with Y scores in the middle. In this example there is no systematic relation between variation on X and

Figure 7.2. Examples of scatter diagrams.

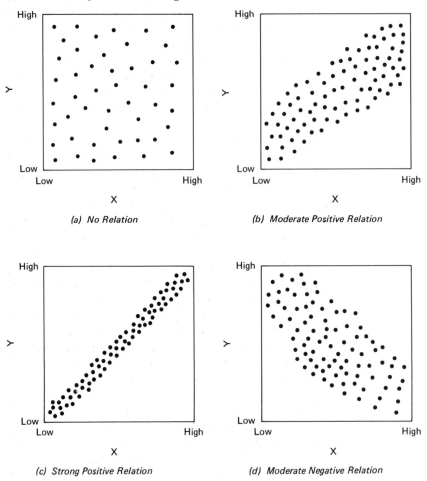

(a) No Relation

(b) Moderate Positive Relation

(c) Strong Positive Relation

(d) Moderate Negative Relation

variation on Y. In other words, knowing that the X score for a particular case is fairly high doesn't really tell us anything useful about what the Y score might be.

Panel (b) is clearly different. Notice that lower scores on X tend to be paired with lower scores on Y and higher X scores with higher Y scores. While there is still some "scatter" (for any particular value on X, the scores on Y cover a little less than half the total range of Y scores), there is clearly a relation between variation on X and variation on Y. Knowing that the X score for a particular case is relatively low, we can expect or predict that the Y score for that case will be somewhere in the lower half of the distribution of Y scores. If the Y score for a case is relatively high, we would expect to find a relatively high X score for that case. When the relation between two variables is generally like that shown in panel (b)— namely, predominantly high–high and low–low pairings—the relation is called *positive*.

The kind of relation shown in panel (c) is of the same general type as that in panel (b), but the relation is stronger. The general pattern is positive (high with high, low with low), as in panel (b). However, any value on X is associated with a narrower range of scores on Y, and vice versa (any value on Y is associated with a narrower range of scores on X). If we knew the X score (or Y score) for a particular case, we could predict rather accurately the Y score (X score) for that case.

In panel (d) the strength of the X–Y relation is about the same as in panel (b), but the direction of the relation is different. Notice that lower scores on X tend to be paired with higher scores on Y, higher X scores with lower Y scores, and so on. When such reverse pairings (high with low, low with high) tend to characterize the relation, it is called *negative*.

As these examples illustrate, there are two aspects of the relation between variables that we must consider. One aspect is the direction or type of relation (positive or negative), while the other is the strength of the relation. Look again at panel (c) of Figure 7.2. Imagine squeezing the "sausage" shape of the distribution in panel (c) such that all the points fall on a nice, straight line. We would have the strongest possible positive relation if all of the points fell on a line running from low, low to high, high. Knowing one of the scores for a case would effectively tell us the other score with perfect accuracy. Similarly, we would have the strongest possible negative relation if all the points fell on a line running from high, low to low, high. Notice that we would wind up with the lack of relation shown in panel (a) as we continued to spread the data points more evenly around the diagram, starting from either a clear positive relation or a clear negative relation. We can thus identify three "marker points" in describing the possible relations between two variables. At one extreme is a perfect positive relation, while at the other extreme is a perfect negative relation; in between is no relation at all.

Clearly, examining scatter diagrams helps in understanding the nature of the relation between variation on one measure and variation on another. However, it also has its limitations. To convey information about a relation, one could always show the scatter diagram, but it would be a little difficult to arrive at reliable rules for calling a relation "moderately positive" or "weakly negative." To allow more precise descriptions of relations, correlation coefficients are computed. A correlation coefficient is a numerical index of both the type and the strength of the relation between variables.

CORRELATION COEFFICIENTS: PEARSON *r*

A correlation coefficient indicates both the direction and the strength of the relation between two variables in a single number. The sign of the coefficient (+ or −) indicates the type of relation, positive or negative, as described earlier. The numerical value of the coefficient indicates the strength of relation—when the relation is "perfect" the numerical value is 1.00, whereas the numerical value is 0.00 when no systematic relation exists. Thus the typical range of values for a correlation coefficient extends from +1.00 for a perfect positive relation, through 0.00 for no systematic relation, to −1.00 for a perfect negative relation. The scatter diagrams in panels (b) and (c) of Figure 7.2 would yield positive coefficients between 0.00 and +1.00, with the coefficient for panel (c) much closer to +1.00, while the scatter diagram in panel (d) would yield a coefficient between 0.00 and −1.00. There are in fact several different kinds of correlation coefficients, each of which indexes the relation between two variables in a slightly different way. In this section, however, I will concentrate on one such coefficient, the most frequently used and most basic correlation coefficient.

If one wishes to index the relation between variation on one interval scale and variation on another interval scale, the most appropriate correlation coefficient is the Pearson Product-Moment Correlation Coefficient, often called Pearson *r* or just *r*. Here is the basic formula for *r*:

$$r = \frac{\Sigma \, z_X z_Y}{N}$$

Understanding Pearson *r* might require a review of some of the concepts we covered in Chapters 2 and 4. Recall that interval scales allow one to interpret distances between scores; Pearson *r* takes the distances between scores into account when a numerical index of the relation between two variables is calculated. As you can see, *r* depends on *z* scores. Recall that a *z* score indicates the location of a score in some distribution of scores. Specifically, a *z* score indicates, for any individual score, how many standard deviations the score lies above (or below) the mean score. If you are not completely sure about the meaning of z scores, you should review the section on standard scores in Chapter 4 before proceeding.

Remember that correlation coefficients are calculated for data in which each case has two scores, one generally called X and the other called Y. Since there are two scores for each case (X and Y), there are two z scores for each case; as you can see, the formula for calculating Pearson r makes use of each individual's two z scores. Examine the formula. The numerator indicates that for each case we should compute the z score in the X distribution (z_X), compute the z score in the Y distribution (z_Y), and multiply the two z scores. Then the z score products (one for each case) should be summed for all N cases and the sum divided by N, the number of cases. Table 7.2 shows the calculation of Pearson r for the test scores of our five imaginary students.

In order to compute the value of Pearson r we need to calculate each student's z score for test 1 (X) and for test 2 (Y). To do this we need to compute the mean and the standard deviation for test 1 (M_X, σ_X) and for test 2 (M_Y, σ_Y), since a z score is defined by dividing the deviation of a score from the mean of the distribution by the standard deviation of the distribution. Table 7.2 shows that the mean and standard deviation of the set of test 1 (X) scores are 61 and 14.0, respectively; for the distribution of test 2 (Y) scores, the mean is 65 and the standard deviation is 6.6. The last three columns in Table 7.2 are the ones we need to compute the value of r. Here we see that, for example, Bill was 1.71 standard deviations above the mean on test 1 and 0.76 standard deviations above the mean on test 2; the product of his z scores is $+1.30$.

The last column contains the product of the two z scores for each student; the sum of these products, which we need to insert in the formula for r, is $+2.05$. Working through the formula results in a value of $+0.41$ for r, indicating (roughly) that a moderate positive relation exists between variation in test 1 scores and variation in test 2 scores. In other words, the average tendency is for students to have somewhat similar z scores on the two tests. As you can see in Table 7.2, this is not uniformly true (Sally is almost half a standard deviation below the mean on test 1 but over one standard deviation above the mean on test 2). For this small set of data, the final value of r reflects mostly the fact that Bill was noticeably above the mean (in z score terms) on both tests while Steve was clearly below the mean on both tests. Of course with larger sets of data no one or two cases have that much influence; the general relation between two sets of scores depends on the overall pattern for all cases.

Later I will explain how to interpret the numerical value of a Pearson r more precisely. Right now, however, let's examine the formula to see what it reflects in the data. Pearson r employs z scores and thus is based on the ideas that underlie the use of z scores as descriptive measurements.

Table 7.2 Calculation of Pearson r

STUDENT	% TEST 1 (X)	X−M$_X$	(X−M$_X$)^2	% TEST 2 (Y)	Y−M$_Y$	(Y−M$_Y$)^2	z$_X$	z$_Y$	z$_X$z$_Y$
Bill	85	24	576	70	5	25	+1.71	+0.76	+1.30
George	68	7	49	64	−1	1	+0.50	−0.15	−0.08
Sally	55	−6	36	72	7	49	−0.43	+1.06	−0.46
Wendy	47	−14	196	66	1	1	−1.00	+0.15	−0.15
Steve	50	−11	121	53	−12	144	−0.79	−1.82	+1.44
Σ	305		978	325		220			+2.05

$$M_X = \frac{305}{5} = 61;\ \sigma_X = \sqrt{\frac{978}{5}} = \sqrt{195.6} = 14.0$$

$$M_Y = \frac{325}{5} = 65;\ \sigma_Y = \sqrt{\frac{220}{5}} = \sqrt{44.0} = 6.6$$

$$z_X = \frac{X - M_X}{\sigma_X} \left\{ \text{Example (Bill): } z_X = \frac{85 - 61}{14.0} = \frac{24}{14.0} = +1.71 \right.$$

$$z_Y = \frac{Y - M_Y}{\sigma_Y} \left\{ \text{Example (George): } z_Y = \frac{64 - 65}{6.6} = \frac{-1}{6.6} = -0.15 \right.$$

$$\text{Pearson } r = \frac{\Sigma z_X z_Y}{N} = \frac{+2.05}{5} = +0.41$$

That is, a good way to characterize an individual score is to relate it to the distribution of scores to which it belongs, and one must consider both the average score in the distribution and the variability of scores in the distribution. Hence, a good way to characterize the relation between sets of scores is to examine how z scores are related. The value of r depends not only on whether the scores for individual cases generally tend to be on the same side of the mean in both distributions (or on opposite sides of the mean) but also on distance from the means (measured in standard-deviation units to take into account the variability of scores in each distribution). For example, while it is important that Bill is above the mean in both test distributions, it is also important that he is *not* the same number of standard deviations above the mean in both distributions.

In order for Pearson r to equal $+1.00$, indicating in its way a perfect positive relation, it must be true that for every individual case the z score in one distribution is exactly the same as the z score in the other distribution. A made-up example of such a situation is shown in Table 7.3.

For each case in the upper part of Table 7.3, the z_X value and the z_Y value are precisely the same; all $z_X z_Y$ products are *positive*, and the product sum is exactly equal to the value of N, yielding $r = +1.00$. In the lower part of Table 7.3, data illustrating a perfect negative relation are shown. In this instance the two z scores for each case have the same numerical value but the signs are reversed, and the result is a Pearson r of -1.00. Such remarkable correspondence between pairs of z scores is extremely

Table 7.3   Hypothetical Data Yielding Pearson r's of $+1.00$ and -1.00

Perfect Positive Relation

CASE	z_X	z_Y	$z_X z_Y$	
A	$+1.5$	$+1.5$	$+2.25$	
B	$+0.5$	$+0.5$	$+0.25$	
C	0.0	0.0	0.00	$r = \dfrac{\Sigma z_X z_Y}{N} = \dfrac{5.00}{5} = +1.00$
D	-0.5	-0.5	$+0.25$	
E	-1.5	-1.5	$+2.25$	
			$\Sigma = +5.00$	

Perfect Negative Relation

CASE	z_X	z_Y	$z_X z_Y$	
A	$+1.5$	-1.5	-2.25	
B	$+0.5$	-0.5	-0.25	
C	0.0	0.0	0.00	$r = \dfrac{-5.00}{5} = -1.00$
D	-0.5	$+0.5$	-0.25	
E	-1.5	$+1.5$	-2.25	
			$\Sigma = -5.00$	

rare in real data, as you might expect. Consequently researchers do not expect or typically obtain Pearson *r*'s of +1.00 or −1.00. The point is that Pearson *r* reflects the *numerical* similarity of the *z* scores associated with each case as well as the similarity of their signs. If every case had either two positive *z* scores or two negative *z* scores but the numerical values were *not* identical within every pair, the correlation would be positive (because all products of *z* scores would be positive) but would be less than +1.00 (because the *z* scores within a pair are not numerically identical). It should be clear that Pearson *r* indexes the relation between two sets of scores in a very sensitive fashion.

PROBLEM

At the end of a course on abnormal psychology the instructor gives two final exams, one based on material in the textbook and one based on material presented in the lectures. Of course all students take both exams. The instructor calculates the correlation between the students' "book exam" scores and their "lecture exam" scores, obtaining a value of +.95 (quite close to perfection). One of the students earned a score of 80 on the "book exam"; would it be reasonable to expect this student to have a score near 80 on the "lecture exam"?

The correlation of +.95 indicates that there is a very strong and systematic relation between scores on the book exam and scores on the lecture exam. It must be true that virtually all students have a pair of *z* scores that are quite similar. Therefore it would be quite reasonable to expect a student's *z* score on the lecture exam to be very similar to that student's *z* score on the book exam. However, this does not mean that the student would have a "raw score" on the lecture exam that is numerically similar to the student's "raw score" on the book exam. What if the book exam was much longer than the lecture exam? Suppose the book exam had a mean score of 140 points and a standard deviation of 30 points while the (shorter) lecture exam had a mean of 50 points and a standard deviation of 10 points. On the book exam a score two standard deviations above the mean would be 200 [140 + 2(30) = 200]; the comparable score on the lecture exam would be 70 [50 + 2(10) = 70]. The essential point is that the value of *r* reflects the relation between *z* scores, and *z* scores "correct for" the mean and the standard deviation.

Using Pearson *r* to Predict Scores

If we know the correlation between two variables, we can use the correlation to predict scores in one distribution (say, Y) on the basis of scores in the other (X) distribution. In standard (*z*) score terms, the prediction formula is quite simple:

$$\text{Predicted } z_Y = r\, z_X$$

The formula indicates that to predict an individual's standard score in the Y distribution you multiply that individual's standard score in the X distribution by the value of r. For example, if the correlation between two distributions were +.40, for an individual whose z_X score was known to be −1.50 we would predict a z_Y score of −.60 (+.40 × −1.50 = −.60). The same prediction formula is used for all cases and is the best way to use a correlation to make such predictions. Table 7.4 shows the z_X and z_Y scores for ten cases (A–J); using these z scores I calculated the value of Pearson r, which came out to be +.68. The last column in Table 7.4 shows the predicted z_Y score for each case, which was obtained by multiplying the value of r (+.68) times the z_X score for that case.

Perhaps you're wondering why one would bother to make the predictions, since for the data in Table 7.4 we obviously know the actual z_Y score for every case. In part, the predictions shown in Table 7.4 are intended merely to show you the mechanics of using Pearson r to make predictions. In practical situations, however, such predictions would be made when a person has a good idea of the correlation but knows only one score for each case. For example, college admissions officers use applicants' scores on entrance exams to make predictions about what their grade point averages are likely to be in college and make admission decisions on the basis of those predictions. Let's look at the predictions in Table 7.4 to get a better understanding of what correlation coefficients tell us.

In a general sense the predictions in Table 7.4 are "fairly accurate." There are obvious discrepancies between the predicted and actual z_Y scores. An essential point is that the predictions in Table 7.4 are the *best* predictions (of z_Y scores) that could be made on the basis of z_X scores and

Table 7.4   Using Pearson r to Predict Standard Scores

CASE	z_X	z_Y	Predicted z_Y
A	+1.88	+1.42	+1.28
B	+1.25	+ .33	+ .85
C	+ .62	+ .51	+ .42
D	+ .42	+1.96	+ .29
E	.00	− .22	.00
F	− .21	− .95	− .14
G	− .62	− .76	− .42
H	− .83	− .40	− .56
I	−1.04	− .58	− .71
J	−1.46	−1.31	− .99

Note: For each case the predicted z_Y value was obtained by multiplying the value of Pearson r (+.68) times the z_X score for that case.

the correlation between the two distributions of scores (z_X and z_Y). Clearly, the accuracy of the predictions will depend on how strongly the two variables are correlated—the stronger the association, the more accurate the predictions will be. If the two variables were perfectly correlated ($r = +1.00$ or -1.00), by definition the predictions would be perfectly accurate. Look again at the prediction formula to see what the formula does when two variables are unrelated ($r = 0.00$). Inserting a value of zero for r in the formula ($r\,z_X$) results in a predicted value of 0.00 no matter what an individual's z_X score might be. Predicting a z_Y score of 0.00 for all cases is simply predicting the mean score in each case. Doing so makes perfectly good sense; if the two variables are unrelated, which is what ($r = 0.00$) tells us, we have no sound basis for predicting that an individual might score above or below the mean. In effect, we can do no better than predicting the mean score for all cases. The data in Table 7.4 represent the broad "middle ground"; there is *some* systematic relation between the two score distributions (z_X and z_Y), which provides a sound basis for predicting that some cases will score above the mean and others below the mean in the z_Y distribution. Because the two distributions are somewhat related, we *can* do better than just predicting the mean for all cases; of course we cannot predict with complete accuracy because the two distributions are not perfectly related.

It is not necessary to use z scores; I have emphasized the z score prediction formula because it is simple and easy to understand. One can use other formulas to make "raw score" predictions. In fact the z scores shown in Table 7.4 are based on the "raw" scores shown in Table 7.5: The z_X scores in Table 7.4 correspond to the heights in Table 7.5; the z_Y scores correspond to the weights in Table 7.5, and the predicted z_Y scores correspond to the predicted weights. Whether the predictions are made in z scores or raw scores, the critical factor determining the accuracy of the predictions is the same—the value of the correlation between the two distributions.

Interpreting the Magnitude of r

What is the proper way of interpreting the numerical value of a correlation coefficient? We have discussed two end points. When r is 0 there is no systematic relation between variation on X and variation on Y. At the opposite extreme, when r equals $+1.00$ or -1.00, there is a perfect relation between the two distributions. What about correlations like $+.35$, $-.80$, or $+.12$—where are they between "nothing" and "perfection"? The value of r itself does *not* directly provide the answer. In fact it is r^2, the square of the correlation coefficient, that best indicates the strength of association between the two variables. (You will have to accept this fact "on faith," since a detailed explanation is beyond the scope of this book.)

Consider once again the idea of trying to predict scores in one distribution on the basis of individuals' scores in the other distribution. At the outset let me emphasize that one does not have to be in a practical situation requiring predictions to find this idea interesting. For example, a researcher might obtain reading and mathematics scores for a number of students for the purpose of finding out how reading ability and mathematical ability are related to each other. To understand this relation it is an excellent idea to ask, "How accurately *could* reading scores be predicted on the basis of mathematics scores (or vice versa)?" Clearly the more accurately the predictions can be made, the stronger the relation between the two variables must be.

To evaluate the accuracy of a set of predictions we would look at the discrepancies between predicted scores and the scores individuals actually have—smaller discrepancies mean greater accuracy. More precisely, a set of predictions would be evaluated by calculating the average squared discrepancy between predicted and actual scores, as follows:

$$\text{Prediction error variance} = \frac{\Sigma \ (\text{actual score} - \text{predicted score})^2}{N}$$

The formula is straightforward. To calculate the prediction error variance one does the following. For each case calculate the difference between the individual's actual score and predicted score and square that

Table 7.5   An Example of Predicting Weights from Heights

PERSON	HEIGHT (INCHES)	WEIGHT (POUNDS)	PREDICTED WEIGHT
A	76	205	201
B	73	175	190
C	70	180	178
D	69	220	174
E	67	160	166
F	66	140	162
G	64	145	154
H	63	155	151
I	62	150	146
J	60	130	139
Mean	67	166	
Standard deviation	4.8	27.5	
Correlation between heights and weights: $r = +.68$			

Note: Each person's predicted weight is based on that person's height and the height-weight correlation.

difference. Do this for every case; sum the squared discrepancies; and divide by the number of cases to get "the average squared discrepancy." Clearly, the smaller the prediction error variance, the more accurate the predictions.

Consider now the "worst possible" situation, namely, $r = 0.00$—no systematic relation between the two sets of scores. In this situation we could do no better than just predicting the mean score for everyone. Notice that if we predict the mean score for all cases, the prediction error variance becomes

$$\text{Prediction error variance} = \frac{\Sigma(\text{actual score} - \text{mean score})^2}{N}$$

which is, of course, the variance of the set of scores we are trying to predict. In other words, the largest (worst) value we could get for the prediction error variance, when $r = 0.00$, is the variance of the set of scores we are trying to predict.

Consider now the best possible situation—$r = 1.00$, a perfect relation. If the two sets of scores were perfectly related, we could predict from one distribution to the other without error—there would be *no* discrepancies between predicted and actual scores. The prediction error variance would have its smallest possible value—zero.

Now we come to all those correlations between 0.00 and 1.00. The question is, What will be the size of the prediction error variance? In general terms, if the correlation is between 0.00 and 1.00, the prediction error variance will be somewhere between the variance of the set of scores we're trying to predict and zero. A more precise answer is illustrated in Table 7.6, where you can see the relation between the value of r and how much the prediction error variance is reduced.

Let's look at a couple of examples. Table 7.6 indicates that if the correlation between two sets of scores is .50 (whether + or −), and we attempt to predict from one distribution to the other, the prediction error variance will be reduced by 25 percent (compared to having no relation at all). If the correlation between two score distributions is .70, the prediction error variance will be reduced by 49 percent. As you can see, a correlation must be quite high before there is a large reduction in the prediction error variance. If the correlation between two variables is only .20, the average squared discrepancy between predicted and actual scores will be just 4 percent smaller than it would be if there were no systematic relation.

We can now return to the importance of the square of a correlation coefficient. For every value of r shown in Table 7.6 the percent reduction in prediction error variance equals the square of the correlation coefficient, times 100. The 16 percent reduction shown for an r of .40 equals $.4^2 \times 100$; the 64 percent reduction shown for an r of .80 equals $.8^2 \times 100$; and so on for all values of r. The rule is well worth remembering: The amount

Table 7.6 Relation Between the Value of r and the Accuracy of Predicting Y from X or X from Y

VALUE OF r	REDUCTION IN PREDICTION ERROR VARIANCE	
1.00	100%	(perfect prediction)
.90	81%	
.80	64%	
.70	49%	
.60	36%	
.50	25%	
.40	16%	
.30	9%	
.20	4%	
.10	1%	
.00	0	(poorest prediction)

by which the prediction error variance is reduced is directly related to the square of a correlation coefficient. Conversely, the square of a correlation coefficient tells you how strong the relation between two variables is.

Reducing the prediction error variance is often referred to as *accounting for* variance in the set of scores we're trying to predict. For example, the typical correlation between entrance exam scores and school grades is about +.50. Looking at Table 7.6, we can see that, with this correlation, predicting school grades from exam scores would result in a 25 percent reduction in the prediction error variance. We could say that variation in exam scores can be used to *account for* 25 percent of the variance in school grades (or that school grades could be used to account for 25 percent of the variance in exam scores, since predictions can be in either direction).

PROBLEM

The correlation between anxiety and performance on a reasoning test is reported to be −.40. The sign of the coefficient indicates that as anxiety scores go up, performance on the reasoning test tends to go down. What percentage of the variance in reasoning can be accounted for on the basis of individual differences in anxiety?

To obtain the answer we would square the value of the correlation coefficient and multiply by 100. Since $-.40 \times -.40 \times 100 = 16$, the answer is that individual differences in anxiety could be used to account for 16 percent of the variance in reasoning scores. Since predictions can be made in either direction, it would also be true that individual differences in reasoning could account for 16 percent of the variance in anxiety. Notice that "accounting for variance" does *not* imply causality; the phrase refers to predictive accuracy, nothing more. Saying that anxiety can account for 16 percent of the variance in reasoning simply means that anxiety scores can be used to predict 16 percent of the variance in reasoning scores, or that using anxiety to predict reasoning (or reasoning to predict anxiety) will result in a 16 percent reduction in the prediction error variance.

Nonlinear Relations. Having examined the properties of Pearson *r*, it is time to introduce a caution: The value of Pearson *r* reflects only *linear* relations between variables. So far any relation we have considered has been a simple, straight-line relation; as scores on X increase, scores on Y tend to increase, or as scores on X increase, scores on Y tend to decrease. Pearson *r* accurately reflects the direction and the strength of such simple, linear relations between variables. However, it is possible for variables to be related in a *curvilinear* fashion. Look at the scatter diagram in Figure 7.3.

There is a rather clear, systematic relation between variation on X and variation on Y, but it is *not* a linear relation. As scores on X increase, scores on Y first increase and then decrease. In other words, a straight line does *not* adequately characterize the relation. If Pearson *r* were calculated for data like those in Figure 7.3, the value would be near zero. To get a numerical index for a nonlinear relation, other calculating methods (which will not be presented) need to be used. Careful investigators always examine

Figure 7.3. Illustration of a nonlinear relation between X and Y. Each point represents a pair of (X, Y) scores for an individual case.

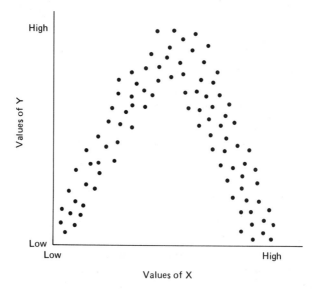

scatter diagrams to be sure that no serious departures from linearity are present in the data, before calculating Pearson *r*. Obviously, just considering the value of *r* could lead to the conclusion that no relation exists when in fact no linear relation holds but a nonlinear relation might exist.

Restricted Ranges. Here is another caution about interpreting the magnitude of Pearson *r*. In order for the value of *r* to accurately reflect the relation between two variables, it is important for the full *range* of scores for both variables to be represented. For example, suppose we wanted to examine the relation between creativity and personal adjustment by giving both a creativity test and a personal-adjustment test to a number of people. Suppose that creativity scores could range from 1 to 40 and that adjustment scores could range from −10 to +10, but that *in our study* we only obtain creativity scores between 25 and 39 and adjustment scores between +1 and +10. If we calculated Pearson *r* for our data, it is very likely that the value we get will *underestimate* the relation between creativity and adjustment. The problem is illustrated in Figure 7.4.

If we look at the whole scatter diagram in Figure 7.4, it is clear that there is a modest positive relation between the two variables. However, if we were dealing with just a restricted portion of the ranges of these variables—say, just high scorers—the scatter diagram *for the restricted data*

Figure 7.4. Illustration of the effects of restricted ranges on correlation. The X − Y relation shown in the whole scatter diagram is not apparent when score ranges are restricted (inset at upper right).

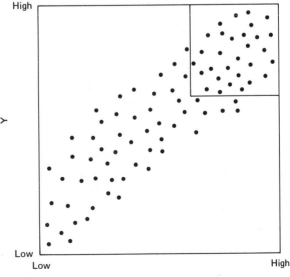

might look like the insert in the upper right-hand corner of Figure 7.4. In that small "scatter diagram" there does not seem to be much of a relation between X and Y. Calculating correlation coefficients for restricted ranges of scores tends to underestimate the relation between two variables.

Restricted score ranges can occur for a number of reasons. Most commonly, restricted ranges might occur when the subjects in a study come from some "special" group. Compared to the entire population, doctors, college students, mental retardates, sixth-graders, and women represent special groups of one sort or another. I am not saying that using some such group as subjects must lead to restricted score ranges, for that is not so. On some measures college students, for example, yield a very representative range of scores; on others, such as an IQ test designed for general use, college students might well yield a restricted score range. A prudent researcher will look at the frequency distributions and at scatter diagrams to check for possible curvilinearity or range restrictions, in addition to calculating a correlation coefficient to obtain a precise numerical index of the relation between variables.

INTERPRETING CORRELATIONAL DATA

Correlational methods are used for many purposes in psychological, educational, and sociological research. Pearson r is the most commonly used coefficient, although other techniques are sometimes employed. In the remainder of this chapter we will consider some of the uses of correlational methods and the issues that arise. Our discussion will include assessments of the reliability and validity of measurements, regression effects, and the relation between correlation and causality.

At the outset let me emphasize that a correlation coefficient is fundamentally *descriptive*—it numerically describes the form and strength of the relation between two variables. For example, finding that the correlation between IQ test scores and school grades is +.50 indicates the extent to which school grades can be predicted from test scores or test scores from school grades. The statistical result itself does not indicate *why*, in any sense of the word, the relation exists. As you will see shortly, trying to explain why a correlation exists, or what a correlation means, is a theoretical endeavor that must be approached with great care.

Reliability Coefficients

In Chapter 2, I stressed the importance of using reliable measures and talked about reliability in terms of the consistency with which values are assigned. In the present context *reliability* refers to the degree to which a measure is correlated "with itself." To evaluate the reliability of measurement we must in some sense use the measure twice for the same cases and examine the correlation between the two sets of scores. We will consider three different methods of investigating measurement reliability; in effect, each represents a different, more precise definition of reliability.

Internal Consistency. One method of assessing reliability is essentially a check on the *internal consistency* of a measure (test). For example, suppose we are examining a "test of mathematical ability" that consists of 100 items. A common method of evaluating internal consistency involves computing two part-scores for each person, one based on the 50 odd-numbered items (nos. 1, 3, 5, 7, etc.) and one based on the 50 even-numbered items (nos. 2, 4, 6, 8, etc.). If the test is internally consistent, we should find a high positive correlation between the set of "odd-item scores" and the set of "even-item scores." How high a correlation is "high enough"? It would be lovely if the correlation were +1.00, but no measure is perfectly reliable. For fairly long tests that are intended to be widely used, an acceptable internal-consistency correlation is often considered to be about +.90. Many standardized tests meet this criterion.

The idea underlying internal consistency is that the various items on a test are measuring the same trait or ability. Inferring "sameness" ought to require a very high correlation. For example, suppose the internal-consistency correlation for a test were +.60. This value would indicate that scores on one "half" of the test can account for or predict just 36 percent of the variance in scores on the other half. Under such circumstances it would be difficult to have much confidence that the various test items were "measuring the same thing."

Test–Retest Reliability. If the construct that a test is supposed to measure is assumed to be stable over time, reliability may be assessed by the *test–retest* method. Using the example of the test of mathematical ability, the test–retest method would involve giving the entire test to the same individuals on two different occasions. Let me emphasize the importance of the assumption that the test measures something that ought to be stable over time. For example, in research on personality a distinction can be made between "trait anxiety" and "state anxiety." Trait anxiety is theoretically assumed to be a characteristic of a person that is stable over time, while state anxiety is assumed to fluctuate from one situation to another. It would make sense to demand high test–retest reliability of a measure of trait anxiety, but it would not make sense to make the same demand of a measure of state anxiety (although it might still be worth while to check into it to see if state anxiety does in fact fluctuate).

To return to the test of mathematical ability, if we assumed that "whatever the test measures" should be stable over short periods, we might give the test twice, with perhaps a few weeks between sessions. There are reasons for expecting that test–retest correlations might be lower than internal-consistency correlations. It is reasonable to expect that any measure is affected by factors that change from time to time and situation to situation (the question is, How much?). For example, performance on a test of mathematical ability is likely to be affected by fluctuations in attention, changes in health, and the like. A person's score will probably be lower if he or she is distracted by personal problems or is feeling sick. These things are likely to change more from one session to another than from item to item during a single session. In addition, there might be real changes in the basic characteristic measured by a test over time, more likely as the interval between test and retest gets longer.

On the other hand, there is a factor that can make test–retest reliability "artificially high." If the test is such that people can remember their answers, if the test–retest interval is fairly short, and if people tend to duplicate their earlier answers during the retesting session, the correlation will be inflated. There is no single test–retest reliability coefficient for any measure; rather, there may be a different level of reliability for each test–retest interval that is considered. It would not be unusual for the correlation to be near +.85 for a short interval such as a few days but drop to +.50 over weeks or months. The manner in which the correlation changes as the test–retest interval lengthens provides information about the stability of the trait or ability being measured.

Alternate-Forms Reliability. A third method of assessing reliability is the *alternate-forms* technique. This method is often appropriate for tests used in school settings. Tests of reading or mathematical ability are frequently constructed in alternate forms. One form might be given at the start of a school year while the alternate form is given at the end of the year. The educational purpose is to assess whether real changes have occurred during the academic year. The assumption is that, in the absence of real change (e.g., over a short interval), the two forms would yield comparable scores. To check on reliability the two forms might be given with a short interval, during which no real changes are expected to occur. Notice that even with a fairly short interval the alternate-forms method involves both changes in content (as does internal consistency) and changes in situation/time (as does test–retest). Of course if both forms are given during the same session, alternate-forms reliability is quite similar to split-half reliability. It is typically most difficult to obtain a high reliability coefficient when comparing alternate forms separated by a long time interval.

By now it must be obvious that reliability takes on different meanings. Nonetheless, reliability coefficients are generally expected to be "high" if a measure is to be trusted. Reliability coefficients below +0.50, regardless of the method used, are a clear signal to treat scores with caution. In this regard I must point out that reliability is affected by test length—in general, longer tests yield higher reliability coefficients than shorter tests. This point is like a two-edged sword. For purely statistical reasons (which I won't go into), longer tests ought to yield higher reliability, other things being equal. At the same time, the fact remains that short tests are likely to have low reliability (it's not "their fault," but it's true nonetheless). The relevance of this point is that you might encounter psychological measurements that involve the administration of many items but are scored not by the "whole test" but in terms of a number of subtests in order to provide a "profile." If, for example, a total of 100 items is scored in terms of 10 scores each based on 10 items, it is the reliability of the 10-item subtests that is the issue. There are instances of psychological measures whose total-score reliability is quite reasonable but whose short-subtest reliabilities are as low as +0.20. Ponder for a moment the fact that a test–retest reliability of +0.20 means that scores on one administration of a subtest can account for (predict) 4 percent of the variance of the scores obtained on another administration! I do not wish to give you the impression that most psychological tests are unreliable, for that is not true. However, problems of low reliability do occasionally occur. It is necessary to decide both what kind and what level of reliability are appropriate, considering the topic that is under investigation.

PROBLEM

A number of researchers have reported that scores on infant intelligence tests (given at about 1 year of age) have a near-zero correlation with scores on intelligence tests given during adolescence. What do such results tell us about the measurement of intelligence?

Basically, the low (near-zero) correlation indicates that infant "intelligence tests" and adolescent "intelligence tests" are measuring different things. Such results indicate a failure to identify a construct of intelligence that can be reliably measured from infancy through adolescence. If we wish to be precise with our language, we should use different terms for the two kinds of tests. For example, if we decide that the adolescent tests measure "intelligence," then we need a different term to use when referring to the infant tests.

Two points about reliability should be kept in mind. First, using Pearson *r* to assess reliability means that the stability of *z* scores is being examined. A high correlation does *not* by itself mean that raw scores are equivalent from one half to another, from test to retest, or from one form to another. For example, it is possible for scores on one form of a test to be systematically higher than those on an alternate form even though the correlation between scores on the two forms is extremely high. For tests with "right answers," such as intelligence tests or measures of mathematical or reading ability, people sometimes generally score higher when the test is given a second time. A test–retest correlation says nothing about whether the average raw score has changed; the coefficient only reflects the extent to which individuals achieve comparable *z* scores on the two administrations. Consequently, if you are concerned about the equivalence of raw scores, a high reliability coefficient (Pearson r) is necessary but not sufficient. Test constructors take pains to design alternate forms that have the same means and standard deviations (in effect, nearly identical score distributions) as well as a very high correlation between them; in this case raw scores from the two forms will be comparable.

The second qualification is that our discussion of reliability has applied to individual scores. Many measurements are used not to characterize individuals but to compare the average (mean) scores of two or more groups. For example, a researcher might be interested in finding out whether the mean score on some test for females is different from the mean score for males. In Chapter 5 we discussed the fact that the mean of a group of scores is more stable than the individual scores in the group. Compared to the standard deviation for individual scores (σ), the standard error of the mean ($\sigma/\sqrt{n}$) can be much smaller. The point is that a measure that does not meet the criterion of high reliability with respect to individual scores might well be good enough for making comparisons between group means, provided that the groups are large enough.

Validity Coefficients

Because reliability concerns the consistency with which "a single characteristic" is measured, reliability coefficients are expected to be quite high. In Chapter 2 validity of measurement was loosely defined in terms of the extent to which a measure reflects the theoretical construct that a researcher has in mind. The concept of validity has many aspects; for example, in Chapter 5 we discussed several factors (e.g., role selection, response sets) that affect the validity of measurements in a particular sense. Correlational analyses are also used to assess validity; scores on some measuring instrument are correlated with some criterion to which they ought to be related. Generally, validity coefficients are expected to be lower than reliability coefficients. The reason is that validity coefficients reflect the relation between two variables that are theoretically distinguishable although somewhat related, whereas reliability coefficients refer to the relation between two measurements that are supposed to measure the same construct.

Suppose a psychologist claims to have devised a test of intelligence. To demonstrate its validity the test scores would be correlated with variation in some criterion behavior that is assumed to involve intelligence. Commonly, scores on intelligence tests are correlated with school grades (or scores on school achievement tests) to demonstrate validity. The reasoning is that since school achievement is assumed to involve intelligence, test scores should be noticeably correlated with measures of achievement. Now, school achievement is not assumed to involve only intelligence; other factors such as motivation, state of health, and the quality of instruction might also be considered important. According to such reasoning, one would expect to find a clear but moderate correlation between intelligence test scores and school achievement (presumably because of the other factors that enter into achievement). In actual fact, the correlation between scores on widely used intelligence tests and measures of school achievement is typically about +0.50. Both test constructors and test purchasers seem to be quite happy with this level of relation.

Perhaps the thought has struck you that a lot of assumptions are made in dealing with validity coefficients (and with reliability coefficients). If so, you are correct. The correlation between two sets of measurements is viewed as a reliability coefficient if the two measures are assumed to represent the same construct, but as a validity coefficient if the two measures are assumed to represent somewhat distinguishable constructs. The process also works in the opposite direction. If two measures (however they are labeled) are very high correlated (e.g., $r = +0.90$), they will surely be considered as measuring the same construct. A moderate correlation leads to the inference that the two measures represent two partially distinct, partially related constructs. If the measures are uncorrelated (i.e., r is near zero), they will be viewed as representing two clearly distinct constructs. A great deal of research involves examining correlation coefficients to see which kind of inference is most appropriate; such research is really more like detective work than a legalistic "determination of the validity or invalidity of this measure."

Validity can be approached from both practical and theoretical viewpoints. The practical question is usually "Is this measure (test) a valid predictor of some designated criterion?" For example, we might want to know whether a test of mechanical ability is a valid predictor of job performance as an automobile mechanic. The issue is straightforward—is the relation between test scores and job performance strong enough to make it worthwhile to use the test in deciding whom to hire? Answering such a question involves many considerations in addition to the value of the correlation between test scores and measures of job performance. The cost of administering the test, the availability of other assessment techniques, and the importance of selecting individuals who will do the job very well are some of the factors that will affect the decision. A test–criterion correlation of, say, +0.50 might be high enough in some circumstances but not in others. Furthermore, a test might be valid for some purposes but not for others. For example, the same test of mechanical ability might be a useful (valid) predictor for auto mechanics but not for airplane mechanics. Each situation requires its own determination of validity; what can safely be said is that a low test–criterion correlation will almost certainly result in the test's being judged invalid (i.e., not sufficiently valid).

Construct Validity. Correlational analyses serve an important function in theoretically guided research on *construct validity*. By examining patterns of correlations a researcher gains information about the adequacy of existing theoretical ideas about a construct and suggestions for further research and theory modification. A theoretically defined construct presumably can be measured in a number of different ways, should be related to some other constructs, and should be unrelated to still other constructs. Construct validation thus involves examination of both *convergent validity* and *discriminant validity* (Cronbach & Meehl, 1955). Does one find strong relations where they are supposed to exist (convergent validity) as well as the absence of relations where they are not supposed to exist (discriminant validity)? Let's look at an example of this approach.

For many years some theorists have argued that the concept of *creativity* should be distinguished from the concept of *intelligence*. Ordinarily it is not argued that creativity and intelligence are completely independent; rather, they are thought to be only weakly related to each other. Intelligence can presumably be measured in several different ways, as can creativity. For the concepts of creativity and intelligence to be theoretically useful, we need to find that various measures of intelligence are strongly related to each other, that various measures of creativity are strongly related to each other, and that measures of intelligence are at best weakly related to measures of creativity. This presentation is oversimplified (what's "strong" and what's "weak"?), but it captures the essence of the method.

Suppose we had four methods of (presumably) measuring intelligence and three methods of (presumably) measuring creativity. If we obtained seven measures for each of a number of individuals (four "intelligence" measures and three "creativity" measures), we would have data that could be used to evaluate our theory. Table 7.7 presents data that would be a theorist's delight.

The table shows that the four supposed measures of intelligence are all highly correlated with each other, as are the three supposed measures of creativity, while very weak correlations exist between measures of intelligence and creativity. This pattern of correlations conforms nicely to theoretical expectations. Real data are seldom so neat. For example, Wallach and Kogan (1965) reviewed the then-existing research on the creativity–intelligence distinction. In general, they observed a discouraging picture, especially for the concept of creativity. While different measures of intelligence tended to be at least moderately related to each other, different (presumed) measures of creativity tended to have quite low correlations (e.g., +.20), showing a lack of convergent validity, and tended to be as strongly related to intelligence measures as they were to each other, showing a lack of discriminant validity.

The pursuit of construct validity does not simply stop when results do not conform to expectations. Wallach and Kogan attempted to redefine creativity, to identify a set of measures of creativity (newly defined) that should be and are highly related to each other and are weakly related to

Table 7.7   Hypothetical Correlations
Between Four Intelligence Measures (I1–I4)
and Three Creativity Measures (C1–C3)
Illustrating High Convergent and
Discriminant Validity

Among Intelligence Measures		Among Creativity Measures	
I1 & I2	.80	C1 & C2	.80
I1 & I3	.80	C1 & C3	.85
I1 & I4	.85	C2 & C3	.85
I2 & I3	.85		
I2 & I4	.80		
I3 & I4	.85		

Between Intelligence and Creativity Measures				
	I1	I2	I3	I4
C1	.10	.15	.10	.15
C2	.15	.10	.10	.15
C3	.10	.10	.10	.15

measures of intelligence. This is the typical course of theoretical research. An observed pattern of correlations allows an evaluation of existing theory and serves as a basis for modification of theoretical notions.

Campbell and Fiske (1959) made an important contribution to research on construct validity. They pointed out that measuring a construct really involves a construct–method combination. That is, measuring, say, anxiety by administering a paper-and-pencil, self-report test yields scores that depend on both the construct (anxiety) and the method ("verbal" self-report). A theoretical construct typically ought to be measurable by several methods; for example, anxiety might be assessed by self-report tests, by behavioral observations in various situations, or by physiological measures. The validity of a construct increases when research shows that measures of that construct based on different methods are highly correlated with each other (or that measures of presumably different constructs are poorly related even though they are based on the same method). The underlying idea is that scores based on the same method might tend to be related whether or not the same construct is being assessed.

Look again at the data in Table 7.7. To illustrate Campbell and Fiske's point, suppose that all three creativity measures were verbal tests while all four intelligence measures were nonverbal, performance measures. If so, the pattern of correlations in Table 7.7 could mean that scores on verbal tests are highly related, that nonverbal scores are highly related, and that verbal and nonverbal scores are poorly related (rather than meaning that relatively independent constructs of intelligence and creativity existed). Consider how much more powerful the pattern of correlations would be if different methods had been used to measure intelligence, different methods to measure creativity, and some of the same methods to measure both intelligence and creativity. In this case the evidence for validity of the constructs of intelligence and creativity would be much stronger because possible confounding by method factors would be minimized.

PROBLEM

A researcher believed that some children are "auditory learners" and some are "visual learners." The idea is that some learn better from visual presentation of materials while others learn better from auditory presentation. This idea translates into the prediction that there will be a low correlation between scores on a visual-learning task and scores on an auditory-learning task. To support his proposal the researcher reported some data that had been collected in a local school. A number of fourth-grade children had each been given several learning tasks, two with visual presentation (call them visual A and visual B) and two with auditory presentation (auditory A and auditory B). Pearson r correlation coefficients had been calculated, with the following results:

visual A and visual B	$r = +.22$
visual A and auditory A	$r = +.15$
visual A and auditory B	$r = +.21$
visual B and auditory A	$r = +.18$
visual B and auditory B	$r = +.24$
auditory A and auditory B	$r = +.25$

Pointing out that the correlations between visual learning scores and auditory-learning scores were quite low, the researcher concluded that his idea was supported by the data. Why is this conclusion questionable?

It is quite clear that visual scores and auditory scores were poorly related. However, the correlations between visual scores, and those between auditory scores, were also quite low. The researcher has not demonstrated that "visual learning" and "auditory learning" were reliably measured. Since we can have no confidence in the visual scores and the auditory scores, the low visual–auditory correlations are rather meaningless. In order to support the researcher's claim, the visual–auditory correlations would have to be low (which they were) while the correlations between visual scores, and between auditory scores, would have to be quite high (which they were not).

Regression Effects

Whenever two variables are less than perfectly correlated, there must be a tendency for individuals who have extreme z scores in one distribution to have, on the average, less extreme z scores in the other distribution. Think about this carefully. If everyone had two identical z scores, the correlation would be 1.00. If the correlation is less than 1.00, then there must be a general tendency for individuals to have different z_X and z_Y scores. Furthermore, the general tendency must be as follows: If you choose individuals with the most extreme z scores in one distribution, you will find that their z scores in the other distribution are less extreme. This will happen whether you choose on the basis of z_X scores and look at z_Y scores or choose on the basis of z_Y scores and look at z_X scores.

The z score prediction formula (predicted $z_Y = r\, z_X$) reflects this fact about the data. If, say, $r = +0.50$, a person with a z_X score of $+2.00$ (two standard deviations above the mean of the X distribution) would have a predicted z_Y score of $+1.00$, one standard deviation above the mean of the Y distribution ($.50 \times 2.00 = 1.00$). If z_X is -1.80, the predicted z_Y is -0.90, and so on. If we "flip the prediction formula over," predicted $z_X = r\, z_Y$, we can see that the same things will happen. It is important to realize that the prediction formula is not magical or arbitrary—rather, it is the best way to predict, *given what the data are like*. If individuals in fact tended to have very similar z scores in the two distributions, Pearson r would be closer to 1.00, and the prediction formula would (sensibly) yield predicted z scores that are more similar to the known z scores used in the prediction. This fact, that predicted z scores are closer to the mean than the known z scores used in the prediction equation, is known as *regression toward the mean,* or simply the *regression effect*. The regression effect means nothing more than that the two variables are imperfectly correlated.

To check your understanding of this issue, suppose that the correlation between IQ scores and school grades is $+0.50$. Suppose further that I tell you that George has the highest IQ score in his class but that he does not have the highest grades. Should you be surprised? The answer is no. If the correlation is only 0.50, then it must be the case that people with the very highest IQ scores do not have "equally highest" grades, that people with the very lowest grades do not have "equally lowest" IQ scores, and so on. This must in general be happening if the correlation is just 0.50. Variation in whatever the IQ test measures and whatever school grades assess are not perfectly related—it's that simple.

Let's look at a concrete example of correlational data to gain greater understanding. In Table 7.8 some hypothetical "test 1" and "test 2" scores are shown for twenty students named *a–t*. I have specially constructed these data such that the means and standard deviations are the same for the two score distributions. This allows us to look directly at raw scores rather than z scores, which is a little easier (note that, because $M_1 = M_2$ and $\sigma_1 = \sigma_2$, any particular score will yield the same z score in either distribution). The left-hand side of Table 7.8 shows the 20 pairs of scores that yield in quite ordinary fashion a correlation of $+0.63$. The correlation

Table 7.8 Correlational Data Illustrating Regression Effects

STUDENT	TEST 1 SCORE	TEST 2 SCORE
a	40	34
b	39	28
c	37	36
d	36	30
e	34	40
f	31	29
g	30	37
h	29	13
i	28	39
j	27	21
k	25	18
l	21	27
m	20	31
n	18	16
o	17	10
p	16	20
q	15	14
r	14	15
s	13	25
t	10	17

Pearson $r = +0.63$
$M_1 = M_2 = 25.0$
$\sigma_1 = \sigma_2 = 9.2$

Selecting Five Best on Test 1

Student	Test 1	Test 2
a	49	34
b	39	28
c	37	36
d	36	30
e	34	40
$\bar{X} = $	37.2	33.6

Selecting Five Worst on Test 1

Student	Test 1	Test 2
t	10	17
s	13	25
r	14	15
q	15	14
p	16	20
$\bar{X} = $	13.6	18.2

Selecting Five Best on Test 2

Student	Test 1	Test 2
e	34	40
i	28	39
g	30	37
c	37	36
a	40	34
$\bar{X} = $	33.8	37.2

Selecting Five Worst on Test 2

Student	Test 1	Test 2
o	17	10
h	29	13
q	15	14
r	14	15
n	18	16
$\bar{X} = $	18.6	13.6

indicates that $r^2 \times 100 = .63^2 \times 100 = 39.7\%$ of the variance in one distribution can be explained or accounted for on the basis of scores in the other distribution (whether we are working from test 1 to test 2 or vice versa). The right-hand side of Table 7.8 illustrates the regression effect.

Notice that if we select the five highest-scoring students on test 1, their average score on test 2 is lower, closer to the group mean, than their average score on test 1 (keep in mind that we can compare raw scores because the means and standard deviations are the same for the two distributions). The same regression effect occurs in the opposite direction; if students are selected for having the highest scores on test 2, their average test 1 score is lower than their average test 2 score. Selecting students who have the worst scores shows a similar regression effect in either direction; the regression toward the group mean is upward in these cases. The essential point is this: When two distributions are less than perfectly correlated, individuals who are selected for having extreme scores in one distribution will tend to have less extreme scores in the other distribution. Such regression effects reflect nothing more than the imperfect relation between the two variables.

Notice the misleading impressions that arise if one does not understand that regression effects are inevitable when correlations are imperfect. If we select just on the basis of test 1 scores, it appears (erroneously) that the better students are getting worse and the worse students better, that the group is becoming more homogeneous. On test 1 the five best students average 23.6 points more than the five worst students ($37.2 - 13.6 = 23.6$), while the difference between these two groups on test 2 is only 15.4 points ($33.6 - 18.2 = 15.4$). If we select only on the basis of test 2 scores, the exact opposite and equally erroneous impression arises. Whereas the best students on test 2 outscore the worst students by 23.6 points on test 2 ($37.2 - 13.6 = 23.6$), they differ by just 15.2 points on test 1 ($33.8 - 18.6 = 15.2$)—the group seems to be getting more varied from test 1 to test 2: Neither impression is correct—the simple fact is that the distribution of test 1 scores is precisely the same as the distribution of test 2 scores.

When variables are imperfectly related, regression effects must be present. Such a fact really presents a problem only for a theorist who predicts that the correlation should be perfect (no psychological theory has yet made such a prediction). The danger lies in a person's failing to understand the inevitability of regression effects in the presence of imperfect relations. Suppose a teacher just picked the best and worst students on the basis of test 1 scores and noticed that their scores were closer together on Test 2—the better students apparently getting worse and the worse students better. The teacher might be pleased with the effect of her instruction on the poorer students but concerned over the apparent negative effect on the better students. She would be reaching improper conclusions by failing to realize that the only fact in existence is that test 1 and test 2 are not perfectly correlated. The lesson is clear: Before trying to "explain" apparent changes in position from one distribution to another, one must examine the correlation between the two distributions and the kinds of regression effects that must be found because of a lack of a perfect relation.

Correlation and Causality

The issue that has received the greatest attention in connection with correlational data concerns attempts to explain *why* a correlation exists between two variables. For example, suppose a researcher tries to figure out why a correlation of +0.50 exists between IQ scores and school grades. Does this correlation indicate that intelligence "determines" school grades, that the amount of school learning "determines" IQs, or what? The answer is that, by itself, the correlation says nothing about why the relation exists. Explaining a correlation depends on the nature of the variables involved and on the nature of existing theoretical knowledge. This issue arises most clearly when the two variables are both natural variables, that is, when the researcher manipulates nothing but simply measures the variation in both variables that occurs under "ordinary" circumstances. The IQ–school grade correlation fits this description—the researcher has not "given" any individual a particular IQ or school grade. Rather, he or she has measured the IQ score and school grade that each individual happens to have.

When a correlation is found between two natural variables, it is typically said that there are three possible explanations for the relation. If the variables involved in the correlation are labeled X and Y, the three possibilities are as follows: (1) Variation in X "causes" variation in Y. (2) Variation in Y "causes" variation in X. (3) Variation in some third, unstudied variable "causes" variation in both X and Y. In Chapter 1, I pointed out that the search for causal explanations is related to the probable effects of intervention or manipulation (reread that section of Chapter 1 if you need to).

Suppose we find a correlation of +0.50 between naturally varying IQ scores and naturally varying school grades. If "IQ causes school grades," then changing people's IQs should result in changes in their school grades. If "school grades cause IQ scores," then changing school learning should result in changes in IQs. If some third, unidentified factor is responsible for the correlation between IQs and school grades, then neither intervention might work, or it might work for a reason other than the one we suspect. What is clear is that the interpretation of a correlation is typically unclear. The correlation itself does not establish any particular explanation, and the researcher needs to choose the most plausible explanation on the basis of existing knowledge. Of course, the probable acceptance of any particular explanation also depends on the lack of plausibility of other explanations. Identifying a single, clearly most plausible explanation of a correlation between natural variables is often quite difficult.

For example, a number of years ago newspapers brandished the headline "Smoking Related to Poor Grades." In one study of high school students a negative correlation had been observed between amount of cigarette smoking and grades in school (more smoking was associated with lower grades). Since cigarette smoking was then getting a fair amount of "bad press," a popular explanation of this finding was that smoking cigarettes had some negative (probably physiological) effect that resulted in lowered concentration or learning ability. Of course this explanation is one possibility. However, consider the alternatives. Given that cigarette smoking is often a response to anxiety, it is also possible that lower grades lead to more anxiety, which leads to more cigarette smoking. In addition, it is possible that, since getting good grades and not smoking cigarettes were both adult-defined "desirable" behaviors for high school students, students who tended to reject such authority were more likely both to smoke more and to get poorer grades. Furthermore, it is plausible that students who spend more time socializing (and thereby smoking) spend less time studying and thus get poorer grades. Perhaps you can see why this finding did not have much theoretical force.

PROBLEM

It has been suggested that social isolation can lead to poor emotional adjustment. A researcher studied the relation between social isolation and mental health in an elementary school. For a sample of 200 children he obtained information about the number of friends each child had and gave each child a standard test of emotional adjustment. In analyzing the results he found that children with fewer friends had lower scores on emotional adjustment—children with more friends had higher adjustment scores. He concluded that social isolation did in fact lead to poorer emotional adjustment. Criticize this conclusion.

The basic finding was that scores on an adjustment test were systematically related to the number of friends children had. The researcher's conclusion, that social isolation (indexed by few friends) leads to poorer adjustment, is one plausible explanation of the result. However, another plausible explanation of the finding is that children who are poorly adjusted will make fewer friends; in other words, poor emotional adjustment leads to social isolation. Both explanations are plausible, and the data do not provide a basis for choosing between them. Therefore the researcher's conclusion need not be accepted—it is not the only plausible explanation of the results.

Considering the plausibility of alternate explanations helps us understand why researchers prefer to manipulate one of the variables involved in a relation. In the example cited earlier, both amount of smoking and school grades were natural variables; each student, for whatever reasons, smoked some amount and earned certain school grades, both of which were measured by the researchers. Contrast this situation with the following: Suppose a researcher obtained the cooperation of a number of high school students such that, for a certain period, the researcher could control the amount of smoking each student engaged in. The idea is that the researcher, on some random basis, chooses one student to do no smoking, another to smoke one cigarette a day, another a pack a day, and so on. As before, school grades are naturally varying—the students get whatever grades they would get according to the ordinary system. Each student will have two "scores," one for amount of cigarette smoking and one for school grades. However, in this case amount of smoking would not be a natural variable but, rather, would have been controlled (manipulated, determined) by the researcher. A correlation coefficient could be computed between variation in smoking and variation in school grades; suppose a negative correlation were observed. In this case it is *implausible* that "school grades 'caused' amount of smoking" because we know that the amount of smoking was controlled by the researcher. Therefore the plausible explanations are reduced to two: that variation in amount of smoking is (directly) responsible for differences in school grades or that in manipulating the amount of smoking the researcher also changed some other variable that led to differences in school grades. This type of study, in which one of the variables is controlled or manipulated by the experimenter, is less ambiguous than one in which the relation between two natural variables is "simply" observed, since there are fewer plausible explanations. Furthermore, it is usually somewhat easier to check out alternate explanations because of the greater control exercised by the researcher—more is known about what might have been varying in the research situation.

While an experiment does have advantages over the study of naturally occurring relations, it also has its limitations. Notice that the researcher could control amount of smoking only for students who were willing to allow such control over their lives. Perhaps these students are unrepresentative of students in general; this would limit the generality of the finding. In a strict sense the experimental result does not necessarily provide an explanation of the relation between two natural variables. While "Grades cause smoking" is an implausible explanation of a relation between experimentally manipulated smoking and school grades, this finding does not rule out the possibility that when both amount of smoking and school grades vary freely or naturally, "Grades cause smoking." Of course, the plausibility of this idea would have to be examined. It is sensible to reason that if the same relation is found between amount of smoking and school grades both when the two variables freely vary and when amount of smoking is controlled (making "Grades cause smoking" implausible in that situation), the general plausibility of "Smoking causes grades" is increased and the plausibility of "Grades cause smoking" decreases.

Another problem with manipulating one of the variables involved in a relation is that the researcher simply might not be able to exercise such control. For example, parents or school administrators or the students themselves might not allow a researcher to assign a student to "smoke two packs a day"; for a variety of reasons the researcher might not be able to manipulate one of the variables. For this and the other reasons I have mentioned, researchers have sought alternate methods of reducing the ambiguity of correlational findings (between natural variables). We will briefly consider one such technique.

Cross-lagged panel analysis. Ordinarily a correlation between natural variables is based on measuring both variables (for a number of individuals) at roughly a single point in time. For example, a correlation between IQ scores and school grades might stem from giving the IQ test and examining school grades in the spring of a school year. As we have seen, an IQ–grade correlation obtained in this way is quite ambiguous, having several plausible explanations. However, if the measurement operations are repeated for the same individuals at a later point in time, it is possible to obtain evidence that increases (or decreases) the plausibility of alternate explanations.

Suppose both IQ scores and school grades are measured for a number of students at two points in time (year 1 and year 2). Figure 7.5 shows the correlation coefficients that could be computed. The two correlations on the horizontal lines represent test–retest reliability coefficients over the time interval for IQ ($r_{I_1 I_2}$) and for grades ($r_{G_1 G_2}$). The two correlations on the vertical lines represent IQ–grade correlations when both variables are measured at the same time ($r_{I_1 G_1}$ and $r_{I_2 G_2}$), the kinds of correlations that we have previously seen to be hard to interpret. Of special interest are the correlations on the diagonal lines, which index relations that are crossed (from one variable to the other) and lagged (over time)—hence the name *cross-lagged* panel analysis. One correlation indicates how well "initial" IQ predicts later grades ($r_{I_1 G_2}$), while the other shows how well initial grades predict later IQs ($r_{G_1 I_2}$). A comparison of these two cross-lagged correlations can be used to evaluate the plausibility of alternate "causal" explanations of the basic IQ–grade relation.

The analysis rests on the idea that, when causal explanations are

Figure 7.5. Illustration of data used in cross-lagged panel analysis. The correlations on the diagonals, $r_{I_1 G_2}$ and $r_{G_1 I_2}$ are most critical.

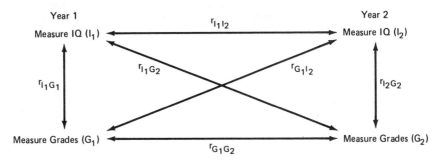

offered, causes *precede* effects in time. If the dominant functional relation is that "IQ causes grades," then initial IQs should predict later grades better than initial grades predict later IQs ($r_{I_1 G_2} > r_{G_1 I_2}$). If the opposite notion is more accurate ("Achievement causes intelligence"), then initial grades should predict later IQs better than initial IQs predict later grades ($r_{I_1 G_2} < r_{G_1 I_2}$). If IQ and grades are *not* causally related or are both effects of some other causal influence, then the two cross-lagged correlations should be the same ($r_{I_1 G_2} = r_{G_1 I_2}$). The comparison of the cross-lagged correlations thus provides much more critical information about the plausibility of alternate explanations than a "simple" IQ–grade correlation. Cross-lagged panel analysis is not quite as simple and straightforward as I have presented it here (see Rozelle & Campbell, 1969 for a complete discussion). However, you should understand the essential logic of the method and realize that it does allow researchers to make reasonable inferences about causal relations on the basis of correlations between natural variables.

This method has been used to study the relation between intelligence and achievement, with the interesting finding that the dominant sequence seems to be that of "Intelligence causing achievement" for suburban schoolchildren, while the opposite sequence, "Achievement causing intelligence," is dominant for inner-city schoolchildren (Crano, Kenny, & Campbell, 1972; Dyer & Miller, 1974). Cross-lagged panel analysis has also been used to study the relation between television violence and agression. Notice that finding a positive correlation between the violence level of TV that children choose to watch and their levels of interpersonal aggression is ambiguous. More aggressive children might choose to watch more violent TV; watching more violent TV might lead to greater aggression; or some other factor might be responsible for both TV-watching habits and aggression. By assessing both TV watching and aggression for a number of children over a period of years, researchers were able to compare the cross-lagged correlations (early TV violence–later aggression vs. early aggression–later TV violence). The findings supported the argument that watching more violent TV leads to more aggressive behavior (Huesmann, Eron, Lefkowitz, & Walder, 1973). These examples illustrate the usefulness of cross-lagged panel analysis, and we should expect to see the method applied to other issues in the future.

SUMMARY

Correlational methods are commonly used to study relations between natural variables; the usual research question concerns the manner in which individual differences in one variable are related to individual differences in another variable. The basic data for correlational analysis consist of (at least) two measurements for each of a number of individuals or cases. When individuals tend to maintain the same relative positions on both variables, the relation between variables is called *positive.* When high scorers in one distribution tend to be low scorers in the other distribution (and vice versa), the relation is called *negative.*

A *correlation coefficient* provides a numerical index of the form (positive or negative) and strength of the relation between two variables. Correlation coefficients range in magnitude from 0.00 (no systematic relation) to 1.00 (perfect relation). Pearson r is the most commonly used correlation coefficient; the value of Pearson r reflects the relation between the z scores of individuals in one distribution and their z scores in the other distribution. A Pearson r of 1.00 indicates that each individual has two z scores of the same numerical value.

If two variables are unrelated ($r = 0.00$), knowing an individual's score in one distribution does not provide useful information for predicting that individual's score in the other distribution. In this situation there is nothing better to do than predict the mean score for all cases. When two variables are systematically related ($r \neq 0.00$), more accurate predictions can be made between distributions. When the relation between variables is perfect ($r = +1.00$ or -1.00), errorless predictions can be made. In general, the square of the correlation coefficient (r^2) indicates how accurately predictions can be made; r^2 is directly related to the percentage reduction in prediction error variance (or, r^2 is directly related to the percentage of variance in one distribution that can be predicted on the basis of scores in the other distribution). Two cautions must be kept in mind when considering the value of Pearson r: (1) Pearson r reflects only linear relations between variables. (2) If the full range of scores for both variables is not represented in the data, the value of r is likely to underestimate the relation between the two variables.

Correlation coefficients are used to assess the reliability of measurements. Reliability may be investigated (defined) in several ways. *Internal consistency* refers to the correlation between parts of a test, while *test–retest reliability* concerns the stability of measurements over various time intervals. *Alternate-form* reliability can involve the stability of measurements over both changes in content and time intervals. Correlational analyses are also used to investigate the validity of measures. In simple terms, the correlation between scores on the measure and scores on some criterion is examined. Validity coefficients are generally expected to be lower in magnitude than reliability coefficients.

Research on construct validity involves the evaluation of patterns of correlations. To demonstrate good construct validity different measures of the same construct (trait or ability) must have high correlations with each other (called *convergent validity*) while simultaneously having low correlations with measures of theoretically distinct constructs (called *discriminant validity*). It is important to separate the methods used to obtain scores (e.g., self-report, behavioral observations, etc.) from the trait that is presumably represented by the scores. More than one method should be used to obtain both the scores that are theoretically expected to be strongly correlated and the scores that are expected to be poorly correlated.

Whenever two variables are less than perfectly related, individuals who have the most extreme scores in one distribution will tend to have less extreme scores in the other distribution. This tendency, which is nothing more than a consequence of the imperfect relation between the variables, is known as *regression toward the mean* or as a *regression effect*. It is important to understand that regression effects are simple consequences of imperfect correlations in order to avoid interpretive errors when examining changes in individuals' relative positions from one distribution to another.

Correlation coefficients are fundamentally descriptive; in principle a correlation between two natural variables might be explained in several different ways. Deriving causal explanations from correlations between natural variables is extremely difficult. To improve the interpretability of correlational data, researchers have invented more complex methods. One such method is called *cross-lagged panel analysis*, which involves measuring (at least) two variables at one point in time and then measuring them again for the same individuals at a later point in time. The researcher's interest lies in comparing the correlation between initial scores on measure A and later scores on measure B to the correlation between initial scores on measure B and later scores on measure A. The comparison of these two correlations can allow the researcher to decide whether the data support the idea that "A causes B" or the contrasting idea that "B causes A." This method has been used successfully in several areas of research.

8

COMPLEX RESEARCH DESIGNS

In earlier chapters I have emphasized relatively simple research designs, such as those involving the comparison of just two treatments, in order to concentrate on the fundamental concepts that apply to all research. We will now consider more complicated techniques that are frequently used in psychological research. First we will discuss factorial designs, which include more than one independent variable but are arranged in such a way that the independent variables are not confounded with each other. Factorial designs provide more information than studies involving just one independent variable. Then we will consider several topics that are related to multiple-stage research. We have previously touched on some aspects of multiple-stage research, for example, in discussing the need to counterbalance practice effects when using a repeated-measures design. In this chapter more complex uses of repeated measures will be presented, with attention focused on research in which the primary interest lies in measuring *changes* in behavior in some way. We will consider factorial designs first because an understanding of such designs will be helpful when multiple-stage research is discussed.

FACTORIAL DESIGNS

In a simple experiment a researcher obtains a number of scores for each treatment and the treatments represent different levels of a single independent variable. We have considered examples in which the treatments represent different levels of illumination or different time intervals or different kinds of instructions. In such experiments each score (on the dependent variable) is associated with one level of one independent variable. If the treatments were, for example, time intervals of 0, 5, or 10 seconds, each score would be associated with either 0 seconds or 5 seconds or 10 seconds. In other words, the data are classified in just one way—according to time interval in this example. In factorial designs the treatments are specially arranged combinations of two or more variables, and each score is associated with a particular combination of variables. In factorial designs the data can be classified in more than one way.

You have in fact already seen examples of factorial designs, because factorial designs are nothing more than *balanced* designs. For example, if a researcher compares two treatments, A and B (which we discussed as levels of *the* independent variable), but also uses two rooms for data collection so that half of the data for each treatment come from each room, the researcher is really using a factorial design. There will be four "kinds" of scores obtained, each representing a particular combination of treatment and room: treatment A, room 1; treatment A, room 2; treatment B, room 1; treatment B, room 2. Notice that each score is associated with both a particular treatment and a particular room—a particular treatment–room combination. The data can be classified with respect to both treatments (A vs. B) and room (1 vs. 2). Such arrangements illustrate the essence of factorial designs.

A researcher "winds up" with a factorial design whenever the treatments are balanced with some "other" variable (rooms, experimenters, etc.) to avoid confounding. In such instances the researcher is usually not really interested in the "other" variable's influence on performance but simply wants to avoid confounding the treatment differences that are of interest. However, the same balancing principle can be used to simultaneously study the influences of two or more variables that are of theoretical interest. For example, suppose a researcher believes that the performance of rats in a learning task might be influenced by both "level of deprivation" and "amount of reinforcement." One way in which these independent variables could be studied is by conducting two separate experiments. In one experiment the researcher could manipulate level of deprivation while holding amount of reinforcement constant. In another experiment amount of reinforcement could be manipulated while level of deprivation is held constant. In this way, through two experiments, the researcher would gain information about both variables. However, by including both variables in a single, factorial design the researcher will not only gain this information more efficiently but also obtain additional information.

Suppose we are interested in comparing two levels of deprivation and two levels of reinforcement (just to keep things simple). The principle of a factorial design dictates that each level of deprivation must be combined with each level of reinforcement equally often. Table 8.1 illustrates a factorial design using these two independent variables. Notice that there are four treatments, each a different combination of deprivation and reinforcement levels, and that equal numbers of subjects are assigned (randomly) to each treatment. Table 8.1 also shows some hypothetical data for this design; I will use these data to illustrate the analysis of a factorial design.

To decide whether performance (trials to learn) is affected by level of deprivation, we would determine whether the sample mean for 2 hours differs sufficiently from the sample mean for 12 hours' deprivation to warrant rejecting the null hypothesis of no true mean difference. The appropriate sample means are 15.3 trials (for 2 hours) and 9.9 trials (for

Table 8.1   Example of a Factorial Design

The Design

AMOUNT OF REINFORCEMENT	Deprivation Level	
	2 HOURS	**12 HOURS**
1 pellet	5 subjects	5 subjects
5 pellets	5 subjects	5 subjects

Hypothetical Data (Trials to Learn)

AMOUNT OF REINFORCEMENT	Deprivation Level		OVERALL MEAN
	2 HOURS	**12 HOURS**	
	(a)	*(b)*	
1 pellet	14	15	
	18	13	
	17	12	
	15	10	
	19	14	
	($\bar{X} = (16.6)$	($\bar{X} = 12.8$)	14.7
	(c)	*(d)*	
5 pellets	13	8	
	14	9	
	15	7	
	16	6	
	12	5	
	($\bar{X} = 14.0$)	($\bar{X} = 7.0$)	11.0
Overall mean	15.3	9.9	

12 hours); both sample means are based on the 10 scores associated with each deprivation level. In other words, to look at the overall score difference between deprivation levels the data are combined across reinforcement levels. Similarly, to analyze the overall difference between reinforcement levels we would combine the data across the deprivation levels and compare the mean of the 10 scores associated with 1 pellet (14.7) to the mean of the 10 scores for 5 pellets (11.0).

It is important to understand the nature of these tests. With respect to deprivation level, the question being asked is whether or not there is a real difference between mean scores for 2 and 12 hours' deprivation *combined across* or *averaged over* reinforcement levels. For reinforcement level, the similar question is whether or not there is a real difference between the mean scores for 1 pellet and 5 pellets' reward *combined across* or *averaged over* deprivation levels. These tests are appropriately described as tests of the *overall* differences in scores between levels of a single independent variable. The conclusion would have the form, "In general (averaged over the levels of the other independent variable(s) in the experiment), there is (or isn't) a difference between the means for different levels of deprivation." A similar conclusion would apply to the overall effect of reinforcement level.

Notice that in examining the overall effect of deprivation level and the overall effect of reinforcement level, *no* comparisons have been made using the sample means for the four basic treatment groups. These means can be used to examine a different question: Does the effect of deprivation level depend on the reinforcement level, or does the effect of reinforcement level depend on the deprivation level? There is really just one question, although it can be asked in either of the two ways just mentioned. Why is this so?

Consider the question of whether the score difference between 2 and 12 hours' deprivation changes or doesn't change from one reinforcement level to the other. The mean score difference between deprivation levels for a 1-pellet reward is $16.6 - 12.8 = 3.8$ ($\bar{X}_2 - \bar{X}_{12}$); for a 5-pellet reward the ($\bar{X}_2 - \bar{X}_{12}$) difference is $14.0 - 7.0 = 7.0$. The question being asked is whether or not these *differences are really different*. The null hypothesis would be that there is no real difference between differences, and the test would involve determining whether the observed difference between differences ($3.8 - 7.0$) is large enough to warrant rejecting this null hypothesis.

Suppose we look at this question "the other way." Does the score difference between reinforcement levels change from one deprivation level to the other? For 2 hours' deprivation the mean score difference ($\bar{X}_1 - \bar{X}_5$) between reinforcement levels is $16.6 - 14.0 = 2.6$; the comparable difference for 12 hours' deprivation is $12.8 - 7.0 = 5.8$. The test would involve determining whether the difference between these differences (2.6

− 5.8) is large enough to warrant rejecting the null hypothesis of no real difference between differences.

Note again that these are not two questions but two ways of asking the same question. Notice that when we look at the question the first way the difference between differences is $3.8 - 7.0 = -3.2$; when we look at the question the second way the difference between differences is $2.6 - 5.8 = -3.2$, exactly the same value. This will always be true and is a consequence of the fact that there is really only one question being asked. If the data allow us to conclude that the effect of deprivation level does change from one reinforcement level to another, it must also be correct that the effect of reinforcement level changes from one deprivation level to the other.

Let's look at this in a different way. In Table 8.1 the four basic treatments are labeled a, b, c, and d. When we looked at the difference between differences the first way, we examined $(a - b) - (c - d)$, which yields $a - b - c + d$. Doing it the second way, we looked at $(a - c) - (b - d)$, which yields $a - c - b + d$. You can see that no matter which way we do it, a and d wind up positive and b and c wind up negative, which is of course why the final value of the difference between differences is the same no matter which way we calculate it.

Notice that the researcher using this factorial design gets answers to three questions: Is there an overall effect of deprivation level? Is there an overall effect of reinforcement level? Does the effect of deprivation level depend on the reinforcement level, or (phrasing the question the other way) does the effect of reinforcement level depend on the deprivation level? By including both independent variables in the same balanced factorial design, the researcher gets not only information about the effects of each independent variable looked at separately but also information about whether the effect of one independent variable changes from one level to another of the other independent variable. A factorial design yields more information than a simple, one-independent-variable experiment, and that is the major advantage of factorial designs.

Terminology

The overall differences between means for a single independent variable are referred to as the *main effect* of that variable. Main effect is the same as overall effect. Remember that when main effects are examined, the data are combined across levels of the other independent variable(s). In a factorially designed experiment with two independent variables, there will be two main effects to examine; we would look at the overall mean differences associated with one independent variable and separately do the same thing for the other independent variable. The question of whether "the differences are different" refers to the *interaction* of the two independent variables. That is, if we concluded that the effect of deprivation level changed with reinforcement level (and vice versa), we would say that there was an interaction between deprivation level and reinforcement level. An interaction means that differences differ, that the effect of one independent variable changes from one level to another of the other independent variable and vice versa.

The principle of a factorial design is that all possible combinations of the levels of the independent variables occur equally often. Each basic treatment is defined in terms of a particular combination. For example, if the design includes 3 kinds of learning materials (nouns, verbs, and adjectives) and 4 intertrial intervals (1, 5, 20, and 60 seconds), there would be 12 basic treatments (nouns, 1 sec.; nouns, 5 sec.; nouns, 20 sec.; nouns, 60 sec.; verbs, 1 sec.; verbs, 5 sec.; and so on). There should be an equal number of scores in each basic treatment (combination) in order to maintain the balanced nature of the design (if this condition is not met, much more complicated methods of analysis must be used, which we will not discuss). The analysis of a factorial design can be viewed in terms of degrees of generality. Since the *main effect* of any independent variable involves combining the data across the levels of the other independent variable(s), the main effect is the most general information available in the experiment. Testing for *interactions* is testing to determine whether there are more complex effects of the independent variables. Let's look more closely at these two kinds of results.

Main Effects

A main effect is fairly easy to understand because it closely resembles the kind of information obtained from a simple, one-independent-variable experiment. Basically, testing for a main effect involves checking to see how scores on the dependent variable change from one level to another of an independent variable. The null hypothesis is that there are no real changes in scores between levels of the independent variable, regardless of the number of levels. Of course to examine any main effect in a factorial design, the data are combined across levels of the other independent variable(s) included in the design. Table 8.2 presents another example of a factorial design that we can use to practice looking at main effects.

This hypothetical experiment concerns making guesses with limited information. The task (made up by me) is as follows: The subject is given a list of names of famous people. On each trial the subject is given a number of clues about the identity of one of these people and must try to guess who the person is. Each subject's score is the percentage of correct guesses over a large number of trials. The experiment includes two independent variables, the number of clues given about the target person's identity (4 levels, 3 through 6 clues) and strategy instructions (2 levels,

Table 8.2   Hypothetical Data (Percent Correct) for a Factorial Design

STRATEGY INSTRUC-TIONS	Number of Clues Given				OVER-ALL MEAN
	3	**4**	**5**	**6**	
Yes	48	81	82	85	
	47	75	75	80	
	50	69	80	72	
	45	77	79	78	
	($\bar{X} = 47.5$)	($\bar{X} = 75.5$)	($\bar{X} = 79.0$)	($\bar{X} = 78.8$)	70.2
No	39	52	63	82	
	35	50	66	74	
	41	54	65	76	
	34	47	59	80	
	($\bar{X} = 37.2$)	($\bar{X} = 50.8$)	($\bar{X} = 63.2$)	($\bar{X} = 78.0$)	57.3
Overall Mean	42.4	67.8	71.1	78.4	

either given or not). Combining the 4 levels of "number of clues" with the 2 levels of "strategy instructions" produces 8 basic treatments, and 4 subjects were randomly assigned to each treatment. Since there are two independent variables, there are two main effects to examine. To test for a main effect of strategy instructions, we would compare the mean of the 16 scores for subjects who received strategy instructions (70.2) to the mean of the 16 scores for subjects who did not receive strategy instructions (57.3). Should these means differ enough (relative to the amount of random error in the data), we would conclude that there is a performance difference between subjects receiving and not receiving strategy instructions, combined across or averaged over the levels of "number of clues." The main effect of "number of clues" would involve comparing the means for the 4 levels of this variable (42.4 vs. 67.8 vs. 71.1 vs. 78.4) to determine whether any differences exist; each mean is based on 8 scores and the test involves combining data across strategy–instruction levels.

As you can see, the main effect of a variable concerns the most general statement about the effect of that variable that can be made from an experiment. The main effect of strategy instructions refers, not to the difference between strategy and no-strategy means for just 3 clues, or for just 4 clues, or for just 5 or 6 clues, but to the average difference between strategy and no-strategy means combined across levels of "number of clues." Notice that the more levels of other variables have been averaged across to get the means for a main effect, the more general that main effect is. For example, had this experiment included just 3 and 4 clues, the main effect of strategy instructions would have involved averaging over just these two levels of number of clues, which would make the main effect less general than when it involves averaging over 4 levels of number of clues.

Interactions

Tests for interactions can be viewed as checks on the general statements based on main effects. For example, the main effect of strategy instructions involved a comparison of the two appropriate overall means, 70.2 percent for yes, 57.3 for no, a difference of about 13 percent. Assume that this difference is statistically significant. If there were *no interaction* between strategy instructions and number of clues, we would expect to find about a 13 percent difference between the strategy and no-strategy means *at every level* of "number of clues." Examination of the means for the eight treatments suggests that this did not happen; the strategy–no strategy mean difference seems to change from one level to another of "number of clues." The eight means are shown in Figure 8.1, which we can use to visually examine the interaction.

Each point in Figure 8.1 represents one of the eight basic treatment means; the points are plotted to show the factorial nature of the design and to allow a visual inspection of the interaction. As you can see, the difference between strategy means seems to vary across levels of number of clues. The largest strategy mean difference occurs with 4 clues, while there is virtually no mean difference for 6 clues. In other words, the data

Figure 8.1 Data illustrating an interaction between strategy instructions (yes–no) and number of clues (3–6).

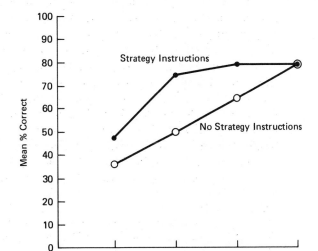

suggest that "the effect of giving strategy instructions depends on the number of clues given." We can also examine the interaction by looking at the effect of number of clues, with and without strategy instructions. Without strategy instructions, adding more clues resulted in consistent increases in the percent of correct responses; there appears to be a linear relation between "percent correct" and "number of clues" when no strategy instructions are given. When strategy instructions are given, however, a different relation seems to occur; there is a rather large increase in performance from 3 to 4 clues but roughly equivalent performance from 4 through 6 clues.

If statistical analysis indicated that the interaction was "statistically significant" (and we'll assume that it is), this would tell us to be cautious about making *general* statements about *either* the effect of strategy instructions *or* the effect of number of clues. The effect of giving strategy instructions is not the same for all numbers of clues—the effect of increasing the number of clues is not the same for strategy and no-strategy conditions. If there were *no* interaction, we could talk about the two independent variables simply in terms of their main effects. When an interaction is present, this indicates that the effects of the independent variables are more complex.

It is important to understand that information about interactions is separate from or independent of information about main effects. The data from a factorial design might yield any combination of results: two main effects and an interaction (as in our example), two main effects but no interaction, no main effects but an interaction, one main effect and no interaction, and so on. We can use graphic displays of the means to illustrate various kinds of possible results (like the display in Figure 8.1). In Figure 8.2 I have graphed several sets of data from factorial designs. In each graph the vertical axis refers to scores on the dependent variable. One of the independent variables (called A, and having levels A1, A2, A3, etc.) is used for the horizontal axis of the graph. The data (means for basic treatments) are plotted to show different functions relating the dependent variable to variable A for each level of the other independent variable (called B, and having levels B1, B2, B3, etc.) To make sure you understand this labeling system, relate it to the concrete example in Figure 8.1. The vertical axis in each graph refers to some measure of behavior (e.g., "Mean Percent Correct" in Figure 8.1). The horizontal axis gives values for one independent variable, which was "number of clues" in Figure 8.1. A separate "line" of data points is plotted for each level of the other independent variable, which was "Strategy Instructions—yes or no" in Figure 8.1. In visually examining such graphs to check on interactions, the essential question is whether the functions relating the dependent variable to independent variable A, one function for each level of variable B, are *parallel* or not. If the functions are all parallel, this indicates that *no* interaction is present. If the functions are not parallel, an interaction is present.

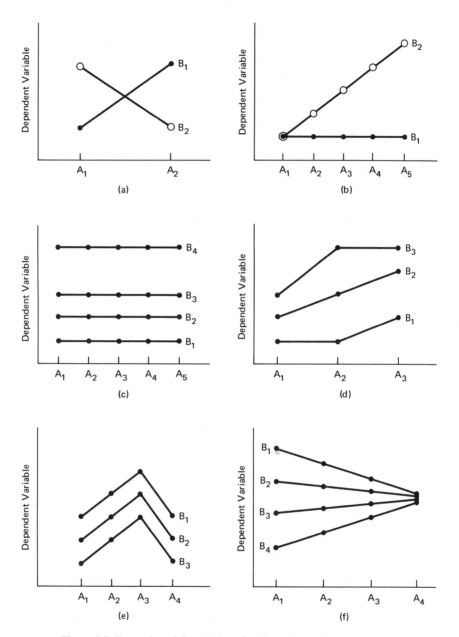

Figure 8.2 Examples of data with and without interactions present.

Panel (a) of Figure 8.2 illustrates the "classic" interaction—a "crossover" effect." Notice that the difference between A1 and A2 is positive at one level of variable B (B2), while the difference is negative at the other level (B1). Looked at the other way, the difference (B1 − B2) is negative at one level of A (A1) but positive at the other level (A2). Clearly, in this instance no general statement about the (A1 − A2) difference or the (B1 − B2) difference would be very appropriate. A similar but less "drastic" interaction is shown in panel (f); in going from A1 to A4, scores decrease for two levels of variable B (B1, B2) but increase for the other two levels (B3, B4). In panels (b) and (d) interactions are present, although there are no "reversals" in the data; in panel (b) the score difference between B1 and B2 gets larger from A1 to A4 or, in other words, variable A has no effect on scores at level B1 while scores increase regularly from A1 to A4 at level B2. Panel (d) shows a very slight interaction; notice that scores generally increase from A1 to A3 for all three levels of B, although the nature of the change varies. At B2 scores increase linearly from A1 to A3, while at B1 there is no change from A1 to A2, followed by a slight increase; at B3 there is a larger increase in scores from A1 to A2 and then no change to A3. Looking at it the other way, B3 > B2 > B1 at each level of variable A, although the sizes of the differences vary. Of the four interactions shown in panels (a), (b), (d), and (f), the interaction in panel (d) is the least "serious."

Panels (c) and (e) do *not* contain interactions. In panel (c) there is in fact no effect of variable A on performance—mean scores do not change from one level of A to another, and this is true at all levels of B; thus there is no interaction. In other words, the differences between the levels of B, B4 > B3 > B2 > B1, are precisely the same at all levels of A; there is a main effect of variable B but no interaction. In panel (e) both variables A and B influence scores, but the effect of A is the same at all levels of B and vice versa—no interaction is present.

Testing for interactions provides useful information to a researcher. If no interaction is present, the researcher can have increased confidence in the generality of the effects of the independent variables, shown in their main effects. If, on the other hand, some interaction is observed, the researcher gains information about the way in which generality is limited. I have argued repeatedly that experimenters need to be concerned with the generality of their findings; factorial designs allow at least some check on generality, whereas a simple experiment, with one independent variable and "everything else" held constant, provides extremely limited information about generality. Factorial designs are also used when theoretical ideas lead to predictions that certain interactions should occur—to test such ideas factorial designs are necessary.

The major reason for using factorial designs is to test for interactions. Factorial designs can be used with independent groups, matched subjects, or repeated measures (even with combinations of these subject assignment techniques). In discussing the analysis of factorial designs I have emphasized how the data are arranged to examine main effects and interactions. In actual research practice the researcher would of course conduct statistical tests to determine whether differences between means (for main effects) or patterns of differences (for interactions) warrant rejecting the appropriate null hypotheses. All of the differences between independent groups, matched subjects, and repeated measures that we considered in Chapter 3 apply whether a researcher conducts a simple, two-treatment experiment or uses a factorial design. Also, factorial designs are not limited to two independent variables; in principle a researcher could include any number of independent variables in the design. For example, it would be perfectly acceptable to include two levels of deprivation (2 or 12 hours), four levels of reinforcement (1, 3, 5, or 7 food pellets), and three types of subjects (rats, hamsters, or gerbils) in a factorial design. Such a design would involve $2 \times 4 \times 3 = 18$ treatments, each a particular combination of deprivation level, reinforcement magnitude, and subject type. The analysis of a more complex factorial design would itself be somewhat more complicated than what we have discussed, but it would follow the principles that we have examined.

PROBLEM

An experiment involved an investigation of two ways of affecting college students' motivational levels and, thus, their performance. The task for all subjects was a fairly difficult problem, which the subject was told to try to solve as quickly as possible. Four different treatments were used. In the control condition, the subject was told what the problem was and asked to solve it. In the threat condition, subjects were also told that performance on the problem was a good measure of general intelligence and that it was therefore important for them to do well. In the money condition, subjects were told that if they solved the problem very quickly (i.e., had one of the four fastest solution times), they would receive a prize of $20. Finally, in the threat-plus-money condition subjects were told both that performance on the problem was a good measure of intelligence and that they could earn a prize. Twenty college students were randomly assigned to each of the four conditions. The average solution times for the four treatments were as follows: control, 13 minutes; threat, 17 minutes; money, 10 minutes; threat-plus-money, 20 minutes. The researcher was interested in determining the main (overall) effect of "threat," the main effect of "money," and their interaction. Assuming that any numerical difference is "statistically significant," determine what the results of the study are.

To do this problem you must recognize that the researcher has used a factorial design and wants information about main effects and an interaction. There are two independent variables in the design, "threat" (yes or no) and "money" (yes or no), and the four treatments consist of all possible combinations of the two values of the two variables. The control condition is "no threat, no money"; the threat condition is "yes threat, no money"; the money condition is "no threat, yes money," and the threat-plus-money condition is "yes threat, yes money." This is a 2×2 factorial design. To examine the main effect of "threat" we need to compare the average score for all "yes-threat" subjects to that for all "no-threat" subjects. Since each basic treatment included the same number of subjects, we can average the averages. The overall mean for "yes threat" is $\frac{1}{2}(17 + 20) = 18.5$; the overall mean for "no threat" is $\frac{1}{2}(13 + 20) = 16.5$. Assuming the difference $(18.5 - 16.5 = 2.0)$ to be "real," we would conclude that, overall, threat leads to increased solution times. For the main effect of "money" we must combine the data in the opposite fashion. The overall mean for "yes money" is $\frac{1}{2}(10 + 20) = 15.0$; the overall mean for "no money" is $\frac{1}{2}(13 + 17) = 15.0$. Since these overall means do not differ, there is no evidence that, overall, offering money affects solution times. Testing for the interaction requires comparing differences, and we can do this in either of two ways. We can compare the effect of threat with no money to the effect of threat with money: $(17 - 13)$ versus $(20 - 10)$. The differences are different: $(+4) - (+10) = -6$, indicating that an interaction is present (assuming the difference between differences to be statistically significant). Or we could compare the effect of money with no threat to the effect of money with threat: $(10 - 13)$ versus $(20 - 17)$. These differences are different: $(-3) - (+3) = -6$, confirming the interaction found when the differences were compared in the other way. We could talk about the interaction in either of two ways. It would be appropriate to say that threatening instructions raise solution times more when subjects are offered money than when they are not. It would be equally appropriate to say that offering money lowers solution times when no threat is given but raises solution times when threatening instructions are given. The researcher could use either verbal description of the interaction.

Factorial designs do not pose any special interpretive problems, although these designs are relevant to a problem that arises from time to time. Specifically, factorial designs can be used to avoid certain kinds of interpretive difficulties. For example, suppose a researcher does an experiment on human problem solving, comparing performance in a "control" treatment with that in a "special-instruction" treatment; uses only college females as subjects; and finds better performance for the "special-instruction" treatment. Another researcher does what appears to be an "identical" experiment except that the subjects are all college males, and finds no significant difference in performance between the two treatments. Of course one possibility is that the special instructions help the performance of females but don't affect the performance of males. However, it would be dangerous to reach this conclusion by *comparing experiments* in this way. As you know, many factors affect the chances of a researcher's rejecting the null hypothesis, and it is also possible that the second researcher (who happened to use male subjects) conducted a less sensitive experiment. It is also possible that the two studies differed in some other important way that is not immediately apparent. To check on the possibility that there really is an interaction between "sex of subject" and the difference between treatments, a researcher should include these two variables in a single factorial design and directly test for the interaction.

Another interpretive problem, related to factorial designs, is slightly different. Consider the following problem:

PROBLEM

A researcher believed that one feature of juvenile delinquency (as a psychosocial "disease") was inability to work well for delayed rewards. She randomly assigned juvenile delinquents from a local institution to two treatments. All subjects were asked to complete a task that consisted of seven successive steps and required several hours to complete. In one treatment subjects were told that they would receive $1.00 each time they completed a step in the task, while in the other treatment subjects were told that they would receive $7.00 when they completed the entire task (of course they were actually paid as instructed). The researcher found that subjects who were rewarded "one step at a time" were more likely to complete the task and did so in less time then those who had to work for delayed reward (full payment at the end). She therefore concluded that the results indicated that inability to work as well for delayed reward as for "immediate" reward is a distinguishing feature of juvenile delinquency. What is wrong with this conclusion?

The weakness in this conclusion is that it implies a comparison that has not in fact been made. The researcher is implying that juvenile delinquents are somehow "unique" in that they work less well for delayed rewards, yet she has not looked at the difference between treatments for nondelinquents! In other words, her conclusion implies an interaction—that the difference in performance between the two reward conditions is different for juvenile delinquents than it is for nondelinquents. But she has not tested for such an interaction because her study did not include nondelinquents. This problem arises occasionally in psychology when a particular group of people is selected for study because there are reasons to believe that they have some "distinguishing" characteristic. The danger lies in studying *only* the selected group and in not contrasting the results for this group with results for other types of subjects. The situation is improved a little if other researchers have provided findings for other groups, but even then there is still the problem of inferring interactions by comparing experiments, which we just discussed. If a researcher wishes to demonstrate that some manipulation affects one type of subject differently than another, the best procedure is to include both types of subjects in a factorial design and test for an interaction.

PROBLEM

A psychotherapist believed that group therapy benefited manic-depressives more than hysterics, but he wanted to collect some data to determine whether this belief was accurate. In the hospital there were 50 manic-depressives and 35 hysterics about to begin the standard, 40-week group therapy program. The therapist decided that a good measure of success would be the percentage of patients who were out of the hospital two years later (and we will accept this measure of success for this problem). He waited patiently for the two years to elapse and then checked the records. Of the 50 manic-depressives, 18 were then out of the hospital, yielding a success percentage of 36 percent ($100 \times {}^{18}/_{50}$).

Only 4 of the hysterics were out of the hospital, which meant that the success percentage was only 11 percent ($100 \times {}^4/_{35}$). Since these percentages differed significantly, the therapist concluded that, at least for the kind of patients seen at this hospital, and to the extent that the measure of success was valid, the data did indicate that group therapy helped manic-depressives more than hysterics. A colleague at the hospital pointed out that even this qualified conclusion was not justified. Why not?

The easiest way to indicate the problem with this conclusion is to ask a question: What percentage of manic-depressives and what percentage of hysterics would be out of the hospital two years later if they had *not* received group therapy? We don't know, and until we know, we don't know whether group therapy helped anyone, much less whether it helped one patient group more than another. Suppose we found that, without group therapy, 50 percent of manic-depressives were out of the hospital two years later while no hysterics were out of the hospital—certainly our opinion of the advantage of group therapy would be considerably altered, and on sensible grounds. The therapist's conclusion implies an interacton—that the difference between therapy and no therapy is larger for manic depressives than for hysterics. Yet obviously no information concerning these differences has been obtained, and thus the effectiveness of group therapy (overall or differentially for the two patient groups) is unknown.

MULTIPLE-STAGE RESEARCH

We will now consider research in which measurements are made repeatedly—observations are made at two or more points in time. I will first discuss a special version of a repeated-measures design, a different one from that presented in Chapter 3. The purpose of the method is to evaluate the effectiveness of some treatment while having all of the data come from the same source. The specific techniques, however, are different from those discussed in Chapter 3 and introduce new complexities. Then we will focus attention on the measurement of change, which is frequently encountered in experimental and nonexperimental research. We will examine both the general issues involved in measuring change and some special problems that sometimes arise. At various points in this section you will see how factorial designs can be productively used and how regression effects (presented in Chapter 7) can raise problems of interpretation.

Time Series and Single-Subject Designs

A method used in a number of disciplines involves a greatly extended series of measurements, with treatments introduced at one or more points in the series. For example, an economist might examine a long series of measurements such as stock market prices or unemployment rates in an attempt to determine the effect of some governmental action or other "treatment" that occurs during the series. In psychology this method is most commonly used in studies of operant conditioning or behavior modification.

The idea behind this method is to measure (something) repeatedly until a *steady state* appears to be reached, that is, until the measurements appear to have stabilized and can be expected not to change *under constant conditions*. When this steady state is reached, the treatment is introduced and the change in the measurements is observed. In some circumstances the treatment might be introduced at several points, or different treatments might be applied at different points in the series. An ideal result from a time series experiment is shown in Figure 8.3. The points labeled "T" along the horizontal axis represent times at which some treatment is applied. The data are rather beautiful; after an initial period of quite unstable scores, the measurements become very steady, and each time the treatment is applied, the scores "pop up" and then return to the steady state or baseline. Such data would be quite convincing with respect to the effect of the treatment, more so with every repetition.

To give Figure 8.3 a psychological flavor, imagine that the measurements are counts of the number of times an animal presses a bar in each of a number of fixed time periods. At first the pressing rate is unstable,

Figure 8.3 Hypothetical time-series data showing the development of a steady state and a clear treatment effect.

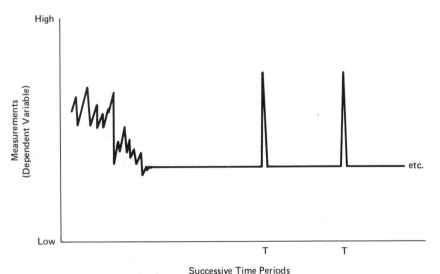

Successive Time Periods

but then it reaches a steady state; when the treatment (reinforcement) is applied, the rate goes up in that period and then returns to the "base rate." As you might suspect, real data are not as neat as those in Figure 8.3. What kinds of problems arise when time series designs (single-subject designs) are used?

A major possible problem concerns the identification of the "steady state." Measurements seldom (if ever) *really* reach a steady state—some variability will be present. In an experiment the researcher might be able to wait until the measurements stabilize before introducing treatments, but this option is not available in nonexperimental uses of the method. Thus one problem can be how to identify a (relatively) steady state. A related problem concerns the assessment of change when the treatment is applied. If the steady state is only approximately steady—some variation in scores is present, and if the treatment effect is "small," it might be very difficult to detect a treatment effect in the presence of the noise produced by the steady-state variation. In Figure 8.4 I have created some approximately steady-state data; notice that the scores for successive periods vary unsystematically over a 20-point range, although they have reached a kind of stability. In the context of this much noise, a treatment that produces a 10-point change will not be detectable—a change of that magnitude will look like a continuation of the (relatively) steady state.

The degree of variability in measurements over successive periods is critical for time series experiments; the greater the variability, the more likely it is that interpretive problems will arise. The usefulness of time series data increases with the number of measurements, the reliability of

Figure 8.4 Hypothetical time-series data illustrating the occurrence of an approximate steady state.

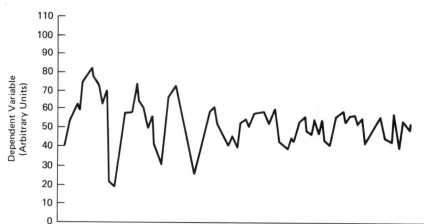

the measurements, and the number of opportunities to evaluate a treatment effect (of course there must be enough spacing between treatment applications). Trying to evaluate the effect of a treatment introduced once into a relatively noisy series of measurements is extremely hazardous. Another possible problem concerns *delayed effects* of treatments. Suppose a treatment does influence the measurements but does so after some delay rather than immediately upon its application. If we look for an effect only right after the treatment, we might erroneously conclude that the treatment is ineffective. Identifying delayed effects is difficult unless there are reasons to expect them, for a "surprising" change in scores some time after a treatment might be interpreted as noise. Also, time series data tend to be clearest when treatments have *local effects,* as in Figure 8.3. In those hypothetical data the treatment produced an immediate and abrupt change in scores followed by an equally abrupt return to the steady state. Such a sharp, local effect is clear and relatively easy to detect. If, however, the effect is gradual or somewhat extended—scores change gradually after the treatment, only gradually return to the baseline, or do *not* completely return to the pretreatment baseline—figuring out what if anything happened can be troublesome. In addition to having many reliable (stable) measurements, investigators using time series need to have a good idea of what kind of effect a treatment might be expected to have.

In a basic time series experiment the treatment is introduced at an arbitrarily chosen point in a series of stable measurements. Sometimes people introduce "treatments" in response to fluctuations in the series of measurements, which can lead to serious errors, as Campbell (1969) has pointed out. The basic idea is that even if the series of measurements does have a general trend, there will be random variation around the trend and occasionally large but random ("chance") deviations from the trend. Figure 8.5 shows such data. As you can see, the scores are generally following an upward trend over time, as depicted by the solid line drawn through the data points. However, the individual data points fluctuate randomly around the trend, and occasionally there is a relatively large deviation, as at the points labeled A, B, and C. It is important to understand that all of the deviations from the general trend are random deviations, including the larger ones; by "chance" there will sometimes be large deviations.

Here's what can happen. To use one of Campbell's examples, suppose the data consist of measurements of accident rates, month by month, for a particular state. The general trend shown in the data is a gradual rise in the accident rate, with fluctuations and an occasional large deviation. When the first large, random deviation (A) occurs, perhaps everyone is pleased (the accident rate seems abnormally low that month), but nothing is done as a consequence. However, when the next large, random deviation occurs (B)—an "abnormally high accident rate"—the governor immediately moves into action ("I know the rate's been generally increasing, but this is ridic-

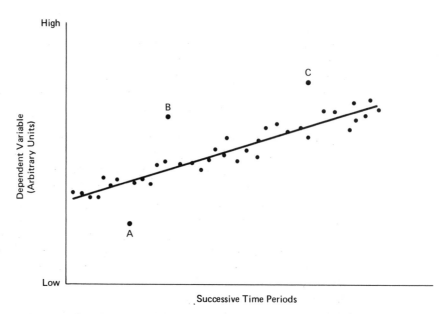

Figure 8.5 Hypothetical time-series data showing fluctuations around a general trend and occasional, large, random deviations.

ulous and something's got to be done," she says) and, with great publicity, orders an instant crackdown on traffic violations. The next month's data point pleases her because there appears to be a large reduction in the accident rate from point B, and she concludes that she did the right thing. The data seem to exhibit their "normal" gradual rise over succeeding months, and perhaps the governor even makes a mental note that "the crackdown seems to have only a temporary effect." Along comes the next large, random, positive deviation (C); the governor decides that she must act again, and does so. Again she is pleased, because the data for the next month show a decrease from the high accident rate at C. This process could continue for a long time.

The point is that since the large positive deviations (B, C, and the others later in the series) are *random*, the next data point is virtually certain to be lower *by chance*. Only occasionally will all the chance factors produce a large positive deviation from the trend, and it is highly unlikely to happen twice in succession. The governor, however, will *erroneously* believe that her crackdowns are responsible for the decreases following "abnormally high" accident rates. Notice that it will be very hard for her to change her mind as long as she consistently introduces the crackdown "treatment" when a large positive deviation occurs. It would be very informative for the governor to avoid the crackdown treatment a few times; in this way she could discover that both the large positive deviations and the reductions that follow them are random.

This problem is a special version of a *regression artifact*. In rough terms, if the large deviations are due to chance, the data will regress back to the trend following them. As this example indicates, applying treatments in response to fluctuations in a time series can lead to interpretive difficulties. In effect, if a treatment consistently follows a large random deviation in one direction, the next, equally random deviation is very likely to be less extreme, giving an erroneous impression of a treatment effect. There might well be some real treatment effect in any case, but it cannot be disentangled from the regression artifact unless the treatment sometimes is and sometimes is not applied when such deviations occur. Perhaps you will have some interesting insights to give a parent, should you encounter one, who says, "I hate to yell at my kid. I mean, he's generally pretty good, but sometimes he's just especially awful. I hate to do it, but I've found that if I yell at him when he's especially awful, his behavior almost always gets better. I really hate to do it, but I guess it works."

Measuring Change:
Some General Issues

Campbell and Stanley (1963) have provided an extensive discussion of the problems involved in measuring change. In this section I will summarize some of the ideas they presented; if you plan to have continuing involvement in research, I strongly encourage you to read their book.

A simple method of measuring change is the *pretest–posttest* design with a single group of subjects. This design is outlined in Figure 8.6. As you can see, there are three stages to the study: First, initial measurements are made of some behavior or trait; then a treatment is introduced; and, finally, the behavior or trait is measured a second time. The idea is to compare the first and second measurements to determine whether the treatment produced any change in scores.

We can use this simple design as a focus in considering some of the threats to internal validity and external validity that Campbell and Stanley pointed out. The various factors may or may not be important in any particular instance of measuring change but they need to be considered in evaluating such results. The first thing to notice is that the pretest and

Figure 8.6 A simple design for measuring change

Time ⟶

Measurement 1 — Treatment — Measurement 2
(Pretest)   (Posttest)

posttest measurements occur at different points in time; we can ask what factors *other than the treatment* might affect the difference between the two sets of measurements.

Practice Effects. Since the measurements are made twice, there is a possibility that posttest scores will be affected by the previous experience with the measurement operations. If the measurement involves some form of test with "correct answers," subjects may "learn" to take the test or otherwise score better the second time because they are familiar with the test. I am sure that you have personally experienced getting used to a particular instructor's exams when taking classes; this phenomenon is not limited to students taking course exams. If choices are measured, as in attitude assessment, and if subjects tend to remember their earlier choices, posttest scores might show little change if subjects are inclined to repeat their choices or "artificial" change if subjects tend to avoid repeating earlier responses. Generally, concern over practice effects increases as the time between pretest and posttest becomes shorter. In addition, the pretest might limit the generality of the findings (as we saw with respect to obtaining matching information for matched-subjects designs). The initial measurements might sensitize subjects to the treatment—the treatment might affect scores only if the pretest is given or more strongly when the pretest is given. The point is that the results regarding the effect of the treatment might not be generalized to situations in which pretests are not given.

History. While the treatment obviously occurs between the pretest and the posttest, it is not the only thing happening during this interval. *History* refers to the collection of other experiences or events that take place during the interval; whether or not posttest scores are affected by the treatment itself, they might be affected by other events. If the pretest–posttest interval is short, history is less likely to confound the results, but as this interval gets longer, the possibility of the results being confounded by "outside influences" becomes more serious. To give a somewhat extreme example, suppose an instructor wishes to see whether "taking introductory psychology" (the treatment) affects students' attitudes toward minorities. These attitudes are assessed at the beginning of the term (pretest) and again at the end (posttest). I am sure that you can see how posttest scores might be influenced by other events occurring during the months between the pretest and the posttest—a crime wave in the ghetto, news stories about the mistreatment of minorities, legislative changes, and the like.

Maturation. Campbell and Stanley use this classification to refer to processes that occur over time but are unrelated to specific events—getting older, tired, and the like. Fatigue or inattention can occur within a single data collection session or over several closely spaced sessions when subjects are performing an effortful task or one that is rather dull and repetitive. Over longer time intervals, especially in research involving children, many changes might occur independent of the specific treatment introduced.

Measurement Changes. Over time, measuring instruments might change in some systematic fashion. There are two noteworthy examples for which caution is very appropriate. When the measurements require judgments by observers or scorers, one must consider the possibility that the judges' criteria might shift over time and repeated exposure to their task. For this reason researchers try whenever possible to have the judgments made after all data have been collected, without the judges knowing whether any particular instance is from the pretest or the posttest. This is a far better procedure than having observers judge pretest behavior at the time of the pretest and judge postest behavior at the time of the posttest. The second example concerns the use of alternate forms of measurement. Sometimes, in order to avoid practice effects that might occur if the same test is given twice, researchers use alternate forms of the test, one for the pretest and the other for the posttest. When this is done it is critical that the researchers ensure that the two forms are really equivalent; it is not enough to know that the correlation between the forms is very high and positive—it must also be true that the two forms yield scores of the same magnitude. There is a possibility that two alternate forms of a test will be very comparable with respect to individual differences (thus having a high positive correlation) but that one form will tend to yield higher scores than another. Should this occur, the measurement of change would be confounded.

Loss of Subjects. The longer an experiment lasts, the more difficult it is to avoid losing subjects. If the comparison is between the scores of all subjects who began the study (pretest) and the scores of those who remain (posttest), the comparison can be confounded by loss of subjects. If the comparison is limited to the pretest and posttest scores of those who completed the experiment, the results are at best limited to that group. "Long" treatments are likely to suffer from this problem. For example, suppose we wished to determine whether a particular weight-reducing technique actually results in weight loss. Fifty volunteers begin the program and have their weights measured (pretest). Six months later 20 people have dropped out of the program, leaving only 30 subjects for posttest measurements. Clearly it will be difficult to assess the impact of the program. Comparing the 30 posttest scores to the 50 pretest scores would be inappropriate. Comparing the pretest and posttest weights for the 30 people who completed the program would at best provide limited information about the effectiveness of the treatment, particularly since it is likely that "staying in the program" is related to "how well the program seemed to be working."

PROBLEM

The dean was trying to settle an argument between the heads of the chemistry and physics departments over which department did a better job of teaching undergraduate majors.

Finally, the two department heads agreed to compare the scores of graduating seniors in the two departments on the Graduate Records Exam, chemistry majors taking the chemistry GRE and physics majors taking the physics GRE. The department heads and the dean agreed that GRE scores in the respective fields were a fair indication of which students were doing better (and we will accept the GRE as a fair test). When the scores were compared it was clear that the average score for chemistry majors was significantly higher than the average for physics majors. The dean and the department heads concluded that the issue was settled—the chemistry department did a better job of teaching its majors. Criticize this conclusion.

The major difficulties with this conclusion concern the question of equivalent subjects (students) in the two treatments (majors). All the comparison shows is that students completing a chemistry major score higher on a standard chemistry test than students completing a physics major score on a standard physics test. We can raise two important questions: Were the two groups of students equivalent in the abilities needed for the two majors before they chose their majors? Do the two departments differ in the percentages of students who start but do not finish the major? Resolving the problems involved in this comparison would be extremely difficult, but you should grasp the basic ideas that apply. Students are not randomly assigned to majors, and perhaps the chemistry department got "better students" than the physics department. In addition, we would need to know how many students were "lost" by each department; for example, if only 20 percent of the students starting a chemistry major actually finished it (and thus provided GRE scores) while 70 percent of "physics starters" actually finished, the comparison of graduating majors would be rather meaningless. By the way, notice that if chemistry got "worse students" than physics and lost a smaller percentage of its majors, the data (while still confounded) would be quite impressive evidence for chemistry's teaching. Since we don't know the answers to these questions, we don't know how to interpret the comparison that was made.

Regression Artifacts. We discussed the phenomenon of "regression toward the mean" in Chapter 7. Briefly, whenever two sets of measurements are *imperfectly* correlated, subjects who are selected because they have the most extreme scores in one set of measurements will have less extreme scores in the other set of measurements. Such regression is a simple fact, reflecting the less than perfect relation between the two measurements. Regression effects occur "in both directions," from measure 1 to measure 2 and vice versa. The amount of regression is inversely related to the size of the correlation. For example, subjects who are chosen because they have the highest scores on one measure will average scores about half as far above the mean score (in standard-deviation terms) on the second measure if the correlation between the two measures is +.50. If the correlation were nearly 0.00, the subjects with the highest scores on one measure would average scores right at the mean score on the other measure. If the correlation were near 1.00, there would be little regression. It might be wise to review Table 7.8 and the accompanying text if you have forgotten the details of the discussion.

With respect to measuring change, regression artifacts can be a problem when the subjects have been chosen because they have extreme scores (in either direction) *on the pretest*. To the extent that the pretest and posttest are imperfectly related, we can expect them to achieve less extreme scores on the posttest simply on the basis of an imperfect relation between the two sets of measurements. Such regression effects do *not* represent real change, and it would clearly be a mistake to attribute such apparent changes to the treatment. The longer the interval between the pretest and the posttest, the lower the correlation between the two sets of measurements is likely to be (recall the discussion of test–retest reliability in Chapter 7). Thus the longer the interval between the pretest and the posttest, the more likely it is that the results might be confounded by regression artifacts, *if the subjects were chosen because of extreme pretest scores.* Notice that the selection might be subtle and need not very obviously involve the pretest scores themselves. For example, choosing students who are generally doing poorly (identified by, say, school grades) and giving them pretest and posttest achievement tests does *not* eliminate the possibility of artificial, regression-toward-the-mean changes from their pretest to posttest scores (they were in effect selected because they were very likely to get low scores on the pretest).

Dealing with the Problems. As you can see, measuring change is fraught with interpretive dangers for the researcher. The simple procedure of pretest–treatment–posttest is particularly subject to difficulties. Of course the importance of any of the factors I have listed depends on the situation. If all subjects who start the experiment finish it, then bias due to loss of subjects is not possible. If the subjects were *not* selected because of their extreme scores, regression artifacts need not concern us. Similar notions apply to the other factors, although some present more difficult problems than others. Researchers have invented a variety of techniques for minimizing such problems (see Campbell & Stanley, 1963), including very complex procedures. Let us look at some relatively simple but useful techniques.

A researcher can gain a great deal by including a "control group" in the study; the design is outlined in Figure 8.7. As you can see, the treatment

Figure 8.7 "Control Group" design for studying change

Time ⟶

| Treatment Group: | Pretest — Treatment | — Posttest |
| Control Group: | Pretest — No Treatment | — Posttest |

group and the control group *both* provide pretest and posttest scores. Between these two events the treatment is administered to the treatment group but not to the control group. The idea is to have "everything else" equal for the two groups during the interval except for the intended treatment–no treatment difference. Accomplishing this equality in practice can be rather troublesome, but the principle is clear. To evaluate the treatment, the change for the treatment group is compared to the change for the control group. In other words, evaluating the treatment involves testing for an *interaction;* the (pretest–posttest) difference for the treatment group is compared to the (pretest–posttest) difference for the control group.

Notice what is gained by using this design. Since both groups of subjects are equally exposed to the measurement operations, practice effects should be the same in both conditions. If the subjects were initially randomly assigned to conditions, maturation and history (as related to individual differences) should be equalized. Likewise, regression artifacts would not be a problem as long as all subjects were selected for extreme scores and then randomly assigned to the treatment and control conditions—in this case regression effects (though present) would be equal. The researcher would have to check for *differential* loss of subjects in the two groups, hoping that there would be no loss or equivalent loss (any loss, even if it is equal for the two groups, will affect the generality of the results to some extent).

While this design is far better than the simple pretest–treatment–posttest procedure, it is not perfect (nothing is!). In practice, when the treatment takes a long time (e.g., months) it is often difficult to avoid differential loss of subjects. It might be more difficult to get "control" subjects to return for posttest measurement if "nothing" is being done to them during the interval. There is also the possibility that the histories for the two groups might differ because of the difference between conditions. In other words, it can be hard to identify a control condition for which "other experiences" will be the same as those for the treatment group. For example, providing some special treatment for students might result in associated changes in the rest of their class schedule, leading them to have different class schedules from those in the control group. Providing special instruction in reading instead of a history course means that the difference between groups consists of "special instruction in reading plus no history course" versus "no special instruction plus history course." The researcher would have to decide how important the impact of the history course would be for the experimental data.

Also, this design would be limited by the pretest with respect to generality. Should the pretest influence the effect of the treatment, the results would not generalize to situations in which no pretest is given. To avoid the possibility of pretest limitations on generality, some researchers eliminate the pretest. Subjects are simply randomly assigned to treatment and control conditions, and scores on the posttest (the only measurement taken) are compared. Random assignment of subjects to groups provides control over initial measurements; in effect the study is reduced to a basic two-treatment experiment like those discussed in the preceding chapters. The lack of pretest scores obviously means that the researcher cannot assess change itself, although he or she can compare posttest scores to evaluate the treatment meaningfully. The researcher would be able to find out whether the treatment leads to different (posttest) scores but would not know how much scores had changed (if at all). Some researchers therefore use still more complex designs, like that outlined in Table 8.3.

In this design there are two treatment groups, one of which takes the pretest and one of which does not, and two similarly distinguished control groups. With such a design the researcher can examine the amount of change that occurs, using the "no. 1" groups for which pretest information is available. In addition, the researcher can test to see whether the pretest influences the treatment effect. Using *posttest* scores for all groups, the researcher would test for an interaction, comparing the treatment-versus-control difference *with* the pretest (treatment group 1–control group 1) with the difference *without* the pretest (treatment group 2–control group 2). If these differences differ, the researcher knows that giving the pretest does influence the treatment effect. If there is no interaction, the researcher can be more confident about the generality of the treatment-versus-control difference. Regardless of how the results come out, researchers using such designs gain much more information than is provided by simpler designs.

PROBLEM

A second-grade teacher felt that one of the reasons why students did poorly on arithmetic tests was that they became anxious when the tests were given and thus got "lower scores than they should." He wondered whether talking to the low-scoring students about staying calm would improve their performance. Since he gave arithmetic tests every Friday, there was a nice opportunity to test this idea. One Friday, after giving a test, he looked at the scores and selected the 10 lowest scorers for "treatment." During the next week (Monday–Thursday) he spent about half an hour talking with each of these students about remaining calm during tests. The following Friday the students took another arithmetic test. The teacher was delighted by the results because the students who had been "treated" scored

Table 8.3   Complex Design for Studying Change

	STAGE 1	STAGE 2	STAGE 3
Treatment group 1	Pretest	Treatment	Posttest
Control group 1	Pretest	No treatment	Posttest
Treatment group 2	—	Treatment	Posttest
Control group 2	—	No treatment	Posttest

somewhat closer to the average—they certainly were not the 10 lowest scorers this time! Of course every student didn't improve, but the group of 10 as a whole did score better relative to the rest of the class. The teacher decided that talking with students about staying calm during tests did work and began thinking about using this procedure more widely.

First, what problems are there with this study? Second, how could the teacher get better evidence about the usefulness of the treatment?

The critical question in this example concerns the correlation between arithmetic tests. It is very unlikely that scores on successive weekly arithmetic tests are perfectly correlated under ordinary circumstances; indeed, for the kinds of tests usually given as class exams a correlation of +.50 would probably be considered rather good. If the tests are not perfectly correlated, it is inevitable that regression toward the mean will be present. If the tests are not perfectly correlated, it must be true that, whether we look from the earlier test to the later one or from the later test back to the earlier one, we will find, without having done anything special, that students who are selected because they have the lowest scores on one test tend to score closer to the average on the other test. In other words, without introducing any treatment we would expect students with the lowest scores on one test to score somewhat nearer the average on the next test if the tests are not perfectly correlated. Therefore the problem is that the apparent improvement of the treated students might reflect nothing more than the imperfect relation between successive tests—there might have been no real improvement.

To test the effectiveness of the treatment the teacher should do something like the following: Having identified the lowest scorers on one test, randomly divide them into two treatment "groups" (on paper, of course). Then talk with the students in one group (call this the treatment condition) while doing nothing special with the students in the "control" group before the next test. When that test is given, compare the scores of the treatment group with those of the control group to see whether there is a difference. Notice that there will be regression toward the mean for both groups but that it will be "equal" in both cases. By comparing the scores of the treatment group with those of the control group, the teacher would be able to assess the effect of the treatment without confounding by regression artifacts.

Special Topics in Multiple-Stage Research

We have now considered the problems involved in measuring change and some of the techniques that researchers can use to deal with these problems. In the remainder of this chapter, I will discuss several special topics relating to multiple-stage research: delayed effects, transfer effects, and developmental changes. Each topic illustrates somewhat different issues that can arise in psychological research.

Delayed Effects. In the research examples that we have discussed so far, the effect of a treatment has typically been measured immediately after the treatment was applied. In some circumstances researchers might be interested not in the immediate effect of a treatment but in changes that might take place over some period after the treatment occurs. For example, a counselor might want to know whether people who have received counseling exhibit changes in their behavior after counseling has ended or show more change compared to people who have not been counseled. In attitude research some attention has been given to "sleeper effects"; the idea is roughly that a persuasive communication might not have an immediate effect on attitudes but that attitudes might change later on. If one wants to know whether different materials are forgotten at different rates, one is concerned with changes occurring after learning has been completed. The general research design that is of interest here is outlined in Table 8.4.

The question that is of interest is how much scores change from point A to point B—notice that this change occurs after the treatment is applied. One could of course use several different treatments in stage 1 and compare the (point A to point B) changes across treatments. Several issues need attention. First, it should be clear that examining just the scores obtained after the time interval, at point B, does not provide the proper information. Here's a simple example: Suppose you want to know whether Bill or George forgets faster. Both individuals are allowed to study some material (say, a list of words) and then, a week later, take a test on the material. Suppose that after one week Bill scores 50 percent correct while George scores 40 percent correct. These scores by themselves do not tell us anything about forgetting, simply because we don't know how much either Bill or George learned in the first place! We need to know the scores at point A (in this example, immediately after study) in order to analyze changes. If, right after studying the material, both Bill and George had scored 90 percent correct, then we could see that Bill had forgotten 40 percent ($90\% - 50\%$) over the one-week interval, less than George's 50 percent forgetting ($90\% - 40\%$).

Table 8.4   General Design for Studying Delayed Effects

Stage 1: treatment applied
    Point A: end of treatment
    (measurement)
Stage 2: time interval
    Point B: delayed measurement

Even if both measurements are available, problems can arise. Suppose Bill scored 80 percent right after study and 65 percent a week later, while George scored 40 percent immediately after study and 30 percent a week later. Who forgot more? If we look at *absolute* losses, Bill's score fell 15 percent (80% − 65%) while George's dropped 10 percent (40% − 30%); it appears that Bill forgot more. If, however, we look at *relative* losses, the picture changes. Bill forgot $^{15}/_{80}$, or 19 percent of what he had initially learned, while George forgot $^{10}/_{40}$, or 25 percent of what he had initially learned. On this basis George forgot more.

The essential point can be summarized as follows. If scores at the end of stage 1 (point A) are very different, then assessing change during stage 2 might be difficult. Comparing absolute changes can yield one outcome while comparing relative changes yields a different outcome. Deciding whether absolute change or relative change is the better measure can be troublesome, and the choice might vary from one study to another, depending on the topic under investigation and the theoretical notions that are being tested.

A different example will illustrate another issue related to this topic. Suppose we wanted to see how people's attitudes change over a one-month period after receiving a persuasive communication. The idea would be to deliver the message and then measure attitudes after different intervals, say, immediately (no delay) and after 1 day, 3 days, 1 week, 2 weeks, and 4 weeks. The question is whether we should measure the attitudes of *the same people* for all intervals. The possible problem is that repeatedly measuring their attitude toward the same topic might affect their attitudes. The data that we would obtain might not accurately reflect changes in attitude over time because of the influence of the repeated attitude assessments. To arrive at a more accurate function it would be better to randomly assign subjects to 6 different conditions. All would receive the persuasive communication, and then the different groups of subjects would have their attitudes assessed just once each, at either no delay, 1 day, 3 days, and so on (one interval per group). In this way we could get an idea of how attitudes change over time without contaminating the results by repeated measurement.

PROBLEM

A researcher noticed that there was a great deal of confusion regarding the question of whether fast or slow learners had better memories (as distinct from learning ability). Previous research had shown that individual differences in learning speed were consistent from task to task. That is, if subjects were sorted into fast and slow learners on one task, the researcher could be pretty sure that, relative to each other, they would also be fast and slow learners on another task. She made use of this fact in the experiment. She had a large number of subjects learn a list of words and selected the 20 fastest and 20 slowest learners from the group (we will accept the notion that these learners will remain "fast" and "slow," respectively). She then gave each of these 40 subjects 10 learning trials on a list of nonsense syllables. One day after completing the 10 learning trials each subject was given a recall test for the list of nonsense syllables. The fast learners recalled more nonsense syllables than the slow learners on the one-day-later test. The researcher therefore concluded that fast learners remember better than slow learners. Why might this conclusion be incorrect?

What the researcher has found is that, one day after learning, fast learners recall more items than slow learners. However, this measurement by itself does not provide information about retention; the one-day scores depend both on how much was learned in the first place and on how much was forgotten (remembered) over the one-day interval. Since all subjects received the same amount of practice on the list of nonsense syllables, the fast learners undoubtedly learned more than the slow learners; unfortunately we don't know how much more. Without knowing how much was learned during the 10 trials of practice, we do not know how to interpret the recall scores obtained one day later. Maybe the fast learners both learned more and remembered *more of what they learned;* maybe the fast learners learned much more but also forgot more, still getting higher scores one day later. We just don't know. To compare the *retention* of fast and slow learners most clearly, it would be advantageous to have the fast and slow learners learn the material equally well (which would require more practice for the slow learners); then differences in retention could be sensibly analyzed.

Transfer Effects. There are many circumstances in which we wish to examine the effect of some form of prior experience on performance on some later task. Interest lies in the analysis of *transfer effects.* The most basic design for studying transfer effects is shown in Table 8.5. Subjects in one condition (transfer group) first experience some sort of treatment and then perform a task, while subjects in the "control" perform the same task without the prior treatment. The groups are compared in terms of performance on the *stage 2, transfer task.* If the transfer group does better in stage 2, we speak of *positive* transfer (from the prior experience); if the transfer group does worse, *negative* transfer has been observed.

Interest in transfer effects occurs most frequently in studies of learning, broadly conceived. Here are some examples of questions that might

Table 8.5   Basic Design for Studying Transfer

	STAGE 1	STAGE 2
Transfer group	Treatment	Transfer task
Control group	"Nothing"	Transfer task

Note: The two groups are compared in terms of performance in stage 2.

be asked: Does prior experience in Head Start programs lead to better performance in school (compared to no Head Start experience)? Is learning French helped by prior learning of Spanish? Will college students perform better in a statistics course if they take an algebra course beforehand? Do people perform better in stressful situations if they have earlier learned the techniques of transcendental meditation?

Transfer effects may be studied in either experimental or nonexperimental situations; the basic question is whether subjects have been randomly assigned to the different groups. In most of the examples just listed it is unlikely that random assignment would have been used, for a variety of reasons. When subjects are *not* randomly assigned to groups, problems that we have already discussed arise (e.g., confounding of treatment differences with subject differences). Researchers also must be concerned with the possibility of differential loss of subjects from the groups during the study. I will not repeat these considerations here; rather, I will concentrate on the issues that are specifically associated with transfer effects.

Let me use a traditional experimental example to illustrate the issues. Suppose we have plausible reasons to believe that there should be positive transfer of learning between "words belonging to the same category." That is, learning a list of words belonging to particular categories should aid subsequent learning of other words belonging to the same categories. A possible (though not very good) design for studying this question is outlined in Table 8.6.

As the table shows, some subjects would learn list A before learning list S, while other subjects would learn nothing before learning list S. We would look at performance on list S to study transfer effects. A possible problem is that not only has the transfer group learned a list of words in similar categories before learning list S, but it has also "learned a list of words" before learning list S. For the transfer group list S is the second task, but list S is the first task for the control group. If the transfer group performs differently on list S, perhaps the difference is due to having learned *any* word list earlier rather than to having learned a list of words in the same categories. To get better information we would want to compare the performance of the transfer group with that of subjects who learned two lists of words that were unrelated to each other. A possible, though flawed, design is shown in Table 8.7.

In this design subjects in treatment 1 learn two related lists while subjects in treatment 2 learn unrelated lists of words. In both treatments subjects learn two lists, thus eliminating the problem found in the simpler design shown in Table 8.6. It would appear that by comparing scores for the two treatments for stage 2 learning we should be able to determine whether transfers between "similars" differ from transfers between unrelated words. The flaw in this design is that the transfer tasks are different for the two treatments. Perhaps list U is easier (or harder) to learn than list

Table 8.6   Basic Design for Studying
"Transfer Between Similars"

	Stage 1 LIST A	Stage 2 LIST S
Transfer group	car	train
	shirt	sweater
	chair	table
	ruby	emerald
	snow	rain
	tulip	daisy
	hammer	pliers
	baseball	tennis
Control group	nothing	train
		sweater
		table
		emerald
		rain
		daisy
		pliers
		tennis

S, even if subjects have *not* learned list A beforehand. To guard against this possible confounding a researcher could use a factorial design, outlined in Table 8.8.

In this design both list S and list U are learned by two separate groups of subjects, one of which first learns list A and one of which does not. To determine whether prior learning of words in the same category leads to a different transfer than learning unrelated words beforehand, we would analyze scores on stage 2 tasks and *test for an interaction*. Looking just at performance in stage 2, if the difference between control groups (S only − U only) is *not* the same as the difference between transfer groups (A, S − A, U), we would have evidence that category similarity affects transfer beyond anything due to "just having learned a list of words beforehand."

In this particular example the transfer question could be approached by using an alternate, "flip-over" design. Notice that the question is whether transfer between related words differs from transfer between unrelated words. There is nothing in the question that dictates that any particular list must be the second, transfer task. Lists A and S are related regardless of which list comes first, and lists A and U are unrelated regardless of which list comes first. Therefore the design in Table 8.7 could be "flipped over," producing the design shown in Table 8.9.

In this design all subjects learn the *same second task* (list A); the two

Table 8.7   Alternative Design for Studying "Transfer Between Similars"

	Stage 1 LIST A	Stage 2 LIST S
"Similars" transfer group	car	train
	shirt	sweater
	chair	table
	ruby	emerald
	snow	rain
	tulip	daisy
	hammer	pliers
	baseball	tennis

	LIST A	LIST U
"Unrelated" transfer group	car	elbow
	shirt	aspirin
	chair	carrots
	ruby	dollar
	snow	lawyer
	tulip	circle
	hammer	purple
	baseball	valley

Note. Each word in list S belongs to the same category as a word in list A, whereas the words in list U belong to categories different from those of the words in list A. Performance in stage 2 would be compared to study transfer effects.

treatments differ in terms of what kind of list was learned in stage 1—either the similar list (list S) or the unrelated list (list U). Since the two groups learn exactly the same task in stage 2, any difference in their performance on that task must have something to do with their prior experiences. To use this design properly we would have to make sure that the different *first* tasks were learned *equally well*, since transfer depends on how well the prior task is learned. If subjects learning list S as their first task learned it just as well as those learning list U first learned their list, then any difference between groups on subsequent learning of list A must be due to the difference in relations between first and second tasks, which is the question that is of interest.

As you can see, studying transfer effects can become quite complicated. It is useful to distinguish between *general* transfer effects and *specific* transfer effects. Compare the designs shown in Tables 8.5 and 8.9. In both

Table 8.8   Factorial Design for Studying Transfer

TREATMENT	STAGE 1	STAGE 2
"Similars" transfer	List A	List S
"Unrelated" transfer	List A	List U
Control S	—	List S
Control U	—	List U

Note: Transfer would be examined by comparing the difference (A, S − S only) to the difference (A, U − U only), using stage 2 scores.

cases the second, transfer task is the same for both groups. However, using the design in Table 8.5 (in which the control group learns nothing in stage 1) makes it impossible to tell whether any differences in stage 2 are due to having learned a list of related words in stage 1 or to having learned *any* list in stage 1. Using the design in Table 8.9 allows the researcher to determine whether learning a related task in stage 1 results in a different stage 2 performance compared to learning an unrelated task in stage 1 (the two groups shown in Table 8.9 are equal with respect to general transfer effects, since both learn "something" in stage 1). When a design like that in Table 8.9 is used it is important to make sure that the two groups achieve equivalent levels of performance by the end of stage 1 (recall our earlier discussion of measuring delayed effects). To use a different example, suppose you gave a test on abnormal psychology to two groups, students who had previously taken a course in personality theory and students who had previously taken a course in psychological measurement. If the students who had previously taken the measurement course had *not* learned that material as well as those taking the personality course had learned their material, any difference in test scores between these two groups would be difficult (strictly, impossible) to interpret.

There are instances in which the second, transfer tasks are different (as in the design shown in Tables 8.7 and 8.8). When the transfer tasks are different for different treatment groups, it is essential to use a factorial

Table 8.9   "Flip-Over" Design for Studying Transfer

TREATMENT	STAGE 1	STAGE 2
"Similars" transfer	List S	List A
"Unrelated" transfer	List U	List A

Note: Treatments are compared in terms of stage 2 (list A) scores; for a clear comparison, performance in stage 1 should be equivalent for the two treatments.

design (see Table 8.8) in order to separate basic differences between second tasks (provided by the control groups) from differences associated with transfer effects. When second tasks differ it is necessary to use the "control" groups and test for an interaction in order to properly study transfer effects.

Finally, note that transfer effects are almost always limited in meaning. For example, if we found that students who had taken a course in psychological testing were better at interpreting tests than students who had not taken a testing course, this result would give us information only about the difference in transfer effects between "prior testing course" and "no course." It would not tell us whether students who had taken a testing course would be better at test interpretation than students who had taken, say, a course on theories of intelligence or personality theory. To see whether prior experience with psychological testing leads to better subsequent test interpretation than prior experience with theories of intelligence or personality theory, we would have to include more treatment groups in the design. All groups would perform in stage 2 of the study (interpreting tests), but groups would differ with respect to the kind of prior experience they have had—testing, intelligence theory, personality, and so on. The essential point is, of course, that this is nothing more than a special example of the generality of findings being limited to the particular treatments used in a study, which we discussed as far back as Chapter 2.

Developmental Changes. A very basic kind of data in developmental psychology consists of "age differences" for various measurements. Researchers might want to know how height, brain weight, reasoning scores, and so on "change with age" as a first step in understanding development. In fact obtaining accurate "age curves" presents researchers with very special problems. There are two frequently used methods of collecting data for age curves: the *cross-sectional method* and the *longitudinal method*. Each method poses its own problems, which are well known to developmental researchers (e.g., Baltes, 1968; Schaie, 1972). The cross-sectional method is basically an independent-groups technique; each age is represented by a different group of subjects. The longitudinal method involves repeated measures; the same subjects are measured at different ages. Let's examine some of the problems that occur when researchers attempt to obtain age curves.

Suppose we wish to know how scores on a reasoning test change from adolescence to old age. We want to look at average reasoning scores for the following ages: 15, 25, 35, 50, and 70 years. To use a cross-sectional method we would obtain independent samples of people from each of the five age groups. Notice that with a cross-sectional design change is *not* assessed for any individual—different people represent different ages. The hope is that the age curve from such a design will represent developmental changes accurately.

A very real problem that arises in such research is that of obtaining representative samples of people in the various age groups. How would you locate a representative sample of 15-year-olds or 50-year-olds? Perhaps you could argue that 15-year-olds could reasonably be contacted in high schools; of course all 15-year-olds are not in high school and there is probably a difference in reasoning scores between those who are in high school and those who are not. You could contact a large number of 15-year-olds in high schools, but how do you find non-school-age subjects? There are no ready solutions to such problems; for example, Schaie, Labouvie, and Buech (1973) obtained subjects from a large medical-insurance group, which is by no means free of difficulties but is better than less systematic techniques. Researchers must try their best and hope that the biases inherent in the various age samples are roughly equivalent. Repeating the study with somewhat different sampling techniques provides some imperfect information about the extent of this kind of sampling bias. The question is whether the age curves look the same or different when subjects in various age groups are obtained in different ways.

Even if each age group is adequately represented, cross-sectional designs contain important risks of confounding. "Age" is a special version of time, and you will recall from the Chapter 3 that time presents special problems as a variable. In a cross-sectional study the measurements are usually obtained at roughly "the same time" for all age groups. Table 8.10 illustrates one of the problems involved. As you can see, "age" is confounded with "year of birth," usually referred to as a *cohort* (the group of organisms born at a particular point in time). When the reasoning scores are obtained, we could just as readily relate them to cohort as to age.

Perhaps it seems obvious that if we measure something for people of different ages at any point in time, the people must have been born at different times and there is no interpretive problem. Remember, however,

Table 8.10   Illustration of Age–Cohort Confounding in Cross-Sectional Designs[a]

YEAR OF BIRTH (COHORT)	AGE
1965	15
1955	25
1945	35
1930	50
1910	70

[a] Time of measurement: 1980 for all subjects.

that the goal is to relate the measurements to *age*. If there have been changes in cohorts over time, the measure–age relation will be confounded with the measure–cohort relation. For example, for various reasons such as improved nutrition and better health care, babies born later (e.g., 1945, 1955, 1965) might be healthier than those born earlier (1930, 1910). If these birth changes affect what is being measured, the "age curve" will be biased, probably in favor of the younger ages (i.e., the later borns). In addition, the general culture in which the people representing different ages grew up is likely to be different. For example, the 70-year-olds went to elementary school (maybe) from roughly 1915 to 1925 whereas the 25-year-olds did so between about 1960 and 1970. If schooling has changed, and if this change affects what is being measured, the age curve will be biased. If we assume that cohort changes and cultural changes are positive over historic time (which is not necessarily so), the "age curve" will be biased by both factors in favor of the younger ages. There is another factor that tends to bias the curve in the opposite way, namely, selective loss of subjects. The basic point is this: Everyone born in 1910 will not survive until 1980 to provide scores; everyone born in 1930 will not survive until 1980; and so on. The longer the time since birth, the greater the loss of members of a particular cohort. If survival is related to what is being measured, the age curve will be biased. For example, if it is true that people who tend to get higher reasoning scores also tend to survive longer, then the 70-year-olds will be most selected for high scores, followed in order by the 50-year-olds, 35-year-olds, and so on down to the 15-year-olds. Such selective loss biases the age curve in favor of the older ages.

As you can see, the "age curve" obtained from a cross-sectional design is in principle a mixture of various relations and is very difficult to confidently interpret as just an "age curve." Notice that the problems associated with cross-sectional designs are likely to increase with the range of ages included in the design. For example, if the ages involved are 5, 6, 7, 8, and 9 years, associated with birth dates of 1975, 1974, 1973, 1972, and 1971 if measurements were obtained in 1980, it is less likely that serious cohort, cultural, and subject loss factors will confound the age curve. With the wide ranges shown in Table 8.10 these problems are much more serious.

Since cross-sectional designs involve so many problems and don't really measure individual change, you might wonder why researchers don't just abandon them and use longitudinal designs. Although researchers seem to have somewhat more favorable attitudes toward longitudinal designs (at least change is in some way assessed for individuals), there are problems with such designs too. First consider the practical aspects, including cost. If you wanted to study changes in reasoning scores from age 15 to age 70 by using a longitudinal design with subjects born in, say, 1965, you would have to measure the same people in 1980 (age 15), 1990 (age 25), 2000 (age 35), 2015 (age 50), and 2035 (age 70): If you began in 1980, you would not only have to keep the research project going for 55 years and maintain contact with the subjects for this period, but the data for the complete age curve would not be obtained for 55 years! Funding agencies tend to have little interest in investing money for such distant payoffs, and indeed, the research question might be theoretically unimportant by the time the project is only 20 percent finished. The practical consequence is that it is very unlikely that a researcher will be able to conduct a longitudinal study over a long period. "Age curves" for wide age ranges thus are most likely to come from cross-sectional designs; and as we have just seen, the problems of cross-sectional designs are greater when wide age ranges are studied.

Longitudinal studies over shorter age ranges are more feasible. Such studies do have inherent difficulties, one of which is most troublesome over short periods. An example of a longitudinal design is shown in Table 8.11. In such designs "age" is confounded with "time of measurement." If there are cultural changes that affect the measurements from one measurement time to another, these effects confound the "age curve" or at least limit its generality. In addition, because subjects are measured repeatedly there is a possibility of *practice effects* confounding the age curve. Furthermore, we must consider loss of subjects over time (and, thus, ages). In addition to the matter of sheer survival, subjects might be lost from the study without being lost from the human race. If the subjects remaining in the study tend to be, say, higher scorers, the age curve will be biased or unrepresentative. Notice that problems due to cultural changes or loss of subjects are less likely when the age range is shorter but that practice effects are more likely to pose difficulties when measurements are repeated over shorter time intervals.

Table 8.11   Illustration of Age–
Time-of-Measurement
Confounding in Longitudinal
Designs[a]

TIME OF MEASUREMENT	AGE
1973	3
1975	5
1978	8
1982	12

[a] Year of birth (cohort): 1970 for all subjects, who are measured repeatedly.

Choosing a method of studying developmental changes is a complex affair, depending on the nature of the question, practical considerations, and the importance of possible problems. Because cross-sectional and longitudinal designs have rather different problems, you might expect that the two designs would yield different "age curves." Indeed, such design differences in curves have sometimes been found, although researchers do not always agree in their interpretation of the differences (e.g., Baltes & Schaie, 1976; Horn & Donaldson, 1976). The two articles just cited provide a spirited example of the complexities of analysis and interpretation involved in obtaining "age curves." Researchers have tried to create better methods for studying developmental changes; basically, the newer methods are mixtures of cross-sectional and longitudinal designs. By comparing the results of both methods and evaluating the various extraneous factors that might cause problems, researchers can arrive at somewhat clearer "pictures" of developmental trends.

PROBLEM

The theory of cognitive dissonance predicts that the simple act of doing something will result in a person's having a more favorable opinion of the activity. In simple terms, the idea is that the person, having actually done something, reasons that "since I did it, it must be a pretty good thing to do." (This prediction holds only under certain circumstances, but we'll ignore the complexities here). One test of this prediction was made by examining the effect of going through college on opinions regarding the value of a college education. At the beginning of the 1969 school year a battery of tests was given to the entire freshman class at a midwestern university and to the entire senior class as well. One of the tests measured opinions about the value of a college education. Analysis of the test results showed clearly that the seniors considered a college education more valuable than the freshmen did. Since the seniors had already engaged in "going through college" for three years while the freshmen had not yet started, the researcher concluded that the results supported the cognitive-dissonance prediction. Do you see any problem?

This study translates into a cross-sectional design, although it is not described as a "developmental study"—rather, it is concerned with the change presumably produced by a treatment (college). The most noticeable problem with the study stems from its cross-sectional nature. Clearly the seniors (in 1969) represent only a portion of their former freshman class— all freshmen do not become seniors! The question is, Do the freshmen who last to become seniors represent a biased sample with respect to what is being measured? Is it plausible that three years earlier, as freshmen, the seniors of 1969 had more positive opinions about the value of a college education than the opinions of former freshmen who did not last to become seniors? This idea is surely plausible, in which case the difference of opinion that was observed would not accurately represent any change in opinion over three years of college. In simple terms, the seniors of 1969 had more positive opinions than the freshmen of 1969, but those seniors might have had more positive opinions even when they were freshmen.

SUMMARY

Factorial designs are balanced designs involving two or more independent variables. Each basic treatment represents a particular combination of one value of each independent variable; to make the design balanced, every value of one independent variable is combined equally often with all values of the other independent variables. Factorial designs yield information about the *overall* or *main effect* of each independent variable and about *interactions*. If the effect of one variable changes from one level to another of a second variable, an interaction exists. Whereas main effects involve looking at differences among means, interactions involve checking to see whether one set of differences among means differs from another set of differences among means. The presence of interactions indicates that treatment effects are complex and provides information about the generality of treatment effects.

Factorial designs do not pose special problems; rather, they can be used to avoid interpretive difficulties. For example, it is very dangerous to conclude that an interaction exists by comparing the results of separate studies; an interaction can be properly studied only with a factorial design. Such designs are also useful for determining whether different subject populations (e.g., neurotics vs. normals, or different age groups) react differently to various treatments.

Multiple-stage research can be extremely useful, but it presents special problems. In a *time series* or *single-subject design* a greatly extended series of measurments is made, with treatments introduced at one or more points in the series. The idea is to introduce a treatment when the measurements have reached a steady, unchanging state; when the method is used successfully it is rather easy to detect treatment effects. Since measurements never reach a truly steady state, problems can arise. If the treatment effect is not noticeably larger than the random variation in measurments, the treatment effect might not be detected. If a treatment has a delayed effect, it might be mistaken for a random deviation unless the researcher expects a delayed effect. If a treatment is introduced in response to a random deviation in the measurement series, any treatment effect will be confounded with regression artifacts (extreme random deviations in one direction are likely to be followed by less extreme deviations, and the regression back toward the trend might be mistaken for a treatment effect).

In many studies some change in behavior is studied by making measurements at two points in time, with a treatment introduced between the two measurements. There are many possible threats to both internal and external validity when change is assessed. Factors other than the treatment might be responsible for the observed change in measurements; these include practice effects, other events occurring between the two measurements, changes in the subjects due to maturation, and changes in the measuring instrument itself. If subjects are lost from the study, it might be difficult to evaluate the treatment, or the results might have severely limited generality. If subjects are initially selected because they have extreme scores, simple regression effects will lead to less extreme scores when the measurements are repeated, and a researcher might mistakenly conclude that the treatment has changed scores. To deal with such problems researchers need to use fairly complex designs; in many circumstances carefully constructed factorial designs are useful.

Researchers are sometimes interested in the delayed effect of a treatment. The research involves (at least) two stages; in stage 1 the treatments are introduced, while stage 2 consists of some time interval after which measurements are made. To obtain clear information it is necessary to make measurements twice—at the end of stage 1 and at the end of stage 2—and evaluate the difference between the two measurements. If scores at the end of stage 1 are quite different for different treatments, interpreting the later changes can be troublesome; comparing absolute changes can lead to a conclusion that differs from a conclusion reached by comparing relative changes. Ideally, scores at the end of stage 1 should be equivalent for all treatments to avoid ambiguity in the findings.

Transfer effects concern the influence of prior experience on later performance of a task. In stage 1 various treatments are introduced; groups are compared in terms of performance on the stage 2, transfer task. To properly interpret differences in stage 2 performance, it is important for treatment groups to reach equivalent performance levels in stage 1. If the stage 2, transfer tasks differ among treatments, it is necessary to have each task performed by (at least) two groups, one of which receives the stage-1 treatment and one of which does not. A factorial design results, and transfer effects are associated with interactions.

In studying developmental processes it is important to know how various measurements change with age. Obtaining accurate age curves presents difficulties. When the *cross-sectional* method is used, subjects of different ages are measured at the same point in time; with this method age differences are confounded with cohort differences (younger subjects were born later in historic time, grew up under different circumstances, and so on). The age curve can also be biased by differential survival—the older the age level, the smaller the percentage of the population that survives, and thus the older ages are represented by more selective samples. The *longitudinal* method, which involves repeated measurements of the same subjects as they age, avoids some of these problems but introduces others. The longitudinal method is impractical for studying age changes over wide ranges; loss of subjects from the study can result in unrepresentative age curves. Age changes can also be confounded with practice effects and cultural changes. In short, it is difficult to avoid interpretive problems; since the two methods involve somewhat different problems, researchers try to use both methods and compare the findings in an attempt to obtain better information about developmental trends.

9

GOING BEYOND THE TEXTBOOK

Our coverage of the fundamentals of psychological research is essentially complete. We have discussed many facets of the research process. I have tried to outline the critical issues, to identify the problems that can arise, and to show you how researchers can deal with the issues and avoid interpretive problems. This brief final chapter is intended to help you use the knowledge you have gained. The chapter begins with a posttest—a series of problems dealing with topics from a number of different chapters. The problems will give you a chance to check on how well you have learned the material and an opportunity to further develop your skills in detecting problems as they might arise in research. The chapter concludes with some suggestions for using and improving your knowledge and skills as you pursue your interest in psychology.

POSTTEST: PROBLEMS IN RESEARCH DESIGN

Most of the problems that follow are brief descriptions of research projects like those used in the earlier chapters. For each problem (with some exceptions that will be obvious), you are to do two things: First, identify the methodological flaw that casts doubt on the stated conclusion. Second, think about how the study could be redesigned so that there would be a more solid basis for the conclusion. Brief answers to these problems may be found in Appendix C. However, it will be to your advantage to try hard to solve the problems before looking up the answers.

1. A researcher wanted to determine whether transfer of learning between words with opposite meanings is different from transfer between unrelated words. To study this question she used a serial-recall task. On each trial the procedure was to present each word in a list for 3 seconds; then, after the last word had been presented, the subject was given 2 minutes to try to recall the words in the order in which they had been presented. The difficulty of learning a list was measured in terms of the number of trials needed by a subject to recall the whole list in the correct order.

The researcher carefully constructed 3 lists of 15 words. List A contained 15 words that were selected arbitrarily; list O contained 15 words, each of which meant the opposite of one of the words in list A; list U contained 15 words that were unrelated to the words in List A. Subjects were randomly assigned to 2 different conditions. Subjects in the "opposites" condition first learned list A and then learned list O. Subjects in the "unrelated" condition first learned list A and then learned list U. The critical comparison concerned the number of trials to learn the second (transfer) list in each condition. Analysis indicated that second-list learning required fewer trials in the "opposites" condition. The researcher thus concluded that transfer between opposites is greater than transfer between unrelated words. Criticize this conclusion.

2. A researcher was interested in the effects of punishment on behavior. He observed the behavior of a number of children in a social play situation, obtaining measures of "hostile–aggressive behavior." From the answers given by these children's mothers during interviews he obtained measures of "severity of punishment." For the problem, assume that both measures are reliable and valid. The researcher found a systematic relation between severity of punishment and aggressive behavior—the higher the severity of punishment, the greater the amount of hostile–aggressive behavior. The researcher concluded that (more severe) punishment leads to (more) aggressive behavior. Criticize this conclusion.

3. A researcher studied the effects of delayed feedback on concept learning. The basic procedure was as follows: A geometric pattern (e.g., a small red square) was shown for 3 seconds; the subject then indicated which category (A or B) he or she thought that pattern belonged to; 10 seconds later the next pattern was shown; and so on. This sequence continued until the subject correctly classified 20 consecutive patterns. The independent variable was the amount of time between the subject's response to a pattern and the indication of the correct category for that pattern (feedback). The conditions were 0, 2, 5, or 9 seconds of delay. Thus, for example, in the 5-second delay condition the subject saw a pattern for 3 seconds, made a response, waited for 5 seconds (the pattern was no longer visible), received feedback, and waited another 5 seconds for the next pattern to be shown (the interval between the offset of one pattern and the presentation of the next pattern was always 10 seconds). When the data were analyzed, the results were clear: The longer the delay of feedback, the more presentations were required to reach the criterion (20 consecutive correct categorizations). The researcher concluded that increasing the delay of feedback makes concept learning more difficult. Criticize this conclusion.

4. An experimenter was interested in associative processes in perception. She felt that people should be better able to recognize words that are related to each other compared to recognizing unrelated words. She selected 8 words that were related (all were animal names) and 8 other words that were not related to each other. Subjects were randomly assigned in equal numbers to either the "related" condition or the "unrelated" condition. Thus each subject saw only one set of words, having his or her recognition threshold measured for each of the 8 words in that set. For analysis, each subject's score was his

or her mean threshold for the 8 words in the set. The experimenter compared the mean scores for the two conditions, finding that the average score for related words was significantly lower than the score for unrelated words. She therefore concluded that relatedness among a set of words facilitates word recognition. Criticize this conclusion.

5. An educational psychologist felt that students become more serious toward their studies as they go through college. Since the research literature showed that amount of time spent studying is a good indicator of seriousness toward study, he decided to compare the study times of freshmen and seniors. He realized that the amount of study required varied from one course to another, but fortunately it was possible to control this factor. At his university there were three elective courses (large lectures) that were commonly taken by students in all years since the courses had no prerequisites and were quite popular. To control for the influence of the course on study time, the psychologist compared study times for only these three courses. He contacted all freshmen and seniors enrolled in these three courses and asked them to participate in his study. Roughly 80 percent of each group agreed to participate. Each student kept a record of the time he or she spent studying for the course during the fourth, fifth, and sixth weeks of the term, turning in the record at the end of each week. All of the participating students turned in their records for all three weeks. The psychologist compared the average study time for seniors to that for freshmen and found that the seniors' average was considerably higher. He therefore concluded that, to the extent that his data were representative of college courses in general, they showed that college students do indeed become more serious toward their studies as they go through college. Criticize this conclusion.

6. A researcher plans to study the effect of the lanaguage in which statements are presented on subjects' accuracy in judging the logical validity of syllogisms. A syllogism requires a person to decide whether a third statement must logically be true if two other statements are true. Three languages will be compared: *abstract symbols* (e.g., "If all X's are Y's and all Z's are Y's, must it be true that some X's are Z's?"), *factual sentences* (e.g., "If all Pontiacs are cars and all station wagons are cars, must it be true that some Pontiacs are station wagons?"), or *meaningless sentences* (e.g., "If all kitchens are truck drivers and all chairs are truck drivers, must it be true that some kitchens are chairs?") Of course the subject's task is to decide whether the conclusion follows logically from the other statements (regardless of the language used). Each subject can be given syllogisms in only one language. Previous research has shown that performance (accuracy) on syllogisms is correlated $+.70$ with scores on the verbal part of the college entrance exam. The researcher has 24 college students who can participate as subjects, and she has their scores on the entrance exam. How should she design the experiment (assign subjects to treatments)?

7. Two researchers study the effects of reward magnitude on performance. Both researchers use the same kind of subjects, the same number of subjects, the same rewards and reward magnitudes, the same apparatus, the same task and performance measure. One researcher uses an independent-groups design and, on the basis of the data, cannot reject the null hypothesis (that reward magnitude has no effect on performance). The other researcher uses a repeated-measures design and finds a "statistically significant" effect of reward magnitude—larger rewards lead to better performance. Assume that neither study has a flaw. There are two fundamental reasons why the two researchers might have reached different conclusions; one concerns the test of the null hypothesis while the other concerns the behavior involved in the two studies. What are the two reasons?

8. A researcher is interested in finding out whether the order of topics in a passage on developmental psychology affects comprehension of the material. He has constructed 5 different passages, all covering the same material but differing in the order in which

various topics are presented (call them simply passages A, B, C, D, and E). The procedure requires the subject to read a passage for 20 minutes and then take a test on the material (the measure of comprehension). The researcher wants to use students in introductory psychology as subjects and wants to collect data during class hours (this is reasonable because reading a passage and taking the test can be completed within a class session). There are 7 sections of introductory psychology currently being taught, all of which may be used for the study. Each contains between 20 and 30 students; each meets at a different time and in a different room; and each is taught by a different instructor. On the basis of this information indicate how the study should be designed.

9. The instructor of a large introductory-psychology course (400 students) was disappointed by the poor performance of some of the students on the midterm exam. She realized that there are many possible reasons for low test scores but felt that in this particular case one likely reason stemmed from the fact that the students were freshmen taking their very first course in psychology. She believed that when faced with a large course dealing with unfamiliar material some students might become alienated or frightened, and this would impair their performance in the course. She decided to try to correct the situation as she saw it. She selected the 40 students who had scored lowest on the midterm and arranged for them to meet once each week with teaching assistants for the remainder of the term. At these meetings the assistants discussed the relevance of psychology to everyday living and engaged in general conversation with the students. On the final exam for the course these 40 students scored closer to the average than they had on the midterm. The instructor concluded that the "counseling" had been successful and made plans to use it again in the future. Criticize this conclusion.

10. Following are the summary results of an experiment on problem solving:
The task involved a "lights-and-switches" apparatus with complex connections between lights and switches (each light connected to several switches, each switch connected to several lights). The subject's task was to figure out which switches had to be activated in order to have just the second light on the panel "on." Two independent variables were involved in the experiment. One was the number of switches available to the subject (5, 7, or 9); the other was the amount of money that subjects were told they could win by solving the problem very quickly ($1, $5, or $20). Subjects were randomly assigned to the nine basic treatments formed by the factorial combination of these two independent variables. Each subject's time-to-solve was measured. The numbers given here refer to the mean solution times for the nine basic treatments. Assuming that numerical differences are "statistically significant," answer the following questions:
1. Is there a main effect of "number of switches?"
2. Is there a main effect of "amount of money?"
3. Is there an interaction?

AMOUNT OF MONEY	Number of Switches Available		
	5	7	9
$1	14	17	20
$5	10	17	24
$20	8	17	26

CONSULTING THE PSYCHOLOGICAL LITERATURE

You will occasionally desire information about research findings, whether out of sheer curiosity, to write a class paper, or to locate information that is relevant to a research project. There are many sources of research information: Textbooks, other books on psychology, review articles, and journal articles providing original reports on research. These sources differ greatly in the amount of detailed information they provide about research (which I will discuss further in a moment). You will have to decide how much detail you desire and then consult the appropriate sources. You have now encountered a fair number of practice problems that illustrate the point that conclusions must be evaluated in relation to the methods used to collect and analyze data and to the actual results obtained. As you gain more information about a research project, you will be in a better position to decide how much confidence you should have in the findings and conclusions.

Textbooks written for undergraduate courses usually present relatively little detailed information about research findings. They are more likely to provide general summaries of research findings, perhaps with some examples of "typical" studies in the area. The information in other books on psychology varies widely, from popularized versions of psychology to original reports of research. In recent years there has been an increase in the number of books containing reviews of research in an area as well as original reports on research. Quite often such books result from special conferences to which a small number of researchers have been invited; when the conference ends, the proceedings are published in book form. It should be apparent that checking the card catalogue in the library can yield no information or information of quite varied quality. Nonetheless, you should not overlook the possibility of finding rather detailed research information in books.

Two main sources of research reviews in psychology are the *Psychological Bulletin* and the *Annual Review of Psychology*. The *Psychological Bulletin* is a journal containing research reviews and articles on research methodology. The *Annual Review of Psychology* will be found among the books in the library. Each year chapters reviewing research in different areas of psychology are published, according to a master plan. For example, there is a chapter every three years on psycholinguistics, one every two years on cognitive development, a chapter on personality every year, and so on. The master plan is presented at the front of each volume, which makes it relatively easy to determine if and when you might find information relevant to your topic. Review articles usually provide some (but not complete) information about the research being reviewed; however, these articles have extensive reference lists that can guide you to sources of more detailed information.

If you rely on any of the preceding sources of information, you are likely to lack the detailed information you need to make your own judgments about the research findings. In effect you must rely on the judgments of the people writing the reviews and the books. If you simply need information about methods and procedures (perhaps for a laboratory project), or if you want more detailed information to make your own judgments, you will have to consult the journals that publish original reports on research. There are very many such journals; the following is a partial list: *Journal of Experimental Psychology: Human Learning and Memory, Journal of Abnormal Psychology, Child Development, Journal of Comparative and Physiological Psychology, Canadian Journal of Psychology, Cognitive Psychology, British Journal of Psychology.* As this list suggests, most journals deal with fairly narrow areas of psychology, although some are broader and are distinguished by the country in which they are published.

The first problem you're likely to encounter is finding the articles that will provide the information you desire. There are several ways of approaching the task. You can consult *Psychological Abstracts,* a large and special journal that publishes abstracts of articles in other journals. It has a table of contents (in the front) and a subject index (in the back) on both a monthly and an annual basis. To be thorough you should check *Psychological Abstracts* both ways. Although you can locate articles dealing with your topic by this method, I have found it to be rather inefficient and tend to use it as a supplement (or, sometimes, a last resort).

Here is a search method that I have found to work rather well. It involves two guiding "principles": work from the general to the specific (with one clear exception), and work backwards over time. Let me explain the second "principle" first. If you begin your search with the most recently published sources, you can use the references contained in those sources to lead you to earlier sources. In effect the author of each source you find will have done some of the work for you. In this way you can search for articles in an efficient fashion.

Textbooks and other books on psychology are, of course, unlikely to directly provide the detailed information you need, but they will have references that may aid your search. Check both the *Psychological Bulletin* and the *Annual Review of Psychology* (starting with the most recent issues); look for reviews that might cover your topic (by checking titles); skim a review to see if your topic is included. Should you find a review dealing with your topic, you are likely to find a reference list that is a veritable gold mine.

The exception to my "general-to-specific principle" is to search directly in journals publishing original reports of research. To do this you need to identify the journals that are most likely to contain articles on your topic. Once you have picked the journals, start with the most recent issue, checking the titles of articles for "possibilities." If the title suggests a promising article, read the abstract of the article (on the first page of the article) to decide whether you want to read further. Obviously, any article you find that deals with your topic should have a list of very relevant references. Using these techniques you can search the research literature rather thoroughly and efficiently. Finally, you can facilitate your search by seeking help—faculty members (who engage in this process regularly) can give you helpful hints about where to look for the information you desire.

When you have found a journal article dealing with your topic, you face another task—extracting the information you need from the article. Reading journal articles is *not* particularly easy—they are written in a technical style and require careful, deliberate reading. The authors assume that the reader has a fair amount of knowledge, which means that there are not many lengthy explanations. In particular, there is a great deal of detailed information about the methods and results of the study. The practice problems I have given you are very brief descriptions; in constructing these problems I tried to avoid giving information that was unrelated to the particular issue that the problem is intended to illustrate. A journal article contains all the procedural information the author deems necessary for the reader to understand what was done. There may be no particular weakness in the methods, but if there is, the relevant information will be surrounded by information about other aspects of the method. You must simply work through this material carefully. The *estimate* mnemonic I described (experimenters, subjects, time, instructions, measurement, apparatus, task, environment) may help you "keep track" of the things to look for. Of course knowing more about the particular topic under investigation will help you identify the variables that should be considered most carefully.

You are likely to have the most difficulty when evaluating the adequacy of the statistical analyses, since you might not have learned about the particular techniques that are used. If so, you will have to assume that the statistical methods were appropriate. In any case, you *can* examine the descriptions of the data—what kinds of scores were analyzed; what do the data look like (means, standard deviations, etc.); what questions were asked about the data? You know that the power of a test depends on the number of observations and that, for example, repeated-measures designs provide more powerful tests than independent-groups designs. You also know that repeated-measures designs pose special interpretive problems. You can use this knowledge to evaluate the results of a study, regardless of the particular statistical tests the author might have used.

The author will draw some conclusions; interpretations of the results will be offered. Examine these statements carefully. Determine which aspects of the results provide the empirical support for a conclusion. In view of the methods used, might there be an alternate explanation of the results? Are there aspects of the results that the author is *not* considering in drawing conclusions from the study? There might be rather speculative conclusions—statements that are not closely tied to the results of the study. Carry out a point-by-point analysis of the author's conclusions. In this way you will be able to see how well the conclusions are related to the results and methods of the study.

I have stressed that doing research and evaluating research are complex, error-prone activities. Do *not* assume that, just because the article has been published in a journal, the research must be free of flaws. The author and the journal editors will have tried their best, but they might have missed something. Or, some aspect of the method might have seemed unimportant from the author's viewpoint but may be critical with respect to your particular interest in the topic. You will have difficulty evaluating some things, but you will be able to evaluate other aspects quite thoroughly. Do not underestimate your own ability.

THE NEED FOR BALANCED JUDGMENT

Whether you are evaluating the research of others or your own, you may sometimes feel discouraged or cynical. Throughout this book I have emphasized the problems that can arise in doing research. Indeed, no research project is perfect—there are inevitably some weaknesses or limitations to be found. I have tried to help you learn to identify those weaknesses. When you apply these skills to journal articles or your own research, you will have to make more complex judgments. If you identify a weakness, you will then have to decide how *important* it is. In the journals, you can find cross-sectional studies of development, research in which data are obtained from only 60 percent of the intended sample, studies involving a very small number of observations or relatively insensitive measures, and many other examples of research that poses some interpretive question. Why are such studies done, and why are they published? While confessing that I sometimes wonder myself, I must point out that many considerations are involved.

Authors and editors ask themselves a number of questions about a research project. Is the topic of theoretical or practical importance? Do the results, even though they are somewhat flawed or limited, suggest the need for modification of a popular theory? Has the researcher "broken new ground" to some extent—are the findings provocative, rich in potential ideas even though they are rather difficult to interpret? Has the researcher employed some innovative method that others should know about, even though the findings are not as clear as might be desired? Are some aspects of the results strong enough to justify publishing them even though other aspects are rather weak? The authors and editors have made their judgments, and if you see the research in print, the decision must have been that, *on balance,* there is enough justification for publishing the research. You will have to make your own judgments. What I wish to emphasize is that perfection is *not* a workable standard for judging research; rather, *progress* is what should be expected from research. A research finding will contribute a small amount to the growth of knowledge; in addition to the positive contributions, there will be false starts, blind alleys, and simple mistakes. To engage in research a person needs to be willing to live with some disappointments and, perhaps above all, uncertainty. If you are planning a research project, you should ask, "How might this research contribute to the growth of knowledge?" and then plan the study as best you can. When evaluating the findings of completed research, the question is, "How do these findings increase our understanding of the issues involved?" In most instances you should find a positive answer.

appendix A

WRITING A RESEARCH REPORT

The written research report is the primary means of communicating research findings. Professional researchers prepare research reports for eventual publication in journals; students are sometimes required to write research reports when they are taking undergraduate psychology courses. This appendix is intended to provide you with guidelines for preparing such reports. Most of the material is based on the *Publication Manual of the American Psychological Association,* although I have included some comments of my own.

Keep in mind that the fundamental purpose of research reports is to communicate factual information and theoretical interpretations. When you have written a section of a report and are examining it, the primary question is, Is this clear and easy to understand? Concentrating on writing *clearly* will help you to write better reports.

The typical research report includes the following sections, in this order: title page, abstract, introduction, method, results, discussion, and references. The main sections of a report are the introduction, method, results, and discussion, which essentially tell a "logical story" (in rough terms)— why I did the study, what I did, what I found, and what the findings mean. We will consider each of these sections separately.

TITLE PAGE

The title page contains the title of the report, the author's name, and (in the case of student reports) the course for which the report is being prepared. You will have to choose a title for your report. The title should be short but should adequately characterize the study that was conducted. For example, if you had examined the relation between individual differences in anxiety (as measured by the Taylor Manifest Anxiety Test) and course grades for a group of students in an educational-psychology course (no. 224 at your college), a reasonable title would be "Anxiety and Achievement in College Students." Including the particular measure of anxiety or the particular course would lengthen the title, to little advantage. Notice also that there is no need to include phrases such as "a study of" in the title. For example, the title "A Study of the Relation Between Anxiety and Achievement in College Students" does not really convey more useful information than the shorter title given earlier.

ABSTRACT

It is quite common to provide an abstract, or very brief summary of the report, at the beginning of the report. Usually the abstract contains about 100–175 words. In journal articles, the purpose of the abstract is to allow readers to get a general idea of the information contained in the report (which they may use to decide whether they wish to read further). For class reports, an abstract is likely to be required by the instructor (for practice, should you later seek to publish journal articles), but in any case it *is* good practice. Trying to summarize your report in so few words makes you really think about what is important and forces you to say things efficiently.

Try to include in the abstract at least one sentence referring to each of the four main sections of the report (introduction, method, results, discussion). In other words, use the abstract to tell your reader "what your purpose was, what you did, what you found, and what you concluded," in 100–175 words, of course. It is a good idea to delay writing the abstract until you have finished the complete report.

INTRODUCTION

The general purpose of the introduction is simple—to provide the reader with background information for understanding your study. Three more specific goals may be identified (1) to identify the central issues that your study will address, (2) to summarize previous research that is relevant to these issues and your study, and (3) to provide the specific reasons for the particular study you conducted. It is useful to remember that the introduction is intended to introduce the reader to *your* study. It is important to keep the introduction focused on *your* study. For example, if you studied the effects of giving hints on problem solving, your introduction should (1) identify the theoretical issues to which a study of hints is relevant, (2) summarize previous research on those issues and on the effects of hints, and (3) present in clear terms what you expected to find out by conducting your study. Your introduction should *not* be a general essay on problem solving.

In your treatment of the issues and relevant prior research, you will need to refer to articles and books published by others. But the fact that you have read something does *not* mean that it should be included in the introduction. References should be included only if they concern issues and findings that are relevant to your study. At the same time, it is necessary to "give credit where credit is due." If an idea that is one of the reasons for your study comes from another's work, then you should cite that work. In a more general sense, you should clearly distinguish between ideas that are your own and ideas that have been proposed by others. Appropriate use of references will make it easier for your reader to make this distinction. As a final suggestion, you should prepare the introduction in such a way that when the reader finishes reading it he or she has a clear understanding of your reasons for doing the study (the questions you hope to answer).

METHOD

In simple terms, the method section should tell your reader what was done. In principle, the method section should be sufficiently detailed to allow the reader to duplicate the important aspects of your methods. It is quite common for the methods section to contain labeled subsections dealing with the design of the study, subjects, apparatus (or materials), and the specific procedures used. These subsections help the reader understand what you did. The design subsection usually includes a brief description of the variables involved in the study (number of values, specific values used) and the method of assigning subjects to treatments. For example, "A 3 × 2 factorial design was constructed by combining 3 levels of reward magnitude (1, 5, or 10 pellets of standard laboratory food) with 2 levels of food deprivation (2 or 12 hours). Subjects were randomly assigned to conditions." The subsection dealing with subjects should provide information regarding who the subjects were, how many there were, and how they were selected for participation in the study. Here's an example of a reasonable description: "The subjects were 45 students from an introductory-psychology class who participated to fulfill a course requirement." It is difficult to state precisely what characteristics of the subjects you should include, since potentially relevant characteristics vary considerably from one study to another. You might consult Chapter 3 to help you decide.

Quite frequently the subjects subsection is combined with the design subsection to form a single "subjects and design" subsection. Basically, the choice is yours—whichever approach seems more informative should be used.

The apparatus or materials subsection may be nonexistent, short, or quite long, depending on the particular characteristics of your study. Commercially available pieces of apparatus may be described in terms of their commercial labels; specially constructed apparatus needs to be described in greater detail. If your study involves a selection of materials for presentation to the subjects, this subsection might be quite long. For example, if you had to choose words for subjects to learn in your study, you will need to indicate the source of the words, how they were chosen, what their important characteristics are, and how they were arranged for presentation to the subjects. Here's an example: "Sixty words were selected from the Smith and Jones (1975) norms. The words were chosen by taking the first 60 words in the norms that began with a vowel, were 5 letters in length, and had frequency ratings of 50 or above in the norms. Two lists of 30 words each were formed by randomly choosing 30 words to form list A (using a table of random numbers), with the remaining 30 words forming list B." Again, referring to Chapter 3 may help you in preparing this section of your report.

The procedure subsection is very important; it should describe precisely what was done when subjects were seen. It should indicate whether subjects were seen individually or in groups (how large were the groups?) The instructions that subjects received should be described in reasonable detail; it is not uncommon for instructions to be presented verbatim (if instructions are viewed as critically important for the topic under study). The sequence of events that occurred (including times between successive events, if important) should be described in simple, straightforward language. When preparing this part of the methods section, keep in mind that the reader needs to know "exactly what happened." In other words, the reader should be able to reproduce your procedure with reasonable accuracy.

RESULTS

The results section includes summary descriptions of the data (e.g., means, standard deviations) and statistical analyses performed on the data (usually related to tests of null hypotheses). Individual scores ("raw data") are typically *not* presented. A well-prepared results section will guide the reader through the findings. Many students tend to just present a bunch of numbers and tests, which produces a rather incoherent section. Instead, they should take their time with the results, concentrating on presenting clear and complete information.

It is quite common for a researcher to collect several different measures or to conduct a number of analyses. To help the reader understand the collection of findings, I suggest the following approach. When you have completed your analyses of the data, consider how many separate results (analyses) you have to present (make a list!). Some of the results are likely to be more important than others, given the purposes of your study. It is a good idea to present the more important results first—doing so tends to focus the reader's attention on these findings.

Once you have decided on the results to be presented (and their order), then treat each result with care. For each analysis be sure to tell the reader the nature of the scores being analyzed (e.g., number of correct words recalled, number of errors, time to solve a problem in minutes), and identify precisely the statistical techniques involved (e.g., Pearson r, t ratio). Present summary data that are relevant to the analysis and direct the reader's attention to their important aspects. Relate the outcomes of the statistical tests to the summary data. If you do this for each result, the section should be clear and easy to read.

Tables and figures (graphs) are often used to present summary data. Choose the form that provides the clearest presentation of the data. Tables and figures should not be used excessively; they are useful when they present relatively large amounts of data that would be difficult to describe clearly in sentences. Each table or figure should have a number and a heading that describe the data being summarized. Preferably, the number of scores should be indicated; for example, for a table presenting mean scores for several treatments, indicate (in the heading or a note) the number of scores that contributed to each mean (if the number of scores varies from one mean to another, include this information in the table itself). In preparing figures be sure to label all axes clearly and to draw the figures accurately (in more than one sense—it would be misleading to present a figure giving the visual impression that two means differ noticeably if your statistical analysis does not support such a conclusion). *Always* refer to each table or figure in the text you are writing; direct your reader's attention to a table or figure (using its reference number) and tell the reader what to look at, that is, how the information in the table or figure is related to the analysis you are presenting in the text.

Keep in mind that the results section typically contains a fair amount of numerical information, which is high-density information—a lot of content in relatively little space. Ease the task for your reader by explaining what the numbers mean, why they are worth attending to, and how they have been used (by you). In short, guide your reader through the results with care.

DISCUSSION

In rough terms, the discussion is the "What does it mean?" section. It is the interpretive part of a research report. There are several possible ways of discussing your findings (you do *not* have to choose just one). The reason for conducting the research was to get answers to certain questions (which are stated in the introduction). What kinds of answers does your research provide? Were your hypotheses supported or not supported by the results? Do your findings support an existing theory, or do they strongly suggest the need for a modification of the theory? What kind of modification seems to be needed?

Compare your results to those of other researchers. Note both the agreements and the differences, and try to provide a plausible, sensible explanation for any diferences. Certain weaknesses in your study might be a basis for alternate explanations of the findings. Do not dwell on minor flaws, but mention plausible alternate accounts and try to evaluate them as dispassionately as you can. If your findings have practical implications, state what they are.

Discussion sections are hardest to write when a study yields "negative" results. If none of your expectations were upheld—if "nothing worked"—it is hard to think of things to say. When this happens accept your fate, do what you can, and above all, avoid a lengthy, apologetic confession. Of course if you feel that you have a very plausible explanation for the negative results, state it and suggest how the study could be redesigned in a productive fashion. Just remember to avoid the "maybe's" and "if only's."

All of the preceding are things that might be included in the discussion. However, the key to writing a good discussion is organization, a firm understanding of what you think the results mean and what you want to say. The discussion should be somewhat assertive, though not overbearing. State your case in a clear and direct fashion—don't overstate it and don't understate it.

Here's a final suggestion: Never, never end your discussion with the statement "More research is needed."

REFERENCES

We need to consider references in two ways. As you are writing your report you will periodically need to refer to someone else's published work (primarily in the introduction and discussion). Keep in mind that it is your responsibility to relate your study to the existing literature and to "give credit where credit is due." For these reasons you will have references in the text of your report. Psychological journals have adopted a convention for indicating that you are citing a published work. Their method is to state the last name(s) of the author(s) and the year of publication in the sentence at the point where you refer to the work. For example, if you were summarizing the results of a study reported in an article by Steven Jones and Marilyn Smith published in 1954, the text would have the following form: "It has been found that injecting small amounts of coffee into the ear raises scores on arithmetic tests (Jones & Smith, 1954)." Here is an alternate form: "Jones and Smith (1954) found that injecting small amounts of coffee into the ear raises scores on arithmetic tests."

If you are quoting from a published work (which is more than just referring to it), you should use quotation marks in addition to stating the author, year of publication, and page number where the material may be found. These are the basic rules for references in the text of the report—identify the reference by author's name and year of publication, and distinguish between "mere" references and quotations.

The last section of your research report will then be a list of all references cited in the text. The list of references provides complete identifying information and allows the reader to consult the source. The standard format for the reference list is to order the references alphabetically by author's last name. If you must list several references by the same author, order them chronologically. Other sensible rules apply to various special cases. Here is an example of a properly ordered list (just authors' names and years of publications are listed):

Abbott, R. H. (1984)
Gershwin, A. R. (1965)
Gorwin, P. (1955)
Gorwin, P., & Smith, R. H. (1978)
Gorwin, P., & Tosca, W. W. (1966)
Manion, R. (1965)
Manion, R. (1967)
Ulrich, D. M., Aaron, B. B., & Acton, K. L. (1935)

The standard formats for individual entries in the reference list are the following (for most common cases):

Journal article: Author's name, article title, journal title, year of publication, volume number, page numbers.
Book: Author's name, book title, place of publication, publisher's name, year of publication.
Chapter in a book: Author's name, chapter title, book author's name, book title, place of publication, publisher's name, year of publication.

Here are some examples of these formats:

Gershwin, A. R. The effects of morphine on eyelid conditioning in the rabbit. *Journal of Neuroscience,* 1965, 44, 240–247.
Gorwin, P. *A Psychology of Reading.* Baltimore, Md.: John Brown & Sons, Publishers, 1955.
Manion, R. Helping people to help themselves. In G. R. Childs, *Psychological Approaches to Better Government.* Boston, Mass.: New Deal, Inc., 1965.

appendix B

STATISTICAL METHODS

This appendix contains abbreviated descriptions of commonly used statistical techniques: correlation coefficients, chi square, *t* ratio, and analysis of variance. Each section provides, for a particular technique, a brief statement of the situations in which the technique is used, the major features of the statistic, the calculating formula, a numerical example, and (where appropriate) a table of values to be consulted when the technique is used.

If your instructor has explained the statistical technique to you, or if you have had other instruction in statistics, this appendix will serve as a handy guide to using the technique to analyze data. *By no means* is this appendix a substitute for instruction in statistics. The treatment is brief and does not include a complete explanation of the techniques.

CORRELATION COEFFICIENTS

Pearson *r*

Purpose: To provide a numerical index of the form and strength of the relation between scores on one interval scale and scores on another interval scale. The basic data consist of two scores, one on each scale, for each of N cases.

Features: Pearson *r* ranges in value from -1 to $+1$; it indexes only a linear relation between the two sets of scores and is affected by the distances between scores in a distribution.

Calculating formula:

$$r = \frac{\Sigma XY - \dfrac{(\Sigma X)(\Sigma Y)}{N}}{\sqrt{\left[\Sigma X^2 - \dfrac{(\Sigma X)^2}{N}\right]\left[\Sigma Y^2 - \dfrac{(\Sigma Y)^2}{N}\right]}}$$

Terms:

X = scores on one scale
Y = scores on the other scale
N = number of cases (number of pairs of scores)

Example: Scores on a vocabulary test (number correct) and on a verbal problem (time to solve, in minutes) have been obtained for 8 individuals, as follows:

PERSON	VOCABULARY	SOLUTION TIME	X²	Y²	XY
A	56	14	3136	196	784
B	72	11	5184	121	792
C	64	18	4096	324	1152
D	46	8	2116	64	368
E	71	4	5041	16	284
F	38	20	1444	400	760
G	41	18	1681	324	738
H	74	6	5476	36	444
Σ	462	99	28174	1481	5322

$$r = \frac{\Sigma XY - \dfrac{(\Sigma X)(\Sigma Y)}{N}}{\sqrt{\left[\Sigma X^2 - \dfrac{(\Sigma X)^2}{N}\right]\left[\Sigma Y^2 - \dfrac{(\Sigma Y)^2}{N}\right]}} = \frac{5322 - \dfrac{(462)(99)}{8}}{\sqrt{\left[28174 - \dfrac{(462)^2}{8}\right]\left[1481 - \dfrac{(99)^2}{8}\right]}}$$

$$= \frac{5322 - 5717.2}{\sqrt{[28174 - 26680.5][1481 - 1225.1]}} = \frac{-395.2}{\sqrt{(1493.5)(255.9)}}$$

$$= \frac{-395.2}{\sqrt{382186.6}} = \frac{-395.2}{618.2} = -.64$$

The negative sign of the coefficient indicates that high scores in one distribution tend to be associated with low scores in the other distribution (and vice versa). The numerical value (.64) indicates a relation that is "41 percent stronger than no relation at all." (See Chapter 7.)

Spearman Rho

Purpose: To provide a numerical index of the relation between two sets of ranks. The basic data consist of two ranks for each case or two scores for each case from which ranks can be determined.

Features: Spearman rho ranges in value from -1 to $+1$. It indexes the linear relation between the two sets of ranks. The sign of the coefficient should be considered in light of the method of assigning ranks. Positive values indicate that "high ranks tend to be associated with high ranks"; negative values indicate that "high ranks on one variable tend to be associated with low ranks on the other." One needs to determine what is meant by "high rank" on either variable.

Formula:

$$ \text{rho} = 1 - \frac{6\Sigma D^2}{N(N^2 - 1)} $$

Terms:

D = difference between rank on one variable and rank on the other variable for an individual case

N = number of cases (number of pairs of ranks)

Example: For 10 individuals, performance on both a motor task (% time on target) and a visual tracking task (% errors) has been measured. Both scales must be assumed to be at least ordinal. To calculate Spearman rho it will be necessary to rank the individuals in terms of both "percent time on target" and "percent errors." (The Spearman rho formula applies *only* to ranks.) Individuals may be ranked in either direction; that is, rank 1 is given to the highest score or to the lowest score. Note that in this example "better performance" would be associated with *high* percent time but *low* percent errors. To have a positive coefficient mean "better with better," percent time scores could be ranked from high to low while percent error scores are ranked from low to high.

PERSON	% TIME ON	% ERRORS	RANK$_T$	RANK$_E$	D	D^2
A	84	33	2	5	−3	9
B	53	52	8	10	−2	4
C	61	16	6	1	5	25
D	42	34	10	6	4	16
E	93	39	1	7	−6	36
F	74	24	3	2	1	1
G	66	50	4.5	9	−4.5	20.25
H	66	26	4.5	3	1.5	2.25
I	58	30	7	4	3	9
J	50	43	9	8	1	1
					$\Sigma =$	$\overline{123.50}$

Note: Rank 1 is given to the highest score for % time, to the lowest score for % errors. For % time scores, cases G and H have tied scores that occupy ranks 4 and 5; the average of the ranks is given to each case.

$$\text{rho} = 1 - \frac{6\Sigma D^2}{N(N^2 - 1)} = 1 - \frac{6(123.50)}{10(100 - 1)}$$

$$= 1 - \frac{741}{990} = 1 - .75 = +.25$$

The value of the coefficient (+.25) indicates a slight tendency for individuals to occupy similar ranks in the two distribution, which means a slight tendency for those with higher percent time-on-target scores to have lower percent error scores (and vice versa).

Phi Coefficient

Purpose: To provide a numerical index of the relation between scores on one two-category nominal scale and scores on another two-category nominal scale. The basic data consist of the assignments of N cases to one of the two categories on each scale.

Features: The phi coefficient varies from −1 to +1. The sign of the coefficient (+ or −) is arbitrary, depending solely on how the categories are arranged. Because both scales are two-category nominal scales, there are only four possible pairs of scores (X_1 and Y_1, X_1 and Y_2, X_2 and Y_1, X_2 and Y_2). To calculate phi one makes use of a 2 × 2 matrix showing the frequency of each pair of scores.

Data arrangement:

	X_1	X_2
Y_1	a	b
Y_2	c	d

Formula:

$$\phi(\text{phi}) = \frac{bc - ad}{\sqrt{(a + b)(c + d)(a + c)(b + d)}}$$

Terms:

a = number of cases having X_1 and Y_1
b = number of cases having X_2 and Y_1
c = number of cases having X_1 and Y_2
d = number of cases having X_2 and Y_2

Example: Each of a number of men and women was asked if he or she preferred movies or books as a form of entertainment. The data display indicates that 20 men said "movies," as did 14 women, whereas 10 men and 34 women said "books."

Sex

		M	F
Movies	a 20		b 14
Books	c 10		d 34

Preference

$$\phi = \frac{bc - ad}{\sqrt{(a + b)(c + d)(a + c)(b + d)}}$$

$$= \frac{(14)(10) - (20)(34)}{\sqrt{(20 + 14)(10 + 34)(20 + 10)(14 + 34)}}$$

$$= \frac{140 - 680}{\sqrt{(34)(44)(30)(48)}}$$

$$= \frac{-540}{\sqrt{2154240}} = \frac{-540}{1468} = -.37$$

The negative sign of the coefficient indicates a tendency for more frequencies in the *ad* diagonal than in the *bc* diagonal. Referring back to the arrangement of the categories in the data matrix, the value of $-.37$ indicates a modest tendency for men to prefer movies and for women to prefer books.

CHI SQUARE

Purpose: To provide a statistical test of null hypotheses concerning the arrangement of frequencies (numbers of observations) over two or more categories.

Features: A distribution of chi square (χ^2) values is a theoretical distribution with values ranging continuously from 0 (zero) to positive infinity. There are many chi square distributions, each characterized by a different number of degrees of freedom (*df*). All chi square distributions range from zero to positive infinity; with low *df*, the distribution is noticeably positively skewed; as *df* increase, the distributions become less skewed (more symmetrical). A chi square test is appropriate when all observed frequencies are *independent* of each other; in psychology this typically means that each frequency (observation) must come from a different subject, with the data collected in such a way that the categorization of one subject does *not* influence the categorization of any other subject.

General formula:

$$\chi^2 = \Sigma \frac{(f_o - f_e)^2}{f_e}$$

Terms:

f_o = the observed frequency in a category
f_e = the expected frequency in a category (based on the null hypothesis)
Note: The sum is taken over the categories; for example, if four categories were involved, the sum of $(f_o - f_e)^2/f_e$ over the four categories would constitute the obtained value of chi square.

General use: The null hypothesis is the basis of the expected frequency of each category (f_e). The alternate hypothesis denies one or more of the equalities stated in the null hypothesis. An alpha level must be chosen (e.g., .05, .02, .01, etc.) for the test. The degrees of freedom (*df*) must be determined in order to identify the appropriate chi square distribution to use for the test. Once alpha and *df* have been set, the *critical value* of chi square for the test may be identified; it is the value (in the appropriate distribution) that has alpha of the distribution *above* it. For example, given *df* = 2, alpha = .05, the critical value would be 5.991 (see Table B.1; in a chi square distribution with *df* = 2, .05 of the values lie above 5.991). The

Table B.1 Values of the Chi-Square Distribution for Selected One-Tailed Significance Levels

Significance Level

Df	.5000	.2500	.1000	.0500	.0250	.0100	.0050	.0025	.0010
1	0.455	1.323	2.706	3.841	5.024	6.635	7.879	9.141	10.83
2	1.386	2.733	4.605	5.991	7.378	9.210	10.60	11.98	13.82
3	2.366	4.108	6.251	7.815	9.348	11.34	12.84	14.32	16.27
4	3.357	5.385	7.779	9.488	11.14	13.28	14.86	16.42	18.47
5	4.351	6.626	9.236	11.07	12.83	15.09	16.75	18.39	20.1
6	5.348	7.841	10.64	12.59	14.45	16.81	18.55	20.25	22.46
7	6.346	9.037	12.02	14.07	16.01	18.48	20.28	22.04	24.32
8	7.344	10.22	13.36	15.51	17.53	20.09	21.95	23.77	26.12
9	8.343	11.39	14.68	16.92	19.02	21.67	23.59	25.46	27.88
10	9.342	12.55	15.99	18.31	20.48	23.21	25.19	27.11	29.59
11	10.34	13.70	17.28	19.68	21.92	24.72	26.76	28.73	31.26
12	11.34	14.85	18.55	21.03	23.34	26.22	28.30	30.32	32.91
13	12.34	15.98	19.81	22.36	24.74	27.69	29.82	31.88	34.53
14	13.34	17.12	21.06	23.68	26.12	29.14	31.32	33.43	36.12
15	14.34	18.25	22.31	25.00	27.49	30.58	32.80	34.95	37.70
16	15.34	19.37	23.54	26.30	28.85	32.00	34.27	36.46	39.25
17	16.34	20.49	24.77	27.59	30.19	33.41	35.72	37.95	40.79
18	17.34	21.60	25.99	28.87	31.53	34.81	37.16	39.42	42.31
19	18.34	22.72	27.20	30.14	32.85	36.19	38.58	40.88	43.82
20	19.34	23.83	28.41	31.41	34.17	37.57	40.00	42.34	45.31
21	20.34	24.93	29.62	32.67	35.48	38.93	41.40	43.78	46.79
22	21.34	26.04	30.81	33.92	36.78	40.29	42.80	45.20	48.27
23	22.34	27.14	32.01	35.17	38.08	41.64	44.18	46.62	49.73
24	23.34	28.24	33.20	36.42	39.36	42.98	45.56	48.03	51.18
25	24.34	29.34	34.38	37.65	40.65	44.31	46.93	49.44	52.62
26	25.34	30.43	35.56	38.89	41.92	45.64	48.29	50.83	54.05
27	26.34	31.53	36.74	40.11	43.19	46.96	49.64	52.22	55.47
28	27.34	32.62	37.92	41.34	44.46	48.28	50.99	53.59	56.89
29	28.34	33.71	39.09	42.56	45.72	49.59	52.34	54.97	58.30
30	29.34	34.80	40.26	43.77	46.98	50.89	53.67	56.33	59.70
40	39.34	45.62	51.81	55.76	59.34	63.69	66.77	69.70	73.40
60	59.33	66.98	74.40	79.08	83.30	88.38	91.95	95.34	99.61
120	119.30	130.10	140.20	146.60	152.20	158.90	163.60	168.10	173.60

From *Analysis of Variance in Complex Experimental Designs* by Harold R. Lindman. W. H. Freeman and Company. Copyright © 1974.

obtained value of chi square is computed (see formula); if the obtained value *exceeds* the critical value, the null hypothesis is rejected.

Example A—Basic Chi Square Analysis

Each of 60 people has been independently asked to select his or her favorite kind of music from a list of four categories (rock, jazz, classical, folk).

Null hypothesis: $p(\text{rock}) = p(\text{jazz}) = p(\text{classical}) = p(\text{folk})$
Alternate hypothesis: at least one $\neq$
Alpha: .01
df: one less than the number of categories $= 4 - 1 = 3$
Critical value: 11.34 (In a chi square distribution with 3 *df*, .01 of the values will be above 11.34.)
Data:

	ROCK	JAZZ	CLASSICAL	FOLK	TOTAL
f_o	20	9	12	19	60
f_e	15	15	15	15	60

Note: The expected frequencies (f_e's) are based on the null hypothesis; if all categories are equally likely to be chosen, then ideally the 60 observations should be assigned equally to the four categories. (See Chapter 6.)

Calculation of obtained value of chi square:

$$\chi^2 = \Sigma \frac{(f_o - f_e)^2}{f_e}$$

$$= \frac{(20 - 15)^2}{15} + \frac{(9 - 15)^2}{15} + \frac{(12 - 15)^2}{15} + \frac{(19 - 15)^2}{15}$$

$$= 1.67 + 2.40 + 0.60 + 1.07$$

$$= 5.74$$

The test: Since the obtained value of chi square (5.74) is *less than* the critical value (11.34), the null hypothesis *cannot* be rejected. With alpha = .01, the observed frequencies do not differ enough from the expected frequencies to justify rejecting the null hypothesis that the four kinds of music are equally likely to be chosen.

Example B—Special Case: Chi Square with Two Categories

Since chi square distributions are continuous but frequencies are discrete, it is necessary (when $df = 1$) to apply a correction for continuity to the obtained value of chi square. This is done by reducing the absolute value of the difference between f_o and f_e by .5, in each category.

Each of 100 people is given a test ride in a Cadillac and a test ride in a Lincoln and then asked which car he or she prefers. (We must assume that each person chooses independently.)

Null hypothesis: p(cadillac) = p(lincoln)

Alternate hypothesis: p(cadillac) ≠ p(lincoln)

Alpha: .05

df: 2 − 1 = 1 (one less than the number of categories)

Critical value: 3.841 (See Table B.1.)

Data:

	CADILLAC	LINCOLN	TOTAL
f_o	36	64	100
f_e	50	50	100

Note: The expected frequencies are based on the null hypothesis.

Calculation of obtained value of chi square (including correction for continuity):

$$\chi^2 = \Sigma \frac{(|f_o - f_e| - .5)^2}{f_e}$$

$$= \frac{(|36 - 50| - .5)^2}{50} + \frac{(|64 - 50| - .5)^2}{50}$$

$$= \frac{(14 - .5)^2}{50} + \frac{(14 - .5)^2}{50}$$

$$= \frac{(13.5)^2}{50} + \frac{(13.5)^2}{50} = 3.64 + 3.64$$

$$= 7.28$$

The test: Since the obtained value of chi square (7.28) is greater than the critical value (3.841), the null hypothesis can be rejected. The data allow the conclusion that the Lincoln is more likely to be chosen.

Note: There are other uses of chi square that result in *df* = 1. Whenever *df* = 1, the obtained value of chi square must be corrected for continuity in the manner just described.

Example C—Two-Way Classifications
(Tests of Independence)

Twenty "fast learners" and twenty "slow learners" have been asked to identify the strategy they used to learn the material, selecting from "just memorized," "used images," or "made up sentences." The question of interest is whether the fast and slow learners differ in the strategies they use (as reported). The subscripts f and s represent fast and slow learners, respectively.

Null hypothesis: $p_f(\text{memorized}) = p_s(\text{memorized})$ and $p_f(\text{images}) = p_s(\text{images})$ and $p_f(\text{sentences}) = p_s(\text{sentences})$

Alternate hypothesis: at least one $\neq$

Note: The null hypothesis says nothing about the precise value of $p(\text{memorized})$—it does assert that, whatever its value, it is the same for fast and slow learners; the same applies to the other categories.

Alpha: .025.

df: (number of rows $-$ 1) $\times$ (number of columns $-$ 1) (see data table) $= (2 - 1) \times (3 - 1) = 1 \times 2 = 2$

Critical value: 7.378 (See Table B.1.)

Data (all entries are observed frequencies):

	MEMORIZED	IMAGES	SENTENCES	TOTAL
Fast learners	2	12	6	20
Slow learners	6	6	8	20
Total	8	18	14	40

The test involves the six cells inside the table; note that each cell can be labeled in terms of a type of learner (fast or slow) and a type of strategy (memorized, images, sentences). For example, the upper left-hand cell is the "fast, memorized" cell ($f_o = 2$). To generate the expected frequency for this cell (on the basis of the null hypothesis), one multiplies the number of fast learners (20) by the number of "memorizers" (8) and divides this product by the total number of observations (40). In formula terms, the expected frequency for the "fast, memorized" cells is

$$\frac{n_f \times n_m}{N} = \frac{20 \times 8}{40} = 4.$$

The same method is used for all cells; for example, for the "slow, images" cell the expected frequency is

$$\frac{20 \times 18}{40} = 9.$$

The expected frequencies for all six cells are shown in the following table:

	MEMORIZED	IMAGES	SENTENCES	(TOTAL)
Fast learners	4	9	7	(20)
Slow learners	4	9	7	(20)
(Total)	(8)	(18)	(14)	(40)

Calculation of obtained value of chi square:

$$\chi^2 = \Sigma \frac{(f_o - f_e)^2}{f_e}$$

$$= \frac{(2-4)^2}{4} + \frac{(12-9)^2}{9} + \frac{(6-7)^2}{7}$$

$$+ \frac{(6-4)^2}{4} + \frac{(6-9)^2}{9} + \frac{(8-7)^2}{7}$$

$$= 1.00 + 1.00 + 0.14 + 1.00 + 1.00 + 0.14$$

$$= 4.28$$

The test: Since the obtained value of chi square (4.28) is *less than* the critical value (7.378), the null hypothesis *cannot* be rejected. With alpha = .025, the observed frequencies in the six cells do not differ enough from the expected frequencies to justify rejecting the null hypothesis that the strategies of fast learners do not differ from those of slow learners.

t RATIO

Purpose: The statistic known as *t* has many different uses, of which this appendix will cover only a few. We will consider the use of *t* to test null hypotheses about (1) the value of a population mean (M) and (2) the value of the difference between two population means $(M_1 - M_2)$. We will also cover the use of *t* to establish confidence intervals (1) for the value of M and (2) for the value of $(M_1 - M_2)$.

Features: There are many *t* distributions, each characterized by a different number of degrees of freedom (*df*). For any *t* distribution the mean is zero and the values range from negative infinity to positive infinity. With low *df*, the variability of a *t* distribution is relatively high; as *df* increase, variability decreases. The *t* distributions can be compared to a normal distribution of *z* values (which also has a mean of zero, with *z* values ranging from negative infinity to positive infinity). As *df* increase, *t* distributions resemble a normal z distribution more and more closely. For this reason tables of t distributions typically do not present values for t distributions with many df (the values of the normal distribution may be used). In Table B.2 you can see that if df exceed 100 one may use values from the normal distribution.

Note: The calculating formula for t and the method of determining the number of degrees of freedom (df) vary with the particular use. These will be presented separately as each use of t is described. Formally, the uses of t covered here rest on the assumption that the measured variable (scores) follows a normal distribution. It has been shown, however, that t ratio works quite well as long as this assumption is *not* seriously violated.

A. Testing a Null Hypothesis About the Value of M

The data from a single sample may be used to test a null hypothesis that specifies a particular value for the population mean (M). The test is based on the difference between the obtained sample mean ($\bar{X}$) and the value of M specified by the null hypothesis.

Null hypothesis: M $= a$ (a is some specified number)
Alternate hypothesis: M $\neq a$
Calculating formula for t:

$$t = \frac{\bar{X} - M}{S_{\bar{X}}}$$

Terms:

$\bar{X}$ = mean of the sample $= \dfrac{\Sigma X}{n}$ where n = sample size

M = value of population mean (given by null hypothesis)
$S_{\bar{X}}$ = estimate of the standard error of the mean

$$= \sqrt{\frac{\Sigma(X - \bar{X})^2}{n(n-1)}} = \sqrt{\frac{\Sigma X^2 - \dfrac{(\Sigma X)^2}{n}}{n(n-1)}}$$

The test: An alpha level must be chosen. The degrees of freedom must be determined; in this use $df = n - 1$ (one less than the size of the sample). The *critical value* for the test is the value of t in the appropriate distribution (determined by df), which is exceeded in absolute value by alpha of the distribution. For example, for $df = 8$, alpha $= .05$ the critical value would be 2.306 (see Table B.2); in a t distribution with $df = 8$, .05 of the distribution exceeds in absolute value the value of 2.306 (more negative than -2.306 or more positive than $+2.306$; in brief, larger in absolute value than 2.306). The obtained value of t is calculated (see formula); if the obtained value of t is numerically larger than the critical value, the null hypothesis is rejected.

Example: For each of 9 people the number of errors made before mastering a task is measured. A mathematical learning theory predicts that the (true) mean number of errors is 14. This specific prediction will serve as the null hypothesis.

Null hypothesis: M = 14
Alternate hypothesis: M ≠ 14
Alpha: .01
df: 9 − 1 = 8
Critical value: 3.355 (see Table B.2)
Data—individual scores (number of errors):

X	X²
5	25
8	64
14	196
10	100
9	81
11	121
15	225
10	100
7	49
ΣX = 89	ΣX² = 961

Needed calculations:

$$\bar{X} = \frac{\Sigma X}{n} = \frac{89}{9} = 9.89$$

$$S_{\bar{X}} = \sqrt{\frac{\Sigma X^2 - \frac{(\Sigma X)^2}{n}}{n(n-1)}}$$

$$= \sqrt{\frac{961 - \frac{(89)^2}{9}}{9(9-1)}}$$

$$= \sqrt{\frac{961 - 880.1}{72}} = \sqrt{\frac{80.9}{72}}$$

$$= \sqrt{1.12} = 1.06$$

Table B.2 Values of the *t* Distribution for Selected Two-Tailed Significance Levels

Significance Level

Df	.500	.200	.100	.050	.020	.010	.005	.002	.001
1	1.000	3.078	6.314	12.710	31.820	63.660	127.300	318.300	636.600
2	.816	1.886	2.920	4.303	6.965	9.925	14.090	22.330	31.600
3	.765	1.638	2.353	3.182	4.541	5.841	7.453	10.210	12.920
4	.741	1.533	2.132	2.776	3.747	4.604	5.597	7.173	8.610
5	.727	1.476	2.015	2.571	3.365	4.032	4.773	5.893	6.869
6	.718	1.440	1.943	2.447	3.143	3.707	4.317	5.207	5.959
7	.711	1.415	1.895	2.365	2.998	3.499	4.029	4.785	5.408
8	.706	1.397	1.860	2.306	2.896	3.355	3.833	4.501	5.041
9	.703	1.383	1.833	2.262	2.821	3.250	3.690	4.297	4.781
10	.700	1.372	1.812	2.228	2.764	3.169	3.581	4.144	4.587
11	.697	1.363	1.796	2.201	2.718	3.106	3.497	4.025	4.437
12	.695	1.356	1.782	2.179	2.681	3.055	3.428	3.930	4.317
13	.694	1.350	1.771	2.160	2.650	3.012	3.372	3.852	4.220
14	.692	1.345	1.761	2.145	2.624	2.977	3.326	3.787	4.140
15	.691	1.341	1.753	2.131	2.602	2.947	3.286	3.733	4.072
16	.690	1.337	1.746	2.120	2.583	2.921	3.252	3.686	4.015

17	.689	1.333	1.740	2.110	2.567	2.898	3.222	3.646	3.965
18	.688	1.330	1.734	2.101	2.552	2.878	3.197	3.610	3.922
19	.688	1.328	1.729	2.093	2.539	2.861	3.174	3.579	3.883
20	.687	1.325	1.725	2.086	2.528	2.845	3.153	3.552	3.850
21	.686	1.323	1.721	2.080	2.518	2.831	3.135	3.527	3.819
22	.686	1.321	1.717	2.074	2.508	2.819	3.119	3.505	3.792
23	.685	1.319	1.714	2.069	2.500	2.807	3.104	3.485	3.768
24	.685	1.318	1.711	2.064	2.492	2.797	3.090	3.467	3.745
25	.684	1.316	1.708	2.060	2.485	2.787	3.078	3.450	3.725
26	.684	1.315	1.706	2.056	2.479	2.779	3.067	3.435	3.707
27	.684	1.314	1.703	2.052	2.473	2.771	3.056	3.421	3.690
28	.683	1.313	1.701	2.048	2.467	2.763	3.047	3.408	3.674
29	.683	1.311	1.699	2.045	2.462	2.756	3.038	3.396	3.659
30	.683	1.310	1.697	2.042	2.457	2.750	3.030	3.385	3.646
40	.681	1.303	1.684	2.021	2.423	2.704	2.971	3.307	3.551
60	.679	1.296	1.671	2.000	2.390	2.660	2.915	3.232	3.460
80	.678	1.292	1.664	1.990	2.374	2.639	2.887	3.195	3.416
100	.677	1.290	1.660	1.984	2.364	2.626	2.871	3.174	3.390
INF	.674	1.282	1.645	1.960	2.326	2.576	2.807	3.090	3.291

From *Analysis of Variance in Complex Experimental Designs* by Harold R. Lindman. W. H. Freeman and Company. Copyright © 1974.

Calculation of obtained value of t:

$$t = \frac{\bar{X} - M}{S_{\bar{X}}} = \frac{9.89 - 14}{1.06} = \frac{-4.11}{1.06} = -3.88$$

The test: Since the obtained value of t (3.88) is numerically larger than the critical value (3.355), the null hypothesis can be rejected. (Note: the sign of the obtained value is unimportant for conducting this test.) The data allow the conclusion that the theory's prediction (M = 14) is incorrect—the mean number of errors is less than was theoretically predicted.

B. Establishing a Confidence Interval for M

The data from a single sample may be used to establish a confidence interval for the value of the population mean. (See Chapter 5.) The interval is a range of values within which the population mean is expected to fall. The confidence level (stated in % terms) depends on the alpha level (significance level in % terms) that is chosen when constructing the interval. The formula for a confidence interval for M is the following:

$$(\bar{X} - t_\alpha S_{\bar{X}}) < M < (\bar{X} + t_\alpha S_{\bar{X}})$$

Terms:

$\bar{X}$ = the sample mean
$S_{\bar{X}}$ = estimate of the standard error of the mean
t_α = critical value of t for stated alpha level

The relation between the confidence level and the significance level is as follows. If one uses the critical value of t for alpha = .05 (the 5% significance level), the confidence level would be $100 - 5 = 95\%$. In general, the confidence level equals 100 minus the significance level (in % terms). Note that, in addition to choosing an alpha (significance) level, one must determine the number of *df* in order to identify the proper value of t_α.

Example (using the same data as in Section A):

$$n = 9$$
$$\bar{X} = 9.89$$
$$S_{\bar{X}} = 1.06$$
$$df = 9 - 1 = 8$$
$$\alpha = .01 \text{ (confidence} = 99\%)$$
$$\text{Critical value} = 3.355$$

Establishing the confidence interval:

$$99\% \text{ confidence interval} = [(\bar{X} - t_{.01}S_{\bar{X}}) < M < (\bar{X} + t_{.01}S_{\bar{X}})]$$

$$= [9.89 - 3.355(1.06)] < M < [9.89 + 3.355(1.06)]$$

$$= (9.89 - 3.56) < M < (9.89 + 3.56)$$

$$= (6.33 < M < 13.45)$$

We would be stating that we are "99 percent confident" that the true value of M lies between 6.33 and 13.45. The "99 percent confidence" means that the procedure used to construct the interval will "work" 99 percent of the time; 99 percent of the intervals so constructed will in fact contain the true value of M. Note that *this particular interval is either right or wrong*—the true value of M either is or isn't between 6.33 and 13.45. The "99 percent confidence" refers to the *procedure* used in constructing the interval; the *procedure* works 99 percent of the time. If one wanted to construct an interval with lower confidence—for example, a 90 percent confidence interval—one would use the critical value of t for alpha = .10, and so on.

C. Testing the Null Hypothesis that $M_1 - M_2 = 0$, Independent Groups

The data from two independent samples are frequently used to test the null hypothesis that $M_1 - M_2 = 0$. [In principle, any specific value for $M_1 - M_2$ could be tested, but zero is the value that is usually tested. (See Chapter 6.)] As in any null-hypothesis test, an alpha level must be chosen; also, the *df* must be determined in order to identify the appropriate t distribution.

Note: The formulas given here are appropriate only when two *independent* groups of scores have been obtained.

Null hypothesis: $M_1 - M_2 = 0$; $\sigma_1 = \sigma_2$
Alternate hypothesis: $M_1 - M_2 \neq 0$; $\sigma_1 = \sigma_2$

Comment: Notice that both the null and alternate hypotheses state that σ_1 equals σ_2. This means that for the test to be appropriate it must be reasonable to assume that, whether the population means are the same or different, the population standard deviations are the same. The reasonableness of this assumption must be evaluated in the context of the particular data to which the test is applied.

Formula:

$$t = \frac{(\bar{X}_1 - \bar{X}_2) - (M_1 - M_2)}{S_{\bar{X}_1 - \bar{X}_2}}$$

Terms:

$\bar{X}_1, \bar{X}_2$ = means of sample 1 and sample 2, respectively
$(M_1 - M_2)$ = the difference between population means stated in the null hypothesis (we will use zero)
$S_{\bar{X}_1 - \bar{X}_2}$ = estimate of the standard error of the sample mean difference

$$S_{\bar{X}_1 - \bar{X}_2} = \sqrt{\frac{\Sigma X_1{}^2 - \dfrac{(\Sigma X_1)^2}{n_1} + \Sigma X_2{}^2 - \dfrac{(\Sigma X_2)^2}{n_2}}{n_1 + n_2 - 2}\left(\frac{n_1 + n_2}{n_1 n_2}\right)}$$

X_1 = score in sample 1
X_2 = score in sample 2
n_1 = number of scores in sample 1
n_2 = number of scores in sample 2
$df = n_1 + n_2 - 2$

The test: The general form is similar to that used for tests about the value of M. (See Section A.) The critical value of t is determined on the basis of *df* and the chosen alpha level. The obtained value of t is calculated; if it is numerically larger than the critical value, the null hypothesis is rejected.

Example: An arithmetic test is given to samples of 15 boys and 12 girls in a sixth grade; each student's score is the number of correct answers. The null hypothesis is that there is no difference between the population means for boys and girls.

Null hypothesis: $M_b - M_g = 0$; $\sigma_b = \sigma_g$
Alternate hypothesis: $M_b - M_g \neq 0$; $\sigma_b = \sigma_g$
Alpha: .05
df: $n_b + n_g - 2 = 15 + 12 - 2 = 25$
Critical value = 2.060 (See Table B.2.)
Data and needed calculations:

Individual Scores

Boys (X_1):   55, 47, 49, 58, 62, 44, 57, 60, 61, 52, 66, 41, 48, 55, 52
Girls (X_2):   49, 55, 59, 63, 67, 69, 70, 61, 55, 70, 58, 55

$$n_b = 15 \qquad \Sigma X_b = 807 \qquad \bar{X}_b = \frac{807}{15} = 53.8 \qquad \Sigma X_b{}^2 = 44123$$

$$n_g = 12 \qquad \Sigma X_g = 731 \qquad \bar{X}_g = \frac{731}{12} = 60.9 \qquad \Sigma X_g{}^2 = 45061$$

$$S_{\bar{X}_b - \bar{X}_g} = \sqrt{\frac{\Sigma X_b{}^2 - \dfrac{(\Sigma X_b)^2}{n_b} + \Sigma X_g{}^2 - \dfrac{(\Sigma X_g)^2}{n_g}}{n_b + n_g - 2} \left(\frac{n_b + n_g}{n_b n_g} \right)}$$

$$= \sqrt{\frac{44123 - \dfrac{(807)^2}{15} + 45061 - \dfrac{(731)^2}{12}}{15 + 12 - 2} \left(\frac{15 + 12}{15(12)} \right)}$$

$$= \sqrt{\frac{1237.3}{25} \left(\frac{27}{180} \right)} = \sqrt{7.42} = 2.72$$

Calculation of the obtained value of t:

$$t = \frac{(X_b - \bar{X}_g) - 0}{S_{\bar{X}_b - \bar{X}_g}} = \frac{(53.8 - 60.9) - 0}{2.72} = \frac{-7.1}{2.72} = -2.61$$

The test: Since the obtained value of t (2.61) is numerically larger than the critical value (2.060), the null hypothesis can be rejected. The data allow the conclusion that the population mean for girls is higher than that for boys.

D. Testing the Null Hypothesis that $M_1 - M_2 = 0$, Matched Subjects or Repeated Measures

The data from a matched-subjects design or a repeated-measures design may be used to test a null hypothesis about a population mean difference. The general logic of the test is the same as when independent groups are involved (see Section C), but the calculating formulas and the degrees of freedom are different.

Keep in mind that when either matched subjects or repeated measures are used (see Chapter 3), each score in one sample is paired with a score in the other sample.

Formula:

$$t = \frac{\bar{D} - (M_1 - M_2)}{S_{\bar{D}}}$$

Terms:

D = algebraic difference between scores in a pair $(X_1 - X_2)$

$\bar{D} = \dfrac{\Sigma D}{n}$ (Note: $\bar{D} = \bar{X}_1 - \bar{X}_2$)

$M_1 - M_2$ = difference between population means stated in the null hypothesis (we will use zero)

$S_{\bar{D}}$ = estimate of the standard error of the sample mean difference

n = number of pairs of scores

$$S_{\bar{D}} = \sqrt{\frac{\Sigma D^2 - \dfrac{(\Sigma D)^2}{n}}{n(n - 1)}}$$

$df = n - 1$ (one less than the number of pairs)

Example: Each of 8 people studies a list of words for several minutes, then puts the list aside and attempts to recall as many words as possible. In fact, the list is composed of concrete and abstract words; thus each subject has two scores: number of concrete words recalled and number of abstract words recalled. The null hypothesis is that there is no real difference between population means for concrete and abstract words.

Null hypothesis: $M_c - M_a = 0$; $\sigma_c = \sigma_a$
Alternate hypothesis: $M_c - M_a \neq 0$; $\sigma_c = \sigma_a$
Alpha: .05
df: $n - 1 = 8 - 1 = 7$ (remember, n = number of pairs for this test)
Critical value: 2.365 (See Table B.2.)
Data and needed calculations:

PERSON	NO. CONCRETE	NO. ABSTRACT	D	D²
A	32	28	+4	16
B	23	20	+3	9
C	19	14	+5	25
D	33	27	+6	36
E	27	26	+1	1
F	24	26	−2	4
G	16	12	+4	16
H	22	23	−1	1
			$\Sigma D = +20$	$\Sigma D^2 = 108$

$$\bar{D} = \frac{\Sigma D}{n} = \frac{+20}{8} = +2.50$$

$$S_{\bar{D}} = \sqrt{\frac{\Sigma D^2 - \frac{(\Sigma D)^2}{n}}{n(n-1)}} = \sqrt{\frac{108 - \frac{(20)^2}{8}}{8(8-1)}} = \sqrt{\frac{108 - 50}{56}}$$

$$= \sqrt{\frac{58}{56}} = \sqrt{1.04} = 1.02$$

Calculation of the obtained value of t:

$$t = \frac{\bar{D} - 0}{S_{\bar{D}}} = \frac{2.5 - 0}{1.02} = \frac{2.5}{1.02} = 2.45$$

The test: Since the obtained value of t (2.45) is larger than the critical value (2.365), the null hypothesis can be rejected. The data allow the conclusion that the population mean for concrete words is higher than that for abstract words.

E. Establishing a Confidence Interval for ($M_1 - M_2$)

The data from two samples (whether from independent groups, matched subjects, or repeated measures) may be used to construct a confidence interval for the value of $(M_1 - M_2)$. The general logic of the procedure is the same as that used for constructing confidence intervals for M. (See Section B.) The general formula for the confidence interval is as follows:

$$[(\check{X}_1 - \check{X}_2) - t_\alpha S_{\check{X}_1 - \check{X}_2}] < (M_1 - M_2) < [(\check{X}_1 - \check{X}_2) + t_\alpha S_{\check{X}_1 - \check{X}_2}]$$

Terms:

$(\check{X}_1 - \check{X}_2)$ = the difference between the two obtained sample means

t_α = the critical value of t for the chosen alpha level, at the appropriate number of df

$S_{\check{X}_1 - \check{X}_2}$ = estimate of the standard error of the sample mean difference

As in the case of the "single mean" confidence interval, the confidence level depends on the alpha level (significance level in % terms) used to determine the value of t used in constructing the interval. If alpha = .05 is used (5% significance level), the confidence level would be $100 -$ (chosen significance level) = $100\% - 5\% = 95\%$.

Example (using the data from the example in Section C):

$$\check{X}_b = 53.8 \qquad n_b = 15$$

$$\check{X}_g = 60.9 \qquad n_g = 12 \qquad S_{\check{X}_b - \check{X}_g} = 2.72$$

$$df = n_1 + n_2 - 2 = 15 + 12 - 2 = 25$$

To construct a 90% confidence interval for $(M_b - M_g)$ we would use the critical value for t with alpha = .10, $df = 25$. The critical value is 1.708. (See Table B.2.)

Construction of the confidence interval:

$$[(\check{X}_b - \check{X}_g) - t_\alpha S_{\check{X}_b - \check{X}_g}] < M_b - M_g < [(\check{X}_b - \check{X}_g) + t_\alpha S_{\check{X}_b - \check{X}_g}]$$

$$[(53.8 - 60.9) - 1.708(2.72)] < M_b - M_g < [(53.8 - 60.9) + 1.708(2.72)]$$

$$(-7.1 - 4.65) < M_b - M_g < (-7.1 + 4.65)$$

$$90\% \text{ CI: } (-11.75 < M_b - M_g < -2.45)$$

Thus we could state that, using a procedure that is correct 90 percent of the time, the true value of $(M_b - M_g)$ is estimated to lie between -11.75 and -2.45.

Note: The same procedure is used whether the data come from independent groups, matched subjects, or repeated measures. If matched subjects or repeated measures are used, note that $\check{D} = \check{X}_1 - \check{X}_2$ and that $S_{\check{D}} = S_{\check{X}_1 - \check{X}_2}$.

ANALYSIS OF VARIANCE

The technique known as analysis of variance actually consists of a variety of methods used to test null hypotheses of many kinds for many different kinds of data. This appendix will cover only the most basic forms of analysis of variance. The uses to be described apply *only* when the scores in each sample come from *independent groups*. Two uses will be described: (1) analysis of variance to test a null hypothesis about two or more population means and (2) analysis of variance for a two-factor factorial design.

Features: The test statistic used in the analysis of variance is the F ratio. There are many distributions of F, each characterized by a particular *pair of values of df*; one number of df is associated with the *numerator* of the F ratio; the other is associated with the *denominator* of the F ratio. In any distribution of F the values range from 0 (zero) to positive infinity. As the df increase (for the numerator and for the denominator), the distributions become less variable (large values of F become less likely).

A. Testing a Null Hypothesis About the Equality of Population Means

When one has scores for two or more independent samples (in general, we will refer to k samples), the analysis of variance described in this section may be used to test a null hypothesis that all population means are equal.

Null hypothesis: $M_1 = M_2 = M_3 = \ldots = M_k$; $\sigma_1^2 = \sigma_2^2 = \sigma_3^2 = \ldots = \sigma_k^2$

Alternate hypothesis: At least one $\neq$ among M's; $\sigma_1^2 = \sigma_2^2 = \sigma_3^2 = \ldots = \sigma_k^2$

Notice that both the null and alternate hypotheses state that all population variances are equal. For the test to be appropriate it must be reasonable to assume that all population variances are equal, whether or not all population means are equal.

Terms and formulas:

N = total number of scores (over all samples)

df_{bg} = degrees of freedom between groups = $k - 1$

k = number of samples (groups)

df_{wg} = degrees of freedom within groups = $N - k$

n_j = number of scores in the jth group (translation: number of scores in a particular group; j is the identifier of a group—that is, j = 1, 2, 3, ... k for the 1st, 2nd, 3rd, ... kth group)

T_j = sum of the scores in the jth group

T_G = "grand total" = sum of all scores in all groups

$$SS_{tot} = \text{total sum of squares} = \sum^{k} \sum^{n_j} X^2 - \frac{T_G^2}{N}$$

$$SS_{bg} = \text{sum of squares between groups} = \sum^{k} \frac{T_j^2}{n_j} - \frac{T_G^2}{N}$$

$$SS_{wg} = \text{sum of squares within groups} = SS_{tot} - SS_{bg}$$

MS_{bg} = mean square between groups = SS_{bg}/df_{bg}
MS_{wg} = mean square within groups = SS_{wg}/df_{wg}

The test: The test statistic is an F ratio calculated according to the following formula:

$$F = \frac{MS_{bg}}{MS_{wg}}$$

An alpha level must be chosen. The critical value of F for the test is then identified from Table B.3 by finding the appropriate F distribution on the basis of the df for the numerator (MS_{bg})—namely, $k - 1$—and the df for the denominator (MS_{wg})—namely, $N - k$. For example, if 5 groups were involved ($k = 5$) and there was a total of 20 scores in all groups ($N = 20$), $df_{bg} = k - 1 = 5 - 1 = 4$ and $df_{wg} = N - k = 20 - 5 = 15$. If alpha were chosen to be .05, the critical value for the test would be 3.056. [In an F distribution with 4 df (numerator) and 15 df (denominator), only 5% of the values would exceed 3.056.] The obtained value of F (see formula) must exceed the critical value for the null hypothesis to be rejected.

Example: Scores (reaction times in seconds) have been obtained for 4 different treatments (circles, triangles, squares, hexagons). Each treatment is represented by an *independent* group of subjects. (Each subject was shown only one kind of figure; the subject's task was to identify the figure as fast as possible when it was shown.) The null hypothesis is that the population means for all four figures are the same.

Null hypothesis: $M_c = M_t = M_s = M_h$; $\sigma_c = \sigma_t = \sigma_s = \sigma_h$
Alternate hypothesis: At least one $\neq$ among M's; $\sigma_c = \sigma_t = \sigma_s = \sigma_h$
Alpha: .01
Data (individual scores):

	Type of Figure				
	CIRCLE	**TRIANGLE**	**SQUARE**	**HEXAGON**	
	1.2	2.3	1.8	2.6	
	1.4	1.9	1.4	2.3	
	0.9	1.8	1.6	2.2	
	1.1	1.5	1.9	2.1	
	1.1	1.6	1.2	2.4	
	1.9	2.2	1.4		
	1.3	2.0			
		1.8			
T_j	8.9	15.1	9.3	11.6	$T_G = 44.9$
n_j	7	8	6	5	$N = 26$
$\sum^{n_j} X^2$	11.93	29.03	14.77	27.06	$\sum^{k} \sum^{n_j} X^2 = 82.79$

Table B.3 Values of the F Distribution for Selected One-Tailed Significance Levels

Df Num	Df Den					Significance Level				
		.5000	.2500	.1000	.0500	.0250	.0100	.0050	.0025	.0010
1	1	1.000	5.828	39.860	161.400	647.800	4052.00			
1	2	.667	2.571	8.526	18.510	38.510	98.50	198.50	398.50	998.50
1	3	.585	2.024	5.538	10.130	17.440	34.11	55.55	89.58	166.90
1	4	.549	1.807	4.545	7.709	12.220	21.20	31.33	45.67	74.13
1	5	.528	1.692	4.060	6.608	10.010	16.26	22.78	31.41	47.18
1	6	.515	1.621	3.776	5.987	8.813	13.74	18.63	24.81	35.51
1	8	.499	1.538	3.458	5.318	7.571	11.26	14.69	18.78	25.41
1	10	.490	1.491	3.285	4.965	6.937	10.04	12.83	16.04	21.04
1	12	.484	1.461	3.177	4.747	6.554	9.330	11.75	14.49	18.64
1	15	.478	1.432	3.073	4.543	6.200	8.683	10.80	13.13	16.58
1	20	.472	1.404	2.975	4.351	5.871	8.096	9.944	11.94	14.82
1	24	.469	1.390	2.927	4.260	5.717	7.823	9.551	11.40	14.03
1	30	.466	1.376	2.881	4.171	5.568	7.562	9.179	10.89	13.29
1	40	.463	1.363	2.835	4.085	5.424	7.314	8.828	10.41	12.61
1	60	.460	1.349	2.791	4.001	5.286	7.077	8.494	9.962	11.97
1	120	.458	1.336	2.748	3.920	5.152	6.851	8.179	9.539	11.38
1	INF	.455	1.323	2.706	3.841	5.024	6.635	7.879	9.141	10.83
2	1	1.500	7.500	49.500	199.500	799.500	5000.00			
2	2	1.000	3.000	9.000	19.000	39.000	99.00	199.00	399.00	999.00
2	3	.881	2.280	5.462	9.552	16.040	30.82	49.80	79.93	148.50
2	4	.828	2.000	4.325	6.944	10.650	18.00	26.28	38.00	61.25
2	5	.799	1.853	3.780	5.786	8.434	13.27	18.31	24.96	37.12
2	6	.780	1.762	3.463	5.143	7.260	10.92	14.54	19.10	27.00
2	8	.757	1.657	3.113	4.459	6.059	8.649	11.04	13.89	18.49
2	10	.743	1.598	2.924	4.103	5.456	7.559	9.427	11.57	14.91
2	12	.735	1.560	2.807	3.885	5.096	6.927	8.510	10.29	12.97
2	15	.726	1.523	2.695	3.682	4.765	6.359	7.701	9.173	11.34
2	20	.718	1.487	2.589	3.493	4.461	5.849	6.986	8.206	9.953
2	24	.714	1.470	2.538	3.403	4.319	5.614	6.661	7.771	9.339
2	30	.709	1.452	2.489	3.316	4.182	5.390	6.355	7.365	8.773

ν_1	ν_2									
2	40	.705	1.435	2.440	3.232	4.051	5.179	6.066	6.986	8.251
2	60	.701	1.419	2.393	3.150	3.925	4.977	5.795	6.632	7.768
2	120	.697	1.402	2.347	3.072	3.805	4.787	5.539	6.301	7.321
2	INF	.693	1.386	2.303	2.997	3.690	4.607	5.301	5.995	6.913
3	1	1.709	8.200	53.590	215.700	864.200	5404.00			
3	2	1.135	3.153	9.162	19.160	39.170	99.17	199.20	399.20	999.20
3	3	1.000	2.356	5.391	9.277	15.440	29.46	47.47	76.05	141.10
3	4	.941	2.047	4.191	6.591	9.979	16.69	24.26	34.95	56.18
3	5	.907	1.884	3.619	5.409	7.764	12.06	16.53	22.43	33.20
3	6	.886	1.784	3.289	4.757	6.599	9.780	12.92	16.87	23.70
3	8	.860	1.668	2.924	4.066	5.416	7.591	9.596	11.98	15.83
3	10	.845	1.603	2.728	3.708	4.826	6.552	8.081	9.833	12.55
3	12	.835	1.561	2.606	3.490	4.474	5.952	7.226	8.651	10.80
3	15	.826	1.520	2.490	3.287	4.153	5.417	6.476	7.634	9.335
3	20	.816	1.481	2.380	3.098	3.859	4.938	5.818	6.757	8.098
3	24	.812	1.462	2.327	3.009	3.721	4.718	5.519	6.364	7.553
3	30	.807	1.443	2.276	2.922	3.589	4.510	5.239	5.999	7.053
3	40	.802	1.424	2.226	2.839	3.463	4.313	4.976	5.659	6.595
3	60	.798	1.405	2.177	2.758	3.343	4.126	4.729	5.343	6.171
3	120	.793	1.387	2.130	2.680	3.227	3.949	4.497	5.048	5.781
3	INF	.789	1.369	2.084	2.605	3.116	3.782	4.279	4.773	5.422
4	1	1.823	8.581	55.83	224.60	899.60	5625.00			
4	2	1.207	3.232	9.243	19.25	39.25	99.25	199.2	399.2	999.2
4	3	1.063	2.390	5.343	9.117	15.10	28.71	46.19	73.95	137.0
4	4	1.000	2.064	4.107	6.388	9.605	15.98	23.15	33.30	53.44
4	5	.965	1.893	3.520	5.192	7.388	11.39	15.56	21.05	31.08
4	6	.942	1.787	3.181	4.534	6.227	9.148	12.03	15.65	21.92
4	8	.915	1.664	2.806	3.838	5.053	7.006	8.805	10.94	14.39
4	10	.899	1.595	2.605	3.478	4.468	5.994	7.343	8.887	11.28
4	12	.888	1.550	2.480	3.259	4.121	5.412	6.521	7.761	9.633
4	15	.878	1.507	2.361	3.056	3.804	4.893	5.803	6.796	8.252
4	20	.868	1.465	2.249	2.866	3.515	4.431	5.174	5.967	7.096
4	24	.863	1.445	2.195	2.776	3.379	4.218	4.890	5.596	6.589
4	30	.858	1.424	2.142	2.690	3.250	4.018	4.623	5.253	6.124
4	40	.854	1.404	2.091	2.606	3.126	3.828	4.374	4.934	5.698

Table B.3 (Continued)

Df Num	Den	|	Significance Level								
			.5000	.2500	.1000	.0500	.0250	.0100	.0050	.0025	.0010
4	60		.849	1.385	2.041	2.525	3.008	3.649	4.140	4.637	5.307
4	120		.844	1.365	1.992	2.447	2.894	3.480	3.921	4.362	4.947
4	INF		.839	1.346	1.945	2.372	2.786	3.319	3.715	4.106	4.617
5	1		1.894	8.820	57.24	230.2	921.8	5764.	199.3	399.3	999.3
5	2		1.252	3.280	9.293	19.30	39.30	99.30	45.39	72.62	134.6
5	3		1.102	2.409	5.309	9.013	14.88	28.24	22.45	32.26	51.70
5	4		1.037	2.072	4.051	6.256	9.364	15.52	14.94	20.18	29.75
5	5		1.000	1.895	3.453	5.050	7.146	10.97	11.46	14.88	20.80
5	6		.977	1.785	3.108	4.387	5.988	8.746	8.302	10.28	13.48
5	8		.948	1.658	2.726	3.687	4.817	6.632	6.872	8.287	10.48
5	10		.932	1.585	2.522	3.326	4.236	5.636	6.071	7.196	8.892
5	12		.921	1.539	2.394	3.106	3.891	5.064	5.372	6.262	7.567
5	15		.911	1.494	2.273	2.901	3.576	4.556	4.762	5.463	6.460
5	20		.900	1.450	2.158	2.711	3.289	4.103	4.486	5.106	5.976
5	24		.895	1.428	2.103	2.621	3.155	3.895	4.228	4.776	5.533
5	30		.890	1.407	2.049	2.534	3.026	3.699	3.986	4.469	5.128
5	40		.885	1.386	1.997	2.449	2.904	3.514			

5	60	.880	1.366	1.946	2.368	2.786	3.339	3.760	4.185	4.757
5	120	.875	1.345	1.896	2.290	2.674	3.174	3.548	3.922	4.416
5	INF	.870	1.325	1.847	2.214	2.567	3.017	3.350	3.677	4.103
6	1	1.942	8.983	58.20	234.0	937.1	5859.	199.3	399.3	999.3
6	2	1.282	3.312	9.326	19.33	39.33	99.33	44.84	71.71	132.8
6	3	1.129	2.422	5.285	8.941	14.73	27.91	21.97	31.54	50.52
6	4	1.062	2.077	4.010	6.163	9.197	15.21	14.51	19.58	28.83
6	5	1.024	1.894	3.405	4.950	6.978	10.67	11.07	14.35	20.03
6	6	1.000	1.782	3.055	4.284	5.820	8.466	7.952	9.828	12.86
6	8	.971	1.651	2.668	3.581	4.652	6.371	6.545	7.871	9.926
6	10	.954	1.576	2.461	3.217	4.072	5.386	5.757	6.803	8.379
6	12	.943	1.529	2.331	2.996	3.728	4.821	5.071	5.891	7.092
6	15	.933	1.482	2.208	2.790	3.415	4.318	4.472	5.111	6.018
6	20	.922	1.437	2.091	2.599	3.128	3.871	4.202	4.763	5.550
6	24	.917	1.414	2.035	2.508	2.995	3.667	3.949	4.442	5.122
6	30	.912	1.392	1.980	2.421	2.867	3.473	3.713	4.144	4.730
6	40	.907	1.371	1.927	2.336	2.744	3.291	3.492	3.868	4.372
6	60	.901	1.349	1.875	2.254	2.627	3.119	3.285	3.612	4.044
6	120	.896	1.328	1.824	2.175	2.515	2.956	3.091	3.375	3.743
6	INF	.891	1.307	1.774	2.099	2.408	2.802			

From *Analysis of Variance in Complex Experimental Designs* by Harold R. Lindman. W. H. Freeman and Company. Copyright © 1974.

df_{bg}: $k - 1 = 4 - 1 = 3$
df_{wg}: $N - k = 26 - 4 = 22$

Critical value of F: 4.938 (See Table B.3; value for 3 and 20 *df* is used.)

Calculations:

$$SS_{tot} = \sum_{}^{k} \sum_{}^{n_j} X^2 - \frac{T_G^2}{N} = 82.79 - \frac{(44.9)^2}{26} = 5.25$$

$$SS_{bg} = \sum_{}^{k} \frac{T_j^2}{n_j} - \frac{T_G^2}{N} = \frac{8.9^2}{7} + \frac{15.1^2}{8} + \frac{9.3^2}{6} + \frac{11.6^2}{5} - \frac{44.9^2}{26}$$

$$= 81.14 - 77.54 = 3.60$$

$$SS_{wg} = SS_{tot} - SS_{bg} = 5.25 - 3.60 = 1.65$$

$$MS_{bg} = \frac{SS_{bg}}{df_{bg}} = \frac{3.60}{3} = 1.20$$

$$MS_{wg} = \frac{SS_{wg}}{df_{wg}} = \frac{1.65}{22} = 0.08$$

Calculation of the obtained value of F:

$$F = \frac{MS_{bg}}{MS_{wg}} = \frac{1.20}{0.08} = 15.00$$

The test: Since the obtained value of *F* (15.00) is larger than the critical value (4.938), the null hypothesis can be rejected. The data allow the conclusion that at least one difference exists between the four population means (M_c, M_t, M_s, M_h). [Note: Rejecting the null hypothesis of this test does *not* indicate which population means differ from each other. It is possible to use further statistical techniques to provide a more specific answer (i.e., which populations means differ); such techniques are beyond the scope of this presentation.]

It is possible to get a "conservative" answer by inspecting the sample means. In the preceding example each sample mean can be calculated—$\bar{X}_j = T_j/n_j$; the four sample means are $\bar{X}_c = 8.9/7 = 1.27$, $\bar{X}_t = 15.1/8 = 1.89$, $\bar{X}_s = 9.3/6 = 1.55$, $\bar{X}_h = 11.6/5 = 2.32$. Notice that the sample means for "circle" and "hexagon" are the furthest apart. Since the test allows the conclusion that at least one difference between population means exists, one could conclude that, *at least*, $M_c \neq M_h$ (the population mean for circles differs from the population mean for hexagons).

B. Analysis of Variance for a Factorial Design

The analysis of a factorial design reflects the special construction of such designs. (See Chapter 8.) This section will describe the analysis of a design including two "independent variables" (factors), variable A, which has levels $A_1, A_2, \ldots A_a$, and variable B, which has levels $B_1, B_2, \ldots B_b$. Each basic treatment group in a factorial design represents a different combination of the levels of variable A with the levels of variable B (A_1B_1, A_1B_2, and so on through A_aB_b). In a factorial design all possible combinations of the levels of A with the levels of B occur equally often.

The methods described here are appropriate for the analysis of a two-factor factorial design if (1) each basic treatment group is represented by an independent group of subjects and (2) the number of subjects (scores) in each basic group is the same.

Features: The analysis of variance for a factorial design begins with the same steps as the simpler analysis described in Section A. The statistic used is the F ratio. However, for a factorial analysis three separate tests are conducted: (1) a test concerning the *main effect* of variable A—differences among $M_{A_1}, M_{A_2}, \ldots M_{A_a}$; (2) a test concerning the *main effect* of variable B—differences among $M_{B_1}, M_{B_2}, \ldots M_{B_b}$; (3) a test concerning an *interaction* effect of variables A and B ["Are the differences among A means the same at all levels of B, or are the differences among B means the same at all levels of A?" (the same basic question can be asked either way)]. Since three tests are conducted, three F ratios must be calculated.

Terms and formulas:

N = total number of scores (over all groups)
a = number of levels of variable A
b = number of levels of variable B
k = number of basic treatment groups (note: $k = a \times b$)
n = number of scores in a basic treatment group (note: for this analysis each basic treatment group must have the same n)
n_A = number of scores at each level of variable A
n_B = number of scores at each level of variable B
T = sum of the scores in a basic treatment group
T_A = sum of the scores at a particular level of variable A
T_B = sum of the scores at a particular level of variable B
T_G = "grand total" = sum of all scores in all groups
df_A = degrees of freedom for main effect of variable A = $a - 1$
df_B = degrees of freedom for main effect of variable B = $b - 1$
df_{AB} = degrees of freedom for the A $\times$ B interaction = $(a - 1)(b - 1)$
df_{wg} = degrees of freedom within groups = $N - k$

$$SS_{tot} = \text{total sum of squares} = \sum^{k} \sum^{n} X^2 - \frac{T_G^2}{N}$$

$$SS_{bg} = \text{sum of squares between (basic) groups} = \sum^{k} \frac{T^2}{n} - \frac{T_G^2}{N}$$

$$SS_{wg} = \text{sum of squares within groups} = SS_{tot} - SS_{bg}$$

$$SS_A = \text{sum of squares for main effect of variable A} = \sum^{a} \frac{T_A^2}{n_A} - \frac{T_G^2}{N}$$

$$\text{SS}_B = \text{sum of squares for main effect of variable B} = \sum^{b} \frac{T_B{}^2}{n_B} - \frac{T_G{}^2}{N}$$

$\text{SS}_{AB} = \text{sum of squares for A} \times \text{B interaction} = \text{SS}_{bg} - \text{SS}_A - \text{SS}_B$
$\text{MS}_{wg} = \text{mean square within groups} = \text{SS}_{wg}/df_{wg}$
$\text{MS}_A = \text{mean square for main effect of variable A} = \text{SS}_A/df_A$
$\text{MS}_B = \text{mean square for main effect of variable B} = \text{SS}_B/df_B$
$\text{MS}_{AB} = \text{mean square for A} \times \text{B interaction} = \text{SS}_{AB}/df_{AB}$

Steps in the analysis:

1. Calculate $\text{SS}_{tot} = \sum\limits^{k} \sum\limits^{n} X^2 - T_G{}^2/N$

2. Calculate $\text{SS}_{bg} = \sum\limits^{k} T^2/n - T_G{}^2/N$

3. Calculate $\text{SS}_{wg} = \text{SS}_{tot} - \text{SS}_{bg}$

4. Calculate $\text{SS}_A = \sum\limits^{a} T_A{}^2/n_A - T_G{}^2/N$

5. Calculate $\text{SS}_B = \sum\limits^{b} T_B{}^2/n_B - T_G{}^2/N$

6. Calculate $\text{SS}_{AB} = \text{SS}_{bg} - \text{SS}_A - \text{SS}_B$
7. Calculate $\text{MS}_{wg} = \text{SS}_{wg}/df_{wg}$
8. Calculate $\text{MS}_A = \text{SS}_A/df_A$
9. Calculate $\text{MS}_B = \text{SS}_B/df_B$
10. Calculate $\text{MS}_{AB} = \text{SS}_{AB}/df_{AB}$

The tests: An alpha level must be chosen; the critical value for each test is then identified from Table B.3 by finding the appropriate F distribution on the basis of the df for the numerator of the F ratio and the df for the denominator.

Note: Three tests will be conducted, and the critical value for each test must be determined separately since the degrees of freedom (might) change from test to test.

Test 1—main effect of variable A:

$$F = \frac{\text{MS}_A}{\text{MS}_{wg}}$$

This obtained value must exceed the critical value in the F distribution with $(a - 1)$ df (numerator) and $(N - k)$ df (denominator) if one is to conclude that differences among the M_A's exist.

Test 2—main effect of variable B:

$$F = \frac{\text{MS}_B}{\text{MS}_{wg}}$$

This obtained value must exceed the critical value in the F distribution with $(b - 1)$ df (numerator) and $(N - k)$ df (denominator) if one is to conclude that differences among the M_B's exist.

Test 3—A × B interaction effect:

$$F = \frac{MS_{AB}}{MS_{wg}}$$

This obtained value must exceed the critical value in the F distribution with $(a - 1)(b - 1)$ df (numerator) and $(N - k)$ df (denominator) if one is to conclude that differences among A means are not the same at all levels of B (or that differences among B means are not the same at all levels of A).

Example: In an experiment on reading comprehension the subject's task was to read a story and then take a test about the story. A factorial design was formed by combining three levels of a "study condition" variable (no study questions, factual study questions, interpretive study questions) with two levels of a "story mood" variable (happy story, sad story). There were thus 6 basic treatment groups, each representing a different combination of the 3 study condition levels with the 2 story mood levels. A total of 24 students were randomly assigned in *equal* numbers to the 6 basic groups (4 students in each group). Each subject's score was the percentage of correct answers on the test.

Data:

	Study Condition			
STORY MOOD	**NO QUESTIONS**	**FACTUAL QUESTIONS**	**INTERPRETIVE QUESTIONS**	
Happy	47	58	75	T_B
	24	55	60	
	32	39	54	
	38	43	50	
	T = 141	195	239	575
Sad	28	48	61	
	46	32	52	
	34	47	43	
	26	29	59	
	T = 134	156	215	505
T_A	275	351	454	$T_G = 1080$

Note: "Study condition" will be labeled as variable A; "story mood" will be labeled as variable B.

Steps in the analysis (note that $N = 24$, $n = 4$, $n_A = 8$, $n_B = 12$, $a = 3$, $b = 2$, $k = 6$):

(1) $$SS_{tot} = \sum^{k} \sum^{n} X^2 - \frac{T_G^2}{N}$$

$$= (47^2 + 24^2 + 32^2 + 38^2 + 58^2 + \ldots + 43^2 + 59^2)$$
$$- \frac{(1080)^2}{24}$$
$$= 52518 - 48600 = 3918$$

(2) $$SS_{bg} = \sum^{k} \frac{T^2}{n} - \frac{T_G^2}{N}$$

$$= \left(\frac{141^2}{4} + \frac{195^2}{4} + \frac{239^2}{4} + \frac{134^2}{4} + \frac{156^2}{4} + \frac{215^2}{4} \right)$$
$$- \frac{(1080)^2}{24}$$
$$= 50886 - 48600 = 2286$$

(3) $$SS_{wg} = SS_{tot} - SS_{bg} = 3918 - 2286 = 1632$$

(4) $$SS_A = \sum^{a} \frac{T_A^2}{n_A} - \frac{T_G^2}{N}$$

(Study condition) $$= \left(\frac{275^2}{8} + \frac{351^2}{8} + \frac{454^2}{8} \right) - \frac{(1080)^2}{24}$$
$$= 50617.8 - 48600 = 2017.8$$

(5) $$SS_B = \sum^{b} \frac{T_B^2}{n_B} - \frac{T_G^2}{N}$$

(Story mood) $$= \left(\frac{575^2}{12} + \frac{505^2}{12} \right) - \frac{(1080)^2}{24}$$
$$= 48804.2 - 48600 = 204.2$$

(6) $$SS_{AB} = SS_{bg} - SS_A - SS_B$$

(Interaction) $$= 2286 - 2017.8 - 204.2 = 64.0$$

(7) $$MS_{wg} = \frac{SS_{wg}}{df_{wg}} = \frac{1632}{(24 - 6)} = \frac{1632}{18} = 90.7$$

(8) $$MS_A = \frac{SS_A}{df_A} = \frac{2017.8}{(3 - 1)} = \frac{2017.8}{2} = 1008.9$$

(9)
$$MS_B = \frac{SS_B}{df_B} = \frac{204.2}{(2-1)} = \frac{204.2}{1} = 204.2$$

(10)
$$MS_{AB} = \frac{SS_{AB}}{df_{AB}} = \frac{64.0}{(3-1)(2-1)} = \frac{64.0}{2} = 32.0$$

The tests: An alpha level must be chosen; let us use alpha = .01.
Test 1—main effect of variable A (study condition):

$$F = \frac{MS_A}{MS_{wg}} = \frac{1008.9}{90.7} = 11.12$$

Since *df* (numerator) = 2 and *df* (denominator) = 18, for alpha = .01 the critical value of *F* is 6.359. (See Table B.3; the value for 2 and 15 *df* is used.) The obtained value of *F* (11.12) is larger than the critical value (6.359); thus the null hypothesis (no differences among M_A's) can be rejected. The data allow the conclusion that at least one difference exists among the population means for the three study conditions. Looking at the obtained means for the three levels of "study condition" ($\bar{X}_{no}$ = 275/8 = 34.4; $\bar{X}_{fact}$ = 351/8 = 43.9; $\bar{X}_{int}$ = 454/8 = 56.8), the test allows the conclusion that *at least* M_{no} differs from M_{int}.

Test 2—main effect of variable B (story mood):

$$F = \frac{MS_B}{MS_{wg}} = \frac{204.2}{90.7} = 2.25$$

Since *df* (numerator) = 1 and *df* (denominator) = 18, the critical value of *F* is 8.68.3. (See Table B.3; the value for 1 and 15 *df* is used.) The obtained value of *F* (2.25) is less than the critical value (8.683); thus the null hypothesis (M_{happy} = M_{sad}) *cannot* be rejected. (In simple terms, we would say that story mood had no effect on test scores.)

Test 3—A × B interaction effect:

$$F = \frac{MS_{AB}}{MS_{wg}} = \frac{32.0}{90.7} = 0.35$$

Since *df* (numerator) = 2 and *df* (denominator) = 18, for alpha = .01 the critical value of *F* is 6.359. (See Table B.3; the value for 2 and 15 *df* is used.) The obtained value of *F* (0.35) is less than the critical value (6.359); thus the test does *not* allow rejection of the null hypothesis (i.e., true differences among study condition means are the same for both story moods). In simple terms, we would say that there was no interaction of study condition with story mood.

appendix C

ANSWERS TO PROBLEMS IN CHAPTER 9

1. The researcher wants to compare transfer between opposites to transfer between unrelated words. The main problem is that the second tasks differ for the two transfer conditions; subjects in the "opposites" condition learned list O as their second task, whereas subjects in the "unrelated" condition learned list U as their second task. Thus any difference in second-task learning might be due either to the difference in transfer conditions (between opposites vs. between unrelated words) *or* to basic differences in difficulty between list O and list U. The design could be improved by using a "flip-over" transfer design. For the opposites condition, subjects would first learn list O, then learn list A; for the unrelated condition, subjects would first learn list U, then learn list A. Since the second tasks would be the same for both conditions (list A in both cases), any difference in second-task learning would have to be due to differential transfer. It would be necessary, in this redesign, to have lists O and U learned equally well during the first stage of the study.

2. The researcher has observed a relation between two natural variables: severity of punishment and hostile–aggressive behavior. Such a relation has, in principle, several possible interpretations. The researcher's conclusion—that punishment leads to aggressive behavior—is only one plausible conclusion. An alternative is that aggressive behavior results in more punishment—a conclusion that is just as plausible as the researcher's.

It would be unethical to use experimental methodology to study the punishment–aggression relation. Randomly assigning children to different punishment treatments and then observing their aggressive behavior would in principle provide clearer data, but doing this is simply unacceptable. An alternative would be to use a cross-lagged panel analysis. Measure the severity of punishment and the amount of aggressive behavior at two points in time. If "punishment leads to aggression," then the correlation between early measures of punishment and later measures of aggression should be higher than the correlation between early measures of aggression and later measures of punishment. (See Chapter 7 for a more complete discussion.)

3. The main problem with this study is that variation in the delay of feedback is confounded with variation in the amount of time between feedback and the presentation of the next pattern (call this interval the postfeedback interval). Since the time between successive pattern presentations was fixed at 10 seconds, as delay increased from 0 to 2 to 5 to 9 seconds the postfeedback interval changed from 10 to 8 to 5 to 1 second. It can be plausibly argued that the more time the subject has after feedback (up to some limit), the more use he or she will be able to make of the feedback and, thus, the better performance will be. Notice that short feedback delays are confounded with long postfeedback intervals, making the results uninterpretable.

There is no simple way of solving this problem. If, for example, delay varied from 0 to 2 to 5 to 9 seconds and the postfeedback interval were held constant at, say, 5 seconds in all treatments, then the time between successive pattern presentations would be confounded with delay. For delays of 0, 2, 5, and 9 seconds, the pattern–pattern intervals would be 5, 7, 10, and 14 seconds. Resolving the issue would require some sound arguments and a fair amount of data collection. For example, if it could be strongly argued that the length of the pattern–pattern interval is un-important, then the redesign just outlined would be satisfactory. It would be useful to try different manipulations. Suppose that, in one experiment, delay varied from 0 to 2 to 5 to 9 seconds, with the postfeedback interval held constant at, say, 5 seconds. Suppose that the results indicated no systematic relation between delay and performance. In a second experi-ment delay is held constant at 5 seconds, but the postfeedback interval varies from 0 to 2 to 5 to 9 seconds; suppose the results indicate that performance is better with longer postfeedback intervals. A pattern of findings like this would favor the interpretation that the length of the postfeedback interval is important whereas the length of delay of feedback is not. Of course more complex findings could be obtained that would require further variations in the procedures for clarification. (Note also that the two experiments described could be combined into a single, larger experiment.)

4. The main problem with this study is that the individual words in the "related" set are different from the individual words in the "unrelated" set. It is possible that the words in the related set, as individual words, are easier to recognize than the words in the unrelated set, as individual words. Here are some examples (I will use just four words per set to save time

and space). Suppose the "related words" were *bear, cow, horse,* and *kitten* (all animal names) while the "unrelated words" were *airplane, garbage, green,* and *diamond.* The question that can be raised is, "If (in principle) each subject saw only one word (and thus related vs. unrelated does not apply), what would the recognition thresholds be for these eight words?" If the words placed in the related set tended to be, as individual words, easier to recognize, then "related" versus "unrelated" would be confounded with "easier words" versus "harder words."

There are several ways of improving the study. The researcher could do pilot work to determine the recognition thresholds for the words as individual words. The pilot data could be used to select related and un-related words that are equally easy to recognize as individual words, or the pilot data could be used to make a different kind of adjustment in the results of the main study (not presented here). An alternative would be to design the study in such a way that, over subjects, the same words are used in the related and unrelated conditions. This might be done as follows:

Sets of Related Words				Sets of Unrelated Words			
A	**B**	**C**	**D**	**A**	**B**	**C**	**D**
bear	car	river	green	bear	dog	horse	kitten
dog	airplane	valley	purple	train	bike	airplane	car
horse	train	hill	red	river	valley	lake	hill
kitten	bike	lake	orange	purple	orange	green	red

Proper materials construction would require more controls than are shown here. However, I want to illustrate the basic method. There are four sets of related words and four sets of unrelated words. Notice that each individual word appears in one related set and in one unrelated set. When collecting data regarding recognition thresholds, one-quarter of the subjects in the "related condition" would receive each set (one-quarter get set A, one-quarter set B, one-quarter set C, one-quarter set D). Similarly, the four unrelated sets would be used equally often; in the "unrelated condition" one-quarter of the subjects would receive set A, one-quarter set B, and so on. When the data are combined over subjects in the two conditions, each individual word would contribute equally to scores in the related and unrelated conditions. Thus any difference in scores between the related and unrelated conditions could not be due to differences in individual words.

5. There are two obvious problems with this study. First, it is a cross-sectional study—freshmen and seniors are assessed at the same point in time. Selective loss of subjects (from the relevant population) is a frequent problem with this method. We could ask, "Is it possible that the seniors

studied more than the average freshman *when they were freshmen?*" This idea seems quite plausible. If this is the case, then the seniors in this study might not have changed their study habits at all since they were freshmen—they studied more than the average freshman when they were freshmen, and they still do.

The second problem is that "outside-of-class" experiences are likely to be different for seniors and freshmen. Although it is true that the seniors and freshmen are being compared with respect to a course that they are both taking, it is reasonable to suggest that the amount of time a student studies for one course will depend on (among other things) the study demands of other courses that the student is taking. For example, if the seniors were, on the average, taking fewer other courses than the freshmen or taking "easier" (demanding less study time) courses, they would then have more time to spend studying for the common course.

As the problem was stated, you were not to question the use of study time as a measure of "seriousness toward study." (The research literature showed that study time is a good indicator of seriousness.) Of course in reality study time may not be a very good indicator of seriousness. It does seem reasonable to state that, *other things being equal,* a more serious student will study more. However, study time is likely to be influenced by many other factors, which means that study time is likely to be a weak measure of seriousness. Suppose we ignore study time as an indicator of seriousness and restate the researcher's question in more limited terms: Given equal course demands, do students study more as they go through college? This question poses difficult problems for the investigator.

It would be better to use a longitudinal method, measuring study times for the same people, once when they were freshmen and again when they are seniors. The subject loss problems would be less serious with this method. If some freshmen failed to become seniors, the data analysis would be limited to those who provided data both as freshmen and as seniors (however, this does not seem to be a serious limitation, since the question sensibly applied only to people who do become seniors). We would need to have comparable courses for the students to take as freshmen and as seniors (and, obviously, they cannot repeat a course). If there were two elective courses available that could be taken by freshmen and seniors, a form of counterbalancing could be used. Call the courses course A and course B. Half the students would take course A as freshmen and course B as seniors; the other half would take course B as freshmen and course A as seniors. Ideally we would want to randomly assign students to the two sequences (which might be difficult in practice). It would be very difficult to "control for" influences stemming from "outside-of-class" factors—the total package of experiences for seniors must be different from that for freshmen. One could try to measure potentially relevant outside influences on study time in both the freshman and senior years (e.g., amount of time spent studying for other courses, time spent working, time spent in social activities, etc.). These measures could then be used to make statistical adjustments of the comparison of (course A or B) study time as freshmen and as seniors (using methods beyond the scope of this book). The comparison would be better, although still not free from interpretive difficulties.

6. Since each subject can receive only one language (treatment), the choice is between independent groups and matched subjects. Since the researcher has information about the twenty-four students that appears to be a good basis for matching them with respect to performance on syllogisms, the matched-subjects design might be preferable. If the matching is good (with respect to syllogism performance), the matched-subjects design should provide a more powerful test of the null hypothesis than an independent-groups design. To construct the matched-subjects design the researcher could do the following: First, rank order the students with respect to their scores on the verbal part of the entrance exam. Second, form eight sets of three matched subjects each. The three highest scorers on the entrance exam would form the first matched set, the next three highest scorers the second matched set, and so on. Third, use some random method (e.g., a table of random numbers or picking names out of a hat) to assign one person in each matched set to one of the three treatments (abstract symbols, factual sentences, meaningless sentences). There would be eight subjects in each treatment group, but each subject would be matched with a particular subject in the other treatment groups.

7. It is important to note that "everything is the same" in the two studies except that one study involves repeated measures while the other involves independent groups. Suppose (just to give a number) that each researcher had 30 subjects. With independent groups, the researcher would obtain 30 scores, one for each subject. With repeated measures, the researcher would obtain 30 scores *for each treatment*. Since increasing the number of observations increases the power of the test of a null hypothesis, the researcher using repeated measures would have an advantage. Even if the total number of scores were the same for the two designs, repeated measures are likely to provide a more powerful test of the null hypothesis. For example, suppose there were two reward levels involved. With 30 subjects, an independent-groups design would result in the assignment of 15 subjects to each reward level. To keep the total number of scores constant, suppose the other researcher had just 15 subjects but that each received both treatments (again, a total of 30 scores). It is still likely that the researcher using repeated measures would have a more powerful test of the null hypothesis. (See Chapters 3 and 6.) Therefore, one reason why the researcher using independent groups could not reject the null hypothesis whereas the researcher using repeated measures did reject it is a basic difference in the power of the test, resulting from the difference in design.

The second reason for a possible difference in results is that the experimental context for subjects in the repeated-measures design is different from the context for subjects in the independent-groups design. With independent groups, each subject receives only one reward level (and has no knowledge that other reward levels are being used for other subjects). However, the subject in a repeated-measures design receives all reward levels and thus is provided with a contrast among reward levels that does not exist with independent groups. It is possible that "larger rewards lead to better performance" when the subject experiences different levels of reward for different tasks but not when the subject experiences only one level of reward.

8. The essential goal is to use as many subjects as possible (more subjects = more reliable data) while avoiding any confounding of "section differences" with the independent variable that is of interest (the order of topics in the passage). Since the treatments involve nothing more than giving students different passages to read (instructions are the same for all passages; the test is the same; etc.), it is feasible to have the different treatments occurring within a single group session (i.e., class session). The fundamental idea is to balance "sections" with treatments (passages). Within each course section students can be randomly assigned to different treatments by some technique such as shuffling the passages and then distributing them to the students as they are seated in the classroom. All five passages (treatments) should be used in each of the 7 course sections. For the analysis of the data each of the 5 passages should be read by the same number of students in a particular course section.

Here is an example of what might be done for a single course section (and for each course section). Suppose the researcher knows that the section will have at most 25 students. He would take 5 copies of each passage (A, B, C, D, E), shuffle them to produce a random order, and distribute them to the students in the classroom. The general instructions would be given; each student would read the passage he or she had received; and then all would take the comprehension test. (Of course the researcher must take steps to make sure he knows which passage each student read when the data are analyzed. One way to do this would be to mark the passages with the letters A–E and instruct the students to indicate the letter of the passage they read on their answer sheet for the comprehension test.) Suppose that on the day the experiment is conducted in that classroom only 23 students are present. Suppose that in that section the number of students reading each passage is A, 5; B, 4; C, 5; D, 5; E, 4. Before analyzing the data the researcher would randomly eliminate one answer sheet for passages A, C, and D; the results would be data for 4 students per passage for that course section. This procedure could be followed for each of the 7 course sections. The result would be that the data for each passage would come equally from each course section. "Section" would be balanced with treatments (passages); a large number of observations would be made (all to the good); and "sections" and "passages" would *not* be confounded. (Note: Sophisticated statistical techniques exist that would allow the researcher to "deal with" unequal numbers of students reading the 5 passages in a given course section. These techniques are beyond the scope of this book.)

9. The fundamental problem with this study concerns regression artifacts in the measurement of change. (See Chapter 8.) The students were selected for "counseling" *because* they had the lowest scores on the midterm exam. The correlation between scores on the midterm exam and scores on the final exam is extremely unlikely to be perfect (+1.00 or, rather strangely, −1.00). Considering the amount of time that elapses between the midterm and the final, and the changes in the content of the exams, the correlation between the two exams is likely to be considerably less than 1.00. If the correlation between scores on the midterm and final exams is less than perfect (which it is virtually certain to be), we can state the following. If nothing were done to anyone, the students who had the lowest 40 scores on the midterm exam would *not* have the lowest 40 scores on the final exam. In fact the lowest 40 scorers on the midterm would tend to be closer to the average score on the final exam. If we looked in the "opposite" direction, from the final "back" to the midterm, we would also find that the 40 lowest scorers on the *final* would tend to be closer to the average score on the *midterm* exam. These "changes in relative position" result from nothing more than the less than perfect relation between scores on the midterm and final exams. Therefore, the fact that the 40 lowest scorers on the midterm, who also received counseling, tended to score closer to the average on the final does *not* by itself indicate that counseling had any effect whatsoever. If the counseling had any *real* effect, the 40 students would have to move significantly closer to the average score than would be expected on the basis of simple regression toward the mean.

The study would be considerably improved if the instructor did the following: Having identified the 40 lowest scorers on the midterm exam, randomly assign 20 of these students to receive "counseling" while the other 20 do *not* receive counseling. Compare the scores of these two groups on the final exam to determine whether counseling had any effect. Notice that regression toward the mean would occur in both the counseled and noncounseled groups, but it would be equal (and, thus, nonconfounding).

10. For this problem keep in mind that we are assuming that any numerical difference is statistically significant. To test for the main effect of "number of switches," compare the mean scores for 5, 7, and 9 switches. The respective means are as follows: 5 switches—$(14 + 10 + 8)/3 = 10.67$; 7 switches—$(17 + 17 + 17)/3 = 17.0$; 9 switches—$(20 + 24 + 26)/3 = 23.33$. Since these means are numerically different, we would conclude that "number of switches" does affect performance.

For the main effect of "amount of money" we would compare the mean scores for $1, $5, and $20. The respective means are as follows: $1—(14 + 17 + 20)/3 = 17.0; $5—(10 + 17 + 24)/3 = 17.0; $20—(8 + 17 + 26)/3 = 17.0. Since these means are identical, we would conclude that there is *no* main effect of "amount of money."

The test for the interaction involves the following question: Are the changes in time-to-solve from 5 to 7 to 9 switches the same at all levels of "amount of money" ($1, $5, $20)? Looking at the data shown in the problem, we can see that they are *not* the same. For example, as "number of switches" varies from 5 to 7, mean time-to-solve changes from 14 to 17 at $1, from 10 to 17 at $5, and from 8 to 17 at $20. Similarly, mean time-to-solve changes by different amounts as "number of switches" varies from 7 to 9, depending on the amount of money. Therefore we would conclude that there is an interaction.

REFERENCES

BALTES, P. B. Longitudinal and cross-sectional sequences in the study of age and generational effects. *Human Development,* 1968, 11, 145–171.

BALTES, P. B., & SCHAIE, K. W. On the plasticity of intelligence in adulthood and old age: Where Horn and Donaldson fail. *American Psychologist,* 1976, 31, 720–725.

BARBER, T. X. *Pitfalls in Human Research: Ten Pivotal Points.* New York: Pergamon Press Inc., 1976.

BRAGINSKY, B. M., & BRAGINSKY, D. D. *Mainstream Psychology: A Critique.* New York :Holt, Rinehart & Winston, 1974.

BRONFENBRENNER, U. Toward an experimental ecology of human development. *American Psychologist,* 1977, 32, 513–531.

CAMPBELL, D. T. Reforms as experiments. *American Psychologist,* 1969, 24, 409–429.

CAMPBELL, D. T., & FISKE, D. W. Convergent and discriminant validation by the multitrait–multimethod matrix. *Psychological Bulletin,* 1959, 56, 81–105.

CAMPBELL, D. T., & STANLEY, J. C. *Experimental and Quasi-experimental Designs for Research.* Chicago: Rand McNally, 1963.

CLARK, D. C. Teaching concepts in the classroom: A set of teaching prescriptions derived from experimental research. *Journal of Educational Psychology,* 1971, 62, 253–278.

CRANO, W. D., KENNY, D. A., & CAMPBELL, D. T. Does intelligence cause achievement?: A cross-lagged panel analysis. *Journal of Educational Psychology,* 1972, 63, 258–275.

CRONBACH, L. J., & MEEHL, P. E. Construct validity in psychological tests. *Psychological Bulletin,* 1955, 52, 281–302.

DEESE, J. *Psychology as Science and Art.* New York: Harcourt Brace Jovanovich, 1972.

DETHIER, V. G. *To Know a Fly.* San Francisco: Holden-Day, Inc., 1962.

DYER, J. L., & MILLER, L. B. Note on Crano, Kenny, and Campbell's "Does intelligence cause achievement?" *Journal of Educational Psychology,* 1974, 66, 49–51.

ERICKSON, J. E. Problem shifts and hypothesis behavior in concept identification. Paper given at the annual meeting of the Psychonomic Society, 1968.

FARR, J. L., & SEAVER, W. B. Stress and discomfort in psychological research: Subject perceptions of experimental procedures. *American Psychologist,* 1975, 30, 770–773.

GRICE, G. R. Dependence of empirical laws upon the source of experimental variation. *Psychological Bulletin,* 1966, 66, 448–498.

HOLMES, D. S. Debriefing after psychological experiments: I. Effectiveness of postdeception dehoaxing. *American Psychologist,* 1976, 31, 858–867. (a)

HOLMES, D. S. Debriefing after psychological experiments: II. Effectiveness of postexperimental desensitizing. *American Psychologist,* 1976, 31, 868–875. (b)

HORN, J. L., & DONALDSON, G. On the myth of intellectual decline in adulthood. *American Psychologist,* 1976, 31, 701–719.

HUESMANN, L. R., ERON, L. D., LEFKOWITZ, M. M., & WALDER, L. O. Television violence and aggression: The causal effects remain. *American Psychologist,* 1973, 28, 617–620.

JOHNSON, D. F., & MIHAL, W. L. Performance of blacks and whites in computerized versus manual testing environments. *American Psychologist,* 1973, 28, 694–699.

KLUGH, H. E. A problem-finding machine. *Psychological Record,* 1969, 19, 313–317.

KUHN, D. Inducing development experimentally: Comments on a research paradigm. *Developmental Psychology,* 1974, 10, 590–601.

LACHENMEYER, C. W. Experimentation—a misunderstood methodology in psychological and social-psychological research. *American Psychologist,* 1970, 25, 617–624.

LAUGHLIN, P. R. Selection versus reception concept-attainment paradigms as a function of memory, concept rule, and concept universe. *Journal of Educational Psychology,* 1969, 60, 267–273.

LEVIS, D. J., & LEVIN, H. S. Escape maintenance under serial and simultaneous compound presentations of separately established conditioned stimuli. *Journal of Experimental Psychology,* 1972, 95, 451–452.

MENGES, R. J. Openness and honesty versus coercion and deception in psychological research. *American Psychologist,* 1973, 28, 1030–1034.

MILLER, D. B. Roles of naturalistic observation in comparative psychology. *American Psychologist,* 1977, 32, 211–219.

ORNE, M. T. On the social psychology of the psychological experiment: With particular reference to demand characteristics and their implications. *American Psychologist,* 1962, 17, 776–783.

REPUCCI, N. D., & SAUNDERS, J. T. Social psychology of behavior modification: Problems of implementation in natural settings. *American Psychologist,* 1974, 29, 649–660.

ROZELLE, R. M., & CAMPBELL, D. T. More plausible rival hypotheses in the cross-lagged panel correlation technique. *Psychological Bulletin,* 1969, 71, 74–80.

SCHAIE, K. W. Limitations on the generalizability of growth curves of intelligence. *Human Development,* 1972, 15, 141–152.

SCHAIE, K. W., LABOUVIE, G. F., & BUECH, B. U. Generational and cohort-specific differences in adult cognitive functioning: A fourteen-year cross-sequential study. *Developmental Psychology,* 1973, 9, 151–166.

SILVERMAN, I. Nonreactive methods and the law. *American Psychologist,* 1975, 30, 764–769.

Siu, R. G. H. *The Tao of Science*. Cambridge, Mass.: The M.I.T. Press, 1957.

Sullivan, D. S., & Deiker, T. E. Subject–experimenter perceptions of ethical issues in human research. *American Psychologist,* 1973, 28, 587–591.

Swensson, R. G. Trade-off bias and efficiency effects in serial choice reactions. *Journal of Experimental Psychology,* 1972, 95, 397–407.

Thorndyke, P. W. Cognitive structures in comprehension and memory of narrative discourse. *Cognitive Psychology,* 1977, 9, 77–110.

Underwood, B. J. *Experimental Psychology* (2nd ed.). New York: Appleton-Century-Crofts, 1966.

Wallach, M. A., & Kogan, N. *Modes of Thinking in Young Children: A Study of the Creativity–Intelligence Distinction.* New York: Holt, Rinehart & Winston, 1965.

Webb, E. J., Campbell, D. T., Schwartz, R. D., & Sechrest, L. *Unobtrusive Measures: Nonreactive Research in the Social Sciences.* Chicago: Rand McNally, 1966.

INDEX